SYMBOLS, THE NEWS MAGAZINES, AND MARTIN LUTHER KING

SYMBOLS,
THE NEWS MAGAZINES,
AND MARTIN LUTHER KING

Richard Lentz

LOUISIANA STATE UNIVERSITY PRESS
BATON ROUGE AND LONDON

Designer: Diane B. Didier
Typeface: Times Roman
Typesetter: The Composing Room of Michigan, Inc.
Printer and binder: Thomson-Shore, Inc.

Library of Congress Cataloging-in-Publication Data

Lentz, Richard, 1942–
    Symbols, the news magazines, and Martin Luther King / Richard
Lentz.
        p. cm.
    Includes bibliographical references.
    ISBN 0-8071-1523-1 (alk. paper)
    1. King, Martin Luther, Jr., 1929–1968—Public opinion.   2. Race
relations and the press—United States—History—20th century.
3. Public opinion—United States—History—20th century.   I. Title.
E185.97.K5L43   1990
323'.092—dc20   89-12852
                                                        CIP

Portions of this book appeared in slightly different form in "The Prophet and the
Citadel: News Magazine Coverage of the 1963 Birmingham Civil Rights Crisis,"
Communication, X (1987), 5–29, © Gordon and Breach Science Publishers, S.A.,
and are reprinted with permission. Other material was originally published in *American Journalism*, IV (1987), 59–81, and is reprinted with permission.

E
185.97
K5
L43
1990

To the memory of my father, Felix Hawkins Lentz, Sr.

CONTENTS

PREFACE AND
ACKNOWLEDGMENTS

The origins of this study are to be found in experiences both personal and intellectual. As a newspaperman, I covered a number of the events of the Memphis garbage strike of 1968. Later, I wrote analyses of the strike and the newspaper coverage of it, including that of the newspaper for which I worked and (not the most comfortable of tasks) some of the stories that I had written.

The study grew beyond my early musings about Dr. Martin Luther King, Jr., and the strike. It became a study of King as a symbol and how that symbol was presented by the news media for more than a decade, from the Montgomery bus boycott of 1955–1956 to the Poor People's Campaign of 1968. Tracking the problem across the longer period struck me as essential because of the transformation from reformer to radical that King underwent in the last years of his life.

Inasmuch as King was a national symbol, it seemed appropriate to study the presentations of national media. I decided to limit my study to the stories in the news magazines *Time*, *Newsweek*, and *U.S. News & World Report*. There were pragmatic considerations for doing this, principally the difficulty of keeping under control an already ambitious undertaking; but there were other reasons as well. The most important was my interest in cultural values and symbol making, rather than in the issues of media-generated effects that have dominated mass communication research for decades. Symbol making is practiced by other media, and cultural values are embedded in the work products of all journalists. Nevertheless, the news magazines offered several advantages for a study of values bound up in news. Unlike other national news media (television, for example), the news magazines provided a range of reasonably distinct political positions during the period studied. *Newsweek* was slightly left of center, *Time* centrist, and *U.S. News & World Report* conservative. While staking out their own patches of political ground, the magazines served audiences composed chiefly of middle-class readers—and thus offered the possibility of striking differences and marked similarities not likely to be apparent in other organs of national journalism.

The stories in the magazines were approached not as reconstructions of events or as descriptions of people in the news but as attempts to structure reality within the social transaction between periodical and reader. Several problems arose because of this approach. One problem was the hazy recollection (or none at all) that readers today would have of such distant news events. Considerable effort was expended, therefore, to provide what might be best described as historical background. The intent was not, however, to give an account against which the magazine stories would be measured, as in, for example, a study of myth versus reality; instead, the material was woven into the text in order to orient readers to now-obscure historical figures and occurrences whose rough edges have been smoothed by the passage of time. I could not rely, of course, upon the magazines' contemporaneous reporting and, therefore, consulted archival and secondary sources. The study required that some attention be paid to the black movement as well as to King. Time after time, King's stock rose or fell with the magazines because of what other black Americans were doing or saying. Just as King was not treated in isolation by the news weeklies, so the analysis of their stories could not be restricted to him.

Another decision was whether to study the stories as institutional or individual products. I chose the former strategy. Some nuances were probably lost as a result, but the sacrifice seemed worthwhile because of what was gained: the picture of news organizations attempting to adjust to the toss and tumble of events occurring on the public stage. Perhaps more important, the decision to analyze the stories as institutional products followed the organizational logic of the news magazines themselves, where the procedures of group journalism minimized the impact of individual journalists.

The stories were read as cultural artifacts in which were embedded social values. More specifically, I sought to establish what tones were sounded, how they related to values and symbols, and how they were ordered and reordered because of the press of events and the expectations of readers. No less essential was the attempt to account for the silence of the magazines, for tones not sounded, for information omitted. Finally, most critical of all, material reported or not reported, tones sounded or not sounded, were related to what was occurring at a given historical moment in order to provide a better gauge of the significance of the journalistic accounts.

Many people generously provided assistance and encouragement. (While acknowledging their help, I acquit them of responsibility for any shortcomings that appear in the work that they helped make possible.) John Erickson knew when to give scope to a fledgling scholar and when to rescue him from his own folly. Jonathan Walton was the source of a number of insights that found their way into the fabric of this work. Both, as I remarked in another setting, are gentlemen and scholars. David J. Garrow took time from a rigorous schedule of researching and writing his last two books on King to give advice and loan research material from his files. Douglas Birkhead read the manuscript critically and sympathetically. Robert Carl Cohen graciously responded at length to an inquiry about his film, *Committee on Un-American Activities*. To James W. Carey, David Eason, Charlotte Jones, James Murphy, and John Pauly I owe intellectual debts that, if less specific, were no less critical to this work. A number of archivists provided assistance. They are: Howard B. Gotlieb, Mugar Memorial Library, Boston University; Esme Bhan and Karen Jefferson, the Moorland-Spingarn Research Center of Howard University; Edward C. Weber, the Labadie Collection of the University of Michigan Library; Beth M. Howse, Fisk University Library; Tom Haslett and Marvin Whiting, Birmingham Public Library; D. Louise Cook, the Martin Luther King, Jr., Center for Social Change; and Nancy Bressler, Seeley G. Mudd Manuscript Library, Princeton University. Coralie Rose, Janice Alcocer, Mary Cullen, and Marian Buckley labored with great cheer through several revisions while preparing the manuscript. Julie Schorfheide edited the manuscript with great patience and meticulous skill. Judy Hoffman endured with grace and good humor the noises emanating from a writer in the act of revising. I thank them, and others whose names may have been omitted inadvertently from this list but whose assistance was nonetheless appreciated.

Symbols, the News Magazines, and Martin Luther King

INTRODUCTION

Martin Luther King, Jr., stood before Lincoln's statue in 1963 and told the quarter-million people assembled there and the tens of millions of others watching televised images of the March on Washington that he still held to his faith in America. His great voice soared over the crowd on that summer's day, proclaiming "I have a dream" and calling on the nation to heed the ideals that had made it free. His dream, his prophecy, was of the sure and certain coming of equality and brotherhood. It was a universal vision, to be sure, but as rendered by King it was replete with American images—of a day when the sons of former slaveholders and the sons of former slaves would reach out to each other as brothers, of a time when even that heart of darkness for the black man, the state of Mississippi, now "sweltering with the heat of oppression," would be transformed into an "oasis of freedom and justice." King's dream was of America made whole, and it was of such power that it fixed him as an inextirpable symbol in the culture, even though the possibility that dream would become reality had begun ebbing before he spoke those words.

Five years later, King's vision was grimmer and far more radical. He had journeyed far afield from the South and the epic campaigns of the old civil rights movement, Montgomery and Birmingham and Selma. He had ventured north, leading an ultimately unsuccessful movement in 1966 against segregated housing and de facto discrimination in Chicago. He had taken up the anti-war cause a year later, decrying his country's war in Vietnam as but little short of genocide. Now, in 1968, King was preparing to embark upon his most ambitious, most radical undertaking. He had begun to organize a class-structured social movement. Joined in common cause, the poor of America—

black men and white men and red and brown—would visit plagues upon Pharaoh, King's word for the national government and the white establishment. Pharaoh must yield, King said in so many words, because there would be no other choice. Justice would be given to the poor, or the cities of the nation would be crippled by civil disruption pushed to the philosophical limits of Gandhian nonviolence. In sum, King intended, before his death in 1968, to create a crisis of such immensity that it could not be ignored.

As a result, King precipitated a different crisis, a crisis of symbols in the American culture, and it was of such magnitude that it required reconciling the contradictions of a prophet who, as a reformer, preached a gospel of American idealism and later, as a radical, symbolically turned upon the society that honored him. This book is a study of the evolution of that crisis and others surrounding the symbolic King and of their resolution by the news magazines *Time*, *Newsweek*, and *U.S. News & World Report*.

Underlying the work is the commonplace that American society is continually confronted by diversity and unity and by the necessity of creating the latter out of the former, a dilemma that is as old as the Republic. Providing cohesion to the nation is a set of cultural values variously identified (often with somewhat different components) as the American consensus, the American dream, or the American Creed. Those values effectively define the society as pluralistic yet united. As Robert Wiebe observed, because "most Americans during most of their history had agreed upon fundamentals, they could fight and still compromise, receive newcomers from many cultures and still assimilate them into one nation, experience economic revolutions and still escape the agony of class conflict." The fundamentals include what Gunnar Myrdal identified as "the most explicitly expressed system of general ideals in reference to human relationships" in Western civilization. The disparity between principles and practices is great, Myrdal acknowledged, but "as principles which ought to rule, the Creed has been made conscious to everyone in American society."[1]

No more moving exposition of those principles has been delivered than King's speech at the March on Washington. Yet what King asked of his countrymen in 1963 was limited. He did not challenge the existing social and political order; rather, his words reaffirmed it, as did his crusades against

1. Robert H. Wiebe, *The Segmented Society: An Introduction to the Meaning of America* (Oxford, 1975), xi; Gunnar Myrdal, *An American Dilemma: The Negro Problem and Modern Democracy* (New York, 1944), 1.

segregation, which violated the American Creed by denying to the black man the political and social rights that were, on the whole, freely available outside the South. As a "conservative militant," to borrow August Meier's description of King as a reformer, King was able to tap a reservoir of white support in America and to channel this force into directions that led to the emancipation of black southerners. All this he accomplished without alienating whites who supported his cause; indeed, to them he offered redemption and catharsis.[2]

There was, however, the later King. By mounting a radical challenge to the society that honored him, King became (to use the sociological term) a deviant. The difficulty in describing King as a deviant is the tendency, traceable to Durkheim, to regard deviance as a mechanism promoting societal cohesion rather than disruption. That is to say, cohesion is maintained or strengthened when the boundaries of acceptable behavior are made manifest by acts of transgression, when those who exceed the limits are punished, and when others are rewarded for conforming to societal standards by experiencing a "tighter bond of solidarity than existed earlier."[3]

Overt response to acts of deviance may indeed promote a sense of unity renewed, but a hidden fault line in society may be unearthed if an inquiry begins with a different perspective. Deviance may also cause enormous stress, particularly during periods in which a society is hit by shock after shock and the sense of unity is being stretched almost to the snapping point. Such was the situation in America during much of the 1960s. The crisis precipitated by King as a powerful symbol turned on its head could not be tolerated; the potential for damage to the severely strained American consensus was too great.

Undoubtedly, a number of institutions attempted to defuse the crisis. Above all, however, the effort engaged the energies of the managers of the symbolic stage, the news media. In modern America, the nation's values—certainly its understanding of those values as associated with specific events and symbolic personages—increasingly have become the province of journalistic institutions. News reports, printed or broadcast, put flesh upon abstractions. One need look no further than the civil rights movement to grasp

2. August Meier, "The Conservative Militant," in C. Eric Lincoln (ed.), *Martin Luther King, Jr.: A Profile* (New York, 1970), 145–48.

3. See Kai T. Erikson, *Wayward Puritans: A Study in the Sociology of Deviance* (New York, 1966), 4. I make no attempt to review the extensive theoretical literature on deviance, except to note that the functionalist explanation has been criticized for failing to account for the dysfunctional effects of deviance.

the principle. Standards of justice and equality were routinely violated by segregation. Yet what moved the nation to respond were the great moral dramas—Birmingham and Selma especially—in which the props were a policeman's club and his snarling dog, the characters violent segregationists and freedom-loving, nonviolent blacks, and the scenario one that could be easily sketched in starkly contrasting tones of good and evil.

Making sense of King's passage from reform to radicalism was the special province of the news magazines. Making sense of the world is something all journalistic media must do, but it is the *raison d' être* of the news weeklies. An editor of *Time* once made that point indirectly when he remarked that a news magazine finding itself in possession of an exclusive story was rather like a whore with a baby: Neither one knew what to do with the strange creature.[4] That readers of *Time* (and its competitors) got their news first from the fleeting images of television or the jumbled patterns of a newspaper page mattered little; what mattered a great deal to the news magazines was to impose order on what they reported.

Making sense of the world of the 1960s for middle-class readers was an enterprise requiring audacity and perseverance—and no little ability to shift rapidly onto new editorial tacks. A number of assumptions held most strongly by the great center of American society were rudely challenged, and some toppled. *Time, Newsweek,* and *U.S. News* direct their stories to the middle class, and any crisis affecting those readers registers most strongly with the magazines; their strategies of address are restricted to the middle class and are unalloyed by the necessity of newspapers to pay homage to local quirks or by the networks' need to dilute messages in order to attract the largest audience.

The process of imposing patterns on news events is not one-sided; rather, it involves a "social transaction between producers and readers."[5] Such a transaction presupposes a number of factors: some necessity for the magazine's existence; the editorial staff's knowledge of, and assumptions about, the audience; some particular style for speaking to that audience; and some means through which the audience may be heard.

For magazines, the question of survival had a sharper edge in the 1950s and

4. David Halberstam, *The Powers That Be* (New York, 1979), 666. *Cf.* Osborn Elliott, *The World of Oz* (New York, 1980), 35. See also Herbert Gans, *Deciding What's News* (New York, 1979), 170–71.

5. Stuart Hall, Introduction to *Paper Voices: The Popular Press and Social Change, 1935–1965,* by A. C. H. Smith with Elizabeth Immirzi and Trevor Blackwell (London, 1975), 22.

1960s, when television all but destroyed the magazine as a general-interest medium and brought about the final triumph of the specialization of magazines.[6]

Information about readers could be secured in a number of ways, the most direct of which was audience research. Assumptions about audiences ran through editorial content. The principal belief of the news magazine was that its readers lacked the time to keep abreast of what was occurring in the world; the corollaries were that this knowledge was necessary for members of the middle class, and that readers required some way of sorting the wheat from the chaff. In theory, all of the important events of the week were to be arrayed before readers. National and international affairs, politics, economics, science, medicine, the law, the arts, and popular culture were presented, complete with tidy interpretations, in editorial departments that may have been the "single most ingenious idea for organizing information since the encyclopedias of the French Enlightenment."[7]

Certain tones were sounded in the social transaction. Often this was a matter of style, but style itself existed for institutional reasons—chiefly to maintain the transaction between magazine and reader. In one telling incident, a college president, who was "thought to have become incoherent as a result of student protest on his campus, was edited to satisfy the expectation that college presidents are coherent." Not all readers were welcome. Other tones were sounded to discourage "downscale" readers—those who, because of age, education, income, or a combination of these and other demographic characteristics, were unattractive to advertisers.[8]

Readers could be "heard" by the magazine staffs, most obviously through the thousands of letters to the editor that arrived each year. Other indicators were available. Editors regarded newsstand sales as a measure of short-term acceptance, believing that direct purchases were tied to cover stories. Another

6. A. J. van Zuilen, *The Life Cycle of Magazines: A Historical Study of the Decline and Fall of the General Interest Mass Audience Magazine in the United States During the Period 1946–1972* (Uithoorn, Netherlands, n.d. [1977]), 181–268.

7. Gans argues that journalists at *Time* and *Newsweek* paid little attention to audience research during his study in the 1970s. *Deciding What's News*, 231. In fact, *Newsweek* employed a polling firm as early as 1963 to amass data for major stories. *Time* used surveys even earlier, probably for in-house purposes. See Robert T. Elson, *The World of Time Inc.: The Intimate History of a Publishing Enterprise, 1941–1960*, ed. Duncan Norton-Taylor (New York, 1973), II, 446. The observation is borrowed from Edwin Diamond, *Good News, Bad News* (Cambridge, Mass., 1978), 183. *U.S. News* used a different system of departmentalization, one more akin to a newspaper's, and, as well, eschewed topics related to popular culture and the arts.

8. Gans, *Deciding What's News*, 131, 219.

gauge was subscription renewals that resulted from promotional campaigns. The number of renewed subscriptions—and the cost of getting them—pointed to the success of the magazine in becoming a part of readers' lives. Finally, there was an indirect but effective way through which reader sentiments could come to the attention of a periodical. Advertisers perceiving that a magazine was not wanted or needed by readers reasoned that it would be a poor vehicle for their messages and withdrew advertising or refused even to meet with the advertising solicitors of a faltering magazine.[9]

In order to maintain the social transaction that ensured survival, a magazine had to develop and maintain a distinctive persona, or editorial personality, that simultaneously kept it in step with its chosen audience and set it apart. The persona was critical because a magazine competed not with all other magazines but with periodicals similar in topics covered and type of readers sought. The sum of many elements constituted the persona—including the "face," or cover that the magazine turned to the world each issue, the "voice," or style used to communicate with readers, and often the particular political position adopted by a magazine.

The distinct editorial identities of the news magazines were established within a general formula created by Henry Luce and Briton Hadden at the founding of *Time* in 1923. More than a simple digest of the news, *Time* was to speak with one voice to one man. After Hadden's tragic early death, the voice became Luce's and the audience that the hypothetical reader represented was middle class. The magazine offered the assurance that within its covers could be found, neatly packaged, knowledge of everything of importance that had transpired in the world during a given week. There was need of certainty thus packaged. With the rise of commercial radio after World War I, the world began pressing in with wars and rumors of wars, with hitherto unquestioned values that flitted like so many leaves before the winds of fashion, and with undreamed-of prosperity that soared until the American economy plunged into the Great Depression in 1929. The news of such matters came first from radio newscasts and newspaper headlines and stories, but it arrived without coherence or organization.[10]

In contrast to other purveyors of news, *Time* sorted the week's events into

---

9. On letters to the editor, see Elson, *The Intimate History of a Publishing Enterprise*, 443. *Cf.* Gans, *Deciding What's News*, 230–31. For other ways in which readers were heard, see Gans, *Deciding What's News*, 219; Elliott, *The World of Oz*, 50; and van Zuilen, *The Life Cycle of Magazines*, 251–95.

10. See Halberstam, *The Powers That Be*, 62.

tidy departments, compartmentalizing incidents and actors on the public stage. *Time* interpreted. It scorned the fallacy of journalistic "objectivity," substituting the promise, which was quickly forgotten, not to plead special causes. To its educated, middle-class readers *Time* offered a plethora of facts that appealed to the notion that people should assimilate information for themselves, but it spared them the trouble of doing so by speaking *ex cathedra* about what those facts meant. *Time* personalized the news. Not least, it did so with its cover, a mirror turned weekly to a world of heroes and villains. In its crisp narrative style, *Time* named other nations, provided devices to help pronounce their names, explained their politics concisely, and used graphics as newspapers had never done. Above all, *Time* dramatized the news, "making of every little item a short story whose point and purpose" could not be mistaken.[11]

Time's powerful sense of audience was demonstrated in other ways. In matters of high culture, its approach was middle-brow. An editor recalled that the "sights" were once set too high in the culture sections, "and we lowered them several times in the months that followed, but never to the contemptibly easy target we had been told to shoot at."[12]

Should his editors and writers become too sophisticated, Luce, a master of his audience, would intervene to get the magazine back on course. It is too simplistic to describe a magazine as merely the lengthened shadow of one man, but the notion is not without merit in the case of *Time* and Luce. In moments of candor, he asserted matter-of-factly that *Time* reflected his views, and that was that. In practice, as one of Luce's editors recalled, that was not so simple as that, but *Time* did reflect Luce's disingenuous self-appraisal, "I am a Protestant, a Republican, and a free enterpriser," as well as his unabashed Americanism and strident anticommunism.[13]

Luce's politics were conservative, and, like most of his readers, he celebrated success. But his was a broader vision, marked by a curious streak of

11. The observation is borrowed from Joseph Epstein, "Henry Luce and His *Time*," *Commentary*, XLIV (November, 1967), 43. For other insights, I am indebted to W. A. Swanberg, *Luce and His Empire* (New York, 1972), 388–89; James Playsted Wood, *Magazines in the United States* (3rd ed.; New York, 1971), 207; Otto Friedrich, "There Are oo Trees in Russia: The Function of Facts in Newsmagazines," *Harper's Magazine*, CCXXIX (October, 1964), 59–65; and Halberstam, *The Powers That Be*, 62.

12. T. S. Matthews, *Name and Address* (New York, 1960), 237.

13. On Luce's control of *Time*, see Swanberg, *Luce and His Empire*, 443; and Halberstam, *The Powers That Be*, 48. *Cf.* Matthews, *Name and Address*, 252. Luce's remark is quoted in Epstein, "Henry Luce," 43.

innocence—exaggerated perhaps, but one not so distant from that of the readers of his journal. Luce saw America as an ideal to be realized. With her technology, America would remake the world in her own image and would transform the twentieth century into the American Century; and with patience, hard work, and persistence, America would rise to meet the magnificent principles that had attended her birth as a nation. Despite its secular overtones, Luce's vision was essentially religious, its articles of faith shaped in China where, as the son of missionaries, he spent the first fifteen years of his life. In America, Luce, the "exile come home," was seduced "by the mythology of the land as no native-born American could ever have been." His boyhood in China "made him more intensely American, more accepting of American values than most men of his intellectual achievement."[14]

Success spurred rather than stilled the missionary in Luce. He was never disillusioned by his country, he once wrote, "but I was from my earliest manhood dissatisfied with America. America was not being as great and as good as I knew she could be, as I believed with every nerve and fiber [that] God himself had intended her to be." One matter in which America had not lived up to God's and Luce's expectation was the lot of the black man; a biographer noted that Luce took a "strong, if academic interest in Negroes, and was as opposed to lynching as Coolidge had been to sin."[15] *Time* had no equal in the task set it by Luce of scourging segregationists who trampled on the ideals to which Luce subscribed. The sympathies exhibited for blacks groaning under the yoke of segregation could also be traced to a perspective shared by magazine and founder. Since *Time* catered to national advertisers and a national audience, its perspective would have been national in any event; but that characteristic was exaggerated because Luce had little sensitivity to regional quirks, even those that were less offensive than segregation.

Luce and his magazine had no more patience with anything smacking of radicalism, whether from blacks or others. *Time* was written and edited for the middle class, especially those in the higher reaches who were, on the whole, comfortable with America. Social reform, implemented with deliberation, was one thing, radicalism another; America was to be set right, not torn asunder.

14. John K. Jessup (ed.), *The Ideas of Henry Luce* (New York, 1960), 115–20. On Luce as exile come home, see Halberstam, *The Powers That Be*, 51. Essentially the same conclusion was reached earlier by Swanberg, *Luce and His Empire*, 25, 35; and Epstein, "Henry Luce," 38.
15. Luce is quoted in Epstein, "Henry Luce," 38; Swanberg, *Luce and His Empire*, 104.

Luce's vision, national in perspective, powerful in motivation, and limited by innocence, dominated his magazine, even if *Time* was never completely swayed by his whims. Luce's control was maintained by the practices of group journalism, which raised by several notches the already considerable bureaucratization of journalistic enterprises. Group journalism centralized power in the hands of editors representing Luce. He and Hadden had inaugurated the procedures in order to pool the skills of reporters, editors, and researchers; the intent was to ensure accuracy and to facilitate the process of reporting events, not in isolation, but within a historical context delimited by the weekly frame of the news magazine. Serendipitously, they produced an instrument of bureaucratic control so demanding that not even Luce escaped its strictures. Luce once wrote an article reporting a speech delivered by Charles Lindbergh. The article was at odds with the style of *Time* and was rewritten extensively. "'Well,' said Luce, upon reading his mangled copy, 'quite a lot of it got through.'"[16]

As practiced at *Time* (and, to a lesser extent, its competitors), group journalism put in place an assembly line, described in 1968 by a writer who had labored at Luce's mill. "The correspondent reports it, the researcher checks it, the writer writes it, the senior editor checks it, and the top editor disposes of it both ideologically and mechanically. The lines cannot be crossed." A correspondent's job was not to write a finished story but to submit the "perfect unfinished research file, containing ten times as much information as 'New York' needed to know." The story thus became a mechanical entity, the essential components of which were facts. Specialization of labor led to an assembly line technique, which Otto Friedrich identified as "The Zip." The writer could "ignore all facts and concentrate on the drama," confident the researcher would supply the missing information. "If he is describing some backward country, for example, he can safely write that oo percent of its people are ravaged by TK diseases. It obviously doesn't matter much whether the rate is eighty percent or ninety percent. Any statistic will sound equally authoritative."[17] Group journalism placed the published story at several re-

16. On group journalism at *Time*, see Curtis Prendergast with Geoffrey Colvin, *The World of Time Inc.: The Intimate History of a Changing Enterprise, 1960–1980*, ed. Robert Lubar (New York, 1986), III, 104–107. See also Wood, *Magazines in the United States*, 207. Luce is quoted in Epstein, "Henry Luce," 45.

17. Andrew Kopkind, "Serving Time," *New York Review of Books*, September 12, 1968, p. 24; Friedrich, "There Are oo Trees in Russia," 62. The codes "oo" and "TK" indicate statistics and facts to be supplied by the researcher.

moves from the direct experience of covering events, and the reporter at several removes from the finished story; the journalist became a unit of production.

As a system, *Time* seemed tailor-made to dominate, the occasional staff uprising notwithstanding. In 1960, Luce found the right man to dominate the newsroom: Otto Fuerbringer, the managing editor from March, 1960, until May, 1968. Power gravitated toward that position in the hierarchy of *Time*. The managing editor was an extension of Luce, and Fuerbringer had Luce's confidence. The politically conservative Fuerbringer also was superbly equipped by temperament, and by the power that flowed from Luce, to keep a potentially too-liberal staff in line. During the Vietnam War, for example, Fuerbringer became outraged when *Time* correspondents strayed from the editorial line that America's war was going well and filed negative dispatches; he ordered a story savaging the Saigon press corps, including his correspondents, as idle, hard-drinking cynics.[18]

Fuerbringer's elevation to a vice-presidency in 1968 was, in fact, a sign that *Time* was changing. Luce had actually begun the process before his death in 1967 because he recognized that a new age was at hand. By 1966, Time Inc. was an international corporation with revenues of more than $500 million annually. Its interests were diversified and far-flung: international publishing of magazines and books; broadcasting in the United States and abroad; pulp and paper mills; a marketing and printing firm. While Luce lived, *Time* retained a missionary flavor, a "pro-Christian, pro-Western aura," but his influence ebbed rapidly after his death. *Time* without Luce became less original, more of a formula.[19]

The formula certainly could be recognized without difficulty at *Time* even after Luce's death. With Hadden, he had created the modern news magazine speaking with one voice to a national audience. After Luce, the voice spoke with less passion and far less sense of its own moral authority, but the formula endured, as did *Time*, as a part of the American landscape and as an idea copied in the United States and abroad.[20]

18. Luce's high opinion of Fuerbringer is cited by Swanberg, *Luce and His Empire*, 325, 430. See also Halberstam, *The Powers That Be*, 356, 456, 464.

19. Epstein, "Henry Luce," 36, and Kopkind, "Serving Time," 27, list business holdings of Time Inc. The implication of the changes at *Time* after Luce's death is borrowed from Halberstam, *The Powers That Be*, 723–28.

20. At least fifty journals throughout the world trace their origins to some extent to ideas first incorporated in *Time*. Epstein, "Henry Luce," 47.

One of the journals inspired by *Time* was, by 1967, becoming a source of concern to Time Inc. The magazine was *Newsweek*. Once a pallid imitation of *Time*, *Newsweek* was winning, by the mid-1960s, a reputation as the hot new "book," as magazines were called in the industry. The reputation had been almost thirty years in coming. The magazine was founded as *News-Week* in 1933 by an English newspaperman, John Cardel Martyn, who, like so many others casting their lot with *Newsweek*, had once worked for *Time*. The true genesis of *Newsweek* occurred, however, in 1937 with the merger of *News-Week* and *Today*, the latter a journal founded by Vincent Astor and Averell Harriman.

The search for a distinctive persona marked its early years. *News-Week* had been a simple digest of the news; its dehyphenated successor sought to establish a three-fold formula "consisting of the news itself, the background to the news, and interpretations of the significance of the news." By claiming to separate fact from opinion, *Newsweek*'s managers were taking an unsubtle dig at *Time*, which never cloaked itself in pretensions to objectivity. *Newsweek*'s intent was less to separate fact from opinion than to separate *Time* from some of its advertisers and readers.[21]

The match was terribly uneven in the early years. *Time* took little note of the pebbles being hurled at it by *Newsweek*. And the latter had competition of its own in the 1950s. When he moved from *Time* to *Newsweek*, Osborn Elliott was dismayed to "find my new magazine measuring itself not against *Time* but against the highly conservative and (to me) unimpressive *U.S. News & World Report*." However vulnerable *Time* appeared to Elliott, *U.S. News* was endangering *Newsweek* far more than the latter was threatening *Time*. Elliott quickly learned this. When he signed on at *Newsweek*, its editor was John Denson, who in a half-dozen years turned the magazine "upside down and shook [it] until all the nuts and bolts came tumbling out," perhaps in the process saving the journal. One of Denson's tactics was the exclusive story, which Denson handled masterfully. He ordered up special issues and exclusive stories, then promoted them.[22] He also set the pattern that Elliott was to use later and more successfully in an intense struggle with *Time* during the 1960s, when the special issue and major exclusive article helped establish a distinctive identity for *Newsweek*.

21. Theodore Peterson, *Magazines in the Twentieth Century* (Rev. ed.; Urbana, Ill., 1958), 302–303.
22. Elliott, *The World of Oz*, 31–33, 36.

But that was years away. *Time* in the 1950s was formidable, and *Newsweek* needed injections of money and talent if it was to mount a challenge. Both were forthcoming after the Washington Post Company purchased the magazine in 1961. The acquisition brought *Newsweek* within the orbit of the publisher-politician Philip Graham. Graham pumped money into the business and editorial sides, buying the talent necessary to challenge *Time*. His influence also helped produce the leftward shift of a magazine considered a dull version of *Time*. Graham was no radical, but he was to the left of what *Time* snidely described as the "neuter approach" of *Newsweek* before its sale to the Post Company. Graham was also accustomed to using his power as a publisher; the Washington *Post* advanced his causes, whether promoting racial integration or castigating Senator Joseph McCarthy. If Graham did not interfere with the magazine's editorial operations (as Elliott and others maintained that he did not), he nevertheless was at least partially responsible for "one of the most remarkable changes made by a major magazine in terms of political and social attitudes."[23]

Newsweek was reasonably profitable, but if it was to make its mark, with advertising revenues and circulation and a reputation in journalism to match, it could not continue as a bland version of Luce's magazine. The way *Newsweek* broke the mold reflected the slightly left-of-center liberalism of Graham. The first sign was the cover story "Thunder on the Right," published in 1961, about groups of the radical Right such as the John Birch Society. Elliott launched the project with Graham's concurrence, a shrewd precaution given the controversy, the loss of advertising revenues, and the hundreds of cancelled subscriptions that resulted. Since the losses could be absorbed by the Washington Post Company, the trade-off was more important. Graham and Elliott "rejoiced at the ruckus" because *Newsweek*, under new management, now "was a magazine to watch."[24]

Newsweek became even more of a magazine to watch because of its "developing atmosphere . . . of missions, of crusades, of *engagé*." *Newsweek* pro-

23. The quotation is from Chris Welles, "*Newsweek* (a Fact) Is the Hot New Book (an Opinion)," *Esquire*, LXXII (November, 1969), 243–44. Graham's political activism is discussed *ibid.*; and in Martin Mayer, "The Lady as Publisher," *Harper's Magazine*, CCXXXVII (December, 1968), 98. On Graham and editorial operations at *Newsweek*, see Welles, "*Newsweek* . . . Is the Hot New Book," 243–44; and Elliott, *The World of Oz*, 11. For the *Post*'s attacks on McCarthy, see Edwin R. Bayley, *Joe McCarthy and the Press* (New York, 1981), 50.

24. "Thunder on the Far Right: Fear and Frustration . . . Rouse Extremists to Action Across the Land," *Newsweek*, December 4, 1961, pp. 18–20, 22, 27–28, 30. Only the cover carried the title "Thunder on the Right." Elliott, *The World of Oz*, 13–14.

claimed its reports from the civil rights campaigns to be "the deepest study of the American dilemma since Gunnar Myrdal." Discounted for hyperbole and qualified to read "the deepest *journalistic* study," the claim would have merit. *Newsweek* effectively used public opinion polling methods and standard reporting techniques to examine conditions in black America and attitudes among blacks and whites about race and the black movement. The first of several such cover treatments, "The Negro in America," appeared in July of 1963, bringing a flood of complimentary mail and approving nods from the Kennedy administration.[25]

A "curious synergy" (Elliott's phrase) between *Newsweek* and the Kennedy administration contributed to the atmosphere of *engagé*. Graham's political connections within the Democratic party no doubt promoted the initial links, which probably were sustained by the identification between a magazine starting the difficult climb up and a political administration that promised to get the country moving again. There was, as well, an element of self-interest: Kennedy exploited "a direct conduit into *Newsweek*" while the magazine used the connection with the president established by its Washington bureau chief, Ben Bradlee, in order "to close the gap on *Time*."[26]

Newsweek was beginning to close the gap by 1964. Its voice of progressive reform was attracting members of the middle class whose politics shaded a bit toward the Left. (Neither the magazine nor its readers argued for any fundamental changes in the economic and political system; as for Luce and *Time*, reform at a measured pace was one thing, revolution quite another.) Eventually, *Newsweek* became not only a hot book but the magazine of the 1960s. It managed the trick because it was a better "fit" for the times, a matter that went beyond money (*Time* was better fixed), stories covered (the news weeklies generally reported the same events), and journalistic innovations such as the adoption of public opinion survey techniques (indeed, on the whole, *Time*'s research usually was superior). Nor could *Newsweek*'s rise be explained by excellence of writing. Chris Welles was not far from the mark when he complained that *Newsweek* often was "bumpy and rickety, crammed with stark cliches and leaden phrases" that would have embarrassed a small

25. Elliott, *The World of Oz*, 30, 76; Welles, *"Newsweek* . . . Is the Hot New Book," 248.

26. Halberstam, *The Powers That Be*, 376. Elliott cleared the coverage of the Bay of Pigs episode with Graham, "this friend of Kennedy's, in order to make sure that we were at least roughly on the same wave-length." Elliott, *The World of Oz*, 10. Bradlee used Kennedy to secure information on *Time* cover stories. Benjamin Bradlee, *Conversations with Kennedy* (New York, 1975), 50.

newspaper. The confluence of progressive ideology and style of a different sort produced a magazine that captured the decade better than did *Time*. Part of that style involved matching interpretations of events to the expectations of readers, but the other news weeklies did the same. *Newsweek* strove as well to convince readers it was ahead of events—and visibly ahead of *Time* in exploring social change and conflict and in unearthing trends and fads. Its cover displayed the latest developments or, better still, developments expected to occur in the coming week; either strategy sought to convey the impression that *Time* was dated and behind the news.[27] Another element was *Newsweek*'s less doctrinaire style. Slogans notwithstanding, it published stories as slanted as *Time*'s (and often their editorial positions did not differ greatly). But where *Time* delivered itself of received truth with one unwavering voice, *Newsweek* had a range of inflections, which better suited the cacophonous 1960s.

Newsweek managed to retain this diversity of tone because it escaped some of the worst excesses of group journalism that left even Henry Luce's prose mangled by an editor's pencil. During the lean years before its acquisition by the Post Company, *Newsweek* had the raffish air of a magazine run on the cheap; the resources necessary for a grinding word-by-word review of correspondents' files simply were not available, and dispatches from the field often were published much as they were submitted. Even with additional resources provided by Graham, Elliott retained enough of the flavor and practices of the old days to keep the editorial process from becoming simply an assembly line with editors as foremen. The looser controls produced a magazine with rough-hewn edges, but as a former managing editor of *Newsweek* said, they also left intact a sense of the texture of "complicated, hectic events, . . . of the quirks and hazards of trying to tell what's going on."[28]

In another decade, these characteristics of style might have mattered less. In the 1960s, however, public protests and displays, bloody clashes, and other events spilled nightly into millions of American homes via television, and the news magazines sketched prose pictures that complemented, reconciled, and made sense of what the reader usually had seen earlier.[29] In the turbulent 1960s, *Time*'s polished prose put it at a disadvantage: It had the smell of a library; *Newsweek* reeked of the streets. Eventually, *Newsweek*'s refinement

27. Welles, "*Newsweek* . . . Is the Hot New Book," 153. On *Newsweek* covers, see Elliott, *The World of Oz*, 56–57; and "Top of the Week," *Newsweek*, March 29, 1965, p. 11.
28. Elliott, *The World of Oz*, 153.
29. For a discussion of news magazine and television stories, see Gans, *Deciding What's News*, 159.

of the formula invented by Luce and Hadden would force *Time* to discard some of the more stifling practices of group journalism.[30]

Three decades after its founding, the magazine had done more than remove a hyphen from its nameplate. *Newsweek* had found its voice, one with various inflections and more range, if less certainty, than *Time*'s—a voice with essentially the same ideology as *Time*'s, but less rigid and predictable in its orthodoxy.

While *Newsweek* was laboring mightily to pull itself from beneath *Time*'s shadow, *U.S. News & World Report* had found a niche from which it was not to be dislodged. Neither its voice nor its audience was problematic. Both had been firmly established by a magazine whose persona was achieved through a posture of contradiction and opposition.

On one level, *U.S. News* contradicted the news magazine formula. *Time* was assured and polished, *Newsweek* vigorous and crusading. *U.S. News*, lacking the bright, splashy covers that beckoned buyers at newsstands, appeared stodgy; its cover soberly listed, poster-fashion, the titles of the major articles. The appearance was misleading. The other magazines, almost certainly by accident, served as foils. *Time* and *Newsweek* were brightened by color photographs, bold cover treatments, and vivid prose, but these same elements also seemed shallow against the more "serious" *U.S. News*. Had its competitors not existed, *U.S. News* almost would have had to invent one or the other so that its drabness would not appear pointless.

Conservative ideology secured the position of *U.S. News* in the market. But its conservatism relied more on what *U.S. News* stood against than on what it stood for. The magazine doubled its circulation in the early years of the cold war and solidified its place during the 1960s, when social conflict and change crescendoed. Questions of ideology aside, *U.S. News* proved most effective when it stood as a watchman at the gates, raising the hue and cry against those forces—most often communism—that it warned were undermining the Republic.

For *U.S. News*, located in Washington, the gates of the Republic were close at hand, and their proximity explained much about the journal. The news weeklies cultivated perspectives appropriate to readers across the country. More so than with *Time* and *Newsweek*, which were headquartered in New York, the character of *U.S. News* was molded by its location. In part, this was

30. *Cf.* Halberstam, *The Powers That Be*, 552; Prendergast, *The Intimate History of a Changing Enterprise*, 339–40, 540–42.

a natural consequence of setting up shop in Washington, a city that lacked industries, financial nerve-centers, and agricultural extremities, but that was affluent and free from the economic catastrophes that convulsed other cities. Washington was inbred, secure, and isolated from the nation it governed. Washington shaped *U.S. News* in another way. More rapidly than in other American cities, the influx of black migrants was pushing Washington toward a black majority; blacks represented a threat to *U.S. News,* and this threat probably strengthened its sympathy for whites struggling against black southerners' demands for equality.

Washington also influenced *U.S. News* by molding the life and career of the journal's founder, David Lawrence, one of the most enigmatic personalities in American journalism in the twentieth century. After more than a half-century as a newspaper columnist, Lawrence was still an unsolved riddle. His obituary in the New York *Times* dutifully recorded the opinions that Lawrence was a "conservative," a "reactionary," and a "Woodrow Wilson-type liberal who simply declined to change his opinions to conform to most of the other national opinion makers."[31]

Lawrence was that rarity, a working journalist who succeeded on the business side of publishing and continued in the grinding occupation of writing daily journalism. Since 1910 he had been a member of a press corps whose members often had to be summoned to home offices in order "to freshen a perspective" too attuned "to the insular psychology of the capital." No such summons beckoned Lawrence. He was a syndicated columnist and a prosperous businessman who enjoyed the accoutrements of being part of the Washington journalism establishment, complete with wealthy friends and memberships in influential clubs.[32]

Lawrence founded *United States Daily* in 1926. He had miscalculated the appeal of a daily newspaper devoted solely to reporting the activities of government, though not until the depths of the Great Depression did he give it up as a futile effort.[33] He was forced to replace *United States Daily* with

31. *New York Times Biographical Edition* (New York, 1973), 265.
32. Edgar Kemler, "The Lawrence Riddle: The Man or the Times?" *Nation,* March 19, 1955, pp. 235, 236; Leo C. Rosten, *The Washington Correspondents* (1937; rpr. New York, 1974), 12.
33. On Lawrence's struggle to keep *United States Daily* afloat, see Kemler, "The Lawrence Riddle," 236. Lawrence quarreled with Kemler's original estimate of five million dollars in subsidy from Lawrence's wealthy friends, claiming that "actually, it was less than one-tenth of that sum." David Lawrence to Edgar Kemler, March 3, 1955, in Box 65, Kemler File, David Lawrence Papers, Princeton University. See also David Lawrence, *U.S. News & World Report: A Two-Way System of Communication* (New York, 1969), 13.

United States News, a weekly newspaper whose scope included not only governmental affairs but also general news of national affairs, analysis, and an editorial written by Lawrence.

The founding of *United States News* in 1933 was one of three attempts by Lawrence to refine the formula that eventually produced *U.S. News & World Report*. A second adjustment, in 1940, changed the format of *United States News* from newspaper to magazine, and "only at this point," Lawrence wrote, "did we begin to make real progress." The greater flexibility of the magazine, especially in the use of graphics, made possible the distillation of long and ponderous government reports in order to show "vividly . . . clearly, and simply the effect of the news on the individual business and planning."[34] Lawrence refined the formula for the third time when he merged *United States News* in 1948 with his magazine, *World Report*, founded two years earlier to report international affairs.

Necessary though the changes were, they do not explain why *U.S. News & World Report* found its voice and its audience. In part, the reason is to be found in the changes occurring in Washington. The depression and the New Deal led not only to centralization of power in the federal government but to a keen awareness throughout the nation of what was going on in Washington. The news from Washington was careering violently from traditional paths and vastly increasing in quantity as Roosevelt led what seemed to be a crusade rather than an administration. The federal government "assumed new powers, invaded new fields, challenged ancient jurisdictions." This expansion aroused hope or hostility in most Americans, depending upon their political persuasion, but in either case the development caused them to become absorbed in the seemingly unending torrent of news from the once-sleepy capital.[35] The popularity of Lawrence's publications did not keep in precise step with the growth of federal power. It was not that they lacked the capacity to report the ponderous affairs of government, labor, and economics; such reports were the selling points for journals that forswore the back-of-the-book sections devoted to the arts, popular culture, and communication that lured middle-brow readers to *Time* and *Newsweek*. Tinkering with the formula was essential, and no doubt the merger in 1948 broadened the audience and increased profits. But *U.S. News & World Report* had to find a way of

---

34. Lawrence, *A Two-Way System of Communication*, 13, 18.
35. See Rosten, *The Washington Correspondents*, 265.

setting itself apart from competitors covering Washington and Wall Street and writing about their affairs more brightly.

Within a few years of the merger, *U.S. News & World Report* began to make its place by tapping a vein of discontent. As Lawrence perceived it during the 1930s, the nation was stumbling into socialism (the title of one of his conservative tracts). One critic, probably oversimplifying the situation, argued that Lawrence's conservative activism grew out of his bitterness at being eclipsed by the new men who rose to the front ranks of Washington journalism, and that "in sounding the anti-New Deal tocsin Lawrence came alive again."[36]

Lawrence sounded the tocsin rather often and not only to alert readers to the expanding power of the federal government. Warnings about the menace of communism recurred in his syndicated column, which at the height of its popularity was published by more than three hundred newspapers. Another recurring theme, the right to associate with others of one's choosing, in practice came down to an editorial struggle against the civil rights movement. The arguments rolled out of Lawrence's typewriter in a daily stream: endorsement of a Court of the Union, whose members, the chief justices of the state supreme courts, could collectively override the judgments of the United States Supreme Court; comparisons of black demonstrators to white lynchers, because neither, Lawrence intoned, were content to let the law take its course; grim suspicions that black leaders and federal authorities were conspiring to precipitate violence that would serve as an excuse to deploy federal troops in the South and thus establish a military tyranny; complaints that the federal government was attempting to alter folkways—segregation—too rapidly; veiled warnings about the dangers of marriage between blacks and whites; and criticism of those who journeyed south to organize demonstrations against Jim Crow.[37]

Lawrence's column was published each week by *U.S. News & World Report*, but he maintained that his opinions did not otherwise influence its editorial content. Some stories contradicting Lawrence's favored themes did appear in his magazine. Much more often, however, the threads of his arguments surfaced. For example, Ben Bagdikian found in 1959 "evidence that

36. Kemler, "The Lawrence Riddle," 236.
37. Michael Bert Shelly, "David Lawrence and Ralph McGill on the Problems of Negro Civil Rights" (M.S. thesis, University of Illinois, 1963), 30, 33, 50, 75, 78. These examples do not exhaust Lawrence's ideas on race and the civil rights movement but, from my reading of *U.S. News & World Report*, are fairly representative.

U.S. News & World Report reaches out for segregationist views [and] in absolute measure . . . tells the reader more of the segregationist view than of the integrationist."[38]

U.S. News did not stake its all on merely getting readers to nod in agreement with the latest conservative broadside. The journal prided itself on furnishing political and economic intelligence directly and immediately useful to readers. These items about the workings of government, primarily the federal government, and about the economy were run in a regular column whose title reflected its intent: "News That You Can Use."

An element of irony attended this approach, as, indeed, it did the magazine's ideology of the Right. A majority of the helpful tidbits could be gathered most easily in Washington, and some could have been unearthed in no other city. The need for much of that information would not have existed had there not occurred the vast expansion of the national government's power. Thus *U.S. News* was not only located *in* Washington, it was part and parcel *of* Washington. Had Washington not existed—the Washington, according to *U.S. News*, that usurped the rights reserved to the states by the Constitution and robbed the people of the fruits of their labor—then neither would the magazine. However much energy and space it expended in denouncing federal intrusions into Americans' lives and businesses, *U.S. News* was a captive of the American consensus. Its voice spoke now and then with nostalgia for a simple, golden past, but its strategies of address were in keeping with what Richard Hofstadter identified as the paranoid style in American politics, the central concern of which is repression of "perceived threats to the dominant status quo-oriented political culture."[39]

For that purpose *U.S. News* was ideally suited. It was situated in the heart of the political culture and guided by an editor whose taste for journalistic inquiry ran to politics, government, economics, and ominous conspiracies. Like its founder, the magazine was limited in perspective and steady of purpose. The gaze of *U.S. News* passed over the allurements of art and the revels of popular culture. It was not to be diverted as long as there were dangers to the Republic and readers who would heed its warning cries.

By 1955, the year that a young and obscure Baptist clergyman reluctantly

38. Ben H. Bagdikian, "The Newsmagazines: I—*U.S. News & World Report*," *New Republic*, February 2, 1959, pp. 14–15.

39. Richard Hofstadter, *The Paranoid Style in American Politics* (New York, 1965). The quotation is from David J. Garrow, *The FBI and Martin Luther King, Jr.: From "Solo" to Memphis* (New York, 1981), 209, who uses the observation in a different context.

agreed to lead a bus boycott in Alabama, *Time* and *U.S. News & World Report* had found their voices. *Time* echoed in many ways the voice of Henry Luce, the exile come home in whose vision America the Perfectible would be realized when power and purpose were joined to make America worthy of its great ideals. *U.S. News & World Report* was satisfied with America as it was; the problem was to protect it against those out to destroy it. Alone among the news weeklies, *Newsweek* was casting about for an identity. In a half-decade or so it would find its distinctive persona, and then *Newsweek* would be sought out by Americans whose sympathies for social reform and whose distaste for radicalism ran equally deep. Millions of readers would turn to the magazines to find the meaning of a new social movement rising in the South and to make sense of the men who led it, one of whom was Martin Luther King.

I

FIRST STRIDES

The Montgomery bus boycott of 1955–1956 came to signify something at once great and terrible in the American experience, the beginning of the black man's long trek toward some distant Promised Land of dignity and citizenship. So powerful was its symbolic force that in years to come the boycott would achieve almost mythic status. The social forces and the accidents of history that led up to the boycott would become cloaked in a sense of inevitability, almost as if the first mass-based civil rights struggle in the South had to appear in Montgomery and Martin Luther King had to emerge as its leader. At the time, however, it was by no means assured that man and movement would rise in the city that proclaimed itself the Cradle of the Confederacy. Indeed, King found black Montgomery riven by factionalism at the top, marked by indifference to social change among the educated, and stifled by the passivity among the masses of the fifty thousand blacks who lived in the city.

Nevertheless, there was reason to hope, and revolution is far more likely to be born of hope than of despair. As southern cities went at the time, Montgomery was by no means the worst of the lot for blacks. Some blacks were registered to vote—a tiny percentage of the total, to be sure, but enough for a taste of political power. And there were a number of black organizations,

1. Martin Luther King, Jr., *Stride Toward Freedom: The Montgomery Story* (New York, 1958), 37.

21

political as well as social, and a body of leaders that had honed its skills in dealings with white officialdom. Furthermore, they lived in the capital of Alabama, whose governor, the populist James Folsom, was a moderate in matters of race.[2]

More reason for hope was generated in 1954, the year King arrived in Montgomery, when the Supreme Court declared in *Brown* v. *Board of Education* that segregation in public schools was unconstitutional. E. D. Nixon, one leader of black Montgomery, recalled, "All of us thought our problems were over with." The problems persisted, however, because the Court's subsequent decision required implementation of *Brown* not immediately but "with all deliberate speed," massive resistance rose in the South, and *Brown* failed to strike down other Jim Crow practices. Thus, the desegregation ruling produced hope and frustration but no concrete evidence of progress. It was into this "terrible vacuum . . . [that] Martin Luther King and the nonviolent technique" moved.[3]

In 1955, however, the odds that King would step into that vacuum were long indeed. Black Montgomery already had capable leaders. Above all, it had E. D. Nixon. Although Nixon was president of the state NAACP chapter, his leadership in a union, the Brotherhood of Sleeping Car Porters, explains more about his activism. The union was founded by A. Philip Randolph, who became both the spokesman for working-class blacks and the leading advocate of mass action to remedy the social ills afflicting them. Randolph was nervy enough to face down President Roosevelt in the early stages of World War II, threatening to bring about a massive march on Washington until Roosevelt issued an executive order assuring blacks jobs in war industries. Randolph was the strongest influence on Nixon, who, while not the only black leader in Montgomery to challenge segregation, was probably the most effective and unquestionably the most forceful.[4]

2. On expectations as a generator of rebellion, see Ted Robert Gurr, *Why Men Rebel* (Princeton, 1970), 46. For black political power, organizations, and leadership, see Lamont H. Yeakey, "The Montgomery, Alabama, Bus Boycott, 1955–1956" (Ph.D. dissertation, Columbia University, 1979), 69–70, 170–74. Folsom is discussed *ibid.*, 476–77; and in Charles Morgan, Jr., *A Time to Speak* (New York, 1964), 29–31.

3. Nixon is quoted in Milton Viorst, *Fire in the Streets: America in the 1960s* (New York, 1979), 19. The statement about the terrible vacuum is in a speech by Wyatt Tee Walker, a former aide of King's, to the Ministers Leadership Training Program, Miami, Florida, February 21, 1968, copy in Box 6, File 33, Mississippi Valley Collection, Memphis State University.

4. For Randolph's influence on Nixon, see Viorst, *Fire in the Streets*, 22–23; and interview with Ella Baker, former director of the SCLC, by John Britton, June 19, 1968 (Transcript of tape 203, in Moorland-Spingarn Research Center, Howard University), 15.

But black Montgomery needed something else to begin a mass movement: a rallying point to reduce factionalism among the leadership and to engage the passions of the tiny middle class and the far larger numbers of laborers and domestics. Just such an issue had been around since the turn of the century, when segregation descended on public transportation. Segregated seating had a particular sting in Montgomery. Most southern cities divided bus seating rigidly by race, with whites in front and blacks in the rear. In Montgomery, the line was not fixed but moved, depending on the number of white riders; drivers could require black passengers to surrender seats to whites, a practice leading to arbitrariness and harassments unusual even under Jim Crow. Since blacks accounted for the majority of bus riders, they found it impossible to escape petty harassments, insults, and incidents that could lead to arrest, injury, even death. The humiliation was sharpened by evidence that segregation was not an immutable fact of life. Nearby air force bases seemed to be islands of equality in a sea of oppression. The military installations were part of everyday life in Montgomery; one of every fourteen employed civilians worked on the bases.[5]

The spark that produced the movement was the arrest and subsequent conviction and fining of a black seamstress, Mrs. Rosa Parks, who refused to surrender her seat on a crowded bus to a white passenger. Mrs. Parks was widely known and respected (she had served intermittently as the secretary of the NAACP in Montgomery), and because of Nixon's efforts, her arrest on December 1 caused an immediate reaction. The day after the arrest, black leaders organized a one-day bus boycott, which was conducted on December 5. It proved successful because of the unwitting assistance of the Montgomery police department and the leading white newspaper.[6]

The stage was set for the rise of King. Fortuitous circumstances led to his

5. King, *Stride Toward Freedom*, 41. On protest against segregated public transportation before the Montgomery boycott, see August Meier and Elliott Rudwick, "The Boycott Movement Against Jim Crow Streetcars in the South, 1900–1906," *Journal of American History*, LV (1969), 756. On racial composition of bus ridership and the work force at the military bases, see Yeakey, "The Montgomery Bus Boycott," 4, 188.

6. The arrest of Mrs. Parks was actually the fourth such incident in 1955, but the other cases did not offer the same symbolic clarity, nor were those arrested so widely known. Interview with E. D. Nixon, by Stanley Smith, February, 1968 (Transcript of tape 139, in Moorland-Spingarn Research Center, Howard University), 9–10. Nixon leaked the story to a sympathetic white reporter whose account got the word to many blacks who had not received notice of the boycott through mimeographed flyers. Police officers trailed buses around Montgomery on December 5 for the announced purpose of ensuring that the boycott organizers did not intimidate blacks who wanted to ride, but blacks believed police were there to keep them off the buses. *Ibid.*, 12.

election as president of the Montgomery Improvement Association, which ran the boycott. King was new to Montgomery, tainted neither by compromising association with the white power structure nor by alignment with any faction of the black leadership. A young man, he could leave town with no wrenching effort should the affair end disastrously. King himself would have been content in a less prominent role, and he recognized that had Nixon wanted the job, it would have been his. Compared with Nixon, King was an unknown quantity.[7]

King soon showed himself to be a considerable quantity, but early in the boycott, it was Nixon who provided the essential spirit of courage. To suggestions that the movement be conducted in secrecy, Nixon responded scornfully. "We are acting like little boys," he said. "Somebody's name will have to be known, and if we are afraid we might just as well fold up right now. We must also be men enough to discuss our recommendations in the open."[8]

Nixon's courage was overshadowed in the end by what King did. No matter his untested leadership, no matter that he had done relatively little to create the movement, King brought important assets to the MIA, as he would to later struggles. First was his ability as a speaker; in time he would mature into the finest orator of his generation. Just as important, King, like Gandhi, would not merely lend respectability to protest but would make it a moral imperative, and for a considerable number of whites as well as blacks. He accomplished this by reawakening the spirit of rebellion in the black church and joining that force to the cult of the Constitution. The great civil rights campaigns would become not simply social movements but crusades. (Nowhere did King join the spiritual and secular to better effect than in his inaugural address as president of the MIA. Their cause was right, he assured the black protesters, because "if we are wrong, the Supreme Court of this nation is wrong. If we are wrong, the Constitution of the United States is wrong. If we are wrong, God Almighty is wrong.")[9] Another contribution was the nonviolent mass movement. Even passing over Thoreau, nonviolence was not new to America.

7. King, *Stride Toward Freedom*, 46, 56. For factors figuring in the selection of King as head of the MIA, see Viorst, *Fire in the Streets*, 32–33; and David L. Lewis, *King: A Biography* (2nd ed.; Urbana, Ill., 1978), 56.

8. King, *Stride Toward Freedom*, 57.

9. On Gandhi's use of moral power for political ends in the struggle against the British raj, see Norman F. Cantor, *The Age of Protest: Dissent and Rebellion in the Twentieth Century* (New York, 1969), 213–16. King's speech is quoted in Donald H. Smith, "Martin Luther King, Jr.: In the Beginning at Montgomery," *Southern Speech Journal*, XXXIV (1968), 15.

Long before Montgomery, the Congress of Racial Equality (CORE) adopted a strategy of nonviolent protest, but the demonstrations it staged in the 1940s and early 1950s were limited. King applied nonviolence on a massive scale. Remarkably, he did it "on the inhospitable terrain" of the South—the terrain being inhospitable not solely because of the hostility of segregationists. In the region's monoculture, shaped as much by blacks as by whites, nonviolence was passing strange. The stereotype of meekness notwithstanding, black southerners created, renewed, and fell heir to a culture of violence quite as much as did their white brethren.[10]

In the remaining days of 1955, representatives of the MIA, the city commission, and the bus company met several times. The meetings were inconclusive. The whites proved stiff-necked, more out of fear of losing face than from the harshness of the blacks' demands. (The MIA initially sought an accommodation within segregation: courteous treatment; hiring black drivers for routes on which the ridership was predominantly black; and seating on a first-come, first-served basis, with black passengers to be seated from back to front and whites, vice versa.) White officials tried to disrupt the MIA's system for transporting black boycotters. A broad hint was dropped that the black-owned taxicabs providing the service would have to charge the minimum fares required by city ordinance. Taking the hint, the MIA quickly organized a car pool to keep the boycott going.[11]

In January, white attitudes began hardening and white violence began to appear. Police started harassing drivers and passengers using the car pool. King was arrested on a trumped-up speeding charge. The three commissioners announced that they had joined the White Citizens Council (a middle-class version of the Ku Klux Klan), which had begun to recruit members across the South. A second ploy, attempted by the commission on January 22, came within an ace of working. The commissioners announced that a settlement had been reached on terms previously offered by them. King got wind of the announcement before it was published, and his representatives made the rounds in the black community denouncing the "settlement" as a hoax. On January 30, King's home was bombed. No members of his family were

10. The quotation is from Viorst, *Fire in the Streets*, 37. King had studied Gandhian philosophy, but the articulation of nonviolence in the boycott came as much from representatives of the Fellowship of Reconciliation, including Bayard Rustin, who figured so prominently in the 1963 March on Washington. *Ibid.* On southerners and violence, see Raymond D. Gastil, "Homicide and a Regional Culture of Violence," *American Sociological Review*, XXXVI (1971), 412–27.

11. King, *Stride Toward Freedom*, 75–76, 111–19.

injured in the explosion, but the bombing attracted an angry crowd. King persuaded its members not to retaliate, admonishing them that "we must love our white brothers" regardless of their actions and requiring his listeners to "meet hate with love."[12] King's appeal served notice that here indeed was an uncommon man who could urge his followers to turn the other cheek even though his wife and family had come close to injury or death.

Time was the first of the news magazines to pick up the story of the bus boycott. In mid-January, it interpreted the boycott as an effective weapon for the black southerner. *Time* spotted something else more important—the religiosity underlying the struggle. But, of course, this element had to be presented in a form acceptable to middle-class readers: "A Negro minister, working for the car pool, stopped to pick up an old woman who had obviously walked a long way. 'Sister,' said he, 'aren't you getting tired?' Her reply: 'My soul has been tired for a long time. Now my feet are tired, and my soul is resting.' " Virtually the same quotation was published later by *Newsweek*. Both versions were at odds with King's recollection of the "ungrammatical profundity" of the remark: "My feets is tired, but my soul is at rest." While the magazines seized upon the quotation as an apt summary of the symbolism of the movement, they could not ignore the belief of readers that proper grammar was a prerequisite for profundity.[13]

Not until early March did *Newsweek* finally catch up with the story. And not until then was King mentioned by it or *Time*. Both depicted him as representing something greater than the cause in Montgomery. In *Newsweek*, for example, King spoke of "one of the glories of America." It was, he said, "the right to protest for right. . . . This bus situation was the precipitating factor, but there is something much deeper. There is this deep determination . . . to rise up against these oppressive forces." To this, *Time* added a note about the possibility of the reconciliation of the races. What was occurring, said King, was not a matter of " 'tension between the Negro and whites. This is only a conflict between justice and injustice.' " *Time* was not content to stop there. More than one hundred of the leading figures of the movement had been arrested in late February, and *Time* underscored the symbolic significance of the arrests by pointing out that they occurred on Washington's birthday.[14] Not

12. *Ibid.*, 135–36.
13. "Double-Edged Blade," *Time*, January 16, 1956, p. 20; "Alabama . . . Why Race Relations Could Grow Even Worse," *Newsweek*, March 5, 1956, p. 25; King, *Stride Toward Freedom*, 10.
14. "Alabama . . . Why Race Relations Could Grow Even Worse," 25; "City on Trial," *Time*, March 5, 1956, p. 21.

for the last time in King's career were event and extrinsic symbol coupled didactically.

The arrests had great symbolic impact because they produced an effect opposite to that intended. The evidence came to King as he was on his way to jail, a destination that inspired terror in southern blacks. No one sought to evade arrest; indeed, some people had "rushed down to get arrested the day before" and others were disappointed to find their names missing from the list of those to be arrested. King exaggerated when he concluded that a "once fear-ridden people had been transformed," but the transformation was under way and being hastened by the bus boycott. The divisions in black Montgomery temporarily were set aside, and "people of all classes . . . joined together for a common cause."[15] It hurt the cause not at all that the white political leaders were so inept. The commissioners' bumbling tactics and transparent maneuvers made MIA's task far easier. The emergence of King's new Negro in Montgomery was helped along by the realization that whites could be beaten at their own game.

Luce's magazine, for one, was starting to note the changes being wrought in black Montgomery. It offered as evidence the demeanor of those attending the trial of King. "For one hundred years Negroes walked soft and spoke low around Alabama's Montgomery County courthouse." During the trial, however, the tramp of their feet "sounded heavy in the dingy downstairs corridors" and their voices "were raised in pain and anger" as, outside, "a Negro crowd roared hope. . . . After a lifetime of taking it quietly, their emotions welled up and overflowed in their testimony. Some began talking before defense lawyers asked for their names; others could hardly be stopped." *Newsweek* had spotted the same phenomenon earlier, but now it emphasized King's spiritual force. In a story replete with symbolism, he became a latter-day prophet whose people grasped at his hem as he passed and for whom a crowd raised the shout: " 'Behold the King! Long live the king!' "[16]

This was strong stuff indeed for a young preacher of the gospel who went to Montgomery with no loftier ambition than the pulpit or a professorship. What was odd was not the sentiment—if anything, a mild taste of the heady wine that King would consume before 1956 ended—but that *Newsweek*, rather than *Time*, reported the incident. *Time* was so caught up in the spectacle of a

15. King, *Stride Toward Freedom*, 146; Smith, "King in the Beginning," 17.
16. "New Sounds in a Courthouse," *Time*, April 2, 1956, p. 24; "The Southern Negro: Two Generations," *Newsweek*, March 5, 1956, p. 25. The quotation is from " 'Long Live the King,' " *Newsweek*, April 2, 1956, p. 26.

people shaking off the shackles of fear that it passed up a chance to celebrate The Hero. The villains, the white city fathers, were ready-made for carica-ture. What was missing was their opposite number, the heroic figure, standing in bold relief and completing a satisfactory symbolic portrait. Luce's maga-zine was never overmatched in the craft of creating villains and heroes, and strangely enough, it paid little attention to King in the early stages of the boycott and, following his trial, all but ignored him for more than seven months.

Neither man nor cause excited the sympathies of *U.S. News & World Report*. When it belatedly covered the movement, both the boycott and King were subordinated to what was framed as the larger issue. An interview with the editor of the Montgomery *Advertiser* was given the headline " 'Hypocrisy of North Incenses Southerner.' " Judging from the interview's emphasis, and its departure from the usual pattern of charge and countercharge characteristic of American journalism, *U.S. News* shared the sentiment.[17]

The tack was entirely in character. For all its surface blandness, *U.S. News* chose, organized, and displayed its stories as purposively as did any of the other news weeklies. Much of its editorial material was hewn to fit the conserv-atism of David Lawrence. The headline was evidence of an undercurrent of almost personal resentment arising at *U.S. News* because of the intense crit-icism being directed at Montgomery. Washington, the provincial southern town where *U.S. News* made its headquarters, was undergoing a population shift that seemed to be leading inexorably to black control—much to the dismay of, among others, *U.S. News*. Thus it was not surprising to find *U.S. News* turning a sympathetic ear to the grumblings of southerners that the pace of change was too forced, or to the tart advice from a southern editor that meddling outsiders should set their own houses in order. Both complaints recurred in the southern orthodoxy of the time, and to that orthodoxy, so it seemed, *U.S. News* subscribed.

17. "Hypocrisy of North Incenses Southerner," *U.S. News & World Report*, February 24, 1956, pp. 47–48. The article failed to set the stage for a reply to accusations. Although a publication must assume its readers hold a certain level of knowledge about given topics, some background information usually is provided to avoid a situation in which a speaker responds to criticism not yet voiced. For King's appearance and the recurring theme of northern hypocrisy on race as repeated and broadened by the editor of the *Advertiser*, see "Montgomery Trouble a Possible Pattern?" 44, 46, and "Editor Says Press Plays Down Northern Discord," 48–50, both in the *U.S. News* issue of March 23, 1956. The editor's complaints were reported, less sympathet-ically, by *Time* in "Tell It Not in Gath," April 23, 1956, pp. 62–63, and by *Newsweek* in "Invasion of the South," April 2, 1956, p. 86.

—As did Montgomery's city commissioners, who had expected the boycott to last no longer than the first stiff rain but were finding the situation out of control. No longer was the MIA seeking an accommodation with Jim Crow; it was challenging the constitutionality of the ordinance requiring segregation on buses. A three-judge federal panel heard the arguments and on May 4 declared the law unconstitutional. The portents could not have been worse for the commissioners—not even when black leaders soon began bickering openly.

One of the MIA's founding officers, a minister named Uriah Fields, issued a statement to the press rebuking the leadership for egotism and misuse of donated funds. No doubt whites, and some blacks as well, nodded their heads sagely. Here, it seemed, was the realization of a widely circulated prediction that the boycott would eventually unravel as its leaders devoured "each other like wounded sharks."[18]

Two elements that make for internecine conflict were present in abundance at the MIA: money and publicity. The latter was both national and international; correspondents from British and Japanese newspapers were among the journalists covering the boycott. The attention being lavished on the movement produced a flood of much-needed donations. The boycott was costing about $5,000 per month. By King's reckoning, the MIA received about $250,000. (King's estimate was disputed by MIA treasurer E. D. Nixon, who recalled writing "checks himself for $415,000, and there may have been more.") Loose accounting procedures caused rumors and disaffection quite apart from the attack on the MIA by Fields. No one seriously alleged at the time that money was sticking to King's hands. But the publicity stuck to him, and that caused grumbling. King made genuine attempts to share the spotlight. He would have broken his health had he attempted to meet all the requests for speaking engagements and personal appearances that came to him. His efforts were to little avail: He became a luminous media personality whose fame spread to the nation and the world.[19]

18. Lerone Bennett, Jr., "When the Man and the Hour Are Met," in C. Eric Lincoln (ed.), *Martin Luther King, Jr.: A Profile* (New York, 1970), 19.

19. On the news media and the boycott, see Frank Adams, *Unearthing Seeds of Fire: The Idea of Highlander* (Winston-Salem, N.C., 1975), 148–49; King, *Stride Toward Freedom*, 80; and Lewis, *King: A Biography*, 74. Nixon's unhappiness with the bookkeeping procedures probably figured in his resignation from the MIA. Viorst, *Fire in the Streets*, 45; Lewis, *King: A Biography*, 77. Years later, Nixon said that he resigned when he realized that "after the boycott, I began to be pushed to the back." *Southern Courier*, September 18–19, 1965, p. 2. On the squabbling

Pique apparently motivated Fields, but unless the MIA had more than its allotment of saints, he was not the only one nursing wounded feelings. King had a crisis on his hands. He interrupted a vacation in California and returned to Montgomery where he persuaded Fields to recant and the membership of MIA to forgive Fields.[20] So whatever smug satisfaction the city fathers had taken in the squabbling was short-lived.

And the commissioners had problems of their own. White housewives, ignoring pleas by officials, continued to provide rides for their black maids, whose services they did not want to lose. More serious were the heavy financial losses being absorbed by the bus company and white merchants. In the first three months of the boycott, the merchants claimed losses of a million dollars in retail sales alone. With that sort of money at stake, the city fathers no doubt were feeling the pressure to get the boycott over with.[21]

They were having no luck at the task. One promising tactic, persuading insurance companies to withdraw liability coverage for vehicles being used in the car pool, was countered when King seized on a suggestion and found an insurance broker in Atlanta who arranged coverage through Lloyds of London. At the end of October, the city government tried a different maneuver to shut down the car pool: Officials petitioned for an injunction against the car pool on the grounds that it was a public nuisance and was operating without a franchise.

The MIA entered its bleakest period. The Supreme Court was still mulling Montgomery's appeal of the order holding the bus segregation ordinance unconstitutional. By November 13, when a court in Montgomery was scheduled to hear the city government's petition to close the car pool, King believed that "the light of hope was about to fade away."[22]

The drama that followed smacked of fiction. While King was sitting in the courtroom, a reporter for the Associated Press handed him a dispatch with the terse announcement that the Supreme Court had affirmed the judgment of

---

and the jealousy caused by King's prominence, see Yeakey, "The Montgomery Bus Boycott," 545; and the polemic in Uriah J. Fields, *The Montgomery Story: The Unhappy Effects of the Montgomery Bus Boycott* (New York, 1959), 32.

20. Lewis, *King: A Biography*, 77. *Cf.* Taylor Branch, *Parting the Waters: America in the King Years, 1954–63* (New York, 1988), 188–89.

21. On the white housewives, see Charles Morgan, Jr., *One Man, One Voice* (New York, 1979), 41. Business losses are discussed by Jim Bishop, *The Days of Martin Luther King, Jr.* (New York, 1971), 170.

22. King, *Stride Toward Freedom*, 157–59.

the lower court striking down the bus segregation ordinance as unconstitutional. The news spread through the courtroom. "'God Almighty has spoken from Washington, D.C.,' said one joyful bystander."[23] So it must have seemed. The hearing turned out as expected. Arguments heard, the judge in Montgomery made his ruling in a matter of minutes: The car pool must be shut down. His decree mattered not at all; the Supreme Court had spoken.

Of these crises and maneuverings there appeared almost nothing in *Newsweek* or *Time*. Most of the events over the summer and autumn of 1956 lacked the dramatic qualities those magazines prized. The allegations by Fields met that standard but were not reported, perhaps out of a desire to avoid giving aid and comfort to segregationists. Not until the courtroom drama, when the bystander heard God Almighty's voice in an AP dispatch from Washington, were there other than scattered references to King.

King emerged as a prophet of moderation in *Time*'s and *Newsweek*'s reports of victory won at the threshold of defeat. There were, of course, differences in their interpretations. *Time*, perhaps reflecting Luce's religious bent, presented King as the "spiritual architect" of the boycott and a prophet of brotherhood. *Newsweek* read King more narrowly, as a defender of justice. Both magazines presented King as a pleader for the middle way, a political position as attractive to them as southern conservatism was to *U.S. News*. In *Newsweek*, King advised his flock, "'don't go back to the buses and push people around . . . we're just going to sit where there's a seat.'" *Time* sounded a more exalted note: "He was too wise to be triumphant; he read to each congregation a statement that should loom large in the Negro's long, patient fight for equality: 'All along, we have sought to carry out the protest on high moral standards . . . rooted in the deep soils of the Christian faith. . . . Go back with humility and meekness.'"[24]

On December 21, 1956, the boycott concluded quietly, 381 days after it was begun. *Time* and *Newsweek* optimistically predicted that the black victory would be accepted by whites; they were quickly disabused of the notion. Snipers fired shots at buses, wounding one black passenger, and a rash of bombings began. On January 10, the homes of a white and a black minister active in the MIA were bombed, as were four black churches. An unexploded

23. *Ibid.*, 160.
24. "Rough Trip by Bus," *Newsweek*, November 26, 1956, p. 49; "Back With Humility," *Time*, November 26, 1956, p. 20. This message was toned down and reiterated in "'A Great Ride,'" *Time*, December 31, 1956, p. 10.

bomb was found smoldering on the porch of King's home. Pressured by businessmen and the Montgomery *Advertiser*, the authorities made seven arrests. No one was convicted of setting off the bombs, but the object lesson of white men being arrested for racial crimes apparently sufficed, and the violence subsided.[25]

So ended a campaign marked by irony. It began as a one-day protest that stretched into more than a year; its initial goal was not to bring down Jim Crow but to achieve an accommodation with segregation; and it was a mass-based, direct-action campaign that won final victory not in the streets but in the courts. Yet the boycott was as much a psychological as a legal victory—a fact demonstrated by the Ku Klux Klan the night after the Supreme Court's ruling. Hooded Klansmen drove a caravan of vehicles into black neighborhoods, expecting the residents to be paralyzed with fear. Most ignored the procession. A few waved or jeered. Frustrated, the Klansmen abandoned their show of terror and rode off into the night.[26]

A poignant irony: As greatness was thrust upon one man, Martin Luther King, obscurity engulfed another, E. D. Nixon. In a sense, Nixon had spent his years preparing for just such a moment as the boycott. More than anyone else, Nixon put the boycott into motion, and his words and example set its tone, a clarion call to courage first heard in his blunt words to the wavering to stand up like men. In the end, the moment passed him by as Nixon himself acknowledged, years later, with a measure of bitterness, the fruit of might-have-beens and constant comparisons of "himself with the young man who took his place in the movement."[27]

The odds were perhaps not so great against Nixon's leading the MIA to victory. To be sure, the factionalism would have plagued him far more than it did King, who was new to black Montgomery and its quarrels. The boycott demanded a unity of spirit, and King promoted unity; he had a knack, which became more and more evident in the years ahead, of drawing into his orbit people of considerable talent, and egos to match, whom he persuaded to work together. Still, Nixon was no cipher, and his straightforward style might have been equal to the demands of a movement limited to Montgomery. But the

25. "Kickbacks," *Time*, January 7, 1957, p. 15; "Integration Under Fire," *Newsweek*, January 7, 1957, pp. 18–19. On the post-boycott violence, see Yeakey, "The Montgomery Bus Boycott," 635, 637–40; and Lewis, *King: A Biography*, 83.

26. See Bennett, "When the Man and Hour are Met," 31. The Klan incident is recounted in Lewis, *King: A Biography*, 80.

27. *Southern Courier*, September 18–19, 1965, p. 2.

movement transcended its origins. King rose to prominence not just on the strength of a bus boycott in Alabama but because of what the movement signaled for the future of the black southerner. On this level, Nixon's courage and dedication counted for little. Nixon did not subscribe to the Gandhian nonviolence that would shape the tactics and much of the strategy of the southern movement.[28] Applied properly, nonviolence offers a way out of the dilemma created when the few attempt to wrest equal rights from the many. Gandhian nonviolence could overcome the weight of numbers by exciting sympathy among Americans for the struggle for fundamental rights. Furthermore, Nixon was far outclassed as a public man by King. He lacked King's ability to make his words count among listeners of different races and classes. By vesting a social and political struggle with moral authority, King legitimated black aspirations for equality in the eyes of many white Americans. Critical to this process of legitimization was King's ability to attract the sympathetic attention of national news media, a matter in which Nixon could not hope to compete.

King's career as a public man was in full swing between the conclusion of the boycott in 1956 and his move from Montgomery to Atlanta in 1959. His office was inundated with letters clamoring for him to speak to this group or that, for favors, for recommendations for scholarships. He had appeared before the platform committee of the Democratic party, had been offered pulpits and professorships, had joined the American contingent at the independence ceremonies in 1957 for the Gold Coast, which became Ghana, and had heard from its prime minister "how heartened he had been by the news of the Montgomery struggle." As a further sign that he had arrived, *Jet*, the black magazine, was hailing him as "a kind of modern Moses" for southern blacks.[29]

The extraordinary prominence rattled King. He told a friend: "A man who hits the peak at twenty-seven has a tough job ahead. People will be expecting me to pull rabbits out of the hat for the rest of my life."[30] Self-doubts haunted him often enough, but he had cause to fret. His rapid climb to national attention could easily be reversed. And, in truth, he would not be able to pull

28. Viorst, *Fire in the Streets*, 39.

29. The voluminous correspondence is in the King Papers, Boston University. On King's participation in Ghana's independence celebration, see William Robert Miller, "The Broadening Horizons: Montgomery, America, the World," in C. Eric Lincoln (ed.), *Martin Luther King, Jr.: A Profile* (New York, 1970), 45. Bennett, "When the Man and Hour are Met," 33.

30. Bennett, "When the Man and Hour are Met," 35.

those rabbits out of the hat without fail; his visibility would ebb and flow for the rest of the decade, particularly when events such as the Little Rock desegregation crisis of 1957 diverted the gaze of the news media, and thus the nation, from the man who had apparently put it all together in Montgomery.

Immediately after the boycott, however, King's visibility was great—the best proof being found in *Time*, which featured his face on the cover in February of 1957. The cover story signaled a significant shift in the interpretations by *Time* and *Newsweek*. The latter, which had celebrated King the more intensely during the boycott, now seemed to regard King with wariness, even suspicion. *Time*, by contrast, all but canonized King beginning in early 1957.[31]

The cover treatment was the first major promotion of King. *Time* had to dispose of several matters first in order to create a King who "is, in fact, what many a Negro—and, were it not for his color, many a white—would like to be." ("Many a reader of *Time* magazine" could have been substituted for "many a white.") The perception of nonviolence demonstrated *Time*'s careful gauge of audience expectations. King's aversion to violence was illustrated by an incident from childhood in which he was slapped by a white woman but did not respond in kind. *Time* anticipated the reaction of readers. "Cowardice? If so it would come as a surprise to Montgomery, where Martin Luther King has unflinchingly faced the possibility of violent death for months."[32] Turn-the-other-cheek Christianity would move few readers to identify with King, even if there were not the complication of Gandhian nonviolence, which smacked of a foreign doctrine. *Time* solved the problem by taking the concrete image of King looking death in the face without flinching, and superimposing it on the abstraction of nonviolent courage.

A discussion of King's ability as a leader also revealed more about *Time* and its audience than about the man himself. If there was one trait the journal worshiped, it was the ability to get the job done. According to *Time*, King was such "an expert organizer" that "the hastily assembled Negro car pool under his direction achieved even judicial recognition as a full-fledged transit system." The car pool had worked efficiently, but even his admirers regarded King as an indifferent administrator. *Time*'s statement was nonsense, but it

31. See *Time*, "Personalities of 1956: Stars in Their Own Orbits," January 7, 1957, p. 24, and "Night of Terror," January 21, 1957, p. 15.
32. "Attack on the Conscience," *Time*, February 18, 1957, p. 17.

was necessary nonsense if its audience of achievers was to be persuaded to identify with a young black preacher with an intellectual bent.[33]

When *Time* took pains to establish King's credentials as a thinker, what it left out was as important as what it reported. There was, for example, a potentially damning association that had wrecked more than one career in the witch-hunt hysteria of the 1950s. The February cover story listed the social philosophers King studied in college. Marx did not make the list—a small but significant omission. Listing Marx on that intellectual tally sheet would have necessitated a forthright denunciation of Marxist thought, which King apparently would have been unwilling to provide, or a lengthy explanation that might have been unsatisfactory to readers. The silence that probably seemed the wisest course to Luce's editors reverberates against a brief item published a month later in *Newsweek* that underscores its wariness about King. The magazine recounted testimony by a former Communist before the Louisiana Committee on Segregation describing King as "a dastardly misleader, leading the Negroes of the South down to destruction." While King was not directly accused of being a Communist, *Newsweek* permitted the witness to add, without challenge or rebuttal, "—but I wonder who is giving him the party line."[34] Although this remark was only in one of four brief items in a roundup story, the reference was significant. A few years hence, after its acquisition by the Washington Post Company and the reputation for liberalism that followed, *Newsweek* would leap to King's defense. But this was 1957, and even if Senator Joseph McCarthy was dead, McCarthyism was very much alive—as both magazines were aware.

King was no less aware of the lingering power of McCarthyism when he and fifty-nine other black leaders founded what became the Southern Christian Leadership Conference. Most of the organizers were clergymen, which partially accounts for labeling it Christian, but the name also helped ward off suggestions that the black group was Communist. Such tactics were to no avail for King. To the end of his life—and beyond—he was chased by allegations, especially from segregationists, that he was a Communist or was

33. *Ibid*. On King's shortcomings as an administrator, see, for example, Bennett, "When the Man and Hour are Met," 32–33.

34. King's synthesis of capitalism and "collective enterprise" probably was unpalatable to *Time*. It is possible, though unlikely, that King's study of Marx slipped through *Time*'s net. In *Stride Toward Freedom* (94–95), King makes no effort to conceal it. "Churning Conflict," *Newsweek*, March 18, 1957, p. 36.

controlled by them. The accusation seemed almost to have a life of its own. In 1957, for example, King delivered a Labor Day speech at the Highlander Folk Center in Tennessee. Modeled after Danish folk schools, the Highlander had acquired a radical reputation because it taught organizing techniques, first to union men, later to civil rights workers. A photographer sent clandestinely to the center by the governor of Georgia photographed King and a journalist from the *Daily Worker* sitting together. Billboards with the photograph started appearing across the South with huge letters proclaiming "King Attended Communist Training Center."[35] Well into the next decade, King was still being called to account for that photograph and his association with the Highlander.

Time was out to polish, not besmirch, King's image, and it was not surprising that the magazine maintained that he was "no radical [and] he avoids the excesses of radicalism." Not surprisingly, as well, *Time* found that King possessed many of the attributes of Henry Luce. If King had been called as a young man to high position, if he had "risen from nowhere to become one of the nation's most remarkable leaders of men," so, too, had Luce. Scholarly credentials did not hurt, but no doubt it was more important to Luce's magazine that King was a Christian leader with a spiritual force who "aspired even to ending prejudice in man's mind." King was to *Time* both missionary and prophet. The prophet brought the gospel of freedom not only to blacks in Montgomery but to "his people." He was, as well, a missionary in a strange land—the South and its peculiar customs could hardly be otherwise to Luce and *Time*—willing to back his principles with his life, willing even to love those who sought to slay him, his family, or his followers. With a tone approaching awe, *Time* told how King turned back from retaliation the mob driven to fury by the bombing of King's home. "'Please be peaceful,' he said from the shattered porch. 'We believe in law and order. We are not advocating violence. We want to love our enemies. Be good to them. Love them and let them know you love them.'" Nothing being more persuasive than the praise of an enemy, this testimony immediately followed: "'I'll be honest with you,' says a policeman who was there, 'I was terrified. I owe my life to that nigger preacher and so do all the other white people who were there.'"[36]

Oddly, the bombing had occurred more than a year earlier, and this was *Time*'s first reference to it. Perhaps *Time* had been unaware of the incident,

35. Adams, *Unearthing Seeds of Fire*, 125–26.
36. "Attack on the Conscience," 17, 19.

but internal evidence, including the lengthy quotations, suggests otherwise. The belatedness of the report can probably be traced to *Time*'s reluctance to confer laurels upon losers. Until the Supreme Court struck down Montgomery's bus segregation ordinance, King and the MIA appeared on the verge of defeat. By the time the cover article appeared, King clearly had "outgeneraled" his white adversaries and attained that most blessed of Lucean states of grace, success. He could, therefore, be celebrated with an adulatory cover spread.

Time's cover treatment appeared shallow when measured against an article published more than six months before by the magazine whose hostility to King was beyond question. The article was a "debate" of sorts that *U.S. News* arranged by reprinting one of King's speeches and a reply by the editor of the Montgomery *Advertiser*. The article provided significant clues not available in the other news weeklies about the course King's career would eventually take. While King exhibited the humility so appealing to *Time*, he also demonstrated a broader vision, particularly in asserting the birth of a "new Negro" who would not be so willing to continue a patient climb to equality. King advocated the reconciliation of whites and blacks, but there was a keener edge to what he said in *U.S. News*. King acknowledged the need for assistance from white allies but attached a significant caveat. "Obtaining full equality," he said, "is a problem for which the Negro himself must assume the primary responsibility. Integration will not be some lavish dish that the white man will pass out on a silver platter, while the Negro furnishes merely the appetite." King recognized as well that race was a national problem. His analysis was that blacks "are far from the promised land, both North and South. In the South we still confront segregation in its glaring conspicuous forms. In the North we confront it in its hidden and subtle forms." (No doubt his remarks occasioned approving nods at a magazine busily condemning northern hypocrisy.) Finally, the article bore evidence that King's social thought already was moving toward a critical perspective on race, colonialism, and oppression.[37]

The King of this "debate" was far more vital than was the somewhat passive figure found in *Time*, which seemed to equate Gandhian nonviolence and the Christian ethic with meekness, not militancy. A magazine of the middle class and the middle way, *Time* derived a certain comfort from King, who promised not race war but reconciliation, not hatred but love, and not revolution but

37. "Alabama's Bus Boycott: What It's All About," *U.S. News & World Report*, August 3, 1956, pp. 88, 89.

reform achieved at a measured pace. *U.S. News* had little sympathy for social change at any pace, and in matters of race its sympathies were with segregationists. By reprinting King's speech, *U.S. News* said, in effect, here is a dangerous man. If the prophet created by *Time* promised peace, the prophet revealed by *U.S. News* promised implicitly that in the future he would bring a sword.

Somewhere between those two positions was *Newsweek*, wary and suspicious. Against the overwhelming tide of opinion, *Newsweek* insisted in 1957 that a collective leadership was responsible for the Montgomery movement. The following year, it found space for a one-paragraph item reporting the arrest of King "while trying to enter a crowded courtroom where another Negro integration leader was testifying." Something appeared to be awry in his attitude. "King asked to be jailed," the story reported, the tone implying he was asking for trouble and getting it. A note was appended: The police commissioner of Montgomery paid King's $10 fine, explaining that "King wanted to become 'a martyr.'"[38]

Following Gandhi's example, King indeed wished to do that, to set an example by accepting incarceration rather than accommodating himself to injustice. It is doubtful, however, that he precipitated the arrest, as *Newsweek* implied. Had police discipline not slipped, the incident probably would not have taken place. Ten minutes after being shoved into a cell, King was permitted to sign out on bond; the arresting officers had apparently violated a departmental policy against arresting highly visible black leaders. King was not ignorant of the value of publicity. "When I go to jail," he remarked to some followers later, "the whole world knows it. . . . But when one of you goes to jail and suffers brutality, no one knows about it." Equally aware that there would be an outcry if King remained in jail, the police commissioner acted swiftly to deny him publicity by paying the fine.[39]

For whatever motive, *Newsweek* seemed bent on denying King his publicity. The brevity and the tone of the item indicated that it was playing down the arrest, as did, for that matter, a caption for a photograph that showed policemen handling King roughly. Not even naming King, the caption merely noted, "Alabama arrests a Negro minister on a loitering charge."[40]

38. "Bid for the Jackpot," *Newsweek*, June 24, 1957, p. 30; "The U.S.—The Issue and a Showdown," *Newsweek*, September 15, 1958, p. 26.
39. King's remark is quoted in Miller, "The Broadening Horizons," 55. On King's arrest, see *ibid.*, 53–55; and Lewis, *King: A Biography*, 96–97.
40. "The U.S.—The Issue and a Showdown," 27.

Time was providing publicity sufficient to make up for any shortage. Particularly striking was a story in 1957 that emphasized the man over the event, which was the Prayer Pilgrimage in Washington on May 17. *Time* did not just depict King as a judicious and moderate leader, but it made those virtues stand out in bold relief against its portrayal of a less temperate black leader. The contraposed figure was the stormy petrel of black politics, Congressman Adam Clayton Powell, of Harlem, with whom King shared the platform at the demonstration. Powell complained shrilly that blacks were "getting more from a dead Republican"—a reference to Lincoln—than from "live Democrats and live Republicans!" By contrast, the reasonable and "softspoken" King was "staking his hopes on the future rather than anchoring his peeves on the past." Unlike Powell, King made an "eloquent plea" for the same right that other Americans enjoyed: the ballot. Once blacks had that most basic right, King said, "'we will quietly and nonviolently, without rancor or bitterness,'" secure equality.[41]

This was the first instance in which *Time* bound King to a contrapuntal symbol, though it was far from the last. In fact, the other news magazines would follow suit. (Even *U.S. News* discovered the usefulness of King as a symbol when an alternative black leader or group looked more threatening. Two years hence, contemplating the deadline "for the extermination of the white race" set by the black separatist sect the Black Muslims, the magazine approvingly quoted a statement by King that "black supremacy is as bad as white supremacy.") By juxtaposing two symbolic figures, the news magazines (and the news media generally) clarify a complex situation and strip it of nuances. As Kai Erikson explained, such symbolic encounters "provide a forum, as it were, in which the issue can be articulated more clearly, a stage on which it can be portrayed in sharper relief."[42] Moreover, as they paint symbols in distinct shadings—radicalism and moderation, for example—the media demonstrate the existence and the efficacy of the latter.

The portrayal of King as an alternative to more radical leaders was an important source of his strength. August Meier's perceptive analysis shows that King held the crucial middle ground in the civil rights movement, the bridge between the radicals of the Left and the conservatives of the Right.[43]

41. "People," *Time*, May 27, 1957, p. 40.
42. "'Black Supremacy' Cult in U.S.—How Much of a Threat?" *U.S. News & World Report*, November 9, 1959, p. 114; Erikson, *Wayward Puritans*, 69.
43. Meier, "The Conservative Militant," 144–56.

The division of the movement into Right and Left had not appeared in any striking public fashion in 1957, but *Time*'s placement of King and Powell side by side in effect designated King as the model for black leadership.

In contrast to *Newsweek*, *Time* named King as the model for black leadership in its report of one of the most dramatic episodes of his life. King had traveled to Harlem in September of 1958 for a series of appearances. A rough reception awaited him: He was jeered and his car pelted with eggs, and it got much worse. While autographing copies of his book, *Stride Toward Freedom*, he was stabbed in the chest by a deranged black woman. King came perilously close to death. Surgeons found the tip of the weapon, a letter opener, resting against King's aorta.[44]

Newsweek's story was favorable in one sense. It promoted King to a status that he had not enjoyed in the magazine since the boycott by reporting that he was regarded "with something close to veneration" in Harlem "as one of his people's most literate spokesmen." However, the story omitted information that would have explained why the venerated King was assaulted. His assailant, *Newsweek* reported vaguely, "shouted something about 'all the trouble [King] had caused for the Negro people' in fighting segregation, and plunged the blade of a letter opener into his left shoulder." By contrast, *Time* emphasized that the incident was an act of madness by a woman, Izola Curry, who "suddenly flashed a steel letter opener and stabbed King in the upper left side of his chest." After an outbreak of panic by customers, some of them "grabbed the deranged woman and held her for police as she babbled incoherently."[45]

Newsweek concluded its account with the bland notation that King was "at Harlem Hospital, [and] on the way to recovery." *Time* carefully established that the wound was a more serious matter than being pinked in the shoulder; it estimated the length of the surgery, two and a quarter hours, and reported a surgeon's announcement that "the blade, narrowly missing the critical aorta near the heart, had been removed." The summary promoted King as "the hero"—first because he "had escaped gun and bomb blasts in Alabama," then because, though gravely wounded, he remained "still conscious and calm" while being taken to a Harlem hospital with a steel blade sticking in his chest.[46]

44. Miller, "The Broadening Horizons," 55–57; Lewis, *King: A Biography*, 98; Bishop, *The Days of Martin Luther King*, 209.
45. "Incident in Harlem," *Newsweek*, September 29, 1958, p. 24; "Accident in Harlem," *Time*, September 29, 1958, p. 14.
46. "Incident in Harlem," 24; "Accident in Harlem," 14.

The details themselves are less important than are the ends to which they were used. The news magazine formula demanded that telling facts be woven into a story to make it complete and satisfying. Not for years would *Newsweek* begin to match *Time* in meeting the requirements for drama, and it was sorely lacking in professional polish in 1958. However, some of the information not supplied by *Newsweek* was so patently obvious—the derangement of the attacker, for example—as to suggest purposive omission rather than incompetent reporting or editing. For whichever reason, *Newsweek* diminished King: At best, he was a victim of ironical circumstances (having stood his ground against hostile whites, King was attacked by a black); at worst, he was set upon because of the trouble he caused his people. By contrast, *Time* elevated King as a powerful symbol; he was a hero who mastered his fear and the wound that threatened his life, and by so doing earned once again his right to lead the black movement.

King's considerable problem was that he had to earn the right over and over again. His doubts that he could continue to pull rabbits out of a hat were justified. As the decade was ending he was slipping into relative obscurity. The Montgomery bus boycott was years past, and the news magazines, no less than other media, prefer history in the making to history already made. They did not report, for example, the dramatic trip to India in 1959 that cemented King's commitment to Gandhian nonviolence. King met the men who had helped Gandhi translate philosophy into action—he reflected that "it was a little like having lunch with George Washington, then tea with John Adams, supper with Jefferson, and an evening chat with Tom Paine"—and they greeted him as one of their own.[47]

By the time he left India, King had come far from the cause that had propelled him to fame. The young preacher of once-modest ambition was gripped with a sense of mission as he prepared to leave Montgomery in 1959. "'I can't stop now,'" King told his congregation in his farewell sermon. "'History has thrust something upon me which I cannot turn away.'"[48]

History had thrust something upon him. It would do so again, but there was little sense of this in the news magazines in the absence of crises that provided the drama the news magazines required. In coming years, there would be crises and drama in full measure.

47. Miller, "The Broadening Horizons," 61.
48. Lewis, *King: A Biography*, 109.

II

STRATEGY OF CRISIS

In the opening years of the new decade, three racial crises significantly altered the course of the southern movement, King's standing in it, and his strategy as a civil rights leader. The first crisis arrived with the sit-ins that swept through the South in the early months of 1960. Both the black movement and American society felt the impact of the sit-ins, which set in motion social forces that eventually made the 1960s a decade of youth in rebellion. The sit-ins themselves produced a revolt of the young not only against segregation but against the elders of the black movement. Succeeding the sit-ins in 1961 were the Freedom Rides. While the sit-ins began as inchoate expressions of anger at the humiliations imposed by Jim Crow, the Freedom Rides were an attempt to create a crisis; the intent was to force the federal government to take action against clearly illegal practices of segregation and discrimination in interstate travel.

Unlike the sit-ins and Freedom Rides, the third crisis, the Albany Movement of 1962, was important not because it succeeded but because it failed. The movement's failure was an indicator of the decisiveness of symbolism as a factor in the crises. The sit-ins and the Freedom Rides were not new tactics, but the demonstrations were unprecedented in scale, and the televised and printed news accounts dramatically focused the nation's attention on the struggle in the South. What the nation experienced vicariously was a series of morality plays. During the sit-ins, young and idealistic black college students, peacefully seeking only what other Americans took for granted, service at a lunch counter, were subjected to insult, assault, injury, and arrest when they challenged the thoroughly oppressive system of segregation. In the Freedom Rides, integrated busloads of young volunteers, whose only offense was sitting beside others of different race, were attacked savagely by white mobs. Victories gave way to defeat the following year during the Albany Movement, led by King. A flaw appeared in the strategy of using moral dramas that King had learned from the sit-ins and Freedom Rides as well as from Gandhi. The lesson of Albany was that if the moral dramas were to arouse sympathy for black southerners groaning under Jim Crow's yoke, they would have to be so charged with symbolism that the evils of segregation would appear brutal, stark, and unrelieved by nuance.

King's accession to leadership in the three crises and in the Montgomery movement held obvious similarities. In Albany, as in Montgomery, King came to lead the struggle by accident, and in the sit-ins and Freedom Rides he was pushed to the forefront of movements he had not created or begun. There were differences no less striking. The obscure young preacher of Montgomery now was internationally known, and he was cast in critical symbolic roles—as a leader restraining the possibility of violence during those unsettled times or as the alternative to more radical elements.

The first crisis was set in motion by four young black students in Greensboro, North Carolina, who tested the local segregation ordinance at a whites-only lunch counter on February 1, 1960. With astonishing rapidity, sit-ins began to appear throughout North Carolina, then in other southern states. Eventually, more than 50,000 persons participated in demonstrations in a hundred or more cities, and more than 36,000 persons were arrested.[1]

With no organization, no headquarters, no acknowledged leader, the sit-ins, spontaneously breaking out in dozens of widely scattered cities, were maddeningly difficult to cover with any perspective beyond the here and now. Reporters are trained to search out sources of authority, and King had the kind of credentials for which they look. The students used nonviolent tactics in the sit-ins, and King had an expert's standing on that subject. He also had an organization, though the Southern Christian Leadership Conference was not much more than a name at the time. Furthermore, King was certified as a news source by the hundreds of times he had been quoted in journalistic accounts or had appeared on broadcast media; not so the youngsters conducting the sit-

1. Howard Zinn, *SNCC: The New Abolitionists* (Boston, 1964), 16.

ins.[2] Nor did it hurt that King, who had just turned thirty, was older than the students. The 1960s passed into history as a decade of the young, but that characterization grew out of the later, increasingly bitter rebellions led by young men and women who would have been regarded as callow in the 1950s. Taking college students as leaders of a social movement undoubtedly struck journalists as too much to swallow early in 1960. All in all, when reporters went looking for a leader of the leaderless sit-ins, it is not surprising that many of them found King.

Among these reporters were the correspondents of *Newsweek*, which had stilled most of its doubts about King and had found, in fact, much to admire in him. *Newsweek* did not anoint King as the black leader in its first story about him in 1960, a report of King's emotional farewell to his congregation in Montgomery. Two issues later, however, he was depicted as the force behind the sit-ins and as a moderate acutely aware of the volatile mood of a people rising from oppression and determined to channel their energies into non-violent protest. The sit-ins, he said in *Newsweek*'s account, help "to ease the frustrations felt by many Negroes as court action on segregation grinds along at 'deliberate speed.'" The black students, he said, must be willing to fill the jails, but should not respond in kind to violence. "'I got it over to them,'" King said, attaching the significant caveat, "'for the moment at least.'"[3]

The article accurately reproduced King's views, but it also justified his leadership of the southern movement. Down one path was violence, perhaps even anarchy; down another, creative protests designed to secure rights for Americans deprived of them. His remark about momentarily winning the students over to the way of nonviolence might have been self-serving, but *Newsweek* was becoming a convert to the way of Martin Luther King.[4]

King's observation had an element of prophecy to it. While taking on Jim Crow, the youngsters of the sit-ins also were challenging the civil rights establishment. Their movement was a protest, the most serious but not the first (a distinction held by the Montgomery boycott), against pace and tactics dictated by elders. The leading black organization, the NAACP, preferred litigation and legislation over demonstrations. King himself had had his troubles with such doyens as Roy Wilkins of the NAACP, and King and others

2. On news currency, see Bernard Roshco, *Newsmaking* (Chicago, 1975), 18.
3. See *Newsweek*, "'Testimonial of Love,'" February 15, 1960, p. 90, and "'Full-Scale Assault,'" February 29, 1960, p. 25.
4. "Next for the South?" *Newsweek*, March 28, 1960, p. 26.

had laid down the path that the students were now taking. But the young warriors of nonviolence regarded all that as the ancient history of the previous decade; they believed King was insufficiently radical, "an old man of the movement," and thought of themselves, in fact, as "the saviors of the world at that point." Although King was remarkably patient, the students rankled their elders, who reacted with predictable snorts of derision about being "down on the boondocks" fighting Jim Crow when the youngsters "didn't know what the word, movement, meant" and grumbled about the students' arrogant belief that "they started the movement."[5]

The students had not started the civil rights movement, but they had prodded it into action, and for the rest of the decade they would set the pace. This happened with the sit-ins, and King was thrust to the forefront of a movement he did not create. This would happen again, in Albany, for example, and it did King's standing with the students no good that he seemed to reap where they had sown.

King's standing with *Time* slipped measurably. Once it had promoted him with glowing phrases; now *Time* was entranced by the compelling drama of the sit-ins and the revolt of the young. Its reading was less of a nascent social movement than of a morality play, appropriately cast. The black students were studiously polite, orderly, resolute in seeking their rights, but not obnoxious; their white opponents were almost Faulknerian in degeneracy. In February, *Time* described them as "familiar flotsam: the duck-tailed, sideburned swaggerers, the rednecked hatemongers, the Ku Klux Klan." The same idea occurred to others less sympathetic to the students' cause, one being an editorial writer for a conservative Virginia newspaper who wrote: "'Here were the colored students, in coats, white shirts, ties, and one of them was reading Goethe and one was taking notes from a biology text. And here, on the sidewalk outside, was a gang of white boys come to heckle, a ragtail rabble,

5. On the students' attitudes, see interview with John Gibson, later a member of the SCLC staff, by John Britton, April 26, 1968 (Transcript of tape 176, in Moorland-Spingarn Research Center, Howard University), 16–17. On the boycott and sit-ins as revolts against civil rights organizations, see Louis E. Lomax, *The Negro Revolt* (New York, 1962), 113–20. On conflicts with the NAACP, see Miller, "The Broadening Horizons," 48. The sit-in was a union tactic applied by NAACP youth groups as late as 1958 in Oklahoma City and Wichita. Clayborne Carson, *In Struggle: SNCC and the Black Awakening of the 1960s* (Cambridge, Mass., 1981), 16. The complaints about students appear in an interview with Wyatt Tee Walker, former executive director of the SCLC, by John Britton, October 11, 1967 (Transcript of tape 56, in Moorland-Spingarn Research Center, Howard University), 42–43. King demonstrated "a great deal of restraint and patience" in his dealings with SNCC. Walker interview, 40. On the generation gap after the sit-ins, see Viorst, *Fire in the Streets*, 212–13.

slack-jawed, black-jacketed, grinning fit to kill . . . Eheu! It gives one pause.'" With middle-class virtues so evident among the black protesters, scant wonder the situation gave pause to the editorialist or caused *Time* to proclaim that "the young Negro . . . is now leading the battle for equal rights. And unless he is tossed into jail and onto a road gang, he is going to lead the battle for a long time to come."[6]

Time was spared a sibylline burden. Many of those students, so inspiring in their youth and earnestness and belief in their country's ideals, in a few years would put away Goethe and pick up Marx and Fanon; would exchange coats and neckties for more proletarian dress; would feel the heady rush of identification with Africa and African freedom struggles, an emotion-filled turning toward their racial homeland already beginning to tug at them in 1960; would come to believe themselves oppressed by domestic colonialism—Fanon's term; and would transmit to clean-cut white American kids a sense of alienation and a spirit of radicalism that would convulse many campuses. Had *Time* that knowledge in early 1960, no doubt King would have fared better. Instead, *Time* subscribed to the belief that youth will be served. It was served well enough by *Time*. Articles published later in the year continued to emphasize that King scarcely figured at all in a movement of the young. Reporting the organization of the Student Nonviolent Coordinating Committee in April, 1960, for example, *Time* said, in effect, that where the students acted, King only talked.[7]

Time's assessment of King's role in the conference at which SNCC was born came tolerably close to the mark. The impetus was provided by Ella Baker, then chief of the SCLC staff. The students met under the aegis of the SCLC in Raleigh, North Carolina. The critical decision was whether the students would become a wing of the SCLC or strike out on their own. Among members of King's staff there was considerable sentiment for the first idea, but Ella Baker resisted the absorption of the student movement. More radical than King, she was convinced that economic questions would come to dominate the black movement, and that black students would become the move-

6. "Complicated Hospitality," *Time*, February 22, 1960, p. 20; Richmond (Va.) *News-Leader*, February 22, 1960, quoted in Zinn, *SNCC*, 27.

7. See *Time*'s reports on the sit-ins and the student movement in "Brushfire," March 14, 1960, p. 21; "Freeze and Thaw," March 28, 1960, pp. 24–25; and "A Universal Effort," May 2, 1960, p. 16. *Time*'s identification of King as a "Negro minister and integration strategist" implied removal from the action. "People," *Time*, June 6, 1960, p. 38.

ment's shock troops—prophecies that would be proven correct. Baker also was openly impatient with the lack of vigor in the SCLC and the conservative ways of King. Concerned about an embarrassing public break with Baker, King backed away from pushing the students into becoming an arm of the SCLC.[8]

As influential as Ella Baker was a young black Methodist minister, James Lawson, who would persuade King to take up the cause of the striking sanitation men in Memphis eight years hence. Lawson was the force behind black students organizing sit-ins in Nashville that were scheduled to begin in February. The first sit-in got under way in Greensboro instead, but the Nashville sit-ins probably were the most effective of any conducted during 1960. A pacifist who chose prison rather than military service during the Korean War, Lawson was paroled and served three years as a missionary in India. His studies and work as a field secretary for the Fellowship of Reconciliation won him a reputation as a theorist of Gandhian nonviolence. Lawson's arguments were persuasive; the members of SNCC accepted nonviolence as the guiding strategy even though some were impatient with talk of philosophy when their preference was for action.[9]

The students' preference for action was causing *U.S. News* to keep a wary watch. Initially it ignored King. Behind the sit-ins, readers were informed in early March, were the NAACP and CORE. A week later, however, the magazine trotted out King in the capacity of symbolic leader. The motivation emerges from a summary that warned of sit-ins "breaking out in city after city," of a "move by Negroes away from reliance on courts and Congress to more direct action," and then posed this question: "Can it mean widespread violence?"[10]

Public order was sine qua non to *U.S. News*, which implied often enough that blacks were barely removed from savagery. Just now, it was having a case of nerves at the prospect of young blacks running wild through Dixie, and settled on King as a restraining influence. King was not quoted in that jittery story about the possibility of "widespread violence," but readers were in-

---

8. David J. Garrow, *Bearing the Cross: Martin Luther King, Jr., and the Southern Christian Leadership Conference* (New York, 1986), 132–33. See also Carson, *In Struggle*, 19–24; Viorst, *Fire in the Streets*, 120–23; and Walker interview, 41.

9. Viorst, *Fire in the Streets*, 106–107; Carson, *In Struggle*, 23.

10. See *U.S. News & World Report*, "Battle of the Lunch Counters: Latest Drive for Integration," March 7, 1960, p. 44, and "Will Negroes Win in South?" March 14, 1960, p. 41.

formed that his "opposition to violence has set the pattern of orderliness [and] discipline that has marked the Negro students' acts."[11]

The theme was strengthened and expanded in a series of interviews published the next week. *U.S. News* gathered its reports in Montgomery, a decision more indicative of the symbols attached to King than of anything else. Montgomery had had some sit-ins, but it was not the city in which they began (this was Greensboro); not the city in which the philosophical and tactical concepts were developed most fully (this was Nashville); and not the center of the sit-ins as a movement (in truth, there was no center). Montgomery was, however, the former home of King, "who inspired the bus boycott and now is active in the new movement." The intelligence provided to readers about the man behind the disturbing phenomenon of the sit-ins was in many ways reassuring. King appeared calm and firmly in control of the situation, speaking for men and women desiring their rights as citizens, knowledgeable of social forces and history, committed to the reconciliation of the races, and, if something of a philosopher, able to translate ideas into practice. The last point was important to *U.S. News* at the moment; a significant portion of the interview dealt with the training of students in nonviolence. That the magazine had little, if any, sympathy for the black cause is beside the point. King held out the promise of order in a situation that *U.S. News* believed could cause racial confrontations across the South, if not the nation.[12]

With an eye cocked to conservative subscribers, *U.S. News* balanced its portrayal of King with interviews of white southerners who reiterated the usual complaints: Communists were inspiring the civil rights movement; outside agitators were stirring up blacks who otherwise would be content to live out their days in segregated harmony with whites. Nevertheless, the theme of King as a restraining influence did not disappear. Five months later, readers were again reassured that King was "advising the students" engaged in protests against segregation.[13] In sum, *U.S. News* had relearned the lesson of the previous year when it fretted about the Black Muslims: When greater dangers threatened, King could be a useful symbol.

Although the southern sit-ins (and sympathy protests elsewhere in the

11. "Will Negroes Win in South?" 45.

12. "Everywhere: Tension," *U.S. News & World Report*, March 21, 1960, p. 73. The King interview was published in "Revolt Without Violence: The Negroes' New Strategy," *U.S. News & World Report*, March 21, 1960, pp. 76–78.

13. "Everywhere: Tension," 72–75. *U.S. News* reiterated the theme in "Now It's a 'Kneel-in' Drive in the South," August 22, 1960, p. 8.

nation) continued throughout 1960 and into 1961, King's name virtually disappeared from the news magazines in the second half of 1960. It reappeared as the result of a curious combination of events. King had been arrested in 1959 and placed on probation for a year because he neglected to get a Georgia driver's license after moving from Montgomery to Atlanta. While participating in a sit-in in Atlanta in October of 1960, King was arrested again. The affair probably would have been smoothed over by the image-conscious white leaders of Atlanta had the matter not been taken out of their hands by a judge who revoked the probation and sentenced King to four months in prison.

The timing of the sentencing and fears for King's safety probably added to the furor that surrounded the event. The 1960 presidential campaign was in its closing days. The Democratic candidate, John F. Kennedy, was persuaded by his advisers to call Mrs. King to express concern. His brother, Robert Kennedy, telephoned the judge and applied pressure to get King out on bail. King was freed. Although it is improbable that King was released because of the Kennedys, their intervention was a political masterstroke that, it was widely believed, swung a number of black votes and ensured Kennedy's victory in an extremely close election.[14]

With the nation preparing to elect a president, the magazines followed their political leanings and maximized or minimized the number of votes that might be shifted to Kennedy. (*Newsweek* emphasized the boldness of what Kennedy had done; *Time*, tilting toward the Republican party, implied that Kennedy's gesture had little to do with setting right an episode that "reeked of redneck justice"; and *U.S. News*, further to the right, ignored the Kennedys altogether, reporting that "the judge said he had been under pressure for and against granting bond, but that he was solely guided by law.")[15] In the years ahead,

14. On the incident, see Garrow, *Bearing the Cross*, pp. 144–49. The apprehensions arose after the almost clandestine transfer of King to a state prison. King's father believed that the authorities were hoping a situation could be created in which King would be killed in a fight with another inmate. Martin Luther King, Sr., and Clayton Riley, *Daddy King: An Autobiography* (New York, 1980), 174–75. *Cf.* Harris Wofford, *Of Kennedys and Kings: Making Sense of the Sixties* (New York, 1980), 18. His lawyer maintained that King would have been released in any event. Interview with Donald L. Hollowell, by John Britton, May 23, 1968 (Transcript of tape 187, in Moorland-Spingarn Research Center, Howard University), 23–24. King remained officially neutral, but his father switched his endorsement from Nixon to Kennedy. King and Riley, *Daddy King*, 176.

15. "Taking a Gamble," *Newsweek*, November 7, 1960, p. 36; "Swift Deliverance," *Time*, November 7, 1960, p. 30; "Negro Leader Jailed, Then Freed on Appeal," *U.S. News & World Report*, November 7, 1960, p. 14.

however, what had been a political gesture became fraught with symbolism. *U.S. News* would see, in that telephone call to Mrs. King, evidence of collusion between King and the federal authorities. More important, however, was the beginning of a process whereby King and the Kennedys, especially John Kennedy, would become associated symbolically. Eventually, after each died a martyr's death, they would become merged symbols in a mythic past stripped of complexity and nuance.

For the present, with the wave of sit-ins receding, presidential politics on hold until after the inauguration, and King out of prison, his name all but disappeared again from the news weeklies. Except for one or two references, it did not reappear until the Freedom Ride crisis was precipitated by CORE the following year. CORE was almost two decades older than the SCLC and its credentials when it came to Gandhian nonviolence were as impressive. But CORE bore the stigma of radicalism because some of its members had pursued a course of militant pacifism during the cold war. King himself spoke out early in his career about the dangers of a nuclear Armageddon, but those statements attracted little notice and, therefore, did not harm his image during the Freedom Ride crisis when he was perceived as the alternative to radicalism.

The crisis grew out of an attempt to embarrass the federal government by demonstrating the disparity between law and fact along the highways of the nation. CORE had tried the tactic before. It had sent sixteen volunteers on a two-week Journey of Reconciliation through the upper South in 1947. Relying upon a Supreme Court decision in 1946 declaring segregation on interstate buses unconstitutional, the volunteers challenged Jim Crow. They received beatings at the hands of segregationists, jail terms from local authorities, and little or no attention from the press and the federal government. In 1961, James Farmer, the director of CORE, had the idea of creating a crisis to which the federal government would have to respond—"a situation that was headline news all over the world and affected our nation's image abroad."[16]

The strategy did not work immediately. Farmer's letters alerting federal authorities to the new campaign were misplaced or ignored. The Freedom Rides began quietly on May 4, 1961, with an integrated party of thirteen

---

16. The best study of CORE is August Meier and Elliott Rudwick, *CORE: A Study in the Civil Rights Movement, 1942–1968* (Oxford, 1973). See pp. 35–46 on the Journey of Reconciliation. See also Inge Powell Bell, *CORE and the Strategy of Nonviolence* (New York, 1968), 9, 33; and Cantor, *The Age of Protest*, 250. Farmer is quoted in Viorst, *Fire in the Streets*, 128.

persons, several of whom were veterans of the sit-ins. As they headed south the Freedom Riders attracted little attention. Ten days into the journey, however, the first bus was attacked in Anniston, Alabama. Police stood aside while the thirty or forty whites ran amok; several demonstrators were beaten, and the bus was damaged before the police finally waved the mob off. The bus departed. A flat tire brought it to a halt six miles away, and the mob, which had been trailing the vehicle, closed in again. A fire bomb was tossed into the bus and exploded; the mob trapped the passengers inside the bus, which was rapidly filling with smoke. After the doors were opened, the fleeing Freedom Riders were attacked again. Police from Anniston arrived finally, along with a rescue party of armed blacks assembled in Birmingham. The beleaguered Freedom Riders were taken to Birmingham by the black party.[17]

Another bus also was attacked first in Anniston and again in Birmingham. In the latter city, young whites armed with iron bars and baseball bats rushed the passengers. As in Anniston, police did not intervene in Birmingham until the mob had almost spent its fury. Asked to account for this failure, Birmingham's fire and police commissioner blandly explained that most of his officers were off duty, visiting their mothers on Mother's Day. Two years later, the commissioner's name would become a synonym for the brutality of segregation. It was Bull Connor.[18]

Farmer had his crisis, which is also to say that the Kennedy administration had *its* crisis, one with international and domestic ramifications. The mobs in Alabama were drawing the attention of the world press. For Kennedy, the timing could not have been worse. Preparing for a summit conference in Vienna with Soviet leader Nikita Khrushchev, Kennedy did not want his position undermined by events implying weakness on his part or division in the United States. Pictures and accounts of jeering mobs and battered Freedom Riders created domestic problems as well for the new administration. Kennedy himself was acutely sensitive to the narrowness of his victory in the 1960 election and to the power of the southern politicians who held his legislative program hostage in Congress. In a situation that called for no bolder step than enforcing settled law, Kennedy heeded the dictates of international diplomacy and Washington politics. He called his civil rights liaison,

17. Viorst, *Fire in the Streets*, 142–45.
18. Connor had apparently promised the Ku Klux Klan ample time to effect the assaults. *Ibid.*, 145. Despite advance warning, Hoover did nothing to alert federal authorities or to prevent the attack. Wofford, *Of Kennedys and Kings*, 152.

Harris Wofford, and ordered him: " 'Tell them to call it off! Stop them!' "[19] The law was so clear and the publicity so glaring, however, that the Kennedy administration was being pushed to the point where it would have to do something about the situation.

The international dimension of the crisis was essentially ignored by the news magazines. The Freedom Rides were regarded as a domestic matter and, except for an article in *Newsweek*, were reported as such.[20] Other factors also shaped the reports. *Time* and *Newsweek*, for example, were confronted by a sticky point, the failure of the federal government to enforce a right settled in constitutional law since 1946. The neglect of ideals and law could scarcely be any less embarrassing to two magazines of the middle way than to the government itself. For *U.S. News* the problem went in the opposite direction. It interpreted the crisis as another unconstitutional imposition of federal authority in the South. Thus, the Freedom Riders and the federal government could not be at odds; in fact, there had to be at least a suggestion of collusion between them.

Upon one thing the news magazines agreed: The crisis produced a wrenching conflict between the national government and the government of Alabama. *Time* and *Newsweek* criticized the outrageous collapse of order in Alabama. *Time*, in its initial reaction, denounced those "from Alabama's Governor John Patterson on down, [who] abdicated their duties of maintaining law and order" and bestowed its approval upon the president, who declared firmly that even if the state government failed to do its duty, the "U.S. Government intends to meet" its responsibility.[21] That declaration of national power and purpose, as much Luce's sentiment as John Kennedy's, recurred in *Time* as the crisis continued.

By no means, however, did *Time* approve of those who, by forcing the crisis, had embarrassed America. The stinging rebuke to the officials of Alabama was matched by the cold disdain for the agitators of CORE; they "were, in fact, hunting for trouble—and found more of it than they wanted." To make the point unmistakable, *Time* offered the contrasting example of a black leader in Nashville whose "willingness to achieve progress in fact rather than seek headline victories . . . made the quiet but vital difference."[22]

19. Wofford, *Of Kennedys and Kings*, 153. Wofford received similar instructions from Attorney General Kennedy. *Ibid.*, 156.
20. "Tension and Justice," *Newsweek*, June 12, 1961, p. 37.
21. "Trouble in Alabama," *Time*, May 26, 1961, p. 16.
22. *Ibid*; "The Nashville Lesson," *Time*, May 26, 1961, p. 17.

And along the way, *Time* rediscovered King's value as a symbol, in part because of another mob episode. The Freedom Rides, interrupted in Birmingham by assaults, resumed. As the bus approached Montgomery on May 20, the state police escort vanished. The Freedom Riders and a representative of Attorney General Kennedy were attacked by a mob of several hundred whites. The attorney general ordered federal marshals sent into Montgomery. The following night, King and approximately twelve hundred Freedom Riders and black and white supporters came under siege. A mob of two thousand whites surrounded the church in which a rally was under way; only the timely intervention of federal marshals and other officers prevented carnage. While the mob howled outside, King told the besieged demonstrators: " 'We hear the familiar cry that morals cannot be legislated. . . . The law may not be able to make a man love me, but it can keep him from lynching me.' "[23]

That lynch mob played a significant role in a *Time* story that underscored the symbolism attached to King as an American prophet. *Time* reported as a crucial symbolic element an extraordinary telephone conversation between Governor John Patterson and Attorney General Kennedy. Patterson, according to *Time*, informed Kennedy that an Alabama National Guard general "could not guarantee the protection of King." Outrage—Kennedy's, *Time*'s, and, no doubt, that of many *Time* readers—echoed in the voice of the attorney general "as he worked over Patterson: 'Have the general call me. I want him to say it to me, I want to hear a general of the U.S. Army say he can't protect Martin Luther King.' "[24] No mistaking the message: The governor of Alabama might claim he was powerless to curb a mob, but the government of the United States was not.

There was another reason why King was back in *Time*'s good graces. The magazine anointed him as the leader of the replacements for the CORE volunteers whom *Time* found so disreputable. Stepping forward were the young men and women of SNCC, King's "tactical disciples" who were "willing to suffer beatings and endure jail." Why *Time* approved of King's disciples and not the volunteers of CORE had little to do with the courage of the former and the cowardice (so *Time* implied) of the latter. Instead, the students' pristine idealism was far more savory than was the radicalism of

23. "Crisis in Civil Rights," *Time*, June 2, 1961, pp. 14–15. On the events in Montgomery, see Walker interview, 19; and Wofford, *Of Kennedys and Kings*, 154.

24. "Crisis in Civil Rights," 15. *Time* added that Patterson wilted and admitted that he, not the general, doubted that King could be protected.

CORE, exemplified by two of its members. One had been a conscientious objector during World War II, the other had sailed a ketch to Eniwetok atoll in 1958 "in an effort to halt scheduled U.S. nuclear tests."[25] In sum, SNCC's members were undergoing the hazards of the Freedom Rides in order to uphold American ideals; CORE was represented by men who had attempted to thwart America's military defense.

Luce's magazine could now sketch a moral drama uncomplicated by nuances: mobs running unchecked through the streets, given free rein by southern lawmen heedless of their duty and their oaths; the governor of Alabama (this was one of those utterly damning details that *Time* correspondents were paid well to unearth) willing to whirl into action to protect a pet toad, but not to save human lives. By contrast, there were brave and idealistic young demonstrators, who sought only to assert their rights as Americans; the president and the attorney general of the United States, who knew their duty and did it; and a moderate leader, Martin Luther King, who spoke in reasoned tones about justice and its coming victory. Two quotations completed the drama. The first was King's assessment of the Freedom Rides as a "psychological turning point" that, once past, "will mean breaking the backbone of massive resistance and discrimination." The second was supplied by Robert Kennedy, who "reminded the world that the U.S. has an Irish Catholic for president, and added: . . . 'In the next forty years a Negro can achieve the same position that my brother has.'"[26]

Newsweek invoked the same political myth but did not emphasize the radicalism of CORE. However, the magazine went out of its way to establish King as the leader of this new campaign. "Flying into Montgomery from Chicago," said its report, "King was ready to rally Negro leaders to take up the cause of the Freedom Riders. 'We're going to see it through,' said one of King's lieutenants. 'We've got to. If we stop now we may lose the psychological advantage.'" The effort to promote King to the leadership of the Freedom Rides thus started before King could have played a role in the campaign. The following edition fixed King even more firmly as a symbolic figure. King appeared with Attorney General Kennedy and Patterson on the cover of *Newsweek*. The captions attached to the photographs etched the symbolism starkly. Kennedy proclaimed that "we must stand for human liberty"; King

25. *Ibid.*, 14; "Trouble in Alabama," 16.
26. "Crisis in Civil Rights," 18.

that "we must be prepared to suffer . . . even die" in that same cause; and Patterson, predictably, that the federal government "encourages these agitators." The inside story reiterated the clearly drawn issue.[27]

Yet *Newsweek* was never as rigid as *Time* when it came to making distinctions between good and evil. It was all very well for *Time* to thump the Constitution, thrash the red-necks in print, and let the matter go at that. *Newsweek* was almost compelled to sound tones of compromise, reconciliation, and even sympathy for the anguish of moderates of the region—"men of good will and good sense"—forced to "make agonizing reappraisals of their traditional way of life." This group included *Newsweek*'s own native southerners, from the correspondents covering the civil rights movement to the magazine's new owner, Phil Graham. Graham agonized over the racial problems of the South; he spent his mental stability while attempting to help resolve the 1957 Little Rock integration crisis without violence, and he killed himself in 1963.[28]

The yearning for compromise and reconciliation was not due entirely to the southern background of *Newsweek*'s new owner and some of its writers. Some of the angst of the progressive wing of the Democratic party crept into the reports as well. As an example, there was *Newsweek*'s portrait of the complex and driven man who was then the attorney general. Kennedy, by *Newsweek*'s account, was a peacemaker who sought the middle way, a man of good will and good sense willing to ensure rights for the black man. The problem was when. The crisis forced by CORE was distasteful to *Newsweek*. It doubted the wisdom of pressing ahead with so divisive a campaign when the sine qua non of Democratic liberalism, the right to vote, remained to be secured. CORE saw the situation differently; the Supreme Court's decisions prohibiting discrimination in interstate transportation had gathered dust long enough, and the time had come to make the federal government enforce the

27. For Kennedy's statement, see "How the World Press Viewed the Days of Tension," *Newsweek*, June 5, 1961, p. 22. The only reference to radicalism and CORE occurred when the already discredited officials of Alabama described CORE volunteers as Communists. "Days of Violence in the South," *Newsweek*, May 29, 1961, p. 22. Journalists use such tenses to report an event that has not yet occurred at the time of the writing, but that will have occurred by the time the article is read. See cover and "Freedom Riders Force a Test . . . State Laws or U.S. Law in Segregated South?" *Newsweek*, June 5, 1961, pp. 18–20.

28. "As the South Turns the Corner on Integration," *Newsweek*, September 18, 1961, p. 73. On the magazine's southern correspondents, see Elliott, *The World of Oz*, 71–80. On Graham, see Chalmers M. Roberts, *The Washington Post: The First 100 Years* (Boston, 1977), 330–31, 363.

law. CORE (along with the SCLC and SNCC), announced that the Freedom Rides would proceed despite the possibility of violence.

Newsweek had to make sense of the situation. That task was simplified immeasurably because the students climbing aboard the buses were so brave, so young—like Boy and Girl Scouts grown into young adulthood: "always . . . polite and composed in the face of adversity, never provocative or . . . unruly," and never afraid. Even though their refrain was insistent—"freedom, freedom," trailing the buses—and their pace was militant—"freedom now," not tomorrow—their presence made it possible for *Newsweek* not to dwell upon the embarrassment of the Kennedy administration because of that insistence upon freedom *now*. And their goal was American to the core, to make "Little Rock and Montgomery . . . someday mean to Negroes what the Alamo does to Texans." Furthermore, King, a reasoned but determined voice for justice, was setting the tone. Not a seeker after martyrdom, he was willing to accept a martyr's fate if it came because "sometimes death can arouse the dozing conscience of the nation" and because "the time is always right for doing right."[29]

To achieve this clarity of symbolism, *Newsweek* filed down some rough edges. The students who took up the banner of the Freedom Riders were brave enough, almost heartbreakingly so in their innocence. *Newsweek*, for example, recounted that they sang "America the Beautiful" on part of the trip into Mississippi. Perhaps on the same bus, James Farmer of CORE watched the youngsters, who did not expect to survive the journey, write the names and addresses of their next of kin and tuck them in pockets and brassieres. The hitch was that *Newsweek* suggested unity always prevailed and ignored the possibility that young men and women so endowed with a sense of destiny, with a belief in the rightness of their cause, and with reckless bravery might be unforgiving of anyone lacking those virtues. King, who had more than his share of the first two qualities and a limited amount of the last, fell into disfavor with the SNCC youths. Farmer recalled that the youngsters expected King to travel into Mississippi with him. When he refused, saying that he would choose the " 'when and where of his Golgotha,' " the students furiously accused him of cowardice.[30]

---

29. "A New Breed—The Militant Negro in the South," *Newsweek*, June 5, 1961, p. 21.
30. "Freedom Riders Force a Test . . . State Laws or U.S. Laws in Segregated South?" 20; Viorst, *Fire in the Streets*, 156–57. Farmer himself tried to make excuses for not traveling into Mississippi, "but the real reason was that I was scared shitless." When a young girl said to him

No coward would have kept to the path King chose in Montgomery. *His* home had been bombed. *He* had come within a hair's breadth of death in Harlem when a deranged woman rammed a steel blade into his chest. *He* had been in the church in Montgomery to which a howling mob laid siege. It was against *his* life that numerous threats had been made. So there was cause for King's well-developed sense of caution, which came into play when the students tried to get him aboard that bus heading for Mississippi. (He offered as well the practical reason that someone with the requisite visibility had to remain behind in order to raise funds and rally others to the cause.) At worst, King's decision was no more reprehensible than that of a general who sends others out on hazardous service—the difficulty being he spoke of death and stayed behind while others went out to face it. If aware of the incident (as it ought to have been), *Newsweek* ignored it.[31] The furor would have detracted from the pristine symbolism of King. If the students could not appreciate the motives of a leader who picked his spots with care, *Newsweek* readers probably would have had equal difficulty with the fine line separating courage from recklessness.

U.S. News, no less attuned to readers' expectations, responded with four themes about the Freedom Rides: They were an invasion of the South; they were characterized by near-anarchy, implying that they were fomented or encouraged by the federal government; the government was unconstitutionally and unnecessarily intruding into the affairs of a sovereign state; and finally, the likely result would be a bloody racial war.

One theme was stated directly. The Freedom Riders had "invaded the South"—a phrase guaranteed to bring to the fore the southern siege mentality. Thereafter, *U.S. News* called into question both their motives (the demonstrators' "announced purpose" was to "discourage" segregation) and their identity (they "called themselves 'freedom riders'"). The "real" motive and identity followed in the next sentence: "Southern officials called them 'rabble rousers' and agitators."[32]

Two other themes appeared in muted form the following week. One story

---

"patronizingly, 'Jim, please,'" he boarded the bus. Viorst, *Fire in the Streets*, 156. See also Baker interview, 92–93; and Stephen B. Oates, *Let the Trumpet Sound: The Life of Martin Luther King, Jr.* (New York, 1982), 176–77.

31. King announced his decision at a press conference. Oates, *Let the Trumpet Sound*, 176–77. See also Branch, *Parting the Waters*, 466–68.

32. "'Freedom Riders'—and Mob Violence," *U.S. News & World Report*, May 29, 1961, p. 6.

examined Attorney General Kennedy's decision to send "U.S. marshals to help keep order, although Governor John Patterson protested they were not wanted." The article delicately skirted the question of whether the marshals were needed. By glossing over or omitting the mob scenes reported by the other magazines, *U.S. News* implied that this was another instance of federal intrusion into matters best left to the states. A headline questioned: "Is South Headed for Race War?" The story to which it was attached was liberally salted with references to that prospect. It also reiterated the invasion theme: The Freedom Riders formed "a succession of waves, battering the South with one challenge after another."[33]

The article was almost restrained, however, when measured against interviews of a CORE official and southern newspaper editors in the same issue. The CORE representative was pressed to answer a number of questions that, while essential to the invasion theme, were not otherwise germane. *U.S. News* wanted to know, for example, where the Freedom Riders lived and where the screening of volunteers was conducted. The editors were questioned about federal intervention and the possibility of racial warfare. The questions posed and the selection of editors to be interviewed—all but one were conservatives—produced responses in keeping with the conspiracy theories favored by the magazine: *Indeed* the Freedom Riders were outsiders; *beyond question* they were invaders; *certainly* they were being aided by the federal government. Another story depicted the Freedom Riders as Communists. Senator James Eastland, of Mississippi, whose pronouncements on matters racial often appeared in the magazine, scourged "'the *agents provacateurs*'" who were sent "'for the sole purpose of stirring up discord, strife, and violence'" and accused CORE of following "'the pattern set by Communist agitators the world over.'"[34]

In this frightening scenario of looming race war, invasion sponsored by an oppressive central government, and an alien conspiracy, King played only a minor role. However often his critics in the region attacked him, King was indisputably a southerner, his organization the *Southern* Christian Leadership Conference. The notion that the Freedom Rides were "directed by organiza-

33. "Is South Headed for Race War?" *U.S. News & World Report*, June 5, 1961, p. 43.
34. See *U.S. News & World Report*'s issue of June 5, 1961, for "Strategy of Integration Leaders," 44–45, "What Southern Editors Say About the Future," 45–46, and "Senator Eastland on the 'Freedom Riders,'" 48.

tions in the North" required that King and the SCLC be relegated to the background. Citing King as the chief threat would have been even less sensible because the once-modest venture of CORE, which had started with thirteen Riders, had grown to include more than a thousand demonstrators penetrating a number of the major cities of the Deep South. *U.S. News* could find space for the grumbling of a southern editor that "King just stirred strife even more," but that complaint did not explain why waves of invaders were battering the South. The label of outsider was attached to King often enough during campaigns in individual cities, but with a region as a battleground, it made no sense.[35]

For much the same reason, *U.S. News* all but ignored the replacement of the original Freedom Riders by SNCC members, the changing of the guard that *Time* made so much of for *its* purposes. CORE fit into the conspiracy theories favored by *U.S. News*: Headquartered in New York City, the organization could be presented as an invader; and the militant pacifism of some CORE members supported its radical image.

Although King's prestige as a symbol rose during the sit-ins and Freedom Rides, it was shaken severely during the third crisis. The Freedom Riders compelled the federal government to begin enforcing rights that were beyond question in constitutional law, and the segregation of interstate travelers began to crumble. But there were pockets of resistance after the Interstate Commerce Commission—at the urging of the embarrassed Kennedy administration—ruled that segregation of terminal facilities was illegal. One such outpost was Albany, Georgia, a city of more than fifty thousand residents, 40 percent of whom were black. Albany became the focal point of the civil rights movement in 1962. It was an unhappy choice: The Albany Movement was beset by divisions in its ranks and frustrated by the maneuvers of its white opponents.

Albany pointed up the weakness of the strategy of crisis. The crisis had to be one that could be drawn in stark tones of justice and injustice. But the demonstrators in Albany were met by nonviolent resistance, not by mobs. Philosophically, Gandhian nonviolence relied on changing the hearts of oppressors. Pragmatically, King's major victories would be won by pricking the

35. On the expansion of the Freedom Rides, see Viorst, *Fire in the Streets*, 141; and Lomax, *The Negro Revolt*, 133–34. The editor's remark appears in "What Southern Editors Say About the Future," 48.

conscience of Americans who would pressure the national government to intervene and guarantee the rights of black southerners.[36] For that strategy to work, Americans had to become vicarious participants in a moral drama staged by demonstrators and sketched by the news media.

Albany posed particular problems for *Time* and *Newsweek*. Almost never first with the news, they needed drama and the thousand bits of journalistic "color"—the details that put flesh on images once seen but since receded in the memory—and they needed to make sense of the half-digested events read in newspapers. The Albany Movement had few dramatic confrontations, and journalists found it much more difficult to make sense of what was occurring. No less than generals, reporters tend to cast new battles in terms made familiar by old struggles, and the events in Albany followed by only a few months the Freedom Rides and their bloodied demonstrators, burning buses, and mobs coursing through the streets. Furthermore, *Time* and *Newsweek* regarded forced confrontations with distaste, as calculated attempts to goad segregationists into violence. Still, there was another embarrassing point they chose not to acknowledge. Without such cold calculation, probably neither foe nor friend, white southerners or the Kennedy administration, would have made any move in 1961 to dismantle segregation in interstate travel, much less in Albany.

For almost a century, blacks in Albany had not seriously challenged segregation. In 1961, however, they began to stir as the result of the sit-ins and Freedom Rides. The earliest attempt to mobilize black Albany against segregation was made by SNCC, which established a field office there in October, 1961. Its staff members began working to register voters and sponsor campaigns to desegregate transportation facilities. Despite the ICC order, students attempting to integrate a segregated terminal in Albany in late 1961 were turned away or arrested. An umbrella organization, the Albany Movement, was created shortly thereafter at the insistence of SNCC. In mid-December, the arrest of an integrated SNCC group led to a series of demonstrations and more arrests. On December 15, King and the SCLC were invited in, and he and his colleague Ralph David Abernathy led a march in downtown Albany. Hundreds of persons were taken into custody. In less than a month, arrests totaled 737.[37]

36. Meier, "The Conservative Militant," 144–56.
37. Howard Zinn, *Albany: A Study in National Responsibility* (Atlanta, 1962), 2, 4; Lewis, *King: A Biography*, 148–49.

It was King's arrest, however, that got the attention of reporters and politicians. King had stumbled into the situation; he had not intended to become embroiled in the Albany campaign. The arrest put his prestige on the line. He announced that he would not pay the fine and that he expected to spend Christmas in jail. Instead, King allowed himself to be released on bail on December 18, ostensibly because a truce had been declared, actually because he and his colleagues feared the damage to the movement if it was revealed that one of their number, also in jail, was on the verge of a mental breakdown. Certainly the truce terms fell short of the original demands. Albany's city fathers conceded little more than that they would discuss integration with representatives of the Albany Movement, and even that promise was not made in good faith.[38]

Once released, King issued a statement maintaining that he believed the problems could be worked out locally. He also praised Albany police for their courteous treatment of the arrested demonstrators. The first statement proved to be optimistic, the second portended the problem of dramatizing the evils of segregation when King's strategy was used against him. Although tension was almost palpable in Albany, there was no violence against demonstrators. Laurie Pritchett, Albany's chief of police, allowed King and his followers an opportunity to disperse, arrested them when they disobeyed his order to do so, and even took steps to ensure the safety of King and other ministers. It was an inauspicious beginning for the Albany Movement.

Perhaps because of the lack of drama in Albany, *Time* turned its attention to the civil rights movement. It reported in January the crumbling of the facade of unity once maintained by the major organizations. CORE was dismissed as "a bunch of loonybirds and crackpots"; though the quote was attributed to an unidentified NAACP official, *Time* had said as much during the Freedom Rides. The NAACP fared little better. Conservative and legalistic, the NAACP was on the decline, according to *Time*; worse, to a magazine ever on the prowl for drama, the NAACP was stuffy and boring. *Time* favored only SNCC—an unexpected position for the magazine, since it had assigned King and the SCLC to the middle ground (usually choice territory, so far as *Time*

38. On King's arrest and the truce terms, see Lewis, *King: A Biography*, 148–51. King's lack of enthusiasm for joining the movement is mentioned by Bishop, *The Days of Martin Luther King*, 259–60. On King's decision to accept bail, see Louis Lomax, "When 'Nonviolence' Meets 'Black Power,'" in C. Eric Lincoln (ed.), *Martin Luther King, Jr.: A Profile* (New York, 1970), 163.

was concerned) somewhere between the NAACP and SNCC. The students of SNCC represented an almost irresistible combination. Young and idealistic, they were the "shock troops of the civil rights front . . . tough and tenacious young Negroes" who measured prestige by "the number of times a member has gone to jail on civil rights charges."[39] They were, in short, crusaders in an American cause, and if they often tried the patience of their elders, *Time*'s patience with them now seemed boundless.

By contrast, King was depicted as a fallen idol. The magazine found SNCC members who complained that he was "far more interested in making speeches across the U.S., than in head-on action." Furthermore, it reported, "King began to lose status with young Negroes last May when he failed to take a Freedom Ride into Mississippi" and lost even more in Albany "when he was taken off to jail vowing that he would stay behind bars indefinitely, then meekly posted bond and went home two days later."[40]

The curious thing was not what *Time* was saying but the moment the magazine chose to say it. Unless *Time*'s reporters required six months to dig up campground gossip to the effect that King was a coward, the reason for the timing of the story probably came down to symbolism. During the Freedom Rides, *Time* packaged SNCC and King as the alternative to the radicals of CORE and cast its morality play with King among the elect and John Patterson of Alabama as the chief villain. In Albany, with clear-cut confrontations lacking, reservations about King rose instead. King was granted space to respond to the complaints of SNCC, but *Time* dismissed his response beforehand with the observation that King "discussed his problems in lofty terms."[41]

U.S. News also sought out examples of discord among the black organizations, but it chose a different approach. Large-scale demonstrations in Albany and other cities represented a "new strategy of . . . 'mass attack.' Instead of sending a few—or a few dozen—Negroes out to create a test case, the new idea is to send out several hundred—or several thousand" to fill the jails to overflowing. Albany represented a new threat to the status quo that *U.S. News* defended mightily, but on this occasion the magazine could report not only a warning but a counterstrategy devised by Pritchett, who had wrested the weapon of nonviolence from his enemy, then turned it against him. Indeed, it

39. "Confused Crusade," *Time*, January 12, 1962, p. 15.
40. *Ibid.*
41. *Ibid.*

seemed Pritchett held to this course despite extraordinary provocation: "Some of the Negro demonstrators reportedly went around the streets saying: 'I love you, God loves you. Hit me. Hit me.' But nobody was hit."[42]

As in the Freedom Ride crisis, King was not featured in the early reports from Albany, and for the same reason—CORE was the more satisfying target. King appeared in the first story as an intruder who came to stir up trouble and departed hastily. Although *U.S. News* managed to find "many Negroes" in Albany who criticized King for dashing to Albany "after the demonstrations began" then back to Atlanta as soon as he got out of jail, the journal was baying after the radicals of CORE, not King.[43]

Newsweek gave the squabbling a different twist: It was evidence that the black organizations were American to the core. Readers were informed that the "wool-hats of the South" believed that the civil rights movement was a monolith financed with "bulging bags of Moscow gold." Not so, the magazine explained; bickering was inevitable because the "several groups, far from dripping Moscow gold, are downright poor and competing for contributions."[44] It was a curious, but nonetheless effective, defense. What, after all, could be more traditionally American than fighting for a piece of the pie?

At the same time, *Newsweek* carefully kept King's image unsoiled by unseemly quarrels. Unlike its competitors, *Newsweek* focused on the Albany Movement, not on the national organizations, and identified the source of the trouble as Wyatt Tee Walker, the executive director of the SCLC, who was accused of attempting to take over the Albany Movement. Walker's clumsiness enabled *Newsweek* to establish King as a peacemaker who promised to "call a meeting soon to try to get something more like the unified front that the wool-hats think already exists."[45]

Much of the article was accurate. The black organizations competed with each other fiercely, often as not over money or publicity, which, as James Farmer later said, amounted to the same thing because publicity would bring in badly needed donations. In the Albany Movement, its attorney recalled, organizational rivalries "took on the specter of a hideous ogre." Some of the friction was produced by the abrasive, take-charge style of the SCLC staff,

42. "New Turn in Race Troubles," *U.S. News & World Report*, January 1, 1962, pp. 43, 44.
43. *Ibid.*, 44. CORE remained the major threat for several months in the eyes of *U.S. News*. See, for example, "Next Big Integration Drive in the South: 'Freedom Highway' Rides—Led by CORE," May 7, 1962, p. 56.
44. "Who Won What?" *Newsweek*, January 1, 1962, pp. 13–14.
45. *Ibid.*, 14.

including Walker. But another problem was King's ability to get the national news coverage. The attention paid to King by the media caused resentment, probably among the elders of black Albany, certainly among the intense young men and women of SNCC, who had worked so hard and with so little notice in Albany before King and the mob of reporters showed up. Within SNCC King became known, derisively, as "De Lawd."[46]

Newsweek seemed to have two reasons for reporting the squabbles in the Albany Movement. First, the disputes were public enough that they could not be ignored. Second, the magazine wanted to reassure its readers by informing them that the segregationists were once more using the red brush to paint civil rights organizations and King as Communist.

The allegations weren't new but were intensifying in late 1961 and early 1962, and King was feeling the pressure. He had lent his name to various controversial causes over the years, including protests against the House Un-American Activities Committee, whose red-hunters bayed after liberals and liberal organizations, including some associated with the civil rights movement, which HUAC regarded as Communist-influenced. King was approached to appear in a documentary film attacking HUAC, and he accepted the invitation. After being informed that one man associated with the film had once been a Communist, he backed out of the commitment because if that fact should surface, explained Wyatt Tee Walker, right-wingers "would create more problems than we have time to deal with."[47]

Southern "wool-hats" were not the only reason for King's caution. He had, in fact, a greater problem with the Federal Bureau of Investigation. Before the Freedom Rides, the FBI took little notice of him. But a notation on King's association with the Highlander Folk School caught the eye of J. Edgar Hoover, who ordered an investigation. It turned up nothing untoward, but the

46. See interview with James Farmer, by John Britton, September 28, 1968 (Transcript of tape 317, in Moorland-Spingarn Research Center, Howard University), 30; and interview with C. B. King, the Albany Movement's attorney, by Stanley Smith, August, 1968 (Transcript of tape 392, in Moorland-Spingarn Research Center, Howard University), 16. On the SCLC staff and the resentment caused by the media spotlight on King, see Lomax, "When 'Nonviolence' Meets 'Black Power,'" 160–61. The pique in some quarters of the Albany Movement, particularly among SNCC workers, is described by Lewis, *King: A Biography*, 152. Understating the friction is William M. Kunstler, *Deep in My Heart* (New York, 1966), 107.

47. See Garrow, *The FBI and King*, 25; and Lewis, *King: A Biography*, 110. On the film, see Robert Carl Cohen to Richard Lentz, April 22, 1981; and Wyatt Tee Walker to Robert Carl Cohen, January 30, 1962, in Box 36, File 3, King Center Archives, Atlanta. Walker appeared in Cohen's film, *Committee on Un-American Activities*, 1963, but there was no mention of his affiliation with the SCLC.

FBI thereafter began looking more closely at King. Early in 1962, the agency discovered his long and close association with Stanley Levison, a lawyer in New York City, who the FBI believed had been involved in the secret financial dealings of the Communist party in the United States. On January 8, Hoover sent a memorandum to Attorney General Kennedy, asserting that two advisers of King's, one of whom was Levison, were members of the Communist party.[48]

After reading the memorandum, Kennedy ordered King informed "of this apparent danger." One of Kennedy's assistants told King that the background of several of his close associates could be used to smear him, and the warning was repeated soon after by the White House civil rights liaison, Harris Wofford. Whether or not they weighed in the decision to back away from the film project, the warnings added to the increasing pressure, which intensified when hostile southern newspapers published stories about a Communist on the SCLC payroll.[49]

Hoover's memorandum had nothing to do with *Newsweek*'s decision to publish that half-humorous article about wool-hats, civil rights organizations, and Moscow gold. But the magazine was well aware of the segregationist smear campaign against King that had been under way since 1957, and this and other stories demonstrated that *Newsweek* remained firmly in King's corner.[50]

Following the truce agreement in December, the news magazines took little note of the Albany Movement. The truce quickly came apart after a former student was arrested for arguing with a bus driver. A boycott forced the transit company to halt operations. A week after the arrest, two SNCC workers were taken into custody and charged with loitering because they were sitting in a lunchroom at a bus depot. City commissioners declined to negotiate in good faith, and more demonstrators were arrested, including some who assembled to protest the death of a black man shot by a police officer in April.[51]

48. Garrow, *The FBI and King*, 42–44. See also David Wise, *The American Police State: The Government Against the People* (New York, 1976), 229; and *Senate Documents*, 94th Cong., 2nd Sess., No. 755, Bk. 3, p. 88.

49. Garrow, *The FBI and King*, 44; Wofford, *Of Kennedys and Kings*, 216. See, for example, Birmingham *News*, October 26, 1962, p. 1.

50. King protested the sabotage of an American dream—"a Negro in the cabinet of the federal government"—in "The Weaver Case: Negro Views," *Newsweek*, March 5, 1962, p. 27. He was cited in "Holy Days and the Atom," *Newsweek*, April 30, 1962, p. 21, which reported resumption of protests against nuclear testing in the atmosphere.

51. Zinn, *Albany*, 5–7.

The national press returned to Albany when King and Abernathy were sentenced in July to pay fines or spend forty-five days in jail. They chose jail. The incarceration brought expressions of concern from the president, the attorney general, and the Republican governor of New York, Nelson Rockefeller. But King's symbolic gesture was thwarted. An unidentified person, described by Pritchett as a "well-dressed Negro," paid the fines. Anxious to remain in jail "as a symbol of Negro resistance," King and Abernathy instead were forcibly ejected. Abernathy quipped, "I've been thrown out of lots of places in my day, but never before have I been thrown out of jail." Plainly, however, the Albany Movement—and King—had been outmaneuvered again.[52]

The reports of King's release followed the thematic lines established earlier. *U.S. News* used the episode as further evidence of federal meddling in local affairs. That theme required the omission of a critical question: How was King's release arranged? Almost in passing, *U.S. News* quoted King as saying: "'I don't know who paid it. We didn't want to leave.'" Ignoring something so obvious that a cub reporter could not have missed it, the article left open the possibility that paying the fine was a political move by the Kennedy administration. Then possibility was converted into probability with this statement: "The flurry of activity recalled the intercession of the President—then a candidate—when Dr. King was jailed in 1960."[53]

Time and *Newsweek* read the unexpected release accurately, as a stratagem to deprive King of martyrdom.[54] But they used the incident for their own purposes no less than did *U.S. News*.

After an absence of several months, King reappeared in early August as that most pathetic of *Time*'s characters: The Loser. King had failed to mobilize black Albany, a point driven home with the cutting observation that "even martyrdom is something that King cannot always depend on. A fortnight ago,

52. *Ibid.*, 9; Zinn, *SNCC*, 134. Abernathy is quoted in Kunstler, *Deep in My Heart*, 99.
53. "When Dr. King Went to Jail Again," *U.S. News & World Report*, July 23, 1962, p. 10. *U.S. News* reiterated its theme three weeks later when President Kennedy argued that if the United States could negotiate with the Soviet Union, Albany ought to be able to do likewise with its black citizens. *U.S. News* trotted out the mayor of Albany, the governor of Georgia, and a United States senator to respond that outsiders, *i.e.*, King, were causing the problems. "Kennedy Says 'Talk,' Georgians Say 'No,'" *U.S. News & World Report*, August 13, 1962, p. 8.
54. "Waiting for Miracles," *Time*, August 3, 1962, p. 12; "Georgia Whodunit," *Newsweek*, July 23, 1962, p. 19. Pritchett recalled that King's release was engineered by a coalition of segregationist whites and conservative blacks. Howell Raines, *My Soul is Rested: Movement Days in the Deep South Remembered* (New York, 1978), 399–400.

he chose to accept a forty-five-day jail sentence. But hardly was he clapped behind bars when a man described by police as a 'well-dressed Negro' paid the fine." Not only was King a loser, he had become too full of himself. "Many Negroes throughout the South" shared *Time*'s suspicions that success had drained King "of the captivating fervor that made him famous." *Time* stopped short of saying that a once-humble black man had become uppity— but not far short. It found "a Negro" to add: "Martin comes in wearing his spiritual halo and blows on his flute and the money comes pouring in. But he doesn't speak for the Baptist ministry, let alone twenty million Negroes."[55]

No doubt *Time* had found someone to grumble that King was working a scam: King had his share of enemies, black as well as white. Still, as a biographer of Henry Luce observed, *Time* had the knack of coming up with anonymous sources to support its position but "seldom to make statements with which *Time* disagreed." And *Time* did more than locate a hostile source. Certain tones transformed King into a Stepin Fetchit. King had not accepted jailing to dramatize injustice but had been "clapped behind bars" or, in a later story, "jugged"—phrases more befitting a weekend spree than a crusade for freedom; in fact, a spree of more than a weekend's duration, judging from the reference to "King, who had been jugged only a week earlier for the third time in eight months."[56]

Newsweek painted a different picture. At the convention of the NAACP in July, King was penetrating in his analysis of the plight of blacks and resolute in his echoing call for the realization of the black man's birthright as an American. He was an even more vital symbol in the reports from Albany. Where *Time* had dismissed King as so inept that he could not effectuate his own martyrdom, *Newsweek* published King's "unhappy comment" that "this is the first time that I'm out of jail and not happy about it." When the mayor of Albany jubilantly proclaimed that black demonstrators "don't have a martyr," *Newsweek* pointedly remarked that this might be a temporary state of affairs inasmuch as "King was talking of leading another march. . . . [A]nd that was likely to land him right back in jail again." Most tellingly, *Newsweek* added an idealistic tone: "In choosing imprisonment, Dr. King declared: 'We had come to this decision because we felt it was the only moral thing to do.'" Moral or no, the gesture was certainly calculated. King had refused to pay a fine or to be

55. "Waiting for Miracles," 12.
56. Swanberg, *Luce and His Empire*, 261–62; "'In Changing Times,'" *Time*, August 10, 1962, p. 14.

released on bail before, and he would use the tactic again with more success than he enjoyed in Albany. The report appeared equally calculated. *Newsweek* separated intent (the decision being "the only moral thing to do") from effect (the gesture "pumped life into the anti-segregation drive") as if there were no connection between the two. No less skillfully than did *Time*, *Newsweek* drew its own pictures of heroes and villains on the public stage of Albany.[57]

One member of the cast was Laurie Pritchett, who heeded the first rule of war: Study the enemy. Pritchett studied King. He outmaneuvered King by eschewing violence, thus denying the Albany Movement the sympathy generated by the attacks on black demonstrators in 1960 and 1961; he set up an efficient transfer system to keep his jail from being inundated because of mass arrests; and he stretched the SCLC's financial resources to the limit by refusing to accept any but cash bonds. Those tactics and the lack of preparation on the part of the SCLC and its partners in the Albany Movement provided the margin of victory for Pritchett.[58]

Pritchett projected a benign public image that proved all but impossible to penetrate. After one demonstration, for example, a black child "showed up in the line of people being booked. . . . 'How old are you?' Chief Pritchett asked. 'Nine,' the boy replied. 'What is your name?' the chief queried. 'Freedom, freedom,' was the response. The chief patted him on the head and said: 'Go home, freedom.' "[59]

With that sort of encounter being reported not in southern newspapers but the liberal New York *Post*, the Albany Movement was indeed hard pressed for dramatic confrontations. Many reporters failed to inquire whether Pritchett's public image matched his private performance or to make much of the hundreds of arrests that had been or would be made under Pritchett's orders. Even fewer looked beyond Albany to nearby counties where they would have found brutality in abundance. Frustrated, the SCLC protested that Pritchett had become "the darling of the press because he has abstained from police brutality." He was walking the tightrope between repression and brutality with such consummate skill that Attorney General Kennedy wired congratulations to Pritchett.[60]

57. "The Indignant Ones," *Newsweek*, July 16, 1962, pp. 22, 25; "Georgia Whodunit," 18–19.

58. Raines, *My Soul is Rested*, 398–401.

59. Zinn, *Albany*, 22.

60. Informal complaints question whether Pritchett was as benign as he seemed. See, for example, C. B. King interview, 13; and John Papworth's mimeographed letter, February 18,

Pritchett was indeed a hero in some quarters; he certainly was so in the eyes of *Time*. In the issue of August 3, its analysis was this: "As much as the pleas of King, . . . Pritchett, an intelligent officer who has dealt unemotionally and with dignity with the Negroes, has kept the activists among them from turning the town upside down." A week later, he rose a notch while King fell one: "More than anyone else, Pritchett is responsible for keeping Albany . . . from turning into a bloody battleground." Pritchett was portrayed as able, tough, affable, cool enough to keep his head and to stay his hand when bottles and rocks were hurled at his men. As a final touch, even King had to admit that "Pritchett is the best Southern police chief he has ever met."[61]

Other outsiders, clergymen who came to Albany at the beck of King, fared little better against the "coolheaded, hard-as-nails police chief." *Time* granted that their willingness to demonstrate was more impressive than the armchair support offered to blacks in the past. It granted them little else. The journal's attitude is illustrated by a crisp account of an incident during which Pritchett demanded to know the clergymen's purpose. The response: " 'Our purpose is to offer prayers to God.' 'You have come to aid and abet the law violators of this city,' the chief shot back," advising them to return home and clear " 'your own cities of sin and violence.' " When the ministers, refusing to disperse as Pritchett ordered, knelt in prayer, they were arrested and jailed. However, *Time* established that they lacked, figuratively and literally, the stomach for martyrdom. "Some fasted—perhaps after glancing at the prison fare of corn-bread, beans, greens, and fatback," and soon after most of the ministers were released on bond and left Albany.[62]

Clearly, *Time* had stayed its hand with Laurie Pritchett. Such forbearance was rare. *Time* routinely scoffed at segregationists' claims that if the outside agitators would go away, so would the trouble. Now, however, *Time*

1964, in Box 2, File 5, Braden Papers, Wisconsin Historical Society, Madison. For the number of arrests and repression of civil rights activities in surrounding counties, see Zinn, *Albany*, 2, 23–25; and Kunstler, *Deep in My Heart*, 117. See also Slater King to President Kennedy, December 26, 1962, and Slater King to Constance Motley of the NAACP Legal Defense Fund staff, August 13, 1963, both in Box 2, Files 6 and 7, Slater King Papers, Fisk University. For the SCLC's protest, see *SCLC Newsletter*, September, 1962, p. 3. On Kennedy's wire and allegations that the Justice Department ignored instances of brutality in the Albany jail, see Viorst, *Fire in the Streets*, 215.

61. "Waiting for Miracles," 12. *Time* did provide, in the same issue, excerpts from a speech by King to Washington news reporters that outlined the case for nonviolence, but it introduced the remarks by quipping that his address "went over noticeably better in Washington than it has in Georgia." " 'Hate is Always Tragic': Martin Luther King's Challenge," August 3, 1962, p. 13. See also, " 'In Changing Times,' " 14.

62. "Act of Belief," *Time*, September 7, 1962, p. 45.

watched, seemingly with approval, as Pritchett advised ministers of the gospel to remove the beam from their own eyes and then arrested them as they prayed for justice and equality. Pritchett escaped the cutting phrases reserved for Patterson when mobs were running amok in Alabama the year before because of what *Time* saw in the juxtaposed symbols, King and Pritchett. King was The Loser—a failure at nonviolence, rejected by his own people, swallowed up by success, unable even (the final indignity) to remain in jail as a martyr. Cool, tough, affable Laurie Pritchett was the winner, gaining the respect of his enemies, certainly King's, while enforcing the law with an even hand.

King could have exhibited all those vices and Pritchett all his virtues without changing the morality of the situation one jot. However ineptly or for whatever motives, King was trying to bring down the system of segregation that denied American principles of equality, and Pritchett, however affable, was coolly doing everything in his power to uphold that same structure. Pritchett at least acted according to his own lights. Not so *Time*, which traded in heroes and villains, and had no equal when the need arose to savage an opponent or puff a rising star. Displaying that capriciousness in Albany, *Time* more often than not lost sight of what it professed as its guiding principles.

As the Albany campaign continued, *U.S. News* drew upon episodes of violence to support its thesis that whites were practicing nonviolence and blacks were running wild. On July 10 and 11, after King and Abernathy went to jail and more demonstrations and arrests followed, the discipline of nonviolence snapped. Crowds, gathered near churches, hurled rocks and bottles at police. Less than two weeks later, there was another outbreak, precipitated by the brutal assault in a neighboring county on the pregnant wife of one of the leaders of the Albany Movement, and by the arrest of about forty persons protesting the assault. By nightfall, almost two thousand persons, most of whom were youngsters, were battling police. Over SNCC's objections, King declared a day of penance, temporarily ending the demonstrations. That night and the following day, he and his lieutenants made the rounds trying to get the volatile situation under control.[63]

The provocations that preceded the demonstrations were essentially ignored by *U.S. News*. Blatantly rewriting the history of the Albany Movement, it maintained: "White people here believe that they have tested a new way to

---

63. Zinn, *Albany*, 9–11; Lewis, *King: A Biography*, 162; Carson, *In Struggle*, 60–61.

meet Negro militance and have proved that it works." The method was non-violence, and according to *U.S. News*, Laurie Pritchett was the originator. "He hammered home the idea that physical contact should be avoided, no police dogs were to be used, no tear gas fired or nightsticks swung except in extreme cases." Only one off-hand remark—"Previously, Negroes had practiced as well as preached a nonviolence of their own"—lessened the symbolism of invaders, chief among them King, and resident militants violating the tranquillity of a "rather moderate Southern city." *U.S. News* passed over the awkward point that, as Pritchett himself admitted, King's weapon was being used against him. To acknowledge that fact would have marred the juxtaposing of moderation versus radicalism.[64]

It almost appeared that *Newsweek* had somehow dispatched its correspondents to another Georgia city, so different were its stories from those of *Time* or *U.S. News*. *Newsweek* consistently attacked Pritchett as a powerful servant of of the evil system of segregation. Its articles evoked the red-neck southern sheriff and explained that Pritchett adopted his strategy out of cunning, not out of devotion to nonviolence.

The thematic elements flowed toward convergence in late July and early August. Despite repeated pleas, *Newsweek* reported, "Albany's implacable city council, supported by shrewd, bull-necked Police Chief Laurie (Bubba) Pritchett, repeatedly countered that it would not negotiate with 'law violators' and 'outside agitators.'" Similarly, when black demonstrators got out of control and hurled rocks at police, it was Pritchett, the red-neck (figuratively) and red-faced (literally) cop who responded ungrammatically with the rhetorical question. "'Did you see them nonviolent rocks?'" Pritchett was simply an adversary who cannily studied his enemy; he had visited "past racial trouble spots" and had even "read up on the prophet of passive resistance, Gandhi. And he had drilled his men: no rough stuff, no firehoses, no tear gas, not even nightsticks, except for self-defense in a man-to-man fight. 'We thought,' he explained, 'we could overcome them with nonviolence.'"[65] Having "read up" on Gandhi (the image being of Bubba Pritchett's lips moving), he was cynically using Gandhian tactics; having drilled his men not to use brutal methods (the implication being that brutality was standard practice for handling

64. "Now It's 'Passive Resistance' by Whites—The Albany, Ga., Plan," *U.S. News & World Report*, September 3, 1962, pp. 43–46.

65. See *Newsweek*, "Marching Shoes," July 30, 1962, p. 15, "Prayers and Brickbats," August 6, 1962, p. 19, and "'Keep Walking,'" August 13, 1962, p. 18.

blacks), Pritchett's talk of nonviolence amounted to a guise and the man himself was a fraud.

If *Newsweek* conceded that Pritchett was firm, it quickly added that he was paternalistic and arbitrary. Arbitrariness, however, was made to stand for the greater brutality of segregation. Readers were brought back to that point again and again with such phrases as "attacking segregation customs in rigidly stubborn Albany"; "discriminatory customs"; "the revolt against segregation"; "recalcitrant segregationist city commission"; and "obstinantly segregationist policies."[66]

Dismissed as a smoke screen for racism was the recurring statement by city commissioners that they would negotiate with residents but not outside agitators. *Newsweek* twice reported that King was willing to leave town when the two sides got together. When they did, *Newsweek* reported in merciless detail the segregationists' response: "The secretary of the Negro coalition group, gangling, gray-haired retired railroader, Marion A. Page (who met the mayor's definition of 'law-abiding' because he is one of the few Albany Negro leaders who has not been arrested for demonstrations) arose. 'Mr. Mayor,' Page said. 'Yes, Marion,' said the mayor." *Newsweek* went on to state that the obduracy of the city fathers "ended the search for a truce."[67] Its scenario made the statement redundant. Addressing the polite, gray-haired, retired railroader by his first name was no better than calling him "boy." Blacks could expect nothing from the whites running Albany.

And what the blacks in Albany expected was no more than their rights—another point *Newsweek* made. Denied their rights, they naturally were angry. In contrast to *Time* and *U.S. News*, *Newsweek* put the riot of July 24 in that context. After a federal court struck down a regulation that prevented demonstrations, "forty Albany Movement members marched toward downtown last Tuesday night to pray and to protest." Despite the court order, "police arrested them by the score. Angered by the arrests (which brought to more than one thousand the number jailed since December), two thousand jeering Negroes ignored" King's exhortations, boiled into the streets and "heaved rocks, bottles, brickbats, and taunts" at police.[68]

Despite the reference to jeering rioters, *Newsweek* did not depict King as

66. "Marching Shoes," 15; "Prayers and Brickbats," 19; "'Keep Walking,'" 17; "Fire and Frustration," *Newsweek*, August 27, 1962, p. 25; "Trouble, Trouble," *Newsweek*, September 10, 1962, p. 47.
67. "Fire and Frustration," 25.
68. "Prayers and Brickbats," 19.

inept. Matters had simply gotten out of hand, and the people had gotten fed up. Instead, the magazine saw in King some singular virtues: a passion for justice; the courage not merely to risk martyrdom but to invite it by going to jail; a firm belief in his philosophy of nonviolence; and the willingness to call for penance and to stop demonstrating when his followers strayed from that path. For all his passion for justice, however, King was no radical but a leader of the middle way. Those characteristics were scattered throughout *Newsweek*'s stories from Albany. But they were refined and collected in an article about the social gospel, which required the clergy to remedy injustice on earth as well as prepare their flocks for the hereafter. *Newsweek* emphasized the willingness of King to sacrifice himself for his cause. A quip made the message not only inescapable but appealing. King had been incarcerated so often, "says Negro comic Dick Gregory, that 'he carries mimeographed sets of fingerprints.'" *Newsweek* turned to the social gospel in order to defend King against the recurring accusation that he was less minister than mischief-maker: "King insists that, in becoming a center in the storm over desegregation, he has not abandoned the basic role of the minister and the church. 'The early church always stood against the evils of the day. When the church fails to do this,' he said, 'it fails to live up to the very thing for which it was created.'"[69]

In the end, *Newsweek*'s best efforts on King's behalf went for nothing in Albany: King had failed. The magazine performed a final service for him, however, as it attempted to keep King's image unblemished by undeniable failure. In the second of two stories published in the first weeks of 1963, *Newsweek* chose King to commemorate the one hundredth anniversary of the Emancipation Proclamation with the message that "'we need a second Emancipation Proclamation'" because "'the segregation we now have is nothing but slavery with subtleties.'" Equally important was something unsaid the week before. *Newsweek* published a historical sketch of the Albany Movement and the results of more than a year of demonstrations, including by that time more than fifteen hundred arrests. It was a bleak picture, replete with "signs of corrosive bitterness and frustration." It was also a story with no mention of King or the SCLC—an omission akin to striking from the history of a battle the name of the general and army on the losing side.[70]

King's reputation was not the only one kept intact by omission. There was,

69. "The Prophetic Ministry?" *Newsweek*, August 20, 1962, pp. 78, 79.
70. See *Newsweek*, "The Wall," January 14, 1963, p. 27, and "Albany Revisited," January 7, 1963, p. 18.

for example, the reputation of the Kennedy administration, which displayed no more eagerness to intervene in Albany than it had during the Freedom Rides.[71] For many in the Albany Movement, particularly the impatient cadres of the SNCC, the failure of the Kennedy administration to intervene in Albany planted seeds of suspicion and distrust that would soon ripen into bitterness and radicalism. Those failures, King's and Kennedy's, were the most important legacies of Albany.

Albany thrust some important lessons on King and the SCLC. Thereafter, when producing such morality plays on the public stage, they would search for a symbolic opponent foolish enough to act out the part in blood and brutality. In 1963, they would find the perfect foil—Bull Connor of Birmingham.

71. Zinn, *Albany*, 26.

III

CONFRONTATION AND CONSENSUS

If the events of any one year could be said to have stamped Martin
Luther King as a symbol on the consciousness of America, the
year would be 1963 and the events the civil rights struggle in Birmingham and
the March on Washington. Together they marked the high tide of idealism in
the 1960s. Despite the rights still to be secured, despite triumphs to come in
other southern cities, Birmingham and Washington would not be overshadowed as symbolic events in American culture.

Birmingham's enduring images were stark and simple. Arrayed on one side
were the forces of good—the black men and women marching by the hundreds for the freedom that was their long-denied birthright as Americans; and
children, the black children of Birmingham, offering up their bodies, their
lives if need be, in a crusade the adults had not won and very likely could not
win alone. Above all, of course, there was King, the refracting symbol, the
instrument that collected, intensified, and focused the elements of the struggle
as no other black leader could. Standing against King and those who followed
him were adversaries representing the antithesis of American principles of
equality and freedom. Their encounters in the streets of Birmingham produced powerful images of brutality—the brutality being real enough but the
images more important—of white men loosing fierce police dogs and training
murderously efficient fire hoses on men, women, and, especially, children,
who wanted no more than the rights of any American citizen. Shock waves

surged through America, indeed the world, leading rapidly to a chorus of demands that justice be brought to the black citizens of Birmingham.

Yet neither images nor brutality sufficed to produce the enduring contrapuntal symbolism. That required another refracting symbol to collect, strengthen, and conserve the force of those events in 1963. Had it not have been for King's opposite, Bull Connor, the personification of the evils of the segregated South, the power of those images would have soon dissipated. Most of all, Birmingham continued to echo in American culture because of its antithesis in spirit, the 1963 March on Washington.

From the March, King emerged as the leading spokesman for black aspirations and as the soaring voice of American principles of justice and equality and brotherhood. Although King's speech moved millions of Americans, not even his eloquence accounts for the impact of his words or of the demonstration at which they were delivered. The dream to which King gave voice was lent particular force by the dynamics of the events of 1963 that made Birmingham and the March one and the same—reverberating against each other first during the March at the end of August, then again in mid-September when four black children were murdered in the bombing of one of Birmingham's black churches. Without the Birmingham of Bull Connor, the March on Washington would have come and gone with little notice, had it occurred at all. Although the largest, the demonstration in 1963 was by no means the first of its kind, but the others vanished with no more than ripples to mark their passing. Nor would the confrontation in Birmingham have taken on such lasting symbolic force had there not followed, three months later, the March on Washington. The blood and brutality of Birmingham would have been incomplete and unsatisfying symbolically without the redemptive quality flowing from the high idealism of the marchers in Washington.

Confrontation and consensus, the consensus formed around American ideals, were the themes threaded through Birmingham and the March that followed. But there also was an intensity, almost an urgency, that grew out of both events and that the symbolism of the moment explains only partly. In 1963, the black revolt was changing far more rapidly, and in ways more dramatic, than could have been foreseen. The clarity and direction of black protests had captured the sympathy of many white Americans since King brought together Gandhian nonviolence and the black church to produce a mass social movement in Montgomery. The sentiment was strengthened subsequently by the crises of Little Rock and Ole Miss, the sit-ins, and the

Freedom Rides. Even Albany, disaster that it was for King, was marked by unity of purpose. By contrast, Birmingham pointed the black movement in two directions. If Birmingham was the citadel of southern segregation, it also was an industrial city that, Jim Crow aside, was almost as much northern as southern in social conditions. The displaced rural migrants of Los Angeles might become as restive, the ghettos of Detroit as tindery, as those of Birmingham. These sobering possibilities became evident during the hundreds of demonstrations King's campaign set in motion across the United States. Initially gestures of solidarity with blacks in Birmingham, the protests became, as well, expressions of outrage at the conditions afflicting blacks in the North and the West as well as the South. The March itself was an expression of a different sort, a celebration of American idealism. Yet the intensity of the event was strengthened greatly by a foreboding that, King's dream to the contrary, would not be stilled. The March was played out against a sense of a coming fury to be unleashed outside the South, as segregationists for their own motives had warned, when blacks throughout America would rise and make demands that could not be so easily satisfied as claims for seats at a lunch counter or for the ballot.

In retrospect, there is a faintly haunting air to the March on Washington, making it akin in spirit to soldiers at dance on the eve of battle. The idealism and camaraderie were real enough, moving, as they did, the quarter-million people assembled in Washington and the millions of others participating vicariously through news media. Still, like the soldiers at sport, who would be tried in a grimmer encounter on the morrow, Americans, especially white Americans, were coming to the realization that much more would be required of them than good will, and henceforth the cause celebrated in Washington would not be so simple nor the solidarity so unwavering.

The knowledge that the black revolt was changing, its demands becoming more insistent, perhaps was only vaguely perceived on that hot August day in Washington. If so, intuition hardened soon enough into certainty—certainty, moreover, edged with a sense of loss and, possibly, with the sadness of innocence squandered. The effect was to hone the spirit of the March on Washington, making of it something even finer than it was. The March would be passed into history, not intact, but as one of those mythic moments to be recaptured and savored anew by Americans whose faith in the essential goodness of their nation would be disrupted in the difficult years ahead. The moment would be reclaimed again and again, and Martin Luther King, against the symbolic images of Birmingham and its police dogs and fire hoses and flailing nightsticks, would assure his countrymen that he still held to his dream of America.

As lived, the events in Birmingham and the March on Washington were not so simple as they have become in memory. *Time*, *Newsweek*, and *U.S. News & World Report* would find themselves hard-pressed to interpret the toss and tumble of events in swift and commanding images in keeping with their editorial positions and in harmony with the expectations of their readers. In King, the centrist *Time* and the left-of-center *Newsweek* would be confronted not by a gentle follower of the way of moderation and sweet reason but by a prophet of Old Testament mien whose strategy was to press his adversary to the wall—nonviolently, to be sure, but to the wall. *U.S. News* would shoulder a burden no lighter. Sympathetic to the segregated South, hostile to black aspirations, *U.S. News* would be forced into the altogether awkward position of having to account for the brutal and open violence against black demonstrators, especially children, that all the world had seen.

Time and *Newsweek* would recall the Birmingham campaign as a crusade for freedom. As the movement unfolded, however, both magazines shared a distaste for a confrontation that they believed was forced by King, as well as a misplaced confidence in the good will of southern moderates—an odd sentiment, considering they had, the year before, labeled Birmingham the citadel of segregation. At almost the same date that *Newsweek* declared the city to be a "hellhole in the eyes of its Negro citizens," *Time* damned it to a Lucean hell as "a backwoods with industrial chimneys [that is] almost totally segregated." They already had caught more than a glimpse of one prominent citizen soon to become a more visible symbol of the city than was the statue of Vulcan atop Red Mountain. He was Bull Connor, the commissioner in charge of the fire and police departments, who had blandly explained that his officers were not on hand to protect Freedom Riders in 1962 because they were fulfilling their filial duties on Mother's Day. Connor was about as unyielding as Vulcan's cast iron, unembarrassed by the grammar, logic, or sentiment of his frequently quoted views on Jim Crow: "We're not goin' to have white folks and niggers segregatin' together in this man's town."[1]

---

1. "Boycott in Birmingham, Ala., Time to Sit Down and Talk," *Newsweek*, May 14, 1962, p. 28; "How Not to Have Anything," *Time*, May 4, 1962, p. 24; Morgan, *A Time to Speak*, 49.

As a symbol of segregation, Bull Connor lacked the subtleties that made Laurie Pritchett of Albany so frustrating an opponent. There was only one problem: Connor was on the way out. The Birmingham electorate had approved a referendum item in November, 1962, that provided for the installation of a mayor-council form of government. Officers of the new government were elected on April 2, 1963. Connor lost his campaign for mayor. He and other commissioners petitioned the courts to delay the date they would vacate their offices. While the case meandered through the state courts for almost two months, Birmingham had two officiaries, the shadow government of the new mayor, Albert Boutwell, and the commissioners, including Connor, who retained control of the fire and police departments.

Into this topsy-turvy political situation strode King, aware that he would be rebuked for not staying his hand until Boutwell could take office but willing to take the heat. King started the campaign on April 3, the day after the election, ostensibly to "take advantage of the symbolic significance of the Easter season." More to the point, King and his advisers were reluctant to pass up the opportunity presented by Connor. The Albany defeat still rankled, a victory was needed to restore his and the SCLC's standing, and Bull Connor, so King was advised, would be unable to walk the tightrope with the skill Pritchett demonstrated the year before.[2] Moreover, Birmingham was a tempting target precisely because it was so tough. Crack segregation there, King believed, and it could be done anywhere in the South.

Newsweek contributed its share of the criticism for which King braced himself. However, its first story waffled a bit. *Newsweek* allowed that King had "his own notions of timing. . . . 'The time is always wrong for some people,' he said. 'The cup of endurance has run over.'" Yet other voices claimed the magazine's attention. What southern moderates were saying in April—"King should call a thirty-day truce and leave town until they can sound out Boutwell's readiness to enter quiet negotiations"—struck it as sensible, and to strengthen the message, the magazine added that "even among Negroes, some question King's timing." *Newsweek* itself questioned King's timing. In reporting the Albany Movement, *Newsweek* had employed

2. Kunstler, *Deep in My Heart*, 174. King's associate Fred Shuttlesworth argued that Connor was "psychologically incapable of adopting Albany's tactics of restraint and that the official savagery would demonstrate the evils of segregation to the world." Viorst, *Fire in the Streets*, 217–18. Birmingham police studied the Albany campaign but, according to Pritchett, were frustrated by Connor. Raines, *My Soul is Rested*, 403.

phrases, such as "apostles of nonviolence," that evoked morality and spirituality. Covering Birmingham, the journal chose terms—siege, army, generals, recruiting troops—that bespoke invasion and militancy. It might be, as one of King's lieutenants put it, that "this is Birmingham's moment of truth," but *Newsweek* doubted seriously this was the proper moment.[3]

Where *Newsweek* entertained doubts, *Time*, as always, had certitude. Connor's defeat meant the end of the symbol of "the nightstick solution to race problems"—unless, that is, the fuss stirred up by King raised Connor's standing among whites. Boutwell was a segregationist, *Time* conceded, but "local Negroes felt certain that they could deal more successfully" with him; that is, but for King, depicted as meddling outsider. "Without consulting most of the Birmingham Negro leaders, King announced that Birmingham is the most thoroughly segregated big city in the U.S. today, [and] said he would lead demonstrations there until 'Pharaoh lets God's people go.'" King's Mosaic allusion was waved away as overblown rhetoric: "Specifically, he demanded creation of a bi-racial commission, fair hiring practices, amnesty for previously arrested demonstrators, an end to lunch-counter and other segregation." To "many Birmingham Negroes," to *Time*, as well, King was part of the problem because his "drive inflamed tensions at a time when the city seemed to be making some progress, however small, in race relations." The headline made the point even more clear: "Poorly Timed Protest."[4]

King's problems were not limited to criticism from *Newsweek* and *Time*. Unexpectedly, his movement was running out of steam. The signs had been promising when he arrived in Birmingham. His presence increased the attendance at rallies conducted at black churches, and protest marches in early April led to a number of arrests. But Birmingham was a gamble, and not just because it was the toughest town in the South. The SCLC and King could ill-afford another drubbing like the one they got the year before. Simply because of Birmingham's size and rock-hard reputation, a defeat there would make Albany seem no more than a minor skirmish. The SCLC went into Birmingham with the attitude that it could "lose everything," recalled executive director Wyatt Tee Walker, "but we knew that as Birmingham went, so would go the South." Dramatic incidents that might rally the faithful had not occurred. King tried to provide one on April 12, when he and Ralph David

---

3. "The 'Bull' at Bay," *Newsweek*, April 15, 1963, pp. 29–30.
4. "Poorly Timed Protest," *Time*, April 19, 1963, pp. 30–31.

Abernathy set out on a march in order to force police to arrest them. They were taken into custody and jailed. Although the incident yielded great dividends in one way—while incarcerated, King wrote his famous "Letter from the Birmingham Jail"—the gesture failed to strike any sparks. Five days after their release, King and Abernathy spent the better part of an hour exhorting a packed church and managed to persuade only a dozen persons to volunteer to go to jail.[5]

The movement had indeed reached a crisis point—though not the sort King was counting on. As Wyatt Tee Walker put the case bluntly: The SCLC had to "have a crisis to bargain with. To take a moderate approach, hoping to get help from whites doesn't work. They nail you to the cross."[6] In contrast to slipshod staff work in Albany, the SCLC had done its homework before going into Birmingham. The problem was that Bull Connor was not taking the bait, not just yet.

The themes of *Newsweek* and *Time* were mostly unchanged as the campaign continued. The former reported the maneuvering in Birmingham as farcical. The buffoonlike Bull Connor was uncharacteristically reining in his forces in a "virtuoso performance in the jail-'em-all school of tamping down the Negro revolt" and snorting that the trouble with the country was due to "Communism, socialism, and journalism." King fared little better. *Newsweek* stripped from King's shoulders the mantle of moral leadership when he maneuvered Birmingham police into arresting him. According to *Newsweek*'s accounts, the same King who made a moral choice in Albany by going to jail now was making a calculated gesture by doing the same in Birmingham. In fact, the magazine sniffed, "King plainly needed a dramatic gesture. . . . Dressed for jail in workshirt and jeans, he met three hundred Negroes at Zion Hill Church. 'This may be my thirteenth arrest,' he told them [before] marching toward his facedown with Bull Connor."[7]

Between King and Connor, there appeared to be little to choose. King set up his own arrest and Connor carried it out, the magazine reported with an

5. Police detectives spying on civil rights rallies reported that attendance increased after King arrived. See detectives' reports, in Box 9, Files 24, 25, Box 12, Files 17, 18, Box 13, Files 2, 3, 4, 5, Eugene Connor Papers, Birmingham Public Library. Walker interview, 52. On King's failure to secure volunteers for jail, see Kunstler, *Deep in My Heart*, 189. Police detectives support Kunstler's observation, though more volunteers stepped forward when asked to register to vote or integrate white churches. See, for example, B. A. Allison to Jamie Moore, April 18, 1963, and R. S. Whitehouse to Moore, April 26, 1963, both in Box 13, File 4, Connor Papers.

6. Lewis, *King: A Biography*, 173–74.

7. "Connor and King," *Newsweek*, April 22, 1963, p. 28.

editorial shrug of impatience, and "each had what he wanted. It was left to history to say which man would have the victory." Left to *Newsweek*, the affair would go into history as pointless. Given a little time, "Birmingham's lame-duck public safety commissioner" would limp off the stage after "the farce at City Hall is played out and the new government takes control."[8]

The most telling evidence of how limited King's standing was at this time with *Newsweek* (and, for that matter, with *Time*) was what did not appear in print. Following the arrest of King, President Kennedy called King's wife in Atlanta to express his concern and to tell her that she would be hearing from her husband. Recognizing a good stroke of publicity, King instructed his wife to get word of the telephone call to the SCLC for an announcement to reporters.[9] No mention of the call appeared in *Newsweek* or *Time*, which was odd, considering that Kennedy was the nation's most visible newsmaker. Both magazines ignored the natural news peg, a similar call to Mrs. King in 1960 when her husband was moved to a state prison. A symbolic linkage between the president and King did not suit their purposes, not when they believed King was attempting to force an unnecessary crisis on Birmingham.

It suited the purposes of *U.S. News* admirably to report the conversation. Not that it regarded King's campaign as either necessary or justified. The city that *Time* and *Newsweek* had described in 1962 as a grim fortress of segregation was depicted by *U.S. News* as a citadel of southern customs and traditions. A year later, Lawrence's journal paid relatively little attention to the Birmingham movement until Kennedy's call to Mrs. King. The incident seemed tailor-made for the recurring theme that black leaders and high officials of the federal government were conspiring to usurp the rightful authority of the southern states.[10]

Kennedy desired no such thing. He was no more enthusiastic about applying the prod in Birmingham than he had been in Albany and was, in fact, no happier than was *Newsweek* or *Time* with the prospect of having another civil rights crisis dumped on his doorstep—particularly when it seemed Boutwell

---

8. *Ibid.*, 33; "The White Sit-ins," *Newsweek*, April 29, 1963, p. 29.

9. Telephone conversation between King and his wife, n.d. [April, 1963], transcript in Box 13, File 3, Connor Papers. Wyatt Tee Walker announced the president's call to a rally. Garrow, *Bearing the Cross*, 244–45.

10. "The Push is on for 'Mixed' Pools and Parks," *U.S. News & World Report*, May 21, 1962, p. 44; "As Racial Conflicts Broke Out Anew—," *U.S. News & World Report*, April 29, 1963, p. 8.

might be amenable to negotiating a quiet settlement. But King was doing what he could to create that crisis, gambling not just that he could win in Birmingham but that the confrontation would generate enough pressure to force Kennedy to move on civil rights legislation.

Even if King's eyes had been raised no higher than the immediate goals in Birmingham, Boutwell remained a question mark. *Newsweek* conceded as much between the lines while struggling to put the best possible face on Boutwell. That task was far from easy because Boutwell had just reaffirmed "his belief in segregation." Still, Boutwell was willing to talk, and for *Newsweek*, "vague as that seemed, it was something. For in the long era of Bull Connor, . . . Birmingham had never even admitted there was a racial problem to solve."[11]

As a magazine that kept to the middle way, *Newsweek* had more than its share of faith in comparative moderation. Boutwell might be a segregationist, but he also was courtly and mannered, unlike that segregationist of the old school, Theophilus Eugene Connor. Given this, would Boutwell not therefore be more likely to negotiate an acceptable democratic solution? Why not simply wait, go to the bargaining table and thrash out the differences there? That, to *Newsweek*, was the moderate way, which is to say the American way, and it was entirely in character for *Newsweek* that such questions were implicit in its stories.

Not to put too fine a point on it, moderation seemed out of place in a city that had earned the gallows-humor sobriquet of *Bomb*ingham. Faith in negotiations and democratic compromise was all very well, but King, fresh from Albany, had learned that arguing against injustice and inequality was not enough; the evil of Jim Crow had to be dramatized with blood and brutality in quantities sufficient to produce shock waves. For such purposes, no better opponent existed than Bull Connor. He had one singular virtue so far as King and the SCLC were concerned: There was no subtlety to the man's style as a segregationist. Years later, after the memories of Birmingham faded, the leaders of SCLC could even wax nostalgic about Connor as they ruefully contemplated campaigns mired in more complex social issues. Ralph David Abernathy once reminisced about that useful characteristic shared by Birmingham's police and fire commissioner and another adversary whom the

11. "The White Sit-ins," 29.

SCLC met two years later in Selma. "Bull Connor and Jim Clark did—in a way—spoil us," Abernathy said. "We knew where they stood."[12]

Connor demonstrated where he stood in the most dramatic way possible in early May. But waiting for the Bull to blunder into the trap made King anxious. Walker recalled that King telephoned him and said, "'Wyatt, you've got to find some way to make Bull Connor tip his hand.'" Walker chose to enlist the black children of Birmingham—and to use some shrewd, if not-so-saintly, tactics, such as turning in false fire and police alarms during the campaign. The turning point came on May 2. Waves of schoolchildren, most of them teenagers, were sent on marches downtown. Before nightfall, more than a thousand were in jail. During subsequent demonstrations, Connor and the police took the gloves off and reverted to form with billy clubs, police dogs, and fire hoses. Americans, King's lawyer wrote, "watched in horror as young boys and girls . . . countered brutality with peace and love. History was being written in the streets of Birmingham."[13]

Indeed, much of the world vicariously witnessed history in the making in Birmingham. More than 250 journalists, from America and from many of the nations of Europe and Asia, covered the story. Among them, of course, were correspondents from the news magazines. *Time*, for example, painted vivid word pictures of whites against blacks, police against children, dogs against humans. Connor dominated the scenes. "'Look at 'em run,' yelled Bull. He saw an officer holding back a crowd of white people near by. 'Let those people come to the corner, sergeant,' shouted Connor. 'I want 'em to see the dogs work. Look at those niggers run.'"[14]

That report captured the quintessential Bull Connor, the stuff of which his savage legend was rapidly being constructed. The tactics were brutal, but the matter went further than that. Police dogs, fire hoses, and clubs had been used before and with equal ferocity against black demonstrators in the South, and, ironically, far deadlier force would cause no such outrage years later when employed during the urban riots.[15] Bull Connor made Birmingham the sym-

12. Speech by Ralph David Abernathy at the National Press Club, Washington, D.C., June 14, 1968, copy in Box 172, File 2, King Center Archives, Atlanta.

13. Walker interview, 62. Walker used the tactics without King's knowledge. *Ibid.*, 31–32, 58–59, 62–63. Kunstler, *Deep in My Heart*, 190. See also Garrow, *Bearing the Cross*, 247–49.

14. "Race Relations—A Candid Report," n.d. [1965], various drafts in Box 3, Files 1, 2, 3, Albert Boutwell Papers, Birmingham Public Library; "Dogs, Kids, and Clubs," *Time*, May 10, 1963, p. 19.

15. For an analogous interpretation, see Garry Wills, *The Second Civil War: Arming for Armageddon* (New York, 1968), 93.

bol that it became—Bull Connor and the black children put on the streets by the SCLC.

Of necessity, the movement had been converted into a children's crusade. King had been unable to unify Birmingham's black community, and the SCLC had "scraped the bottom of the barrel of adults" able or willing to go to jail. But the use of children as marchers set off a storm of protest inside and outside the movement, occasioning, for instance, the caustic remark by Malcolm X of the Black Muslims that "any man who puts his women and children on the front lines is a chump, not a champ."[16]

Time and *Newsweek* were no less critical. The former reported that King "decided to throw schoolchildren into the Negro battle line." What awaited them—"club-swinging cops, police dogs, and blasts of water from fire hoses"—made his action all the more reprehensible. "There were no winners in Birmingham last week," *Time* declared decisively. *Newsweek* heard "even some friendly voices" raise "the prickly questions: if it was wrong for police to put the children in jail, was it right for the integrationists to start them on the way?" Returning to its theme that King should wait for Boutwell to come to power, *Newsweek* added: "Indeed, should there be any demonstrating at all?" As a further sign of displeasure, *Newsweek* lodged a complaint that questioned the ruthlessness of King's decision and, sotto voce, King's manhood in the same breath. "And if the man's work of fighting for freedom fell to children," *Newsweek* snapped, "so be it."[17]

"So be it" was reserved for moments when King plunged ahead, disregarding the counsel of *Newsweek* or of people it respected. The phrase was being used now not only because children were on the front line—black children had been on that line in Little Rock, for instance—but also because King was being called back to the way of moderation by the attorney general. Robert Kennedy, worried about the crisis, was urging negotiations; he was appealing to moderates on all sides to help alleviate the growing tension in Birmingham. He echoed *Newsweek* (or vice versa) when he said that blacks "should press their case against segregation in meetings, in 'good-faith negotiations, and not in the streets.'"[18]

16. On Birmingham's divided black community, see Andrew J. Young, "And Birmingham," *Drum Major*, I (Winter 1971), 23. The remark about scraping the bottom of the barrel is from the Walker interview, 62. Louis E. Lomax, *When the Word is Given* (Cleveland, 1963), 85.

17. "Dogs, Kids, and Clubs," 19; "Birmingham, U.S.A.: 'Look at Them Run,'" *Newsweek*, May 13, 1963, pp. 27–28.

18. "Birmingham, U.S.A.: 'Look at Them Run,'" 28.

Time agreed. King was flying in the face of Kennedy's wise counsel that "an injured, maimed, or dead child is a price that none of us can afford to pay." *Time* warned that the cost would be all the more grievous because it was unnecessary: Boutwell was waiting in the wings until Connor was turned out of office. *Newsweek* had called Boutwell a "walk-soft segregationist"; *Time* went even further. Boutwell was a "relative moderate"—shorn by *Time* even of his professed belief in segregation—and a pleader for "'restraint and peace' until his administration takes effective power."[19]

Where *Time* and *Newsweek* had urged moderation on King, then turned on him when he failed to respond, *U.S. News* depicted him altogether differently, as a sinister and ruthless leader "helping to mastermind the Birmingham protests" and promising to escalate demonstrations in a city already suffering from violence. Care had to be taken when reporting the violence. Like its competitors, *U.S. News* acted upon the knowledge that its audience had already read or seen news accounts of the event. Making the magazine's task harder was the fact that taking those blows, tumbling under the blasts of powerful fire hoses, recoiling from the snapping jaws of police dogs were black *children*. More awkward still, the attacks were directed against people, children and adults, peacefully seeking their rights. That Americans should enjoy those rights was a notion firmly fixed in the American consensus, no matter the number of times practice triumphed over principle. However reactionary its voice, however intense its hostility toward King and his cause, *U.S. News* could not deny the essential *rightness* of the ideals without denying America. All in all, the task was demanding.

U.S. News turned to the task with a will. The drama recreated by *Time* and *Newsweek* was diluted by *U.S. News*, which reported a clash between the forces of law and order and groups of marching blacks. "Firemen doused them with high-pressure hoses. Many were sent sprawling across the pavements. There were screams. The water streams passed. The crowd surged forward again, and was hit by another blast of water. Police brought dogs, let them loose on long leashes. Officers on motorcycles chased Negroes back into the church. One used a nightstick on stragglers."[20]

The story contained masterfully crafted understatements. The "high-pressure" hoses lacked the power, as *Time* would put it, to strip bark from a

19. "Dogs, Kids, and Clubs," 19.
20. "As Racial Troubles Broke Loose in Alabama . . . ," *U.S. News & World Report*, May 13, 1963, p. 8.

tree, and their use was justified by the notation that the crowd (to be read as mob) "surged forward" twice. Only one policeman used a nightstick, and then merely to prod stragglers. Dogs were employed—but carefully, on long leashes, and dogs and demonstrators did not even meet. Even more important than such delicately etched details was the absence of the looming symbolism of Bull Connor. Connor had to be fitted in somehow, and of course he could not be shown gleefully watching vicious dogs, fire hoses, and clubs being used on children. The following week, he became the exemplar of even-handed law enforcement. No one was seriously hurt, Connor said in *U.S. News*, nor had there been "really bad trouble." Indeed, it seemed that he had clamped down on *all* trouble-makers: "'I've kept the Ku Klux Klan and the Citizens Councils out of this—and I'm going to make sure they stay out.'"[21]

There was no need for such delicacy of hand, however, when it came to reporting on black demonstrators. After some minor episodes the following week, *U.S. News* published a scenario of concerted attack upon the forces of law and order. "The demonstrations were run with almost military precision. The Negroes would gather in a church to listen to exhortations and instructions, then set off in waves toward downtown Birmingham. Police, using trained dogs and fire hoses, turned back wave after wave. Hundreds were arrested daily under an ordinance which forbids parading without a permit. Eventually, however, police were overwhelmed. On May 7, hordes of Negroes escaped police control and surged through downtown streets and stores, snarling traffic and shoving white people from their path."[22] The report showed that any action taken by the police was justified because blacks were one step removed from savagery.

The SCLC's enlistment of children did not shock *U.S. News*, which reported that almost 90 percent of the city's schoolchildren were truant during the height of the demonstrations. The magazine supplied brief but telling quotations clearly establishing the militancy of the youngsters and their knowledge of what was at stake. Then it tut-tutted and let the matter go: Blacks were blacks, demonstrators, demonstrators. *U.S. News* was more concerned with warning its readers to "watch out for the Birmingham pattern [thousands of demonstrators, children among them] to show up in other cities around the country," and to be wary of the man behind the protests. King was

21. "Tension Growing Over Race Issue," *U.S. News & World Report*, May 20, 1963, p. 39.
22. *Ibid.*, 38.

vilified as an intruder inciting racial hatred in Birmingham and preparing to do the same elsewhere. King's statements, at least those selected by *U.S. News*, matched that thesis nicely. "'If we can crack Birmingham,'" King said, "'I am convinced we can crack the South.'" Additional evidence appeared in his response to the magazine's question about whether the Birmingham pattern would be showing up in other cities: "'Yes, that's a real possibility.'"[23]

Tensions were rising together with the demonstrations, which peaked on May 6 and 7. More than 2,000 persons had been arrested and jailed, and several thousand others were still willing to march. On May 7, two demonstrations were staged involving more than 2,500 persons. Rioting erupted downtown. Bricks, rocks, and bottles were thrown at policemen and firemen. More violence seemed likely, and that possibility, along with pressure from the Kennedy administration, pushed Birmingham's establishment into negotiations. On May 8, King assented to a truce of twenty-four hours. A day later, he announced that agreement had been reached on most of the black demands. A major sticking point, the fate of 900 demonstrators remaining in jail, was cleared away by a bond fund established by the Kennedy administration and national labor unions. The demonstrations were scheduled to resume on May 10, but before they started, King reported that a settlement had been reached.[24]

King's moment of triumph was disrupted on May 11. Dynamite explosions demolished the home of his younger brother, A. D. King, a Baptist minister, and blew a hole in the side of a motel being used as the SCLC headquarters. Perhaps as many as 2,500 angry blacks gathered on the streets after the bombings. More rioting erupted, covering nine city blocks and lasting for about three hours. The outbreak caused numerous injuries and considerable property damage. As he had done in Albany, King made the rounds of pool halls and other black establishments urging that violence be avoided. Relative quiet descended after President Kennedy ordered riot-trained troops dispatched to nearby military bases and Governor George Wallace sent in state troopers who, if anything, had a worse reputation among blacks than did Birmingham police.[25]

23. *Ibid.*, 37, 39.
24. See Lewis, *King: A Biography*, 194–96; Viorst, *Fire in the Streets*, 218–19; and Walker interview, 67–68.
25. Walker interview, 71; Garrow, *Bearing the Cross*, 260–62; Morgan, *A Time to Speak*, 7; Reese Cleghorn, "Crowned with Crises," in C. Eric Lincoln (ed.), *Martin Luther King, Jr.: A Profile* (New York, 1970), 114–15.

With white leaders lining up behind the settlement, two final hitches were taken care of. On May 22, a federal court overturned the Birmingham school board's suspension of about a thousand schoolchildren who participated in demonstrations. A day later, the Alabama Supreme Court ruled that Connor and the other commissioners had to surrender their offices to Boutwell's mayor-council government.[26]

King had won, though the local gains were not especially impressive. They amounted to not much more than desegregating some downtown stores, hiring and promoting blacks in commercial and industrial establishments, and forming a biracial committee. But the changes were a start—if no more than that—for Birmingham. In June, the real victory became apparent. The Kennedy administration had publicly expressed sympathy for the goals of the Birmingham campaign and almost in the same breath had deplored King's timing. Now, with hundreds of demonstrations occurring across the United States because of the events in Birmingham, Kennedy was forced to act. The president announced he would send a civil rights bill to Congress.[27]

The same events prodded *Time* and *Newsweek* to resurrect King as a symbol, in part because King emerged the victor; *Time*, for one, was no more disposed to award laurels to losers now than it had been in Albany. The magazines were more influenced, however, by what was occurring elsewhere in the nation. Increasing militancy among black Americans was producing demonstrations "mounted to protest discrimination in education, jobs, and housing"—grievances that applied as much outside the South as in it.[28] Prophecies other than Gandhian nonviolence and prophets other than King were emerging or gathering strength in black America in mid-1963. The most ominous threat appeared to be the Nation of Islam, popularly known as the Black Muslims, which represented the antithesis of King's doctrine of reconciliation with whites. The Black Muslims' charismatic proselytizer Malcolm X damned the white man as not only an oppressor but a devil. The sect had been dismissed previously as a perversion of Islam with no attraction for black

26. Viorst, *Fire in the Streets*, 220; Kunstler, *Deep in My Heart*, 193.

27. *Cf.* Aldon D. Morris, *The Origins of the Civil Rights Movement: Black Communities Organizing for Change* (New York, 1984), 258, 280, 322n114. Morris argues the Birmingham campaign was organized primarily to generate sufficient economic pressure to defeat local segregationists rather than bring about federal intervention. On the strictly local issues, see Lewis, *King: A Biography*, 199–200.

28. On the spread of the demonstrations, see Viorst, *Fire in the Streets*, 221–22; Lewis, *King: A Biography*, 211–12; and Bishop, *The Days of Martin Luther King*, 338.

Americans. That was not so easy to do now, when even the conservative NAACP, reacting to the pressure of black militancy, was taking part in street protests as well as engaging in dignified litigation and lobbying in courtroom and legislative chambers.

With social unrest so evident, *Newsweek* and *Time*, which had no taste for extremes, now depicted King as a moderate. Peculiarly, but not uncharacteristically, *Newsweek*'s coverage of King ran on two parallel tracks as the Birmingham crisis was coming to a head. To begin, the magazine criticized him for recklessness. Its report of the rioting on May 11 and 12 put the Birmingham police—not King—in the role of peacemaker. The "integrationist field marshal Martin Luther King" could not even recognize, when he proclaimed victory after the negotiations started, the consequences of his own folly: " 'This day,' King said, 'is truly a moment of great victory.' In the smoky, acrid dawn Sunday, the words echoed full of tragic irony." While scourging King, *Newsweek* also defended him. It did this by picturing him as a leader scrambling to catch up with the "restive mood" of black Americans—following the example of Gandhi, whose aphorism " 'There go my people, I must catch them, for I am their leader' " was "much cherished by his American disciple." Had *Time* published those two stories, it would have been startling indeed. But *Newsweek* had been known to speak with disparate voices on the same event. Soon enough, the voices would take on the same tones, and the differing themes would converge. They were converging now—partly because Birmingham was a national story requiring a perspective broader than could be supplied by reporters in the field. Another reason for the convergence of themes was suggested by a black leader, who was quoted in a related context: " 'He may be an s.o.b.,' says one, 'but he's our s.o.b.' "[29]

Opinions heeded by *Newsweek* held that King might be an s.o.b., but the moderates had to claim him. From the intelligentsia came the warning, voiced by Walter Lippmann, a *Newsweek* columnist, that the "crucial question is whether these moderate men will continue to be followed, or whether the movement will become explosive in a mood of desperation"; from the arts, the novelist James Baldwin spoke of " 'the cat in the Harlem barber shop' who listens to Black Muslim Malcolm X rather than moderate Martin Luther

29. See *Newsweek*, "Explosion in Alabama," May 20, 1963, p. 27, and " 'I Like the Word Black,' " May 6, 1963, pp. 27–28.

King"; from the Oval Office, Kennedy was pleading with southerners to recognize that "if moderates do not solve the race problem . . . the Negro advocates of nonviolence will give way to extremists who teach violence"; and from the other side in the South came what could be taken as an endorsement of King, considering the source—Governor Wallace's tirade against "appeasers" who played into King's hands. With such statements and the recognition that "every inch of progress" whetted the black man's "hunger for a yard more," small wonder that *Newsweek* was hastily draping the cloak of moderation about the man who conducted himself so recklessly in Birmingham.[30]

Newsweek had not much choice in the matter in any event. Bull Connor had made the theme of King's recklessness untenable. Compelled to make sense of the situation, *Newsweek* subtly rewrote the history of the Birmingham movement, beginning with the decree of the Alabama Supreme Court that pushed Connor and his fellow commissioners out of office. Previously, the magazine had emphasized that the commissioners were on their way out, as indeed they were, the question being when, 1963 or 1965. Dwelling on the might-have-beens only when it needed to transform King into a moderate, *Newsweek* pointed out that had the commissioners won their lawsuit, they would have remained "in office until their terms ran out in 1965." The prospect of two more years of Bull Connor (who was changed from "a lame-duck segregationist" into a "hoses-and-dogs segregationist") justified almost anything King did. Nor was Connor the only one altered; so was the new mayor. *Newsweek* found it too awkward to confess disillusionment with Boutwell's vague promises. Still, something had to be done about the man on whom so much hope had once been pinned for a reasonable solution. So *Newsweek* settled for de-emphasizing his relative moderation, describing Boutwell now as a "peace-and-quiet segregationist." The Birmingham school board's suspension of pupils who marched in the demonstrations provided another opportunity to display King's moderation. The decision "angered . . . two of King's lieutenants who cranked out four thousand mimeographed handbills urging a full-scale boycott of Negro schools." Trouble was averted by King.

---

30. Walter Lippmann, "The Racial Crisis," *Newsweek*, May 27, 1963, p. 23. Baldwin's statement was reported in "Kennedy and Baldwin: The Gulf," *Newsweek*, June 3, 1963, p. 19. The remarks of Kennedy and Wallace appeared in "Birmingham's Choice," *Newsweek*, May 27, 1963, pp. 26–27. The desire for more black equality was reported in "'I Like the Word Black,'" 27.

He "overruled" his less reasonable aides; he "reasoned with rebellious students"; and he sent his lawyers into court, getting the school board's rash decision reversed just in the "nick of time." Then King "sighed: 'The truce still holds. It has not been broken.'"[31]

With the "integrationist field marshal" newly anointed as peacemaker, *Newsweek* had to eliminate the military titles conferred during the Battle of Birmingham. A battle that struggle remained in *Newsweek*'s prose, but King became, variously, "Negro leader," "integrationist leader," and one of the "nation's top Negro leaders." Most telling of all, King was restored to his symbolic position as "the nation's best-known apostle of nonviolence."[32]

The resurrection of King as a prophet of the middle way occurred also in *Time*. King represented the reasonable approach that, much to the consternation of Luce's magazine, was going out of style. The outsider who pushed his way into Birmingham without bothering to consult the city's own black leaders underwent a transfiguration in mid-May. Birmingham *needed* King; *Time* said as much in this picture of Birmingham before and after King:

> Birmingham Negroes had always been a docile lot. Downtown at night, they slouched in gloomy huddles beneath street lamps, talking softly or not at all. They knew their place: They were "niggers" in a Jim Crow town, and they bore their degradation in silence.
> Last week they smashed that image forever. The scenes in Birmingham were unforgettable. There was the Negro youth, sprawled on his back and spinning across the pavement, while firemen battered him with streams of water so powerful that they could strip bark off trees. There was the Negro woman, pinned to the ground by cops, one of them with his knee dug into her throat. . . . And there was the little Negro girl, splendid in a new starched dress, who marched out of a church, looked toward a massed line of pistol-packing cops, and called to a laggard friend: "Hurry up, Lucille. If you stay behind, you won't be arrested with our group."

No less than *Newsweek*, *Time* had been forced by events to acknowledge that King had lifted up blacks cowed by "hoarse threats and club-swinging cops." As a sop to King's critics and to its previous stories, *Time* noted that King was sometimes inept, but it added that he also was the "Negroes' inspirational leader."[33]

31. "Changing Order," *Newsweek*, June 3, 1963, p. 20.
32. See *Newsweek*, "Focus on Washington," June 3, 1963, p. 19, "The Other Side," June 10, 1963, p. 30, and "An End and a Beginning," June 24, 1963, p. 33.
33. "Freedom—Now," *Time*, May 17, 1963, p. 23.

Time smoothed over another matter. If King indeed had been reckless, that now appeared to be the better part of wisdom. It seemed he had been "obsessed by the fear that other groups, more aligned to violence . . . , might move into Birmingham." *Time* all but heaved a sigh of relief: "But [King] got there first." King's virtues shone when the magazine juxtaposed him against radical alternatives, the "most baleful" of which was the Nation of Islam. The Black Muslims were taking full advantage, so *Time* maintained, of the rioting in Birmingham. Luckily, they were headed off by King, whose rapid and decisive (no longer reckless) action meant that for the moment Malcolm X "could only sneer" at the "gospel of nonviolence."[34]

Implicit in such statements was a question: What if Malcolm X could do more than sneer? *Time* reassured its readers that the Muslims could be forestalled by a prophet who preached not violence but love, not hatred of but reconciliation with whites. However, proof was required that nonviolence worked in the streets as well as in the abstract. Birmingham provided the evidence, and if nonviolence worked in the city of Bull Connor, who could doubt that it would work anywhere? *Time* recounted a miraculous change of heart when blacks encountered the massed forces of segregation: "A police captain demanded their parade permit. They had none. Seeing the fire hoses, they knelt in silence as a Negro minister solemnly began to pray: 'Let them turn their water on. Let them use their dogs. We are not leaving. Forgive them, O Lord.' Suddenly, inexplicably, in a moment of overt mercy, Bull Connor waved the Negroes through the police line."[35]

The prophet King was as compelling as the parable of Bull Connor's uncharacteristic mercy. As "the Atlanta integration leader," King remained an outsider, but he appeared to advantage juxtaposed with other outsiders. These were the state police ordered into Birmingham by Wallace, "a militant segregationist who seemed to be spoiling for a fight." The officers acted like storm troopers, "shouting threats, shoving Negroes into doorways, and menacingly snapping the safety catches off their weapons." By contrast, King made his rounds after the rioting, pleading "for peace in a pilgrimage through Negro pool halls." King was touchingly earnest as he ministered to his errant flock: "Facing embarrassed pool sharks, he said, . . . 'We must make it clear that it is possible to fight against all this evil without having to resort to violence.'" Later, "he shouted: 'Violence is immoral, but not only that—

34. *Ibid.*, 23–24. See also "The Resounding Cry," *Time*, May 24, 1963, p. 22.
35. "Freedom—Now," 23. *Cf.* Lewis, *King: A Biography*, 194, who maintains that firefighters disobeyed Connor's orders to use hoses against the demonstrators.

violence is impractical.'" To avert disturbances, King even accepted "pallid promises" from white businessmen in Birmingham, and he worked to preserve a fragile truce when the promises were not kept. *Time* reported at the end of May that "King, obviously disappointed, would only say that he would try to hold off further demonstrations until it was clear exactly what the white men had meant to promise." In short, King was a prophet of moderate reform. While telling his followers, *Time* reported, that "we will turn America upside down,'" King nevertheless added "'in order that it turn right side up.'"[36]

The spreading black revolt threatened to turn the ordered America of *U.S. News* upside down. This development occasioned both smugness and disquietude at a magazine that for years had warned of the racial troubles approaching for those Americans who had diverted "to the South all the onus for discrimination."[37] To the satisfaction of *U.S. News*, the shoe now appeared to be on the other foot—and pinching. But the conservative *U.S. News* was also alarmed by the racial problems occurring across America.

As the racial demonstrations multiplied, Lawrence's journal provided political intelligence to its readers about the leader of the black revolt. In its early Birmingham coverage, *U.S. News* dismissed King as but "one Negro leader." His victory and the magazine's prediction that human wave protests would be used across the nation demanded that King get a promotion. In early June, King was designated the "Top Man of the Negro Revolution." That title recognized King's importance; it did not confer approval. The journal implied that King preached nonviolence but practiced the opposite: "He has been in the midst of violence many times—bombings, burnings, riots." And it suggested that King's civil rights campaigns were undertaken to reap a harvest of donations. Furthermore, King hungered for power. He was exploring the idea of founding a national organization—not interracial like the NAACP, *U.S. News* made a point of saying—that would raise him to "a level of power and prestige unmatched by any Negro in American history."[38]

Equally piquant were stories in the next two issues. One reported a suggestion, attributed to King, that President Kennedy should escort black students when they desegregated the University of Alabama. King seemed cavalier

36. "The Resounding Cry," 22; "Freedom—Now," 25.
37. See *U.S. News & World Report*, "Tomorrow," June 10, 1963, p. 30, and "Tomorrow," September 2, 1963, p. 15.
38. See *U.S. News & World Report*, "Top Man of the Negro 'Revolution,'" June 10, 1963, p. 21, and "What the American Negro Wants," April 29, 1963, pp. 46–52.

when responding to a newsman's suggestion that this might endanger the president's life. "Dr. King replied: 'The risk to his life is not the major consideration. The Negro risks his life every day.'" For further proof of King's radicalism, *U.S. News* returned to Birmingham, which had been brought to the "brink of disaster" when King fanned the fires of racial hatred. The vehicle for expressing this view was an interview with an unnamed newspaper editor who complained that "much more progress would have been made toward granting Negroes more rights in Birmingham if . . . King and his crowd had not come in." Another lesson *U.S. News* wanted taught throughout the country was summed up by the same editor, who warned that King "has set a frightening pattern. It is already spreading across the country. And who has gained from it?"[39] *U.S. News* was sounding the tocsin once again about a false prophet who divided Americans and brought bloodshed and unnecessary suffering.

The period between the conclusion of the Birmingham campaign and the March on Washington was a season of doubt. The public outcry touched off by the events in Birmingham had been thunderous, but a question remained unanswered: How far would the nation go to put ideals into practice when the cause was not so clearly dramatized or its location so comfortably distant? Before Birmingham, there had been a fairly general belief among whites sympathetic to black aspirations that most problems of race would be resolved once the South was brought into line with the rest of America. The notion was rudely jolted in 1963.

King himself was pondering the burdens of race and musing "whether I should be limiting myself to the South." Two years before the Selma campaign that capped the southern movement, King wrote of "brothers and sisters who are suffering discrimination that is even more agonizing, in a sense, than in the South. . . . In the South, at least the Negro can see progress, whereas in the North all he sees is retrogression."[40] While overstating the progress in the South, King had put his finger on something important. However limited and however slowly, changes clearly were occurring in the lot of black southerners. They could see the evidence of movement, as could blacks outside the

39. See *U.S. News & World Report*, "Should President 'Risk His Life' for Integration?" June 10, 1963, p. 35, and "After Birmingham Riots: 'Who Has Gained?'" June 17, 1963, p. 46. The theme was developed earlier in "After Birmingham Riots—Troubles Linger On," May 27, 1963, p. 40.
40. Cleghorn, "Crowned With Crises," 122.

region, who, quite correctly, did not sense that *their* life was improving. What their southern brethren were struggling to win, other blacks in America already had—the right to vote, the right to eat at lunch counters, the right to sit where they pleased on public transportation. The sting of de facto discrimination was felt no less keenly for all that, and it was altogether likely that demonstrations outside the South would not only continue but become more militant, with or without Martin Luther King to lead them.

Time and *Newsweek* did not lack understanding of the burdens of black Americans or of the rising tide of militancy. Segregationists to the contrary, both magazines had devoted ample space to racial problems across the country. But the impediments of color existed more in the abstract than in the flesh for the two journals that shared the comfortable supposition that good will and devotion to justice, so noticeably absent in Bull Connor's South, would be enough to dispose of racial problems elsewhere. When these virtues did not suffice—in part, because they were not exhibited to the extent anticipated—comfortable notions began to crumble. There was, for example, the violence directed in July against civil rights demonstrators in the citadel of liberalism in the United States. As *Newsweek* put it, "This, incredibly, was New York." Picketing and sit-ins could "no longer be regarded as the monopoly of the Birminghams"—but "neither could white mobs," in this instance "running riot for four nights, waving rebel flags, yelling racist jeers, [and] pitching rocks and garbage at pickets." *Newsweek* managed to swallow its shock: "Demonstrations might be provocative, but if they had worked in Birmingham, why not in the Bronx? . . . [O]ne demonstrator—a white schoolteacher—said: 'We've got our own Birmingham right here.'"[41]

Time grasped the same implications. With some effort, *Time* admitted that henceforth "if the U.S. North thought it could view the South's spectacle with any complacency, it was wrong. The Negro revolt had burst all regional boundaries." The disciplined black demonstrators in the South seemed far less threatening, however, than the masses huddled in, to take one example, Chicago, the site of the "nation's biggest and most potentially explosive Negro ghetto." Inhabitants of that ghetto and others like it across America shared the problem of not being *Time* subscribers; that is to say, they were poor, the crime rate where they lived was high, as was the rate of illegitimate births among them. The black man deserved his rights, *Time* said in the

41. "New York, N.Y.," *Newsweek*, July 22, 1963, p. 23.

patronizing, middle-class view of that period, but thereafter it was up to him "to take, and deserve, his place in American society."[42] No other response could have been expected from the house organ of the American Dream. Hard work by blacks to correct their own failings, and time—the passage of it, not the magazine—would set aright the problems of race in America.

The auguries were not favorable for that solution. The Lucean scheme relied on the premise that blacks would queue patiently for admission into the Promised Land of middle-class America and for the acceptance to be found there for those cleansed of crime, poverty, and other stigmata. Such saintly patience was not much in evidence at a time when even the staid NAACP was taking to the streets, but it would have been out of character for *Time* to examine an article of faith so ingrained in its persona.

The menace of black militancy appeared all too clear to *U.S. News.* "Threats: Negroes' Latest Weapon in Rights Drive" its headline proclaimed shrilly in the issue of July 1. The principal threat came from King, who intended to bring about a "reign of terror and violence." Journalistic sleight-of-hand effected that image. The magazine first quoted a statement by an underling of King's that the SCLC "'will tie up public transportation by laying our bodies prostrate on the runways of airports, across railroad tracks, and in bus depots.'" Immediately thereafter was inserted a partial quotation from King—"there will be a nation-wide reign of 'violence and terror' unless civil rights legislation is passed by Congress"—purporting to show his true intentions.[43] The stratagem made it appear that King was preparing a bloody insurrection rather than predicting one.

Three weeks later, David Lawrence pitched in with a broadside aimed directly at the mob spirit and almost as directly at King. The questions were rhetorical, the message unmistakable, as was the target, even if not identified by name: "Why . . . have so many Negro ministers become the active leaders and managers of street 'demonstrations' that have resulted in disturbance of the peace, arrests, bloodshed, and death? Do [they] really feel that people of other races cannot be impressed with the merits of their cause except through so-called 'nonviolent demonstrations' which so often lead to violence?"[44] The

42. "The Revolution," *Time*, June 7, 1963, pp. 17, 18.
43. "Threats: Negroes' Latest Weapon in Rights Drive," *U.S. News & World Report*, July 1, 1963, p. 39.
44. David Lawrence, "What's Become of 'Law and Order'?" *U.S. News & World Report*, August 5, 1963, p. 104.

missing identification was not critical. Lawrence could flail away editorially at "so many Negro ministers" and be reasonably certain of hitting King, as far as his readers were concerned.

If a few readers somehow remained oblivious to Lawrence's message, they needed only wait a week for a "debate" about civil disobedience. The issue was framed in the headline "Is It All Right to Break the Law?" The parties to the discussion were King and an obscure judge in New York City, who complained that civil disobedience damaged respect for law. King's side was taken from his "Letter from the Birmingham Jail," which had been written four months earlier. The intent was not to debate the merits of nonviolence but to portray King as a trouble-maker on the eve of the March on Washington.[45]

The prospect of a major demonstration staged by blacks in Washington set off alarm bells at *U.S. News.* Its apprehensions, which were shared by others to one degree or another, were not entirely groundless, given the turmoil of the times. And there was another reason for the case of nerves. Although the March on Washington ended as a placid celebration of American ideals, it was not conceived in that spirit.

The March was the idea of by A. Philip Randolph, founder of the Brother- hood of Sleeping Car Porters and the nation's leading black labor unionist. Randolph revived his plan from World War II, when he threatened to stage a massive demonstration by blacks in Washington if Roosevelt did not issue an executive order prohibiting discrimination in employment in war industries and in government.[46]

Randolph proposed a march in November, 1962, and again in 1963. Other black leaders received his plan coolly until the goals were broadened to include dismantling other racial barriers as well as opening up jobs for blacks. The tenor of the demonstration also was altered. Initially, the event was to have been more militant than placid, possibly even including sit-ins in Senate

---

45. "Is It All Right to Break the Law?" *U.S. News & World Report*, August 12, 1963, p. 6. Considering the space allotted, King's remarks were not distorted. But it was scarcely the case, as *U.S. News* maintained, that the letter was just then being publicized. Nearly a million copies had been circulated before King was released. Young, "And Birmingham," 26. The juxtaposition of King's comments about civil disobedience and the remarks by the judge, who had lectured a group of persons arrested during an act of civil disobedience at a construction site, further strengthens the argument that *U.S. News* chose to dredge up King's already famous epistle in order to paint him as a radical.

46. Interview with A. Philip Randolph, by Robert Martin, January 14, 1969 (Transcript of tape 384, in Moorland-Spingarn Research Center, Howard University), 57–58.

and House buildings—an idea quickly jettisoned because Congress was considering civil rights legislation. When Kennedy met with black leaders in Washington on June 22, he argued that the March would hurt the chances of passage of his civil rights bill. Kennedy lost his argument, but he won his point. The March, conceived "as an instrument for stirring up the black masses," was transformed "into a channel for containing them." On July 17, Kennedy made a public statement of support for the March.[47]

Like Kennedy, *Newsweek* initially opposed the March, preferring a "consensus of conscience" to demonstrations likely to cause resentment among congressmen. Those heedless of the magazine's warnings—including King, who had issued a warning of his own, that a filibuster against the civil rights bill would set in motion a "Negro march on Washington and a massive sit-in at the Capitol"—were labeled militant. Still, *militant* was a slippery word when used by *Newsweek*. Depending on the circumstances, the term might signal approval or the opposite. In this case, *Newsweek* was vexed. In the same issue, another article looked into the causes of disharmony among the civil rights organizations. It found two—money and Martin Luther King. The acrimony was ascribed to the fact that "the Negro groups need funds, and to get funds they need publicity. Thus they are jealous when someone else comes poaching on their preserves. Especially when it's King." *Newsweek* did not stop with that entirely accurate analysis. Its catalog of the sins of King and the SCLC was far more critical than any it had previously published. *Newsweek* could not quite bring itself to print the derisory nickname "De Lawd," which would have jolted the sensibilities of liberal readers. Despite the euphemism substituted, its message was transparent. King, "The Lord," "rushes in, gets everybody stirred up, marches hundreds to jail, then leaves with minimal gains for the Negroes but enough publicity to get the money rolling in to SCLC. 'We're always watching . . . ,' said one Negro, 'when he will throw the people a bone and take off.'" The evaluation was reiterated a paragraph later, and *Newsweek* raised a question: Where does the money go? "A principal criticism of King is that he doesn't closely account for money received and spent." Furthermore, the SCLC was "top-heavy with self-perpetuating ad-

47. On the earlier plans, see interview with Norman Hill, associate executive director of the A. Philip Randolph Institute, by James Mosby, March 12, 1970 (Transcript of tape 532, in Moorland-Spingarn Research Center, Howard University), 15–16, 28–29. The quotation is from Viorst, *Fire in the Streets*, 222–23. See also Wofford, *Of Kennedys and Kings*, 174.

ministrators" and "sometimes seems to spend most of its funds raising more funds."[48] The focus, timing, and tone of the article indicated a desire to take King down a peg or two, to remind him that he still needed the support of white moderates disturbed by his talk of a sit-in at the Capitol.

Nevertheless, the article was an exception to the pattern. Despite a tone approaching petulance, King remained *Newsweek*'s s.o.b., a moderate in a hard season for moderation, when black leaders were "beset, not only by recalcitrant whites but by militant Negroes." Two weeks after taking him down a peg or two, *Newsweek* rushed to defend him as a leader. During a visit to Harlem, King watched "incredulously" as hecklers pitched eggs at his car. King's disbelief was matched by *Newsweek*'s: How could *this* be happening to the hero of Birmingham? Its story hastily smoothed over the embarrassment. There were only a half-dozen eggs, the crowd welcoming King numbered five hundred persons, and, in any event, the incident was said to be the handiwork "of black nationalists."[49]

Newsweek found that King's name still was magic among black masses and black leaders. A remarkably clumsy headline attached to the story about a public opinion survey proclaimed, "The Big Man is Martin Luther King, Jr." There were dissenters of course (one complained that King has "'sold the concept that one man will come to your town and save you'"), but *Newsweek* observed that "a devoted and overwhelming majority agree that King 'has proved himself to be a leader of the Negro people.'" In fact, King and the members of Kennedy's New Frontier had much in common, according to *Newsweek*—they were "young, talented, articulate, educated, middle-class, and, most of all, militant." Militancy now implied not radicalism but moderation in the service of social change—a point illustrated by the satisfaction *Newsweek* took from poll results. Blacks rejected the importunings of the Black Muslims and accepted Kennedy "to a degree stunningly close to unanimity" as a hero of the black revolt. Thus if King was a Joshua-like figure who fought the Battle of Birmingham, the walls that came tumbling down were those of segregation. And while challenging his white countrymen, King did so primarily to reawaken their sense of justice. Militaristic titles would not have been appropriate; an aura of spiritual leadership was. Thus, when King issued a call for reverse discrimination to help blacks seeking jobs,

48. See *Newsweek*'s issue of July 1, 1963, for "Reveille in Washington," 18, and "Hotter Fires," 20.

49. "Worried Leaders," *Newsweek*, July 15, 1963, pp. 19, 20.

his was not a political position but a summons to "a sort of national atonement for the sins of the past."[50]

Luce's magazine harbored no liberal guilt. Blacks would have to solve their own problems and work their way into the middle class. The leader and the organization most likely to make this possible on *Time*'s terms were not King and the SCLC. For one thing, black organizations were fiercely competing with each other, believing the most militant "will wind up on top," said *Time* through an unnamed official of the Justice Department. Whichever organization managed that feat, *Time* believed, ought not be the sort that welcomed the "knife and club type" of black. The NAACP had won *Time*'s favor for the moment. *Time* did not doubt King's credentials as a disciple of Gandhi. But he had already disregarded timetables laid out by others and now was venturing out of the South and into the tinderbox cities of the North, where he seemed even less safe. In Chicago, for example, King proclaimed an unseemly impatience with the gradualism recommended by *Time* and a willingness to fan the volatile temperament that seemed to be appearing everywhere. His address to an audience of about 5,500 people "brought them shouting to their feet." Segregation in Chicago was as bad as in Birmingham, King said, and ought to be pulled down just as decisively. Had he stopped there, *Time* would have been less disturbed. But King pressed on: "'We're through with tokenism and gradualism and see-how-far-you've-comeism. We're through with we've-done-more-for-your-people-than-anyone-elseism. We can't wait any longer. Now is the time.'" Now was certainly not the time to Luce's magazine, not when "the fever was everywhere and every act seemed to fan the flames." Rhetoric about being through with gradualism and tokenism has been made shopworn by repetition, but in the summer of 1963 the black revolt disconcerted *Time* to the point that it piled adjective on top of adjective to describe "a feverish, fragmented, spasmodic, almost uncontrollable revolution . . . with a torrent of Negro demands."[51]

Time yearned for simpler days when blacks and whites made common cause against those lacking a decent regard for the principles of American

50. "The Big Man is Martin Luther King, Jr.," *Newsweek*, July 29, 1963, p. 30. Kennedy's standing among blacks was reported by *Newsweek* in "The Negro in America," July 29, 1963, p. 16. See also "The Right to a Job," *Newsweek*, August 5, 1963, p. 52.

51. "The Inexorable Process," *Time*, June 14, 1963, p. 23. King's speech in Chicago was reported in "The Revolution," 17–18. A shortened version described King as "crying" his message, a verb designating semi-hysterical demagoguery. "The Long March," *Time*, June 21, 1963, p. 14.

democracy. It yearned also for orderly ways of bringing about the perfection of the society it regarded as perfectible—a society in which blacks and, for that matter, segregationists shorn of bigotry would be brought within to share the promise of the dream. This was a dream of the center, of course, and in this new America of 1963 the center appeared not to be holding. There was disagreement, and it was becoming acrimonious, over how rapidly America should be changed, and through what means. Should black leaders persist in their plans for marching on Washington even though "it is unanimously agreed by legislators of all political stripes that any such pressuring attempt might mean the death of the whole [civil rights] package?" *Time* thought not. There was disagreement about tactics. An idea making the rounds in the black movement was particularly flustering. President Kennedy, so it held, should escort black students as they desegregated the University of Alabama. Should that idea be treated seriously? *Time*'s reaction probably matched Attorney General Kennedy's when he heard it—the laughter of disbelief that such a thing could be seriously suggested by serious men. *Still, in such times, who could be certain? Time* was discovering a world of black America it did not know, not even understanding the hostile epithets used to describe whites.[52]

The "dangers of militancy" prompted the magazine to turn to Roy Wilkins and the NAACP in the weeks before the March on Washington. The voice of Wilkins seemed safer and saner than the one King raised in Chicago. The NAACP, for example, initially resisted the idea of the March on Washington for reasons similar to *Time*'s. It helped, so far as *Time* was concerned, that black militants were jeering at the NAACP, and it didn't hurt that Wilkins got himself arrested in a demonstration to prove his militancy. Wilkins and the NAACP believed in gradualism and orderly change, not in upending the system.

Time commended gradualism often enough in the summer of 1963, doing, in fact, just what King complained about in his Chicago speech— pontificating about the progress blacks had made. It published excerpts from a number of documents, some famous, others obscure, that represented milestones in the black struggle for freedom. The tumult in the streets, *Time*

52. The quotation is from "The President's Package," *Time*, June 28, 1963, p. 15. The proposal that President Kennedy escort the students is reported in "The Revolution," 18. *Time* attempted a lexicon of black street phrases in "Beyond the Ears of the Greys," August 2, 1963, p. 14.

maintained, "would be far less effective were it not for the words on those documents." There were limits to legalism, it conceded, but then added that mass demonstrations might alienate sympathetic whites who stood ready to correct discrimination because it "violates justice and morality." In short, whites must be persuaded, not pressed to the wall. Not long after, a similar message was issued by Wilkins, who, in *Time*'s approving phrase, sensed that militancy was nearing the danger point. "'We are not fighting white people,'" he told blacks. "'We are fighting for an idea. You don't need guns; you only need this dynamite-like idea of freedom. You don't have to be discourteous or rude, to be militant or even stubborn.'"[53]

King had uttered similar messages. But *Time* was skittish about him, his impatience, and his mass demonstrations. Therefore, King suffered in comparisons with Wilkins. *Time* located little in King's record to suggest that he was a national leader; indeed, even in the South he seemed to owe his success more to good fortune than to wisdom and leadership. Birmingham was a case in point. King ignored the advice of many civil rights leaders, *Time* said, and pressed ahead with demonstrations that seemed "singularly ill-timed." That he won reflected less to his credit than to the discredit of Bull Connor, who "became an international symbol of blind, cruel Southern racism."[54]

By contrast, Wilkins, while a rebel of sorts, retained the reassuring ability to "analyze rationally even the most emotional of problems"; King could whip up a crowd. Wilkins' mind was driven toward the concrete rather than—an implicit jab at King—"fuzzy generalization." Wilkins was willing and able to use a variety of techniques including nonviolence; others—King, presumably—were "limited in their tactics." Finally, Wilkins was the realistic executive of a group that whites had helped found and in whose history whites played an important role. *Time* was willing enough to defend King against the thrusts of segregationists, but that was about as far as it was prepared to go on the eve of the March.[55] Thus King, who once appeared wise beyond his years

---

53. See *Time*, "A Legal History of Negro Progress," June 21, 1963, p. 15, and "The Dangers of Militancy," July 19, 1963, p. 17.

54. "'The Awful Roar,'" *Time*, August 30, 1963, p. 12. *Time* also gave credit to white businessmen for helping to sort out Birmingham's racial problems, in "Race and Realism," July 5, 1963, p. 77.

55. On whites and the NAACP, see "'The Awful Roar,'" 9–10. The points made about Wilkins are *ibid.*, 12–14. For *Time*'s defense of King, see "To Fulfill a Historic Role," July 19, 1963, p. 18, and "With George and Sam on Capitol Hill," July 26, 1963, p. 11.

to *Time*, passed out of favor again—an inept leader with no organization to speak of, heedless of the counsels of moderation, and distinguished only by luck and the ability to bring a crowd to its feet.

King's power of oration was demonstrated magnificently during the March on Washington. His "I have a dream" speech caught the mood of the event. In truth, however, the tone had emerged weeks before when a demonstration conceived as a confrontation with American practices became a celebration of American principles—a transformation that accounts for much of the favor that it found with *Time* and *Newsweek*.

Despite significant thematic differences, *Time* and *Newsweek* reported the March as a rite of national idealism. *Time* found that "those scores of thousands of marching Negroes" proved they "were able to accept the responsibilities of first-class citizenship," an analysis indicating the magazine had had some doubts about this. But the triumph was less the black man's than America's; America had dared do what other societies would not or could not do. The possibility of rioting had been present, *Time* wrote, and had disorders occurred, they "would have been plainly visible for the whole world to see. But the marchers took that chance, and the U.S. took it with them."[56]

King's stock rose with *Time* because his oratory was "catching, dramatic, inspirational"; he became the "civil rights leader who holds the heart of most American Negroes in his hand." Yet King rose in its estimation as well because he stood in bold relief against other symbols representing extremes of Right ("the nitwit American Nazi Party") and Left (represented here by John Lewis, the "aggressive chairman of aggressive SNICK," who was prepared to deliver a threatening speech until dissuaded by other black leaders).[57]

Actually, within SNCC, Lewis was a moderate, not a radical. SNCC originally entertained the idea of turning the March into a massive exercise in civil disobedience, but had to give it up. Then Lewis got caught up in a dispute with Stokely Carmichael, later to become chairman of a radicalized SNCC, who refused to take part in the March and objected to Lewis doing so on behalf of SNCC. Lewis won that battle, but another one arose. An advance copy of Lewis' speech came to the attention of a prominent clergyman who threatened to withdraw from the platform unless the speech was changed. The elders of the movement persuaded Lewis to delete some of the more embittered pas-

56. "The March's Meaning," *Time*, September 6, 1963, pp. 13–14.
57. "Beginning of a Dream," *Time*, September 6, 1963, p. 14.

sages in order to prevent a rift in the liberal forces supporting the March. One passage appeared to be particularly inflammatory: "We will march through the South, through the heart of Dixie, the way Sherman did. We shall pursue our own 'scorched-earth' policy and burn Jim Crow to the ground non-violently. . . . We will take matters into our own hands and create a source of power, outside any national structure, that could and would assure us a victory."[58]

Time was not appeased by the fact that this "bold threat" was unspoken and even less by the statement that Lewis did make: " 'We want our freedom—and we want it now!' " Yet much of what occurred and much of what was said that day comforted *Time*. The militancy of Lewis (which *Time* dismissed as petulance by punctuating the text with "now!" "now!" "now!" "now!" "now!") was nullified by sound men of the center such as Roy Wilkins, "introduced as the 'acknowledged leader' of the civil rights movement," who talked "quietly of the necessity" of winning passage of the civil rights bill. And when some voices shrilly expressed distrust of whites, *Time* found one black marcher who "snapped satisfiedly: 'Salt and pepper—just what it should be.' "[59]

Just as it should be was King's challenge to America. With Birmingham and Bull Connor looming in the background, King's voice could be heard as a ringing call for Americans to bring their ideals into practice—but more so in the hills of Alabama, or Georgia, or Mississippi than in the dark corners of Chicago. And King's faith seemed as strong as *Time*'s: America could rise to the challenge, it could march toward its destiny in the American Century prophesized by Luce. Indeed on that day in Washington, much seemed possible to *Time* magazine.

So it seemed also to *Newsweek*, if with less smugness. Where *Time* counseled patience, *Newsweek* preached the urgent necessity of action. Where *Time* regarded the March as blacks tapping for admission into the system, *Newsweek* saw those quarter-million demonstrators as Americans come "to their Capital to lay their grievances in peaceable assembly before their government and their nation." The March thus was a cause made sacred by the Constitution. *Newsweek* threaded this idea through its description of a "solemn, massive sacrament in which thousands of Negroes and their white

58. Carson, *In Struggle*, 91–95; Zinn, *SNCC*, 190. On the disputes between Lewis and Carmichael and SNCC's notion of using civil disobedience, see Viorst, *Fire in the Streets*, 355–57. The passage from Lewis' speech draft is quoted in Viorst, *Fire in the Streets*, 229.

59. "The March's Meaning," 13; "Beginning of a Dream," 14–15.

friends in churches, unions, and liberal circles could share." Accentuating the theme were numerous invocations of the nation's symbols, whether "the larger-than-life statue of the President who tendered freedom to 3.5 million slaves" or the constitutional right to assemble in order to petition government for redress of grievances.[60]

Another symbol was present as well. As it had during the Freedom Rides, *Newsweek* placed King at the head of an event before it occurred; "only the charge of electricity generated by the Battle of Birmingham" set the demonstration in motion, the magazine maintained. *Newsweek* also made King the principal spokesman for American ideals even before his speech, having him proclaim that "'the presence of hundreds of bodies presenting living witness to the truth . . . will help Congress see the determination of the Negro.'" Still, there was a sticky point to clear away. In July, the magazine reported that King had warned that sit-ins might take place at the Capitol. Now, apparently, the warning had been issued not by King but by "one King subaltern." Furthermore, "King said his man had spoken out of turn on civil disobedience; it wouldn't happen again." Indeed, the whole tone of the demonstration had changed, *Newsweek* noted with visible relief. It selected a quote that made the point: The March "'has become too respectable and popular and stuffy to spark an explosion.'"[61]

The March was respectable enough for almost anyone's taste, fine words and good feelings in abundance, effects on congressional deliberations of the civil rights bill almost nil. If the March had any impact beyond the symbolic, it probably went no further than the respectability thereafter attached the struggle in the South.

For *Newsweek*, symbolism more than sufficed. Searching for meaning, the journal found a crusade with "the elusive, gossamer sense of communion that seemed to A. Philip Randolph a dream fulfilled," that made the novelist James Baldwin "want to cry or sing." (This passage was published after the March, but the tone differed little from those sounded beforehand.) *Newsweek* found

60. See *Newsweek*, "Big Day—End and a Beginning," September 9, 1963, pp. 19–20, "On the March," September 2, 1963, p. 18, and "'Peaceably to Assemble and Petition, . . .'" September 2, 1963, p. 19. See "Big Day—End and a Beginning," 19–22, for *Newsweek*'s references to these symbols.

61. "On the March," 18, 20, 21. The March occurred on August 28, but because issues are postdated, this was an advance story, not an after-the-fact report. Although it is possible that *Newsweek* simply corrected an earlier misattribution of the statement, in late June *Newsweek* was irked with King and other black leaders for not heeding Kennedy's call for restraint. By this time, Kennedy had reversed his position—as had *Newsweek*.

much to its liking, not least the evidence that this revolution would achieve its ends through "temperate methods." For example, the respectable revolutionary Martin Luther King demonstrated his adherence to moderate tactics when he persuaded John Lewis to take some of the sting out of a "fire-eating peroration." King was even more convincing when he invoked that sacred American document in his challenge to America to " 'rise up and live out the true meaning of its creed: "We hold these truths to be self-evident, that all men are created equal." ' " And King was reassuring, cautioning that militancy must not lead to distrust of all whites, "for many of our white brothers— evidenced by their presence here today—have come to realize that their destiny and their freedom is inextricably bound to our freedom."[62] It was fitting to *Newsweek* that King would say these things to preserve unity. And this was perhaps the final meaning of the March: Its unity, like America's, endured in the midst of "many voices and many moods."

Except that one voice was subdued to match the expectations of white middle-class readers. The summary of King's speech made it seem almost as if King were not a black preacher, the son of another black preacher. As *Newsweek* had carefully edited the ungrammatical profundity of the black woman who proclaimed during the Montgomery bus boycott that "my feets is tired, but my soul is rested," as it translated King's nickname "De Lawd" as "The Lord," now *Newsweek* also shrank from the crescendo of King's speech, when he located the meaning of freedom not only in the pristine rationalism of the Declaration of Independence but in the fiber of black experience—giving voice to the black spiritual's exuberant shout of faith in the Promised Land: "Free at last, free at last, thank God Almighty, we are free at last!"[63]

Measured against the reports of *U.S. News*, *Newsweek*'s retreat into respectable middle-class rhetoric was a minor omission. *U.S. News* did its utmost to ignore King and, when he could not be ignored, took care to strip him of his dream, to depict him as an ineffectual leader and, most important, to label him the author of more of the threats that *U.S. News* believed were coming from most quarters of the black movement. King prophesized that the

62. "Big Day—End and a Beginning," 21, 22. Lewis did not appear quite the fire-eater in *Newsweek*. King's remark appears in "A Dream . . . I Have a Dream," *Newsweek*, September 9, 1963, p. 21.

63. " 'A Dream . . . I Have a Dream,' " 21. The excerpts ended with the insipid quotation, " 'This is our hope.' " King's closing was impromptu, but *Newsweek* had ample time to report the changes from his prepared text. The phrase from the black spiritual probably was deleted because its tone clashed with Jefferson's phrases—and with the expectations of readers.

"whirlwinds of revolt will continue to shake the foundations of our nation until the bright day of justice emerges." "Day of justice" meant little to *U.S. News*; its mind's eye beheld those whirlwinds, and what registered was a remark by King congratulating "the Negro marchers on their 'marvelous new militancy.'"[64] *Newsweek* used the same quotation to show King urging moderation and reconciliation of the races, but that thesis did not fit the needs of *U.S. News*. It would have been an even poorer fit to allow King to quote the Declaration of Independence and maintain that its promises were unkept. So *U.S. News* made the best of a bad job by ignoring the speech by King that the other news magazines found so compelling.

U.S. News also ignored King, except to point up his militancy, by designating A. Philip Randolph as the true leader of the March on Washington. In one sense, *U.S. News* was correct; Randolph was the father of the idea. But the March had outgrown Randolph's original concept, and its leadership was drawn from the major black organizations—making King at least an equal of Randolph's. Furthermore, King had already vividly demonstrated his impact in the black movement by leading more than 125,000 people on a march through downtown Detroit in June. And it was most peculiar that the conservative *U.S. News* would side with a labor leader, much less a black labor leader. But the journal did just that, probably for the reason it once made King a spokesman against the Black Muslims: Randolph looked better than the alternative, and in August, 1963, the alternative was King.[65]

U.S. News also made the best of a bad job when it came to the March—no easy matter, considering its intimations that demonstrators would run riot through Washington. There was no bloodshed, no violence, no untoward intrusion into congressional deliberations; instead, a story conceded, the March wound up as "a combination of church picnic and political rally"— hardly the stuff with which to construct a scenario of danger to the Republic. Lacking better material, *U.S. News* interjected some might-have-beens: "As the size of the crowd swelled, neither police nor leaders of the march knew what to expect. You got the feeling that there was always the possibility that

64. "As 200,000 Marched in Washington—"*U.S. News & World Report*, September 9, 1963, p. 40.

65. "'March Leader' Randolph: Struggle Just Begun, He Says," *U.S. News & World Report*, September 9, 1963, p. 24. King attracted crowds of about 25,000 in Los Angeles and 10,000 in Chicago. Lewis, *King: A Biography*, 210–11.

the throng, ignited by some spark, some taunt, might turn into a heaving, frightened mob. But such a moment of terror never came. Toward the end, the crowd was exultant . . . but it never really 'caught fire.' There was no need to call in the four thousand military troops who were standing by, in full battle dress."[66]

The report made it appear that only the lack of a spark prevented an explosion of black anarchy. Other articles hinted of menace and conspiracy, but the cries were feeble and unconvincing.[67] No mob had gone storming through Washington; indeed, the affair was so respectable as to be almost stuffy.

Respectability had come late to the March on Washington, only after its leaders turned away from confrontation and members of both races joined in common cause, despite some mutterings in the black movement about distrust of whites. In the end, however, the March endured as a symbol because of King's great speech and the Birmingham campaign. What King said on that hot August day lent form and direction to the inchoate spirit of the March. "Black men and white men," he said, "Jews and Gentiles," all of God's children, but, more important, all right-thinking Americans, marching toward that dawning when men could gather as brothers, voices raised in the insistent chorus—"Free at last, free at last, thank God Almighty, we are free at last"—that now had passed from the black experience into the American experience. Yet the power of King's oration ultimately derived from the confluence of two antithetical symbols—the Birmingham of Bull Connor with its snarling police dogs and lashing fire hoses, and the March with its assemblage of Americans sharing King's dream of America made whole. Twice those events-as-symbols reverberated against each other in 1963, once on the day of the March, August 28, then again a little more than two weeks later.

What occurred on the morning of September 15 forced Birmingham abruptly back into the nation's consciousness. A bomb was exploded in a black church used as the site of civil rights activities, killing four young black girls and shocking America, if not the world. Before the day was out, two

66. "As 200,000 Marched in Washington," 39, 40.
67. "'The March'—Gains and Losses," *U.S. News & World Report*, September 9, 1963, p. 33; David Lawrence, "Church Control of the State," *U.S. News & World Report*, September 23, 1963, pp. 116–15. (The latter article was continued to the previous page.)

young black boys were killed in other incidents, and there were a score of injuries as a result of the church bombing and subsequent violence.[68]

As their attention returned to Birmingham, *Time* and *Newsweek* portrayed King as a moderate. The former contraposed him against Governor Wallace, the "international symbol of the demagogic segregationist" because of his farcical "stand in the school house door" during the desegregation of the University of Alabama earlier in 1963. Although Wallace had retreated from a confrontation with federal authorities, *Time* argued that "he had aroused violent passions . . . which led to the Sunday school bombing." Completing this picture of extremism was a sketch of Wallace as a political opportunist who interfered in the affairs of the local governments in Alabama that were attempting to preserve the peace and obey the law. The former outsider King now became the "Alabama Negro leader" who practiced the Sunday school lesson "The Love That Forgives," which was scheduled to be taught in the church where the girls were killed. Black leaders led by King understandably were angry, demanding at first that "President Kennedy send troops to take over Birmingham." But, *Time* added, being reasonable men they responded to another reasonable man and accepted Kennedy's offer to send two mediators instead.[69]

King appeared even more restrained in *Newsweek*. He did not originate the demand for federal troops to "take over Birmingham" after the bombing; that was the idea of his associate, the "passionately gesturing" Fred R. Shuttlesworth. *Newsweek* implied, in fact, that King toned down the extreme position that an American city should be occupied by federal troops. After King's arrival, black leaders were willing to accept far less. "At least, they said, [Kennedy] could attend the funeral himself—or proclaim a day of national mourning for the four dead children." And when Kennedy discussed the crisis with black leaders, the moderate King agreed that reopening the "dialogue between deadlocked Negroes and whites . . . was a crucial objective," even though other blacks bitterly criticized Kennedy for doing no more than dispatching mediators to Birmingham. *Newsweek* also designated King to make sense of the seemingly pointless deaths of the four children. The

68. Morgan, *A Time to Speak*, 162–64; Lewis, *King: A Biography*, 105.

69. "Where the Stars Fall," *Time*, September 27, 1963, pp. 17, 20–21. While delivering the sound thrashing *Time* reserved for villains, the article was (for *Time*) an uncommonly sensitive treatment of the state and, for that matter, Wallace, a sometime Populist whose merit as governor—racism aside—was considerable. *Time* reported the details of the deaths separately in "Sunday School Bombing," September 27, 1963, p. 17.

struggle must continue, he said, because "their death says to us that we must work passionately and unrelentingly for the realization of the American dream. And so, my friends, they did not die in vain."[70]

King did not figure so prominently in the coverage by *U.S. News*, which emphasized the rising racial tensions in Birmingham. Its theme was that people of influence were caught between ill-educated whites convinced " 'that if they don't keep the Negro down they'll lose out to him on jobs and starve to death' " and blacks who stood ready to dynamite the city into rubble. The magazine did not regard King as one of those ready to level Birmingham. What he proposed was, in a way, worse; he wanted the president to send federal troops " 'to take over the city.' " That suggestion sufficed to paint King as a radical. The appeal for soldiers was given a particular twist. The magazine identified the forces requested as "Regular Army troops," a reference cut to fit the siege mentality of the South. The Union army's occupation still rankled white southerners born long after Reconstruction ended, and there were more recent memories of army detachments deployed at Little Rock and Ole Miss. The details also were tailored to the expectations of readers who lacked the white southerner's ingrained sense of history as a projection into the present but shared his distrust of central government and the fear that it would upend the established order. To get that point across, *U.S. News* made King the sole author of the appeal for troops and did not show him being persuaded by the rational argument that mediators were preferable to soldiers.[71]

In sum, *Time* and *Newsweek* portrayed King as a leader acting reasonably in circumstances that tried the limits of patience. *U.S. News* used the same circumstances to paint him as a radical determined to bring about a military dictatorship in the South.

No less dexterity was demonstrated when the news magazines, following the twists and turns of events in 1963, chose their material to suit their needs. By setting out to create a crisis in Birmingham, King became a reckless militant in the eyes of *Time* and *Newsweek*: Once he got his crisis, they converted him into a moderate. They transformed, as well, Bull Connor from

70. "Birmingham: 'My God, You're Not Even Safe in Church,' " *Newsweek*, September 30, 1963, pp. 22, 23.
71. "Birmingham After the Bombing," *U.S. News & World Report*, September 30, 1963, pp. 38–40. On the siege mentality of the region, see Lewis M. Killian, *White Southerners* (New York, 1970), 14–65.

lame-duck buffoon to savage racist, and Albert Boutwell from relative moderate to a Bull Connor with manners. *U.S. News* interested itself in the campaign when presented with evidence—Kennedy's telephone call to Mrs. King—that could be made to support its thesis of sinister collusion between black leaders and federal authorities. Thereafter, the magazine depicted King essentially as a radical threat. Similarly, the three magazines were irked or frightened or both during the weeks before the March on Washington. Once it became patently obvious that the March would celebrate America, not confront its national government, King won the favor of *Newsweek* and *Time*, though *U.S. News* did its best to both ignore him and portray him as a menace.

Man and event—two events no longer but a symbolic entity, Birmingham and the March, blending all but invisibly into one—continued to echo powerfully in American culture. The conjoined symbolism was made possible because something important went astray in the process. King's campaign in the citadel of segregation also loosed the black revolt throughout the country. In 1963, black voices started insisting "Freedom Now"—and freedom not only from Jim Crow but from other burdens, especially economic, borne by black Americans. Very soon the voices would become shrill, no longer asking, not even insisting, but demanding, and the spirit of the March would be rudely shaken. In the end, that spirit lingered. When Americans looked for the meaning of Birmingham and the March that followed, they found a pristine symbolic truth of such power that it eclipsed the social forces at work in 1963. Long after Birmingham and Bull Connor became reduced to catchphrases, long after the inevitable dulling of the horror and shock produced by the massacre of innocents in the bombing, long, even, after the fading from faulty recollection of all but King's final soaring passage, the moment would be recaptured.

His sojourn had almost five years remaining. Great honors would come to him in 1964, he would lead another great crusade in Selma in 1965, and thereafter would settle onto the course leading to a crisis of symbols. But King's image already was fixed at that one moment in Washington when he preached the sure and certain coming of justice to a South sweltering in the heat of oppression.

IV

HONORS FOR THE PROPHET

King's year began in 1964 with one honor, designation as *Time*'s "Man of the Year," and concluded with another, the Nobel Peace Prize. Both recognitions paid tacit tribute to the drama of the Birmingham campaign and to King's speech during the March on Washington. Like the awards, most of the major events in which King took part in 1964 grew out of forces set in motion the year before: Birmingham yielded to a bloody confrontation in the Florida city of St. Augustine, St. Augustine provided the final push for the enactment of the 1964 Civil Rights Act, and, most important of all, the black revolt continued to spread across the nation, its pace quickening as blacks copied tactics used successfully in the southern movement and invented others of their own.

Black protests against economic deprivation, de facto discrimination, and Jim Crow produced anxiety North and South. As C. Eric Lincoln observed: "The white man feels that he has given up something that was uniquely his. Perhaps he has given up too much? And yet the blacks are not satisfied. They push. *They continue to push!*" And blacks felt no gratitude for getting gradually and grudgingly what "was not the white man's to withhold or bestow." There was another source of tension. The focus was shifting from individual opportunity, which under the American Creed could not be seriously questioned, to removing the barriers confronting a group, another matter entirely.[1]

1. On the tactics, see Arthur I. Waskow, *From Race Riot to Sit-in, 1919 and the 1960s: A Study in the Connections Between Conflict and Violence* (Garden City, N.Y., 1966), 239–43. C.

The strains tugging at the fabric of American society registered with the news magazines. *Newsweek* seemed particularly affected in the first quarter. As blacks continued to push, the magazine developed a siege mentality probably mirroring that of its readers. Cities with reputations for enlightened race relations were feeling the pressure of militant protests by impatient blacks who pointed out the gap between reputation and reality. This might be the case, *Newsweek* agreed, but "even friendly whites found the issues blurrier, the goals touchier, and the demonstrations more abrasive." Another shock: The coalition of liberal-minded Americans seemed unable to hold; indeed, some liberals seemed bent on ripping the alliance apart. The tactical organizer of the March on Washington, Bayard Rustin, for example, said that whites would have to learn "to share the burden"; fair enough, but then he added: "We will force them to learn—and I say force."[2]

Other black leaders alarmed *Newsweek*. Malcolm X was one source of disquiet, curiously enough, even though he severed his ties with the Nation of Islam in March. His relationship with Elijah Muhammad had been deteriorating since 1963. He was suspended by Muhammad in December of that year, ostensibly for the remark that the assassination of President Kennedy demonstrated that the "chickens were coming home to roost." C. Eric Lincoln noted, however, that Malcolm X had made intemperate remarks before without incurring the wrath of Muhammad, and that Muhammad believed his chief lieutenant was "seeking exaltation." Whether or not that was the case, Malcolm X was entering a new phase in which he would question, then repudiate, some of the doctrines of the Black Muslims. After his break with the Muslims, Malcolm X traveled to Africa in May, intending to strengthen ties between American blacks and African nations. He made a pilgrimage to Mecca and visited several Islamic states, being welcomed by light-skinned Algerians and Egyptians as a brother in Islam and a fellow revolutionary. He returned to the United States more accepting of whites and their value to the black man's cause and with a new regard for black American leaders, including King. In 1963, Malcolm X had scorned King's nonviolent strategy as the "approach . . . of an Uncle Tom." In the spring and summer of 1964, however, he extended the olive branch, asking civil rights leaders to join in "united efforts

Eric Lincoln, *My Face is Black* (Boston, 1964), 107–108. On the shift to group grievances, see David Danzig, "The Meaning of Negro Strategy," *Commentary*, XXXVII (February, 1964), 45–46.

2. "New Wave," *Newsweek*, February 10, 1964, p. 24.

toward solving the unending hurt that is being done daily to our people here in America." On March 26, he met with King in Washington, and they agreed to work together to pressure Congress to pass civil rights legislation.[3] In sum, Malcolm X was moving closer to King's perspective as, eventually, King would move closer to the militancy of Malcolm X.

In the normal course of events, *Newsweek* would have welcomed Malcolm X's break with the Black Muslims as a sign of confusion in the enemy's camp. Now, however, it fretted that Malcolm X might set the fires roaring in America and was confronted by the unsettling sight of King smiling, shaking hands with Malcolm X, and agreeing that a parliamentary maneuver during congressional debate over the 1964 Civil Rights Act was a victory. Considering the confusion in its own camp, *Newsweek*'s dismay over those two "strange bedfellows" King and Malcolm X was no surprise.[4]

By contrast, *Time* opened 1964 by naming King its "Man of the Year," but the honor represented less of a change in its regard for him than was immediately apparent. In fact, a fair amount of space was given over to King's deficiencies. He lacked the "quiet brilliance" and "sharp administrative abilities" of Roy Wilkins of the NAACP. He had "none of the sophistication of the Urban League's Whitney Young, Jr." James Farmer of CORE was his master in inventiveness, and King could not match the "raw militancy" of SNCC's John Lewis. For bristling wit, *Time* looked to the novelist James Baldwin.[5] Fainter praises had seldom been used to disparage King.

Still, *Time* had to admit that King was a vital symbol of the black revolt. The question was which wing he represented—the northern or the southern? *Time* chose the latter: "Birmingham with its bombs and snarling dogs . . . and death in the streets and in the churches." King's role as an American symbol was strictly limited; he was a prophet from the South, which Luce's journal reckoned to be another country.[6] The limitation, which lasted throughout the

3. See Lincoln, *My Face is Black*, 103, 104, 109; and Lewis, *King: A Biography*, 271–72. For Malcolm X's remark about King, see interview of Malcolm X on radio station WUST in Washington, May 12, 1963, transcript on Reel 2 (microfilm), FBI Surveillance File on Malcolm X.

4. "Malcolm's Brand X," *Newsweek*, March 23, 1964, p. 32. The photograph of King and Malcolm X and the remark about strange bedfellows appear in "Long Day," *Newsweek*, April 6, 1964, pp. 20, 22.

5. "Man of the Year: Never Again Where He Was," *Time*, January 3, 1964, p. 13.

6. *Ibid. Time* continued to limit King to the role of the prophet from the South for the remainder of the first quarter of 1964. See "People," February 7, 1964, p. 44; "A Lincoln Man," February 21, 1964, p. 76; and "Go Ahead and Say It," March 20, 1964, p. 78.

first quarter of 1964, was accomplished in several ways. The most striking was that *Time* permitted King to speak in the tones and cadences of the black southern preacher. Four months after the fact, *Time* became the first of the news weeklies to report the culmination of King's "I Have a Dream" speech: "'Free at last. Free at last. Thank God Almighty, we are free at last.'" The magazine also reproduced the dialogue between preacher and congregation:

> King: I hear they are beating you!
> Response: Yes, yes.
> King: I hear they are cursing you!
> Response: Yes, yes.
> King: I hear they are going into your homes and doing nasty things and beating you.
> Response: Yes, yes.
> King: Some of you have knives, and I ask you to put them up. Some of you may have arms, and I ask you to put them up. Get the weapon of nonviolence, the breastplate of righteousness, the armor of truth, and just keep marching.[7]

It was all very well for King to offer such rhetoric to ignorant people groaning under the burden of southern racism. Middle-class readers, however, would find some of his metaphors "downright embarrassing." *Time* explained: "For Negroes, he says, 'the word "wait" has been a tranquilizing Thalidomide'; segregation the 'adultery of an illicit intercourse between injustice and immorality,' and it 'cannot be cured by the Vaseline of gradualism.'"[8]

For readers inclined to snicker at phrases such as "the Vaseline of gradualism," another level of rhetoric, at once familiar, reassuring, and uplifting, had to be located. Thus was resurrected, with no cough of editorial embarrassment, the "Letter from the Birmingham Jail," which had been ignored by the news magazines until it could serve their purposes. As excerpted by *Time*, the epistle was reassuring because it situated the black man's struggle within the context of the fight against southern oppression, and it was couched in terms of American ideals. Blacks will win their freedom, King said, "because the sacred heritage of our nation and the eternal will of God are embodied in

7. "Man of the Year: Never Again Where He Was," 14.
8. *Ibid.*, 13–14.

our echoing demands."[9] The epistle was even more reassuring because *Time* omitted King's pointed observations:

> Over the last few years I have been gravely disappointed with the white moderates. I have almost reached the regrettable conclusion that the Negro's stumbling block in the stride toward freedom is not the . . . Ku Klux Klanner, but the white moderate who is more devoted to "order" than to justice; who prefers a negative peace which is the absence of tension to a positive peace which is the presence of justice; . . . who paternalistically feels that he can set the timetable for another man's freedom. . . . Shallow understanding from people of goodwill is more frustrating than absolute misunderstanding from people of ill will.[10]

The rebuke edged uncomfortably close to the spirit of Malcolm X's stated preference for racist rattlesnakes over "Northern snakes who grin and make you forget you're still in a snake pit." Thus *Time* selected a quotation matching the theme of the cover treatment. King quoted "an old Negro slave preacher, who said, 'We ain't what we ought to be and we ain't what we want to be and we ain't what we're going to be. But thank God, we ain't what we was.'"[11] That was one message to black Americans. Other messages embedded in the story were that America was responding to the calls for justice in the South and in the rest of the nation, and that the black man was becoming part of the great middle ground of American society that *Time* served.

The question was whether blacks were entitled to a leg up into the Promised Land. Plainly, *Time* believed the contrary. A seven-page photographic essay accompanying the cover story devoted a single paragraph to the economic plight of blacks. The remainder of the essay documented the careers of a handful of talented blacks—entertainers, clergymen, surgeons, diplomats, military officers, even the odd millionaire—whose achievements reaffirmed the American Dream. For the black masses, as the *Nation* commented acidly, the success stories had "hardly more meaning than the fact that, before the

9. *Time* commented that King's letter "in the tumble of events then and since . . . never got the notice it deserved." "Letter From the Birmingham Jail," January 3, 1964, p. 15. The magazine neglected to point out that the letter was passed over because *Time* was scourging King for ignoring the counsel of moderates to await the seating of Mayor-elect Boutwell.

10. King to Bishop C. C. J. Carpenter *et al*. ["Letter from the Birmingham Jail"], April 16, 1963, uncataloged, in William C. Hamilton Papers, Birmingham Public Library.

11. "Playboy Interview: Malcolm X," *Playboy*, X (May, 1963), 62; "Man of the Year: Never Again Where He Was," 27.

Civil War, the South boasted a few manumitted slaves who were themselves slave owners."[12]

Time's paean to success signified something else. After the black revolt spilled out of the South in 1963, *Time*'s complaints about blacks raising immoderate demands grew shriller, and success stories were one way of saying to blacks they should not be too impatient. Still, Luce's magazine was about success—success *in* America, the success *of* America. According to reader profiles, most of *Time*'s audience already had gotten a taste of success, as had Henry Luce, who had risen to wealth and influence at breathtaking speed. So *Time* could not have done otherwise than to compile its *Who's Who* of black America, not if it was to remain the journal Luce dedicated to the celebration of the American Dream.[13]

Readers of *U.S. News* found a symbol that differed greatly from the one portrayed in *Time* or *Newsweek*. In general, King was depicted as a false prophet and a dangerous radical who preached the necessity of social disruption and increasing militancy throughout the nation. On occasion, however, *U.S. News* would provide a revealing and balanced sketch of King. In late February, a question-and-answer interview supplied a more detailed and broader treatment of King than did any that appeared in 1964 in the other news weeklies, including the "Man of the Year" cover story. Included among the topics of King's far-ranging discussion were de facto discrimination, problems with public accommodations in the South, the failure of the civil rights movement to alter the lives of most of black Americans, and differences in tactics employed by the major black organizations. Yet the story did not signal a change of heart. Two weeks earlier, in fact, *U.S. News* had launched a campaign against King that would continue, with brief interruptions, until his death. As it began the campaign, *U.S. News* tacitly acknowledged the existence of a dilemma created by the mingling of King's force as a symbol with the power exerted by the American Creed. *U.S. News* had to pick its way carefully. The greater King's standing as a symbol, the more his identification with the egalitarian ideals that, as Myrdal noted, were accepted as principles that ought to rule in America.[14] The magazine could not directly deny the

12. "Man of the Year," *Nation*, January 13, 1964, pp. 41–42.

13. On *Time*'s readership, see Gans, *Deciding What's News*, 219, 224; and Elson, *The Intimate History of a Publishing Enterprise*, 437. On *Time*, Henry Luce, and success, see Swanberg, *Luce and His Empire*, 81, 106, 425–29.

14. "'Boycotts Will Be Used,'" *U.S. News & World Report*, February 24, 1964, pp. 59–61.

justice of King's cause—equality for the black American—without calling into question the consensus about the Creed.

One way out of the problem was to assert that blacks were unfit for citizenship. *U.S. News* published pseudo-scientific theories of genetic inferiority and cited approvingly the hoary school of southern historiography that damned black political power exercised during Reconstruction as the rule of the ignorant controlled by the corrupt. As well, *U.S. News* sought to divert attention from inequality by arguing that demands for federal intervention, legislative or otherwise, represented a heretical interpretation of the Constitution that would destroy states' rights, if not the Constitution itself. The mustiness of those themes—long since demolished by scientists, historians, and the centralization of governmental power in Washington—detracted little from the message because the magazine was preaching to the faithful.

When it came to dealing with King himself, the solution was more convoluted. *U.S. News* had no choice but to confront the prevailing definition of him as a living symbol of American principles by asserting that he was a false prophet. That did not end the matter. Occasionally, the magazine found itself in urgent need of the symbolic force it sought to destroy. When other black leaders or organizations represented greater dangers, King would be offered as an entirely different symbol, one whose moderate attributes were left intact or augmented. At such moments, King was contraposed against the more frightening threat, his symbolism making the radicalism of the other party all the more apparent.[15] *U.S. News* had little choice in the matter. A black leader would not suffice to counter rising threats in the black movement; a certified symbol had to be located. In King, *U.S. News* found one and, however reluctantly, used him as such.

U.S. News managed this trick because of the indirect ways the journal attacked King. Sometimes it published its own assertions condemning King outrightly. But the effectiveness of the campaign was actually derived from a series of echoes. Statements from other sources were selected because they parroted its editorial position. The magazine created other damaging echoes by printing variations of the first statement elsewhere in the same issue, in subsequent editions, or both.[16] The campaign resembled a chamber filled with

15. On contraposed symbols, see Erikson, *Wayward Puritans*, 69.
16. On journalistic selection as a structuring of reality, see, for example, Todd Gitlin, *The Whole World is Watching: Mass Media in the Making and Unmaking of the New Left* (Berkeley, 1980), 6. The selection process of *U.S. News* appears vividly in the Albert L. Warner Papers,

reverberations untraceable to a single source. In many instances, contextual rather than direct identification of King was supplied. After 1964, for example, mentioning the Nobel Peace Prize adequately identified King even if his name was not cited. Similar were the grindingly repetitious references to a black leader or leaders who preached nonviolence but whose activities produced the exact opposite. More than any other American, King was associated in the public mind with nonviolence and civil disobedience, and his civil rights campaigns often were marked by violence. It mattered little to *U.S. News* whether the violence was caused by policemen, by white mobs, or by King's followers who strayed from the discipline of nonviolence; the point was that where King went, violence often appeared.

It would have been simpler, of course, had the magazine supplied the requisite identification of King—and not only simpler but a matter of journalistic routine. Whether this method would have been as effective is another question. When *U.S. News* warned that King was a threat to the Republic, ominous tones implied the existence of a Fifth Column. Inasmuch as a conspiracy is secret, vagueness amplifies the sense of danger and makes a threat seen in hazy outline all the more frightening. Vagueness also preserved an important part of the persona of *U.S. News*. The magazine's surface drabness, its publication of dry official reports, its question-and-answer interviews, even the space given views contrary to Lawrence's created an aura of journalistic objectivity not enjoyed by the other news magazines.[17] An open and unremitting attack on King would have damaged the facade that was nurtured in order to set *U.S. News* apart from its competitors. And, of course, *U.S. News* need not identify King directly; it could be reasonably assured that its audience would hear certain tones and draw certain inferences from them. Otherwise, the magazine would have been embarking on a perilous course, roughly analogous to publishing the warning that a dangerous intruder was at

---

Wisconsin Historical Society, Madison. See, for example, Warner to "IH," February 25, 1964, Reel 3; and Warner to "OLS," July 27, 1967, Reel 4.

17. *Time* spurned the notion of objectivity. See, for example, lecture by Otto Fuerbringer at the University of Missouri School of Journalism, October, 1958, pp. 6–9, copy in Box 25, File 7, T. George Harris Papers, Wisconsin Historical Society, Madison. On *Newsweek*'s claims to objectivity, see Elliott, *The World of Oz*, 31. Sociologists have all but destroyed the notion of journalistic objectivity. See, for example, Gaye Tuchman, "Objectivity as Strategic Ritual: An Examination of Newsmen's Notions of Objectivity," *American Journal of Sociology*, LXXVII (1972), 660–79.

large in a given neighborhood but neglecting to provide the information necessary to identify him.

The reverberations began in February. *U.S. News* complained of senseless militancy in Atlanta, which it labeled a "Model City" for race relations. "Many Negro leaders feel that the younger Negroes are trying to go too far, too fast," reported *U.S. News*. King, however, believed "all along that the demonstrations were necessary." The statement was echoed more strongly in the issue of March 30, when King appeared to threaten yet more racial trouble: in the South, where he wanted to line up " 'ten thousand recruits who will be willing to spend vacations in jail' "; in Washington, where there would be unspecified action with an ominous ring to it " 'in connection with a Senate filibuster' " over the civil rights bill; " 'in the North,' " where he expected " 'a very massive, intensified registration drive' " to sign up black voters; and throughout the nation, where the effects of a " 'nationwide selective-buying program' " would be felt.[18]

In the next two issues, *U.S. News* used the tactic of establishing guilt by association. It juxtaposed King with Malcolm X, who "urges Negroes to arm themselves with guns for defense against white people," thus tingeing King with some of the radicalism of Malcolm X. Initially, the symbolic linkage between the two men was subtle. There was an indirect reference to King in the remark by Malcolm X that "when our people are being bitten by dogs"— as they were in Birmingham—"they are within their rights to kill those dogs." The idea was reiterated in the caption of a photograph taken during King's Birmingham campaign. A week later, another caption stated that King and Malcolm X "agreed that a long filibuster could provoke Negroes to 'direct action.' " Although *U.S. News* conceded that King "personally favors peaceful demonstrations," this point was subordinated to a warning delivered by a "close associate" of King, who "predicted flatly that the civil rights campaign will produce almost unprecedented violence this summer." So it must have seemed to readers. First they saw King and Malcolm X shaking hands and agreeing on the prospects for "direct action" in Washington; then an accompanying story informed them that Malcolm X was advocating formation of rifle clubs in areas where blacks "are the constant victims of brutality" and was

18. See *U.S. News & World Report*, "Race Trouble in a 'Model City,' " February 10, 1964, p. 78, and "In South: Racial Trouble—and a Threat of More," March 30, 1964, pp. 8–9.

muttering that a long filibuster against the civil rights bill would produce another march on Washington—"except this time it won't be orderly."[19]

No less disquieting was a plan by the New York chapter of CORE to inaugurate civil disobedience on a major scale. The most visible element of the campaign was to be the disruption of the New York World's Fair, which was to be accomplished by deliberately stalling cars on the highways leading to the Fair. Laboring under the disadvantage of opposition from its own national organization, the chapter failed to bring off the stall-in, but the scheme disconcerted those who counted themselves sympathetic to the black cause. The plan was only one in a series of rude shocks those supporters had in 1963 and 1964. Several major tactics were being tried out in the black move-ment: economic boycotts, rent strikes, blockades of building sites designed to force contractors to hire black craftsmen and tradesmen, and school boycotts involving hundreds of thousands of black children. Such tactics, as Arthur Waskow pointed out, amounted to the nonviolent equivalent of insurrection. Short of sustained armed revolt, nothing was more radical than Gandhian civil disruption.[20]

King had used some of the same tactics, but he generally escaped being censured as a radical (other than by segregationists) because his campaigns produced relatively limited disruption, they were closely associated with the exercise of constitutionally protected rights (such as the right to peaceably assemble), and they took Jim Crow as their target. More radical disruption had occurred to activists in the southern movement. SNCC floated a proposal in the fall of 1963 for demonstrations that would paralyze the transportation systems of some southern states, and the SCLC's executive director Wyatt Tee Walker delivered the warning in 1963 that "at some appointed hour" America might be "literally immobilized by widespread acts of civil disobe-dience."[21] All this amounted to little more than talk at the time, though King would revive the ideas in the last years of his life when he was on a collision course with the federal government. In 1964, however, King was not as bold as was the CORE chapter that wanted to bring the New York World's Fair to an abrupt standstill.

19. See *U.S. News & World Report*, "Now It's a Negro Drive for Segregation," March 30, 1964, p. 39, and "A Summer of Race Violence on the Way?" April 6, 1964, p. 34.
20. Bell, *CORE and the Strategy of Nonviolence*, 13–14; Waskow, *From Race Riot to Sit-in*, 239–43.
21. Waskow, *From Race Riot to Sit-in*, 244. Walker is quoted in Lewis, *King: A Biogra-phy*, 232.

Naturally, that chapter was painted as radical by the news weeklies. Oddly enough, *U.S. News & World Report*'s coverage was the most restrained, presumably because disrupting the World's Fair struck the magazine as business as usual in the black movement. The plan for a stall-in hit nerves at *Time* and *Newsweek* that were as sensitive as the one twitching at *U.S. News* before the March on Washington. The World's Fair was a glittering symbol of things right about America—its progress and its wealth and its yeasty pride in both. The notion the Fair should be rudely disrupted was bad enough; worse was the timing. Hostility to the black movement was rising, going at the time by the name of white backlash, and already a surprising harvest of presidential primary votes was being gathered in the North by Alabama's segregationist governor George Wallace. *Time* complained of the failure to distinguish "staunch" friends from enemies, and disruption—"pointless, . . . destructive, and sometimes dangerous tactics"—from legitimate demonstration. *Newsweek* agreed about this "calculated act of social sabotage," though it conceded that the stall-in was "conceived in despair at the faltering pace of progress toward equal rights." The demonstration, said *Newsweek*, seemed to "unsettle the Negro's friends more than his enemies."[22]

The demonstration unsettled *Time* and *Newsweek*, even if it was, in the former's characterization, "a flop." *Time* piled on these adjectives: "wild-eyed, harebrained," and "crackpot," and was no more generous in analyzing the results: "It tried the patience of national, state, and city officials, wasted taxpayers' money for protective measures, set a city of eight million on edge, and hurt the cause of civil rights." *Newsweek* was even more acid when it reported the demonstrations at the Fair conducted, interestingly enough, not by the New York chapter but by CORE itself, which had managed to head off the plans for the stall-in. To *Newsweek*, it "was as if the uninvited kid from the other side of the tracks had crashed the party, plunked himself on the floor and thrown a tantrum," except this party was "a five hundred million dollar distillation of American affluence through which ranged a raucous army of civil rights demonstrators, whooping, singing, sloganeering, picketing, courting arrest, and very nearly shouting down the president of the United States."[23]

22. "Will a Racial Protest Tie Up the World's Fair?" *U.S. News & World Report*, April 20, 1964, p. 6; "The Backlash," *Time*, April 24, 1964, p. 17; "'To the Sound of a Different Drum,'" *Newsweek*, April 27, 1964, p. 25.

23. "The Flop," *Time*, May 1, 1964, p. 22; "A Cry of Foul at the Fair," *Newsweek*, May 4, 1964, p. 20.

As demonstrations went at the time, this was pretty tame. Indeed, each of those tactics (with the exception of shouting down the president) had been used in civil rights campaigns. *Newsweek* missed the irony. So did *Time*, which drew a line between using these maneuvers in the South and using them elsewhere in the nation by quoting a liberal friend of the black cause, Senator Hubert Humphrey. A "great public outcry" arose when Americans saw "police dogs and policemen with clubs being used against peaceful demonstrations" in Birmingham, Humphrey said. But, he cautioned, "if extremists in the civil rights movement decide to inconvenience hundreds of thousands of people, it's going to have the same reaction in reverse." *Newsweek* made the contrast implicitly when it complained of the cavalier treatment of President Johnson. The "demonstrators were shouting too loud to hear him talk about the value of the nation's 'constant process of criticism and examination,'" the magazine reported defensively. "Some of them laughed when he invoked God's help in fashioning 'a world in which all men are equal, in which all people are free.'" Another spurned symbol was the national anthem; two demonstrators showed their disrespect by reclining "in a puddle while a band played 'The Star Spangled Banner.'"[24]

These protesters were a far cry indeed from the inspiring examples of the earnest legions marching through segregated Birmingham and of King rising in Washington to celebrate, not deride, America. Therefore, *Newsweek* implied, King must have disapproved. In an advance story on the stall-in, *Newsweek* felt compelled to explain away King's failure to sign a statement rebuking the organizers of the protest. He *would* have done so, *Newsweek* reported, but (quoting "one insider") "'his board just ranted and raved. They wouldn't let him sign.'"[25]

King *did* disapprove of the chapter's plan for what he described as "a meaningless protest in general with no specific demands or goals in mind."[26] Why he disapproved was another matter. King was willing to use the weapons of nonviolent disruption, but he wanted the preparations made to ensure the disruption would be effective and planned for the right moment. The implications ought to have caused a chill at a magazine fretting about demonstrators thumbing noses at symbols while sitting in puddles of water. The black leader

24. "Backlash," 18; "A Cry of Foul at the Fair," 21.
25. "'To the Sound of a Different Drum,'" 18.
26. Martin Luther King, Jr., "The 'Stall-in' in Retrospect," *Amsterdam News*, May 1, 1964, in Box 27, File 46, King Center Archives, Atlanta.

with the widest following in black America was not condemning civil disruption but was arguing instead that it ought to be better timed and better planned. No such thought struck home, *Newsweek*'s King being a symbol affirming, rather than challenging, America.

For *U.S. News*, black demonstrations, at the World's Fair and elsewhere, were part of a pattern stretching over a decade. The echo chamber signaled that King was the principal threat. In April, *U.S. News* reprinted a column written by Joseph Alsop, who warned that American Communist party agents were infiltrating the SCLC, SNCC, and CORE. A week later appeared a warning by FBI director J. Edgar Hoover that the Communist party was attempting to "exploit the militant forces of the Negro civil rights movement." Editor David Lawrence assembled Hoover's and Alsop's statements in a neat package. Lawrence reprinted a significant portion of Hoover's testimony, which also was reported in the issue. While conceding that most black leaders were untainted by communism, Lawrence noted that "there is a small minority of misguided Negroes and whites who are fanatical about the racial movement and actually have been much influenced by the Communist techniques."[27]

King was among those fanatics; so it seemed from a report three weeks later. King was selected as the leading example of black leaders unwilling to follow the democratic way and compromise on proposed amendments to the civil rights bill pending in Congress. *U.S. News* carefully strengthened its point by reporting that King was unwilling to accept any amendments even though sponsors of the bill from both parties saw no harm in them and Attorney General Kennedy pronounced the amendments "perfectly satisfactory." *U.S. News* went a step further: King would not be satisfied even if he got what he wanted. He predicted there would be demonstrations whether or not Congress passed a civil rights bill, adding only the faint encouragement that a civil rights law might make it "possible to keep the demonstrations much more disciplined and nonviolent."[28]

Assurances about nonviolent demonstrations did not convince *U.S. News*; the journal expected King to lead an invasion of Alabama for which he was

27. See *U.S. News & World Report*, "Reds and Negroes—'An Unhappy Secret,'" April 27, 1964, p. 34, "J. Edgar Hoover Speaks Out on Reds in the Negro Movement," May 4, 1964, p. 33, and David Lawrence, "The Enemy Within Our Gates," May 4, 1964, p. 108.
28. See *U.S. News & World Report* issue of May 25, 1964, for "Civil Rights Tangle: Where It is Heading," 37, and "Negro Leaders Warn: More Race Troubles," 38.

already "'recruiting students by the hundreds and thousands . . . who will engage in these demonstrations all over the state.'" This statement spelled trouble to *U.S. News*. After echoing Hoover's remarks about Communists infiltrating the black movement, Lawrence cited Communist infiltration of student movements elsewhere in the world, implying the same might occur in the United States. "The Communists find it easy to brainwash the young," Lawrence said, "and to inspire them to engage in street demonstrations, 'sit-ins,' 'stall-ins,' and violence." Now King proposed to do just what Lawrence had warned about and invade Alabama to boot.[29]

Later in the year, *U.S. News* focused on civil disobedience, which the magazine regarded as a prelude to the breakdown of law and order. It published, in August, an interview with the conservative police chief of Los Angeles, William Parker, who asserted that the federal government was condoning anarchy when it permitted the "violation of local laws." King was brought into the picture when *U.S. News* posed this question: "Yet aren't clergymen and politicians saying that it's all right to violate some laws?"— eliciting this response from Parker: "'Oh, I'm sure of that. Without quoting names, I have read public statements by such persons saying that if the law was not based in justice then it need not be obeyed. This is what they call civil disobedience.'" Continuing, Parker raised the specter of lawlessness that would destroy a free society; the instrument would be "'the man on the white horse [who] will come forward and lead you into slavery under the pretext of solving your problem.'"[30]

Parker was far from the only conservative to find the makings of tyranny within public pronouncements about disobeying unjust laws. Thus, no names were necessary for the message about King to get through. For the echo chamber to be effective, an occasional direct reference and more numerous indirect references (such as to prophets of civil disobedience) would suffice. Over time, this technique produced a continuing portrait of a false prophet who collaborated with Communists or was the instrument whereby the mob would be loosed on the Republic.

In fact, mobs had been running free in one American city, producing something tolerably close to the sort of anarchy predicted. Not much attention

29. "Negro Leaders Warn: More Race Troubles," 38; Lawrence, "The Enemy Within Our Gates," 108.

30. See *U.S. News & World Report*, "A Police Chief Talks of 'Police Brutality,'" August 10, 1964, p. 34, and "The Road to 'Anarchy,'" September 14, 1964, p. 40.

was paid to the situation by *U.S. News* (other than to publish an abbreviated chronology that made it appear that King had sniffed out trouble and exploited it) because the mobs were composed of whites, the city was St. Augustine, and the scenes of savage attacks upon demonstrators were too reminiscent of Birmingham.[31]

St. Augustine was the last major struggle against segregation in public accommodations before the enactment of the 1964 Civil Rights Act. While King provided assistance to the local movement, his goal was to generate more pressure for passage of the civil rights bill. A repeat of the campaign in Birmingham in many ways, the struggle in St. Augustine turned out to be as difficult. The pattern was set during the sit-ins of the early 1960s when the white leaders turned a deaf ear to black demands, and white toughs launched violent reprisals against demonstrators. In 1963, four blacks narrowly escaped being murdered at a Klan rally. One of them was Robert Hayling, a black dentist and a leading civil rights activist in St. Augustine. Hayling and his companions brought criminal charges, but their attackers were acquitted; Hayling was subsequently found guilty of assault and fined $100.[32]

Hayling quit the NAACP chapter after an argument with Roy Wilkins about the conduct of the campaign in St. Augustine. He appealed to King for help, and King sent Hosea Williams and later journeyed himself to St. Augustine to join the demonstrations. In the early stages, however, King played a minor role. The SCLC recruited college students and prominent New Englanders for demonstrations around Easter. By April 1, approximately 285 persons were packed into St. Johns County Jail. Among the SCLC volunteers arrested was Mrs. Malcolm Peabody, the mother of the governor of Massachusetts and an authentic grande dame of a New England dynasty. The prominence of those arrested, especially Mrs. Peabody, and the publicity value of staging demonstrations in the nation's oldest city were bringing the SCLC a rich harvest of national media coverage.[33]

The SCLC was confronted by serious problems, some expected, others not.

31. "Race Violence in the 'Oldest City,'" *U.S. News & World Report*, June 22, 1964, p. 8.

32. The best study of the campaign is David R. Colburn, *Racial Change and Community Crisis, St. Augustine, Florida, 1877–1980* (New York, 1985); on King's goals, see 208–10; on the Klan rally, see 51–53. See also Kunstler, *Deep in My Heart*, 285, 293; and Arnold Foster and Benjamin R. Epstein, *Report on the Ku Klux Klan* (New York, n.d. [*ca.* 1965–66]), 32.

33. Robert Wayne Hartley, "A Long, Hot Summer: The St. Augustine Disorders of 1964" (M.A. thesis, Stetson University, 1972), 43–44, 51. For the arrest of Mrs. Peabody, see Colburn, *Racial Change and Community Crisis*, 66–67; and Robert K. Massie, "Don't Tread on Grandmother Peabody," *Saturday Evening Post*, May 16, 1964, pp. 74, 76.

The division of the black community into conservative and activist camps was no surprise; King or his staffers had encountered disunity in Birmingham and in a number of other towns. Violence was not unexpected, either, though its intensity and its form probably were. Police officers initially attracted attention by using dogs and electric cattle prods against demonstrators, but as a rule they did not mistreat blacks as openly as had Birmingham police; instead, the St. Augustine police force sanctioned violence by white segregationists, including members of the Klan. King regarded St. Augustine as "the most lawless community that we've ever worked in the whole struggle over the past few years." The situation had gotten so out of hand that a federal judge admonished the attorney general of Florida that "rigid law enforcement, arrests, and real charges against the hoodlums" were needed to restore order.[34]

Order eventually returned to St. Augustine, but only after the state government brought its police powers to bear, a federal judge curbed the leaders of white mobs, and the 1964 Civil Rights Act destroyed the legal basis of segregation in public accommodations. In the period beforehand, however, hundreds of marchers demonstrated almost nightly for five weeks during June and July, nearly up to the date President Johnson signed the bill into law.

A strange tone, almost one of relief, ran through the reports published by *Time* and *Newsweek*. After the World's Fair, where blacks seemed unable or unwilling to separate friends from enemies, the events in St. Augustine were unclouded by nuances. Blacks and their white sympathizers sought no more than the right to swim or to eat together undisturbed. Arrayed against them were mobs whipped up by, among others, "a California rabble-rouser named Connie Lynch." *Time* could scarcely have asked for a more appropriate surname for the man who became its chief villain in the scenario that followed. Lynch "cried" (that was *Time*'s verb of choice for a demagogue) his message of hate: "'I favor violence to preserve the white race. . . . Now, I grant you, some niggers are gonna get killed in the process, but when war's on, that's what happens.'" What happened was as brutal as the attacks in Birmingham, except those assailing the black demonstrators were not policemen. For the most part, the police stood aside in St. Augustine while assaults on dem-

34. See, for example, Hartley, "A Long, Hot Summer," 1–3, 112. King's statement is quoted in Pat Watters, "The American Middle Ground in St. Augustine," *New South*, XIX (September, 1964), 11. The judge is quoted in Kunstler, *Deep in My Heart*, 299.

onstrators were carried out. Even when the policemen intervened, as in an incident reported by *Time*, the mob ran amok, attacking the civil rights demonstrators for fifteen minutes. The pitched battle ended when the blacks retreated with forty of their number injured.[35]

Amid the scenes of mobs assaulting peaceful demonstrators appeared King, the peacemaker, the voice of reason and reconciliation. *Time* reported, in July, the formation of a biracial committee "to try to talk out" the conflict. However, the journal gave the credit to King, who made the peace possible by calling off demonstrations and telling his followers: "'Every thousand-mile journey begins with a first step. This is the first step on our journey here in St. Augustine.'"[36]

The journey toward equality was under way in other cities outside the South. While white mobs ran unchecked through St. Augustine, blacks were rioting in the North. A longstanding feud between Harlem residents and the New York City police erupted into a riot on July 18. Other disorders soon followed, first in Rochester, New York, then in the New Jersey municipalities of Jersey City, Elizabeth, and Paterson. The last episode of rioting occurred in Philadelphia at the end of August. There was, said *Time* even before the disorders started in New Jersey, "something terrible about the discovery" that large-scale rioting could happen in the North. The terrifying and bewildering situation was summed up for *Time* by a "perplexed Michigan housewife" who asked: "What do they want?" and "Why don't they stop?" *Time* had few answers (a good gauge of just how serious the situation was), but it seemed imperative to offer blacks some sign that their race was finding a place in American society. Grasping at straws, *Time* had to settle for the selection of a black woman as a finalist in a beauty contest.[37]

Time used King in much the same fashion. He became a symbol of what America had done, what, according to *Time*, America would continue to do to solve its racial problems. To strengthen King's symbolism, *Time* contraposed him against Malcolm X, who represented the "worst kind of element." Side by side with Malcolm X, who counseled blacks to "demand 'an eye for an eye, a tooth for a tooth, a life for a life,'" King indeed seemed an attractive

35. "This Time, Things Changed," *Time*, July 10, 1964, p. 27.
36. *Ibid.*
37. On the summer disorders, see Waskow, *From Race Riot to Sit-in*, 255–59. "The Talk is Race," *Time*, August 7, 1964, p. 17.

alternative.[38] King's impatient denunciation of tokenism that brought a crowd surging to its feet in Chicago in 1963 now appeared to be pretty mild stuff. Furthermore, King had joined other civil rights leaders in calling for a moratorium on demonstrations during the 1964 presidential election campaign.

Whatever its uses for the symbolic King, Luce's magazine still harbored suspicions about the man himself. There was, for one thing, this business of civil disobedience. To a magazine fervently arguing that law and the Constitution would correct racial injustice, civil disobedience was troublesome "even in the name of what . . . King calls 'the moral law or the law of God.'" Luckily for King, he was engaged in civil disobedience against segregation and not the sort of "guerrilla warfare" at the New York World's Fair.[39] Put another way, *Time* wanted King to restrict himself to the South and remain out of the turmoil spreading across the country.

What *Time* wanted, *Time* could make happen—in its own pages. Its varied treatments of King in two cities made as much clear. *Time* reported, for example, that King had visited New York City in an attempt to assist the administration of Mayor Robert Wagner in resolving some grievances in the aftermath of the Harlem riots. First, the story omitted the fact that King had been invited to New York by Wagner. Then it added: "Before long, local Negro leaders were complaining publicly that King had ignored them, and, anyway, he was not speaking for them. . . . Not much of substance came out of the meeting." Very little had come out of that venture into the tangles of New York politics, to be sure, but the striking element was the depiction of King as a visiting fireman who was out of his depth. The curt designation "Atlanta's Martin Luther King, Jr." implied that King was an outsider in New York, not a particularly prominent one at that. By contrast, *Time* identified King simply as the "leader of the demonstrators" in St. Augustine and vigorously defended him when the inevitable chorus arose that he was an outside agitator. This complaint was revived by the white-owned newspaper that "hammered on this theme: that trouble would subside if only the agitators would get out of town" and the affair would be settled if King would agree "to withdraw and let us work it out among ourselves." That statement was waved away in advance as segregationist propaganda, and *Time* scornfully dismissed

38. "The Talk is Race," 17.
39. "How to Change Laws You Don't Like," *Time*, July 17, 1964, p. 63.

as well the newspaper, a "modest little daily . . . with even more modest ambitions . . . [that] tried to ignore the South's biggest story, on the hopeful assumption that if nobody pays any attention, the race problem just might go away."[40]

With some stretching, that assessment fitted *Time*. Not that it ignored the race crisis; indeed, more and more space was being devoted to what was turning into the nation's, not merely the South's, biggest story. But *Time*'s response, listing black success stories and beauty contest finalists and offering the courts as a remedy for economic disabilities beyond the reach of law, betrayed a desire that some of the complexities of race problems would go away. Wishful thinking of that sort was not without precedent at *Time*. Hearing of the Supreme Court's ruling in 1954 that struck down segregation in public schools, Henry Luce turned to his editors and said: "Well, that's good, . . . that takes care of the problem."[41] But the problem refused to go away, and the stark tones of the southern movement were blurring as the black revolt took different forms, whether civil disobedience that seemed like "guerrilla warfare" to *Time* or rioting that frightened perplexed housewives in Michigan.

The spreading protests confronted *Newsweek* on two fronts as well, and its coverage of St. Augustine followed a pattern similar to its coverage of Birmingham. The opening article included militaristic terms and references such as "legions," "pitching a tent," and "open warfare." And the magazine said the motivation behind King's "gesture of going to jail for the cause" was that the ranks of demonstrators in St. Augustine were thinning. When matters took a more violent turn, *Newsweek*'s coverage shifted, washing out the elements that might detract from the symbolism of King as a nonviolent prophet. Because St. Augustine lacked a relative moderate on the order of Albert Boutwell, *Newsweek* turned King himself into the moderate. King was willing to compromise, the magazine said, but he insisted that gestures made by whites have more behind them than symbolism. *Newsweek* made it clear that attitude could only be regarded as realistic because of the collapse of law and

---

40. "The Talk is Race," 18; "Covering St. Augustine," *Time*, July 10, 1964, p. 75. *Newsweek* depicted King as an inept peacemaker in New York, but its account was neither unfair nor inaccurate. " 'Calculated Risk,' " August 10, 1964, p. 27. On King in New York, see Garrow, *Bearing the Cross*, 342–44.

41. Halberstam, *The Powers That Be*, 51.

order. Witness the episode in which "a county sheriff's deputy grinned and extended his club to a shaggy young segregationist in a T-shirt. 'Here,' the deputy said, 'do you wanta use this for a few minutes?'"[42]

Against the scenes of mobs in St. Augustine, the symbolism associated with the signing of the 1964 Civil Rights Act rang hammer against anvil the following week. *Newsweek* reported the ceremonial signing of the act as an example of American ideals in action. President Johnson spoke for justice and equality. The law, he said, "'does not restrict the freedom of any American so long as he respects the rights of others. . . . It does say that those who are equal before God shall now also be equal in the polling booths, in the classrooms, in the factories, and in hotels and restaurants and movie theaters, and other [public] places.'" King was among the black leaders present when Johnson signed the bill. To *Newsweek*, King was more than a mere onlooker; he was an instrument whereby the law would be put into practice and the races reconciled.[43]

Newsweek had good reason to promote King. For one considerable matter, he threatened no one except segregationists. He certainly was no danger to the suburban dwellers whose distaste for pushy blacks was registering in public opinion surveys. *Newsweek*'s pollster was finding a contradictory mix of attitudes. "More than half the suburbanites feel that Negroes must be kept in their place," Louis Harris wrote in a report commissioned by the magazine. On the other hand, "they protest vigorously against Southern attitudes and claim they are moderate on all things, including civil rights." Those suburbanites, according to Harris, "could be aroused this summer and at the polls next November" and turn against the Democratic liberalism espoused by *Newsweek*. The magazine's relief was almost palpable when King and other black leaders resolved "what could prove the most ominous crisis in the history of the U.S. civil rights movement" by seeking a moratorium on the demonstrations that were setting suburbanites' nerves on edge and that might contribute to a white backlash against Johnson's reelection in 1964. "Plainly," *Newsweek* wrote, "the Negroes felt they should not rock the boat."[44]

Clearly, *Newsweek* agreed, perhaps not solely out of concern for the Demo-

42. See, for example, *Newsweek*, "King's Targets," June 22, 1964, p. 26, "Acid Test," June 29, 1964, p. 26, and "No Man's Land," July 6, 1964, pp. 16–17.

43. "'. . . Shall Now Also be Equal . . . ,'" *Newsweek*, July 13, 1964, p. 17.

44. Louis Harris, "The 'Backlash' Issue," *Newsweek*, July 13, 1964, p. 27; "'Calculated Risk,'" 26.

crats. Suburbanites might also direct their anger against a magazine too many steps ahead of its readers. *Newsweek* was building an audience not so different from those well-to-do Americans who at once spoke well of the black southerner and fled the cities in order to escape his kind. With relief, *Newsweek* turned to King, contraposing him to Malcolm X, "a man with a menacing word for every occasion." King was the moderate, the reconciler; Malcolm X, the fiery alternative. In effect, *Newsweek* presented its comfortably fixed readers with a choice: Support King, a believer in the middle way (as was *Newsweek*), or wind up with Malcolm X, "whose claim to leadership rests on little more than the anger in their hearts."[45]

This approach might get *Newsweek* momentarily off the hook with readers rattled by black militancy, but some blacks persisted in rocking the boat. A leading example was the furor created at the 1964 Democratic National Convention in August when the Mississippi Freedom Democratic party challenged the seating of an all-white delegation from Mississippi and in the process raised a question about the survival of the liberal coalition that supported the black movement.

The origins of the Freedom Democratic party can be traced to a mock vote for governor and lieutenant governor in 1963, a compelling demonstration of disfranchisement of blacks in Mississippi; more than eighty thousand votes were cast in the mock election, four times the number of blacks registered to vote in the state. The party itself grew out of community organization and voter registration work by SNCC. In the early 1960s, SNCC began to turn away from direct action tactics, partly for ideological reasons, partly because of the infusion of money and the encouragement for voter registration provided by the Kennedy administration. The difficult and dangerous work contributed greatly to the alienation and later radicalization of SNCC's tight little band; gnawing at its members was the belief that the federal government had urged them to undertake their hazardous work and then left them without protection against the savage reprisals that followed. Almost as intense was a cultural clash between the black volunteers of SNCC and the white college students recruited for the Mississippi Summer campaign of 1964. Most of the media attention went to the "young white army gone to save the Negroes of Mississippi." That interest caused resentment among black volunteers who had been laboring much longer and had undergone severer tests. Another

45. "'Calculated Risk,'" 27–28.

source of discontent was the conviction that brutal attacks on blacks would be ignored while intense publicity would follow if white students, particularly those with prominent parents, were arrested, attacked, or killed.[46]

Despite SNCC's suspicions and anger, the Freedom Democratic party was an attempt to make the system work. But American politics works through compromise, and the Freedom Democrats were in no mood to cut a deal. Inasmuch as the state Democratic party had bolted the 1960 national convention and continued to bar blacks from the political process, simple justice seemed to demand that the regulars lose their seats at the 1964 convention. President Johnson, anxious to keep both southerners and northern liberals in his camp for the 1964 election, offered a compromise. Two at-large seats would be awarded to the Freedom Democrats, though Johnson specified that only moderates, not militants, would get them. Johnson also offered a rule prohibiting lily-white delegations at future conventions.[47]

The compromise struck the fancy of *Newsweek*. Because of its sensitivity to boat rocking, *Newsweek* was the only news weekly to catch the significance of the struggle, the first public sign that the civil rights coalition would come unglued. (*Time* scoffed at the Freedom Democrats as publicity seekers who spent "most of their time shouting into ever-ready television mikes." *U.S. News* misread the situation altogether, reporting that Johnson's offer "ended the threat, and harmony prevailed.") *Newsweek* reported that Senator Humphrey, as Johnson's emissary, pleaded with King and the Freedom Democrats to accept the compromise and thus avert the possibility that southerners would bolt the convention and boycott the election. The magazine was outraged by the refusal to strike a bargain. However, it was not King but Bob Moses, the representative of SNCC and the radical wing of the Freedom Democrats, who bore the brunt of *Newsweek*'s displeasure. *Newsweek* grumbled that the "undisciplined, mistrustful Freedom Democrats" did not understand their own best interests, did not understand, even, that they had won a

46. On the origins of MFDP, see Pat Watters, *Encounter with the Future* (Atlanta, 1965), 11. For information on black voter registration, see *Race Relations in the U.S.A., 1954–1968* (New York, 1970), 195. The cultural clash is described by Sally Belfrage, *Freedom Summer* (New York, 1965), 79–81. On SNCC's suspicions that violence against blacks was regarded less seriously than violence against whites, see interview with Marion Barry, first chairman of SNCC, by Katherine Shannon, October 3, 1967 (Transcript of tape 54, in Moorland-Spingarn Research Center, Howard University), 33.

47. Viorst, *Fire in the Streets*, 264; Garrow, *Bearing the Cross*, 345–51.

victory and then had "frittered away its psychological impact by treating it stubbornly as a defeat."[48]

From its perspective, fretting about white backlash, disgruntled suburbanites, and an "ominous crisis" in the black movement, *Newsweek* had a point about confusing politics with principles. It missed another. The Freedom Democrats were taking notions of justice and equality rather more literally and urgently than was *Newsweek*. As Milton Viorst noted, the blacks had suffered the casualties, had built their organization in Mississippi without the party's help, and looked to the convention in Atlantic City "only to ratify" what they had accomplished. "Understandably consumed by a sense of righteousness, they considered themselves betrayed when the Democrats rejected them."[49] The struggle at the 1964 convention cracked the coalition that had grown up around the civil rights movement. Other strains from the evolving black revolt eventually would shatter the alliance.

Tensions of a different nature appeared in the coverage of the clash between King and Hoover. Symbol measured against symbol, the match was even: The hero of Montgomery and Birmingham, the unequaled orator of the March on Washington, the American prophet soon to be a Nobel laureate locked in public conflict with the doughty public servant who had transformed a corrupt federal agency into the mythic band of courageous G-men who tracked down the country's enemies, kidnappers and bank robbers, Nazi spies during World War II and their Communist counterparts in the cold war. Their public brawl was unseemly, if only rhetorical, with King questioning the devotion to justice of Hoover's handpicked agents, claiming they preferred to remain on good terms with segregationist policemen rather than protect black demonstrators, and Hoover denouncing King as the "most notorious liar" in the United States.

More than symbolism was at stake. Hoover's outburst was the first visible tip of a campaign to destroy King that was set in motion by an agency far more dangerous than segregationists or right-wing politicians. As early as 1962, Hoover scrawled on a memorandum that "'King is no good,'" and in May of that year King's name was added to the list of persons to be rounded up and

48. "Trying to Paper It Over," *Time*, September 4, 1964, p. 32; "Now the Real Race Begins," *U.S. News & World Report*, September 7, 1964, p. 28; "Battle of Credentials," *Newsweek*, September 7, 1964, pp. 26–27.
49. Viorst, *Fire in the Streets*, 267.

detained in the event of a national emergency. Thereafter, the FBI attempted to ruin King in what was the "single most extensive program on an individual in the Bureau's history." Although King got some private advice from the Kennedy administration to mind his back, neither Kennedy nor Johnson made any serious attempt to halt the FBI effort. The FBI's electronic surveillance and wiretapping of King and the SCLC were authorized by both administrations. The FBI recruited an informant within the SCLC and attempted to discredit King with the executive branch, Congress, foreign heads of state, American diplomats, churches, universities, and the press. Hoover's aides tried to plant stories to the effect that King had pilfered funds and had secret Swiss bank accounts, that he caroused with women, and that he was influenced or controlled by Communists. In a catalog of persecutions, perhaps the most outrageous occurred when the FBI mailed King a package containing an anonymous letter and tape recordings. The letter specified that King had "just thirty-four days" in which to take the "one way out for you" and advised him to "take it before your filthy, abnormal fraudulent self is bared to the nation." King's aide, Andrew Young, later testified that King "felt somebody was trying to get him to commit suicide" and assumed the FBI was behind it.[50]

While the FBI continued its campaign, *U.S. News* had one of its own under way. Whether or not there was any connection between the two campaigns, *U.S. News* paid respectful attention to Hoover and the FBI; in turn, the journal was regarded by the bureau as a friendly source—and not without reason, judging from the magazine's stories on the public dispute between Hoover and King. It reprinted most of the text of Hoover's comments to a press conference on November 18, including headline-making disparagement of King as "the most notorious liar in the country." King got an opportunity to reply, but the magazine's placement of his short remark and photograph muted the response. Furthermore, the magazine tried to strengthen Hoover's position by implying that President Johnson sanctioned the criticism of King.[51]

---

50. The best study of the war on King is Garrow, *The FBI and King*. The FBI's letter to King and its recruitment of a spy within SCLC are treated *ibid.*, 125–26, 175–76. On attempts to discredit King, wiretapping during the Kennedy administration, and Hoover's notation, see *Senate Documents*, 94th Cong., 2nd Sess., No. 755, Bk. 3, pp. 11, 82, 111–12. The wiretapping during the Johnson administration is cited in Wise, *The American Police State*, 287–88. The scope of the FBI's campaign is outlined in Frank M. Sorrentino, "Bureaucratic Ideology: The Case Study of the Federal Bureau of Investigation" (Ph.D. dissertation, New York University, 1978), 78, 214. On the FBI leaks, see Morgan, *One Man, One Voice*, 37–38. Young is quoted in Christy Macy and Susan Kaplan (comps.), *Documents* (New York, 1980), 179.

51. On Hoover's regard for Lawrence, see their correspondence in Box 58, Hoover File, David Lawrence Papers, Princeton University. Despite the magazine's respect for the FBI, it did

U.S. News also painted King as a radical bent on destroying American liberties. In early December, it refocused on the issue of establishing a national police force. On one level this was logical. It was widely believed at the time that Hoover's outburst was motivated by King's complaint that FBI agents had failed to protect civil rights workers. Yet *U.S. News* took the matter much further than the debate over the wisdom of, or the constitutional authority for, providing federal protection for civil rights workers. On one side in the scenario was Hoover, proclaiming that " 'We don't want a Gestapo.' " On the other, "Negro spokesmen" (to be read as including King) were determined to establish centralized police forces such as those that had trampled freedom elsewhere in the world. It was a simple choice: either a national police system "such as exists behind the Iron Curtain," or Hoover's "objective investigative force." Conveniently at hand were the examples of the "terrorism of Hitler's Gestapo, the atrocities committed by the Soviet secret police, and the reign of terror today in Communist Cuba," which, *U.S. News* reminded readers breathlessly, was a "police state only ninety miles from the U.S."[52] In other words, the enemy was at the gates of the Republic and getting assistance from a Fifth Column within. The thesis demanded judicious selection of facts. *U.S. News* avoided weakening its argument with citations of national police agencies in Western democracies that were less oppressive than were the Gestapo and the KGB.

As *U.S. News* sketched the situation, King, if not at the head of that Fifth Column, at least belonged to it. This point was made obliquely in the same issue that raised the specter of an American KGB. One story reprinted excerpts from an address by Hoover, who complained of "the zealots of pressure groups . . . carping, lying, and exaggerating with the fiercest passions, spearheaded at times by Communists and moral degenerates." No individual was cited by name; at the time, however, it would have been all but impossible

---

refuse to print an article about King that the bureau was trying to place. Sorrentino, "Bureaucratic Ideology," 210. "The FBI and Civil Rights—J. Edgar Hoover Speaks Out," *U.S. News & World Report*, November 30, 1964, p. 56. King's response was in "Martin Luther King's Reaction—A Statement and a Disagreement," 58, in that same issue. An echo was heard in "Dispute Between Hoover and King: The FBI's Answer to Criticisms," *U.S. News & World Report*, December 7, 1964, pp. 46, 48—from all appearances a reprinted FBI document or press release. "Washington Whispers," *U.S. News & World Report*, December 7, 1964, p. 26, implied the White House sanctioned Hoover's statement.

52. The phrase "Negro spokesmen" undoubtedly was intended to include Wilkins of the NAACP, another critic of the FBI's operations in the South, but the previous emphasis suggests strongly that the primary target was King. "Next: A National Police Force?" *U.S. News & World Report*, December 7, 1964, p. 44.

not to believe that Hoover had King in mind. Similar references to "carping" and "lying" critics of the FBI who were influenced by Communists had been published as *U.S. News* reported the dispute. Hoover's remarks were echoed in a somewhat milder version two weeks later. Another article, a brief excerpt from testimony before the Warren Commission by an FBI official, sounded again the warning about the threat of centralized power and, because of its placement, tarred King as a Communist. The report included this statement: "We have been asked many times why we don't pick up and jail all Communists. . . . [But] if action, unrestrained action, is taken against a particular group of people, a precedent is set which can be seized on in the future by power-hungry or unscrupulous authorities."[53] The statement was tacked onto the end of the FBI's point-by-point rebuttal of King's statements—at least the statements the FBI said he made.

The *U.S. News* portrait of King as a radical differed markedly from the reports of *Time* and *Newsweek*, which ascribed Hoover's outburst to senility, organizational or personal. *Time* leaned toward the latter theory. Six months earlier, *Time* had pronounced Hoover to be "hale and hearty," but now it depicted him as feeling the pressures of age: "J. Edgar's outburst left a lot of people puzzling over what had happened to the tight-lipped old G-man. . . . [U]ndoubtedly, there will be increased pressures on the White House from now on to boot the old fellow out of his job." Careful editing added an extra edge to King's "cutting statement." According to *Time*, "King said that Hoover's assertion seemed to indicate that the G-man 'has apparently faltered under the awesome burdens, complexities, and responsibilities of his office.' "[54]

Newsweek diagnosed the incident as symptomatic of bureaucratic senility.

---

53. Hoover undoubtedly intended the reference to "moral degenerates" to apply to King, but that implication cannot be used here because the FBI had been unsuccessful in its attempts to persuade the press to publish stories about King's sex life. King's philandering is treated candidly but sensitively by Garrow, *Bearing the Cross*, 374–76, 423, 587. See *U.S. News & World Report*, "What J. Edgar Hoover Says About 'Pressure Groups,'" December 7, 1964, p. 45, which was echoed in a five-page article, "Interview with J. Edgar Hoover," December 21, 1964, p. 38. See also "How the FBI Regards Its Responsibilities," *U.S. News & World Report*, December 7, 1964, p. 48.

54. See *Time*, "People," May 15, 1964, p. 50, and "Off the Chest and Into the Fire," November 27, 1964, p. 31. In the statement, King said he could not imagine Hoover making such a statement unless he had been under extreme pressure and added: "I have nothing but sympathy for this man who has served his country so well." *SCLC Newsletter*, October-November, 1964, p. 9. *Newsweek* printed the milder version of King's statement in "Off Hoover's Chest," November 30, 1964, p. 30.

The episode provided a news peg for a searching examination of the FBI. The bureau was found wanting on numerous counts: foot dragging in investigations of civil rights violations and organized crime, providing false or puffed-up statistics in order to get larger appropriations, and exaggerating the danger from domestic Communists. *Newsweek* also provided an alarming account of the bureau's extensive files that posed an "enormous potential danger—a kind of arsenal of defamation that might someday be put to political use." The FBI's investigative skills had been put to political use for years, most recently when it tapped King's telephones at the 1964 Democratic convention. *Newsweek* probably was unaware of the tapping, but its reporters were certainly aware the FBI was out to get King. One of Hoover's aides had offered a transcript of surveillance materials from the file on King to the magazine's Washington bureau chief, Benjamin Bradlee, before the publication of that cover story on the FBI. (Bradlee declined the offer.) *Newsweek* misread the situation, believing that President Johnson would persuade Hoover to retire. Possibly out of a desire to raise no barrier to Hoover's graceful withdrawal, the magazine did not cite the FBI's attempts to discredit King. It noted instead that Hoover had "access to knowledge that could ruin countless thousands" and, ironically, that there was a danger that the files could be used by a successor "less rigidly nonpolitical" than Hoover.[55]

Another bloody episode in the South overshadowed the controversy. During the Mississippi Summer civil rights campaign, three young volunteers, two whites from the North and a black Mississippian, disappeared in June near the town of Philadelphia. President Johnson ordered the FBI into the case. The bodies of the three men were found buried in an earthen dam, and in December, FBI agents arrested twenty-one persons and charged them with violating the constitutional rights of the three murdered civil rights workers. Despite the tragic elements, there was a satisfying denouement to a case that had outraged the nation. The principles of justice were underscored by the arrests, particularly because the local sheriff, Lawrence Rainey, previously was involved in the killings of two blacks and seemed to be a rural counterpart of Bull Connor.[56]

55. "J. Edgar Hoover and the FBI," *Newsweek*, December 7, 1964, pp. 23–24, 26. On the attempt to leak material to Bradlee, see Garrow, *The FBI and King*, 127.

56. Walter Lord, *The Past That Would Not Die* (New York, 1965), 237; Watters, *Encounter with the Future*, 3; Florence Mars, *Witness in Philadelphia* (Baton Rouge, 1977), 76–78, 93, 106.

The solution of the case served to reaffirm the mystique of the FBI and Hoover and enabled *Time* and *Newsweek* to work a reconciliation of the embarrassing clash of symbols, though not the parties to it. In such a symbolically charged atmosphere, the discord between Hoover and King now appeared of little moment.

Time's and *Newsweek*'s reports reduced the affair to the dimension of a family spat. A meeting in Hoover's office in Washington appeared to "cool the controversy," a phrase used in both headline and text by *Time*, which now regarded the "fuss" as settled. *Newsweek* took the controversy more seriously, but still reduced it to a ripple in the prevailing harmony. *Newsweek* implied that Johnson had restored peace. In fact, it all but said that he had spanked the two errants, inasmuch as "both Hoover and King evidently acted with an eye cocked on the president, who had evinced pointed displeasure with their feud."[57] *Newsweek* exhibited relief—that King was out of another scrape, that harmony was restored, that *Newsweek* could get on to other matters.

One such matter was the assiduous promotion of King after he won the Nobel Prize. In contrast to *U.S. News*, which labeled King a "Man of Conflict" and questioned why a prize for peace should go to someone whose "activities often led to violence," *Newsweek* and *Time* celebrated the new Nobel laureate. King was anointed as a latter-day American saint ("Nobelman King," as *Newsweek* turned the phrase)—dedicated, self-sacrificing, and self-effacing. A prophet being not without honor save in his own country, *Time* went looking for evidence to support that biblical aphorism and found it in the Deep South, from which "there were, of course, outraged howls." One came from old foe Bull Connor, who "cried" (that verb of scorn favored by *Time*), " 'They're scraping the bottom of the barrel.' "[58] The howl from Connor served *Time*'s purpose, which was to limit King as a symbol inspiring Americans to right the wrongs in the South.

Naturally, in covering King's Nobel Prize acceptance speech, *Time* and *Newsweek* had to take into account their readers' expectations of what would be said on such an occasion. Some strained metaphors were dropped. How-

57. "Cooling the Controversy," *Time*, December 11, 1964, p. 30; "The Hoover-King Meeting," *Newsweek*, December 14, 1964, p. 22. In this story, *Newsweek* abandoned its critical stance on the FBI and Hoover.

58. See *U.S. News & World Report*, "Man of Conflict Wins a Peace Prize," October 26, 1964, p. 24, and "How Martin Luther King Won the Nobel Peace Prize," February 8, 1965, p. 76; "Nobelman King," *Newsweek*, October 26, 1964, p. 77; "The Youngest Ever," *Time*, October 23, 1964, p. 27.

ever valid the sentiment, King's statement that the Nobel Prize "honored the ground crew without whose labor and sacrifices the jet flights to freedom could never have left the earth" fell considerably short of the elevated tone readers would require. Both magazines selected excerpts that narrowed King's perspective on black problems. King opened his address with a reference to the 22 million black Americans "engaged in a creative battle to end the long night of racial injustice." *Newsweek* substituted the vaguer passage that King accepted the prize on "'behalf of a civil rights movement which is moving with determination and a majestic scorn for risk and danger to establish a reign of freedom and a rule of justice." *Time* chose excerpts evoking the stark images from Birmingham, where "our children, crying out for brotherhood, were answered with fire hoses, snarling dogs, and even death," and from Mississippi, where "young people seeking to secure the right to vote were brutalized and murdered."[59]

The remainder of the reportage was remarkable more for what was omitted than for what was included. Lack of space undoubtedly led to some omissions. However, *Time* and *Newsweek* had their own ideas about what comments the occasion demanded. King was not permitted to speak in their pages of the "debilitating and grinding poverty [that] afflicts my people and chains them to the lowest rung of the economic ladder." Nor was King allowed to establish a wider context for the black struggle in America, whether through comparisons to Third World movements or an unobjectionable tribute to Gandhian nonviolence. Those ideas would have not meshed smoothly with the theme threaded through the stories: While King and his foot soldiers were receiving the acclaim of the world along with the Nobel Prize, so also was America; America was being honored for translating her magnificent ideals into practice, for hastening the day when in Birmingham, and in Philadelphia, Mississippi, and in a thousand nameless hamlets in the South, the black man would know the heady taste of freedom.

The difficulty was, of course, that that crusade had broken its bounds, and leaders and foot soldiers alike were at this moment loudly proclaiming the existence throughout America of a glaring disparity between ideals and practices. King's was one of those voices, if not one of the more raucous ones. His

59. "Two Perspectives—One Goal," *Time*, December 18, 1964, p. 21; "Up From Montgomery," *Newsweek*, December 21, 1964, p. 41. *Time*'s and *Newsweek*'s reports were collated with the full text of King's speech, printed by the New York *Times*, December 11, 1964, p. 33, from an Associated Press dispatch.

voice had to be altered now as the world watched and honored America. Symbolism demanded that editorial silence smother King's disconcerting notions about race and poverty, that other elements be located that would fit neatly into what the mayor of New York, as he welcomed King back to his country, called "the moral epic of America."[60]

Indeed it had been a moral epic, if one marked by the tawdry as well as by the pristine spirit of the tales spun by *Time* and *Newsweek*. Much went unsaid in those stories. When it came to the black struggle for justice, for example, considerable prodding had been required in order to move the nation to uphold the principles at stake. King's prodding had taken the form of staged moral dramas, one of which remained to be played out in an obscure corner of Alabama, not far from where King had begun it all. There, in Selma, King the prophet from another country of *Time*, the prophet of the middle way of *Newsweek*, and the false prophet of *U.S. News*, would create another crisis that forced the nation to look south again with shock and horror.

60. "People," *Time*, December 25, 1964, p. 29.

V

SELMA

King's Selma campaign copied the strategy used in Birmingham
two years earlier. His intention was to create a crisis that would
put irresistible pressure to bear on voting rights legislation. Crises were created in Birmingham and Selma, King wrote later, because "we have learned
from bitter experience that our government does not correct a race problem
until it is confronted directly and dramatically." After some prodding, Bull
Connor supplied the crisis in Birmingham, and King was counting on the
same unwitting assistance from James G. Clark, Jr., the sheriff of Dallas
County. Just as it studied Connor, the SCLC scouted Clark; King "had to have
someone like Clark to do in public, before the cameras, what whites had done
to blacks . . . largely without notice." Although never so clearly etched a
symbol as Connor, Clark played the role so well that Ralph David Abernathy
quipped that Clark ought to be voted membership in the SCLC in recognition
of his contribution to the cause.[1]

The SCLC got its crisis after Alabama state police and posse members
deputized by Clark brutally attacked civil rights demonstrators. The resulting
outcry was all the stronger because the right to vote was at stake. The outrage
stirred by the attack in Selma was best caught by President Johnson in an
address to Congress. Johnson emphasized his determination to secure a strong

---

1. King to "SCLC Supporters," February 15, 1968, in Box 6, File 29, Mississippi Valley
Collection, Memphis State University; Charles E. Fager, *Selma, 1965* (New York, 1974), 34.

voting rights act by declaring at the conclusion of his speech, "We shall overcome," a phrase taken from the anthem of the civil rights movement. The legislation later enacted was the legal capstone of the struggle in the South, but the symbolic conclusion of the Selma campaign occurred months earlier when King led a march from Selma to Montgomery. By the time the marchers made their dramatic entrance into the Cradle of the Confederacy, almost thirty thousand Americans had joined in.

Although the legislation and the march to Montgomery gave rise to intense symbolism, Selma differed from Birmingham in one important respect. Less than a week after the voting rights bill became law, rioting erupted in Watts. Like Birmingham and the 1963 March on Washington, Selma and Watts were seeming opposites: Selma was the last great milestone of the southern movement; Watts, a reminder writ in fire and blood that black Americans were as discontent as their brethren in the South, if for different reasons. Selma and Watts produced no overarching consensus. The coalition of conscience was coming unstuck, the era of good feelings fading rapidly. One sign of this change was the course taken by King after Selma, away from reform and toward the radicalism that eventually would bring him into conflict with the national government and lead him into the volatile ghettos of Chicago.

Initially, *Time* and *Newsweek* used King as a symbol contraposed to radical elements. *Newsweek* offered him as the alternative to the "apostles of despair," whose number included racists, black and white, hoodlums, and Communists. For "apostles of despair" *Time* substituted "extremist Northern Negroes" and had one in mind: Malcolm X. He cried menacingly, "'The white man should thank God that Dr. King is holding his people in check'" and threatened that should King's tactics fail, some "'other ways' will be tried."[2]

King became a far less reassuring figure when he took nonviolence out of the abstract and put it on the street. King opened the SCLC's campaign in Selma on January 2, 1965. It was a late start. SNCC had sent cadres to Selma in 1963, but, by late fall of 1964, only 335 of approximately 15,000 eligible blacks had been registered to vote in Dallas County. The meager results were due to the unvigorous action of the Justice Department and the byzantine state

2. "The Negro in America—1965," *Newsweek*, February 15, 1965, p. 27; "Victory in Jail," *Time*, February 12, 1965, p. 16.

voter registration procedures. Sheriff Clark was another obstacle. In the fall of 1963, more than 300 persons were arrested during the voter registration campaign. Such a rock-hard segregationist was Clark that once he even rushed into the federal courthouse to arrest 3 demonstrators. Clark was winning himself a name as a segregationist of the old school.[3]

That reputation was not welcomed by the city fathers of Selma, who wanted no reprise of Birmingham. Mayor Joseph Smitherman, while a committed segregationist, wanted to bottle up the unpredictable Clark by persuading him to yield control of the law enforcement strategy to Wilson Baker, Selma's public safety director. With Baker following the example of Laurie Pritchett, meeting nonviolence with nonviolence, Smitherman hoped to avoid confrontations and the national publicity that they would generate. For a time, Smitherman's plan worked.[4]

The strategy was succeeding well enough with *Time* and *Newsweek* in January and February. The latter reported, for example, that King went in search of a symbolic opponent and found in Clark "a foil as good as any since Theophilus Eugene Connor played Bull to King's matador in the Battle of Birmingham two years ago." Clark was, however, not simply King's adversary but an anachronism in the moderate New South. On one side were the officials of Selma, who were less abrasive than was Clark. On the other were Clark and his "irregulars"—whites deputized and organized into a posse "armed with clubs, electric cattle prods and pistols . . . symbols of repression." The distinction was driven home when Baker "bulled through a crowd" to arrest a racist who had struck King; by contrast, Clark arrested demonstrators, manhandling a woman and black teachers. *Time* developed the same theme. The moderates included Smitherman, a "self-described segregationist" who nevertheless wanted "to maintain the dignity of the town, and peace." Smitherman and Baker were allied against Clark in a "small civil war." The reports implied that King was preparing yet another unnecessary confrontation. "A new Selma city administration, with the cooperation of many businessmen," *Time* maintained, "is trying hard to clear the town's dark racist reputation by steering a more moderate course." *Newsweek* observed

3. On the number of voters, see David J. Garrow, *Protest at Selma: Martin Luther King, Jr., and the Voting Rights Act of 1965* (New Haven, 1978), 34. On the arrests, see Zinn, *SNCC*, 149, 158.
4. Garrow, *Protest at Selma*, 35.

that "Selma had already become—in spite of herself—an arena for a black-and-white symbolic clash she could not control."[5]

The moderates of Selma, caught between the extremes of Clark and King, were in about the same position as were the two news magazines: They were disconcerted or frightened by the relentless black movement and frustrated by stiffening white resistance to the social change necessary if violence was to be averted. To this extent, Selma was a microcosm of the nation. Naturally, *Time* and *Newsweek* held no brief for Clark or King. Almost without exception, Clark and his "squirrel-shooting posse" (*Newsweek*'s phrase) were depicted as "remarkably stupid law enforcement officials" (*Time*'s description) who "fell hook, line, and sinker for [King's] bait." King was treated similarly: His followers, according to *Newsweek*, deliberately provoked Clark to attack, then reaped a harvest of publicity.[6]

For once, *Newsweek*'s tones were the harsher. But it redounded to King's benefit very little. *Time* was preoccupied with its theme of an unnecessary confrontation. King led a mass march despite the admonition of Wilson Baker, "who has been desperately trying to keep peace in the strife-stricken town and who kept running out to pluck at Parade Leader King's sleeve and saying: 'This is a deliberate attempt to violate the city's parade ordinance. You know the law. You've been abiding by it for two weeks. You've had plenty of time to apply for a parade permit, and you haven't done it.' As the Negroes marched on, Baker ordered them all arrested." Furthermore, King appeared determined to bring about another, equally unnecessary confrontation in nearby Montgomery. "As Dr. King should have known," *Time* reported, "Montgomery Negroes who are interested enough to register have mostly been able to do so since 1962."[7] The article implied, of course, that King knew and went ahead anyway.

King was getting nowhere in Montgomery, a fact stressed by two magazines busily promoting moderation. White leaders, as *Time* put it, "fell all over themselves to help out" when King staged his unnecessary demonstration. From this situation was derived a general lesson: "Whenever one of . . .

5. "Shades of Bull Connor," *Newsweek*, February 1, 1965, pp. 21, 22; "The Aim: Registration," *Time*, January 29, 1965, p. 21.

6. "Black Eye," *Newsweek*, February 8, 1965, p. 24; "Victory in Jail," 16. The theme also appears in *Time*, "Rare Tribute," February 5, 1965, p. 24, and "Difference of Impact," February 19, 1965, p. 23; and in *Newsweek*, "Forced March," February 22, 1965, p. 24. Provocations were reported by *Newsweek* in "Black Eye," 24, and "By the Book," March 1, 1965, p. 34.

7. "Victory in Jail," 16; "Difference of Impact," 23.

King's nonviolent civil rights drives is met by white nonviolence, the result is something like driving a tack into a marshmallow; there is very little impact." *Newsweek* offered southern lawmen some folksy advice to mind their media images. "Handled with care, demonstrations stop making news—and eventually stop happening at all. That was the central lesson of Albany, Georgia, where new-breed Police Chief Laurie Pritchett boned up on Gandhi" and defeated King with "nonviolent mass arrests."[8] This lesson was made possible by a rewriting of *Newsweek*'s own reports. In 1962, the magazine had shown Pritchett propping up the oppressive system King was attempting to pull down. Now Pritchett had become a model for police who wanted to make black demonstrations ineffective.

Newsweek's new editorial course had nothing to do with Albany and not much more to do with Selma—but almost certainly a great deal to do with what was occurring elsewhere in America. The magazine was beginning to get edgy about King and his tactic of filling the streets with marchers. About midway through the Selma campaign, a journalistic distinction was drawn between appropriate and inappropriate demonstrations. Unlike the complex issues arousing blacks in the North and West, argued *Newsweek*, denial of voting rights and access to public accommodations in the South was straightforward, and therefore "old-fashioned direct action is appropriate." Outside the South, direct action seemed slightly "ragged and funky," and King, in the words of a "Negro influential in Washington," was sapping energy and funds that could be put to better use. Less than a decade after mass direct action was inaugurated in Montgomery, two years after Birmingham, less than a year after St. Augustine, the major weapon in King's arsenal had become "old-fashioned."[9] In fact, King's fill-the-streets and fill-the-jails style of campaigning had not received a real trial other than in his native region; judging from its comments, *Newsweek* was reluctant that his strategy or tactics ever have such a test.

Time also was getting edgy about King. Earlier, it had offered King as an alternative to Malcolm X. Now, after the murder of Malcolm X in New York, *Time* was not so certain. The problem was that black leaders, King being the only one mentioned by name, had not denounced Malcolm X as a radical and troublemaker but had "sanctified" him, saying he was "brilliant" and had

---

8. "Difference of Impact," 23; "Forced March," 24; "By the Book," 34.
9. "Now—'The Era of Complexities,'" *Newsweek*, February 15, 1965, pp. 27, 28.

recently "moderated" his extremist views, *Time* complained. What King added was bound to anger *Time*: He blamed Malcolm X's death on a " 'society sick enough to express dissent with murder.' " The remark did not square with the magazine's thesis that the death of Malcolm X was part of a squalid quarrel within a gang of thugs. Malcolm X was disparaged as a former "pimp, a cocaine addict, and a thief" who had become even worse, "an unashamed demagogue" whose gospel was hatred and whose creed was violence. King and others who saw redeeming virtues in Malcolm X were implicitly dismissed as fools unable to recognize that "in life and in death [he] . . . was a disaster to the civil rights movement."[10]

The choler carried over into the following issue when King proposed martyrdom for Jimmie Lee Jackson, a young black demonstrator mortally wounded by an Alabama state trooper in Marion, a town near Selma. Ordinarily, *Time* would have condemned the shooting as an outrage. However, after the "sanctification" of Malcolm X, *Time* scorned Jackson as a "woodcutter" and a "woodchopper" and emphasized the burlesque qualities of the memorial services in which King participated. The affair became a tawdry bit of show business in which the coffin "was paraded" to a drab black church where "King offered the dubious consolation. Cried King: 'Farewell, Jimmie! You died that all of us could vote, and we are going to vote.' " Interestingly, while stripping Jackson of dignity, the article restored it to the bucolic, bumbling Jim Clark. When King led some demonstrators on a march to the courthouse, "Clark was, as usual, standing in the way," and not merely standing but standing "resolutely." Clark came across as a man of common sense seeking only to maintain a necessary degree of public order, not as a club-swinging segregationist.[11] King had managed—no inconsiderable feat—to make Jim Clark palatable to Luce's magazine.

While *Time* and *Newsweek* agreed that the moderates of Selma were caught between King and Clark, *U.S. News* sowed suspicions about King and ignored the symbolism of Clark. The only faintly discordant note sounded was the report that Clark made prospective black voters "stand in an alley, [and] use a rear entrance." However, the blacks matched Clark's intransigence. "Later," *U.S. News* reported, Clark relented and "opened one of two main

10. "Death and Transfiguration," *Time*, March 5, 1965, p. 23. *Time* printed police mug shots of Malcolm X taken twenty-one years before his death, presumably to establish that he was a criminal as a young man and remained one until his death.
11. "Eulogy for a Woodchopper," *Time*, March 12, 1965, p. 23B.

entrances to them. When Negroes refused to go into the alley, [and] insisted on using both entrances, he ordered arrests." *U.S. News* also passed over controversial actions such as the episode when Clark was struck by a black woman and then was photographed poised to hit her with his club as his deputies held her. Nor did it report what *Newsweek* described as a "Forced March" of black children arrested during demonstrations. Instead, *U.S. News* published a bland photograph showing the pupils being escorted to jail.[12]

Lawrence's magazine kept some issues in the background. *U.S. News* emphasized the efforts of Selma's city fathers to keep the peace and ignored the difficulties blacks had in registering to vote. (By contrast, *Time* noted that even the Chief Justice of the United States might have trouble passing Alabama's voter test.) Examining the "Real Stakes" on the table in Selma, *U.S. News* announced ominously that King's intent was "to touch off a chain of events that could put Negro voters in the drivers' seats in some areas."[13]

The idea was certain to excite the deepest apprehensions of readers haunted by the prospect of black political power. One of the cities in which blacks might soon be in the driver's seat was Washington, D.C., the magazine's headquarters city. Little more than a month before, President Johnson had proposed legislation granting a measure of political autonomy to Washington. Opposition to the bill, *U.S. News* reported, was motivated in part by "the fact that fifty-eight percent of Washington's residents are Negroes, and their vote could elect a Negro as mayor of the nation's capital." Judging from its tendency to trot out political horror stories from Reconstruction, *U.S. News* counted itself among the "some" who opposed black rule in Washington—or anywhere else in the nation.[14]

Legislation to secure the ballot for black southerners was becoming a distinct possibility, in part because of King's new campaign. Casting about, *U.S. News* could find only two hopeful signs. One appeared in the almost wistful report that even "some of the closest friends of the civil rights movement are unhappy about the latest pressure" from King for "new civil rights

12. See *U.S. News & World Report*, "No Peace for Winner of Peace Prize," February 1, 1965, p. 19, and "As Alabama Arrests Neared 3,500—," February 15, 1965, p. 10. "Forced March," 24.

13. "The Aim: Registration," 21; "The Real Stakes in Negro-Vote Drive," *U.S. News & World Report*, March 8, 1965, p. 37.

14. See *U.S. News & World Report*, "Home Rule for D.C.? What Johnson Proposes," February 15, 1965, p. 10. For its version of Reconstruction history, see "When Federal Registrars Were Last Used in the South," March 29, 1965, p. 33.

legislation." Another was that the warring between followers of the murdered Malcolm X and the Black Muslims—"a round of murder, bombing, and arson," *U.S. News* called it—"took the spotlight away from" the scenes in Selma of "clashes between white segregationists and Negroes."[15] If King's political friends wearied of his demands, if King were denied publicity, *U.S. News* said in so many words, he would fail.

U.S. News was grasping at straws. King got his crisis on March 7 when about six hundred demonstrators set out from a church in Selma on a march to Montgomery, the state capital. King having returned to Atlanta briefly to resume his pastoral duties, the march was led by Hosea Williams, of the SCLC, and John Lewis, chairman of SNCC, who won his organization's grudging consent to take part in the event. The march had been prohibited by Governor Wallace. At the Edmund Pettus Bridge, the marchers were met by a contingent of about fifty Alabama state troopers. After the demonstrators refused to disperse, the troopers and Clark's possemen attacked. About fifteen mounted deputies charged their horses into the throng. Tear gas, clubs, and cattle prods were used freely. The marchers were driven back across the bridge, into Selma and their homes and churches. At least seventeen demonstrators were seriously injured, including John Lewis, whose skull was fractured, and another forty persons were given emergency treatment at a black hospital.[16]

Scenes of charging horsemen and flailing clubs and screams of hurt and terror were filmed by television news crews. The symbolism was absolutely stark: Courageous marchers nonviolently demanding their rights were being attacked by sadistic policemen. Writing years later, a reporter only slightly exaggerated the time element when he maintained that "the sound of clubs on heads echoed all around the world and returned to Selma within a few hours." Large demonstrations were mounted in New York, Chicago, Los Angeles, and Detroit. SNCC volunteers staged a sit-in at the White House, and picket lines were later established outside to protest inactivity by the Johnson administration. Governors' offices, state legislatures, and local governments issued messages and adopted resolutions condemning the attack in Selma. In Con-

15. See *U.S. News & World Report*, "Washington Whispers," 22, and "Now It's Negroes vs. Negroes in America's Racial Violence," 6, both in the issue of March 8, 1965.

16. Sources consulted in preparing this account included Lewis, *King: A Biography*, 272–77; Viorst, *Fire in the Streets*, 327–30; Garrow, *Protest at Selma*, 73–77; and Morgan, *One Man, One Vote*, 32–33.

gress, forty-three representatives and seven senators, including some conservatives, rose in their respective houses to denounce the assault and to demand voting rights legislation.[17]

King issued a call, asking clergymen to journey to Selma to support the movement. He specified that the protesters would begin another trek to Montgomery on March 9, but an injunction issued by a federal judge temporarily halted the march until a hearing could be held. King was caught between pressure from the federal government to obey the injunction and from rebellious SNCC workers to proceed with the march and damn the consequences. He chose a curious compromise. King proceeded with the march a day late as if, for the first time, he would defy a federal court order. He led about three thousand demonstrators across the Edmund Pettus Bridge and there encountered a federal marshal who advised him of the order and stepped aside. Also present in force were state troopers whose commander admonished King that the march could not continue. Then the troopers inexplicably moved out of the line of march. With the road to Montgomery open, King turned his followers back, in keeping with his agreement with federal negotiators.[18]

The evening after King halted the march, several whites in Selma, armed with clubs, attacked three white clergymen, one of whom, Unitarian minister James Reeb of Boston, died of his injuries two days later. Against this backdrop of renewed violence came the symbolic culmination of the outrage that had arisen. During a presidential address viewed by millions of Americans, President Johnson told the Congress and the nation that the black cause in Selma was America's cause and concluded his address with the firm declaration that "we shall overcome."[19]

These events forced *Time* and *Newsweek* to reshuffle their stocks of symbols. *Time* accomplished an almost dazzling change in the actors in the drama. Clark, the buffoon of its earlier coverage and the resolute figure of the week before Bloody Sunday, became the "bully-boy segregationist who leads a club-swinging, mounted posse of deputy volunteers, many of them volunteer

17. The observation is from Bishop, *The Days of Martin Luther King*, 384. On the public responses to the attack, see Viorst, *Fire in the Streets*, 328; Lewis, *King: A Biography*, 276–77, 283; and Garrow, *Protest at Selma*, 87–88.

18. See Lewis, *King: A Biography*, 277–78; Garrow, *Protest at Selma*, 273–74n9; and Carson, *In Struggle*, 159–60. King denied that he made any agreement to halt the march, but his statement is dismissed by Lewis, *King: A Biography*, 281–82.

19. Fager, *Selma*, 108–109, 117.

Ku Klux Klansmen." Also transformed were the former moderates caught between Clark and King. So thorough was *Time*'s handiwork that only Wilson Baker remained essentially unaltered, portrayed as a "bitter enemy of Clark's who has done his thankless best to keep peace in the city." But Baker fitted awkwardly into the morality play and was passed over quickly. *Time* did not record, for example, Baker's intervention to protect demonstrators from state troopers and Clark's possemen. Luckily for *Time*, Mayor Joseph Smitherman stepped into a leading role in another morality tale in April. Previously, the journal had described Smitherman as a segregationist, but one bent on keeping the peace. After Bloody Sunday, Smitherman became "the race-baiting mayor of Selma." *Time* took an almost savage joy in recounting the gulling of Smitherman by a black con artist during a trip to Washington—poetic justice for an oppressor.[20] *Time* also tailored another character to fit the expectations of readers. Gone was the King who had "cried" out the maudlin, almost hysterical eulogy for a "woodchopper" slain by a state trooper. Now King was a spellbinding orator and charismatic leader.

As it happened, King was attracting a good deal of criticism from SNCC and others rankled by his absence on Bloody Sunday and his decision to turn back the march to Montgomery. King explained that he felt duty-bound to fulfill his pastoral obligations in Atlanta on March 7 and that he expected, at most, mass arrests but no bloodshed. His statement was received skeptically. Openly critical of King before, the increasingly militant SNCC complained angrily that he had backed down rather than expose the whites marching with him to injury or death. There was enough resentment against him that King briefly went into seclusion in Selma.[21]

On both counts *Time* defended King. Explaining his absence, its story said that "King planned to lead the march himself, but at the last minute was persuaded by aides to stay at his Atlanta headquarters for his safety's sake." The statement shifted the blame from King to his aides, and its placement within the article obscured the controversy; not until two pages further into the text was note taken of the criticism directed at King for "having absented

20. "The Central Point," *Time*, March 19, 1965, pp. 23–24. Baker's intervention prevented several deaths on March 7. Lewis, *King: A Biography*, 275. "Mr. Smitherman Goes to Washington," *Time*, April 16, 1965, p. 26.

21. On King's absence, see Bishop, *The Days of Martin Luther King*, 385; Garrow, *Protest at Selma*, 73; and Fager, *Selma*, 92. On the bitterness that arose after King turned back the march, see Wofford, *Of Kennedys and Kings*, 184. On King's decision to go into seclusion, see Garrow, *Protest at Selma*, 92.

himself from the Sunday march." This arrangement not only reversed the usual journalistic order of charge and response but put an unusually wide gap between the two elements. Turning back the march was cited as an example of the virtues of a peacemaker. King put it this way: " 'Maybe there will be some blood let in the state of Alabama before we get through, but it will be our blood and not the blood of our white brothers.' " Similarly, by turning back the march King had averted a confrontation with the federal government, to which (a graduate student argued this point for *Time*) "the civil rights movement owes its life and accomplishments."[22]

Moving relentlessly, the nation would bring justice to Selma. That Lucean thesis required the transformation of another symbol. Selma was no longer "trying hard" to clear its racist past but was now portrayed as a city where blacks "are supposed to know their place." *Time* came upon the evidence in the form of a "Selma ordinance of 1852 [that] declared that 'any Negro found upon the streets of the city smoking a cigar or pipe or carrying a walking cane must be on conviction punished with thirty-nine lashes'—and the place has not changed much since."[23] Certainly *Time* could have found far more grievous injustices with which to belabor Selma, but none would have served its symbolic purposes as well as the exotica of antebellum racism. By using the ordinance, *Time* made two points. The first was that Selma was clinging to its ancient and peculiar racism—quite likely correct. The second point was that Selma was not America when it came to race and justice. If the spread of the black revolt is any evidence, that was a more questionable proposition among large numbers of black Americans.

Perhaps with those doubters in mind, *Time* sought to prove that the cause in Selma was America's cause, that the cossack-like charge at the Edmund Pettus Bridge trampled not only on the rights of blacks but on American principles. Evidence was provided by the living symbol of the Republic; President Johnson's "strong, yet measured words made it perfectly plain that the day was not far off when all American citizens would be equal in the polling place." Another example, quite as impressive to *Time*, was the martyr Reeb. If blacks had found a martyr in Jimmie Lee Jackson, *Time* had found a

22. "The Central Point," 23, 25, 28.
23. *Ibid.*, 23. The message was reiterated when *Time* published editorial cartoons caricaturing "[Governor] Wallace, Alabama law enforcement officers, and Selma's red-neck hoodlums . . . as fascist bullyboys, Neanderthal dimwits, or lumbering ogres." "Indignation in the North," March 19, 1965, p. 71.

more satisfactory one in Reeb. Luce's magazine could not ignore the missionary fervor that drew Reeb to the dark and brooding South, especially as he was bent upon performing good works in order to perfect America. The irony was missed by *Time* (if not by some in Selma), which reported: The "white racists in their blind ferocity" had created a new martyr whose murder—unlike the death of a humble woodchopper—caused "telegraph wires across the country [to burn] with expressions of outrage."[24]

Newsweek made similar alterations to its stock of symbols. It relished, as much as *Time* did, the symbolic justice meted out by the black confidence man to the former moderate, now the "vehemently segregationist" Smitherman. In the tale unfolded by *Newsweek*, Smitherman was bested by a black man who pursued his quarry with not merely "professional" but "racial pride." *Newsweek* did not bear down so heavily on Jim Clark, but he also was transformed symbolically. Less than two weeks before Bloody Sunday, one of the magazine's columnists described Clark as "almost the ideal patsy," who was "so grossly inept that even some Northern sympathizers with the cause of Negro voting rights have wondered whether he shouldn't be more pitied than blamed." After March 7, demonstrators once depicted as manipulated by the SCLC or as manipulating Clark by goading him, became citizens exercising their fundamental right to protest the denial of another right that "is supposed to be beyond debate: the right to vote." When these Americans attempted to assert their rights, they were met by police "on foot and on horseback, swinging billies, brandishing bullwhips, and chucking tear-gas grenades," and, most memorably, by Clark's "cavalry that mounted a cossack charge into the scattering column." Burlesque laments eliminated, the Selma campaign became a crusade. The term had been used before by *Newsweek* but had hardly squared with the picture of the SCLC goading a buffoon. Now that was past, and Selma's name was "forever linked with those of Little Rock, Oxford, Birmingham—the great battlegrounds of the American Negro revolt."[25]

Most important of all, King was transfigured. After taking backhanded swipes at him for "ostensibly" tending to church business while his followers were trudging toward the Edmund Pettus Bridge and for cutting a "face-

---

24. "The Central Point," 26–27, 28. For public responses to the deaths of Reeb and Jackson, see Fager, *Selma*, 111.

25. "$107 Misunderstanding," *Newsweek*, April 19, 1965, p. 27; Kenneth Crawford, "Right to Vote," *Newsweek*, March 1, 1965, p. 39. Although a columnist, Crawford kept fairly close to the magazine's editorial line. The attack was covered in "An American Tragedy," *Newsweek*, March 22, 1965, pp. 18–20.

saving deal" with federal authorities to turn back the second march, *Newsweek* set out to polish King's image. No longer was King trying to create a crisis. Instead, he escalated "his Selma voter-registration campaign toward the state he calls 'creative tension'—the setting for a paroxysm of segregationist violence that can shock the nation to action."[26] If the words amounted to the same thing, the tone was considerably more savory: "Creative tension" would force the racists to show their true colors, and once that happened, America would rise up in righteous anger.

And of course the nation *had* responded, its righteous anger almost awing *Newsweek*. The demonstrations that had followed Bloody Sunday for "breadth and depth of feeling, for sheer geographical scope, had never been equaled in the history of the civil rights movement." The spirit that drove the demonstrations was a revulsion against those who violated the great principles of the Republic and a willingness to do something to correct injustice. The evidence of this came to *Newsweek* in the form of the response to the call King had sent. Even his strategists, the article reported, were surprised at what happened. "Overnight, some four hundred ministers, priests, rabbis, and lay leaders streamed into town from points as far as California—and they came to march."[27]

They came to march. In so many words, America was on the move to restore vitality to principles violated in an obscure corner of Alabama. *Newsweek* did not trail off into silence there, and what it said marked *Newsweek* as a magazine struggling toward greatness. Its prose was seldom as facile as *Time's*, its editing often ham-fisted, but *Newsweek* more often captured the flow of events that defied easy characterization and demonstrated a willingness, rarely seen in *Time*, to swim against the tide. A case in point: *Newsweek* found the faddishness of "civil rights buffs" troubling; many went to Selma "like the lame to Lourdes." Two pointed questions were raised: Would the clergy challenge racial injustice when they returned home? "Or will the spirit of Selma dissolve in the teacups of a thousand rectories and parish houses across the nation?"[28] *Newsweek* supplied no answers and in a week's time skirted these very questions. But the act of raising such questions set it apart. Where *Time* had drawn a distinct line between Selma and America, *Newsweek* communicated the disturbing message that resolving America's racial prob-

26. "An American Tragedy," 18.
27. *Ibid.*, 20; "Impact and Anger," *Newsweek*, March 22, 1965, p. 21.
28. "Selma, Civil Rights, and the Church Militant," *Newsweek*, March 29, 1965, p. 78.

lems would require far more than the chastisement of Jim Clark. *Newsweek* had performed that rarest of journalistic acts. Questioning the commitment of the liberal-minded church militant, *Newsweek*, after a fashion, had questioned itself.

U.S. News had no questions, but it did have a problem arising out of the brutal attack upon demonstrators exercising one constitutional right in order to secure another. The justice of their cause could not be gainsaid, so the journal chose to emphasize the illegality of a demonstration "banned as a menace to public safety" by Wallace. The demonstrators proceeded "in defiance of the Governor's order"; when ordered to disperse, they refused, instead kneeling in prayer. Thus, the state troopers and Clark's posse, in effect, had to disperse the rabble.[29]

A narrative of unlawful defiance and just retribution put the scenes from Selma in a different light. "When two tense minutes had ticked by," *U.S. News* reported, "the troopers charged, swinging their clubs." The marchers continued their challenge of the forces of law; they "fell back but did not disband." Only then did troopers lay "down a tear-gas barrage" and Clark's possemen "spur their mounts and pursue the marchers, who fled through thick, yellow clouds of gas." The report noted, to be sure, that the "men on horseback swung clubs, whips, and knotted lengths of rope," but it justified such actions with the explanation that "some of the Negroes fought back with rocks, bricks, and bottles."[30]

Selma's "racial explosion" required explanation. *U.S. News* ascribed the problems to a "deliberate strategy by Negro leaders to 'draw blood.'" A Selma businessman sounded the requisite tone of conspiracy. King "'had a master plan to keep agitating here until hell broke loose. He knew that would give him the psychological impact he needed to make nationwide TV drama and stir up a loud outcry all over the country. He wants federal bayonets pointed at our throats, and it looks as though he'll get them.'"[31] No doubt King would have agreed about his need for a crisis to stir the country. Naturally, *U.S. News* added its own twist, preferring the word *agitating* to a phrase such as *creative tension* and making certain readers could hear the sounds of

29. "It Looks Like a 'Hot Summer'—With Selma the Beginning," *U.S. News & World Report*, March 22, 1965, p. 32.
30. *Ibid.*
31. *Ibid.*, 33.

federal bayonets being unsheathed—which fitted the recurring theme of a second Reconstruction.

Quite effectively, the magazine joined two contradictory themes. The first was that there was collusion between King and federal authorities, the second that King was so reckless and radical that he ignored his own allies. Democratic and Republican leaders had pledged that a voting rights bill would be "pushed hard" in Congress. Even this was not enough for King, who refused to stop the demonstrations, saying that "'I would rather die on the highways of Alabama than make a butchery of my own conscience.'" Here were deftly mingled the two contradictory themes. King was practicing a form of political blackmail; should "anything happen to Dr. King," reported an article elsewhere in that issue, there were fears that "major violence would be likely to flare in the country's big cities."[32]

Combining the two themes served another purpose. While *U.S. News* reported, usually in passing, the attempts to register black voters in Selma, that issue was subordinated to Lawrence's longstanding crusades for states' rights and against mob rule. At the end of March, Lawrence described the demonstrations after Bloody Sunday as the handiwork of "the new extremists" to whom the federal government was surrendering the nation's constitutional heritage. King's name did not appear in the column, but there can be no doubt that Lawrence counted him among those extremists and not much doubt that the idea registered with faithful readers. The timing of the column would have ensured by itself that the message got through, but Lawrence provided other clues. One hint was his description of civil rights demonstrations as portents of "mobocracy."[33]

The consequences of "mobocracy" were explored in three articles in the same issue. One article examined the potential political effects of black voting rights, consequences that distressed *U.S. News* because those who stood to gain—liberals, most Democrats, and union leaders—were not counted among its loyal subscribers. More alarming was the magazine's prediction of a second Reconstruction. While it did publish opinions to the effect that black

32. The agreement to halt the second march was cited as further evidence of collusion. *Ibid.* The consequences should harm come to King are mentioned in "Washington Whispers," *U.S. News & World Report*, March 22, 1965, p. 26.

33. David Lawrence, "Bowing to the New Extremists," *U.S. News & World Report*, March 29, 1965, p. 112.

voting would be relatively benign over the long run, *U.S. News* raised the specter of government by ignorant blacks, of ignorant blacks, and for ignorant blacks. An unidentified businessman from Mississippi supplied the quotation underscoring this theme: "'What is to happen here . . . when the Negroes, many of them quite ignorant, vote themselves into command of county affairs?'" The point was reiterated in another article as a lesson taken from history. Standard fare in *U.S. News*, the article painted a dismal picture of Reconstruction governments controlled by "Negroes, 'carpetbaggers'— spoils-seeking Northerners—and 'scalawags'—Southerners supporting the Republicans" that "brought what historians have termed an era of corruption, incompetence, and extravagance."[34] Thus, unions and the national Democratic party could be read as modern-day carpetbaggers out to line their pockets, and moderate southern politicians willing to court black voters could be seen as unprincipled scalawags. Exploiting the black vote, scalawags and carpetbaggers would usher in a new era of corrupt government.

The third article raised fears of black insurrection. Conveniently available, "a Negro in touch with all areas of racial tensions" sounded the alarm. King had opened a Pandora's box because "'the national furor stirred up by events in Selma has given many Negroes the idea that they can force compliance with their demands.'" Bad enough in the South, the situation was far worse elsewhere: "'There are tens of thousands of Negro racists and hotheads in Northern slums who just can't be controlled.'" Grudgingly, *U.S. News* gave King some due; at least in the South, according to that same source, "'Negro demonstrations are planned . . . [and] this gives police a chance for control.'"[35]

U.S. News had to reorder its symbols much less drastically than did *Time* and *Newsweek*, even though Lawrence's magazine trimmed the news from Selma to fit its recurring theme. The radical King had forced a crisis; he was a reckless leader for whom the end justified the means and an extremist whose actions would distort the Constitution. That was far from the last word that *U.S. News* would have about King. Soon enough, the journal would have urgent need of him, not as an exemplar of radicalism, but in a different role.

The culminating drama of the march to Montgomery had been temporarily

---

34. See *U.S. News & World Report*, "What the Negro Vote Will Do to South," March 29, 1965, pp. 30–32, and "When Federal Registrars Were Last Used in South," 33. The message was echoed in the same issue in "Tomorrow," 21.

35. "Climax Near in Negro Revolt," *U.S. News & World Report*, March 29, 1965, pp. 27, 28. Portions of the story were echoed in the same issue in "Tomorrow," 21.

stalled by an injunction issued by a federal judge, so the attention of the news media shifted to Montgomery. In the state capital, SNCC, disaffected in about equal measure with King and conventional liberalism, was organizing black college students and staging a series of demonstrations. On March 15, there were violent clashes between the students and the police, and the following night there was another charge by mounted policemen that caused serious injuries to eight people. SNCC began hurling threats. King hurried over to Montgomery as a peacemaker. While the attack aroused much indignation, it was, in a way, less dramatic than what followed. Mindful of the national furor aroused by Bloody Sunday, the local sheriff apologized for the methods used to disperse the crowd. Before, wrote a civil rights lawyer, "not only would such a concession have been unthinkable, but no Southern official would even have met with militant Negroes. The movement had come a long way."[36]

The movement had indeed come a long way if it could force a concession of that sort from a Black Belt sheriff. The southern movement, as distinct from the black movement, had just under fifty miles to go, the distance from Selma to Montgomery. Injustice would not vanish magically as King strode into Montgomery at the head of a triumphant procession; there would be many more marches, many blows struck, more killed and crippled before segregation was destroyed. Still, Jim Crow's death rattle was unmistakable now, even if racism would survive its passing. Henceforth, the burdens of the black southerner, poverty and neglect in particular, would not differ greatly in kind from those afflicting the blacks in the North and the West. As one of King's aides recalled, before the end of the Selma campaign "life seemingly was very black and very white, [and] good and evil were pretty well established."[37] Thereafter the choices would not be so simple or the way so certain.

On March 17, the way was clear for the march to Montgomery. Federal Judge Frank Johnson lifted his injunction. The final touch was President Johnson's. He maneuvered Wallace into the public admission that the state government would not assume the responsibility of protecting the marchers, thus depriving Wallace of the opportunity to denounce the sending of federal troops into Alabama. Protected by four thousand troops and a contingent of FBI agents, the marchers trudged along the highway to Montgomery for five

36. See Carson, *In Struggle*, 159–60; and Fager, *Selma*, 140–41. Kunstler's observation appears in *Deep in My Heart*, 355.
37. James R. McGraw, "An Interview with Andrew J. Young," *Christianity and Crisis*, January 22, 1968, p. 1.

days. What they set out to do was strictly symbolic; the announced goal, petitioning Wallace for redress of grievances, was quixotic. The demonstration was nonetheless arresting as a symbolic ordering of good and evil. On the last day, King led his tens of thousands on the last three miles to the state capitol.[38] The moment evoked the 1963 March on Washington, in part because King's speech celebrated the nation's rapid and determined response to the brutality of segregation, in part because of another murder.

The martyr, a white volunteer from Michigan, Mrs. Viola Gregg Liuzzo, was driving demonstrators back to Selma after the march ended. Mrs. Liuzzo was shot to death by segregationists firing into her automobile on the highway. An SCLC volunteer with her escaped the same fate by feigning death when the murderers returned to ensure their victims were dead. Arrests were quickly made because an FBI informant was one of the four men in the car from which the shots were fired.[39]

Of the news weeklies, *Newsweek* was the most struck by the march and the martyr. It had to acknowledge the obvious, that "by the hard measure of concessions won" the march to Montgomery "accomplished nothing at all." But *Newsweek* was well aware of the powerful symbolism of King and the drama on Highway 80, and took measures to intensify these elements.

A week after elevating King almost to equal status with Martin Luther, *Newsweek* raised him another notch. King became a biblical prophet, introduced, in fact, by his "apostle [Ralph David] Abernathy to the wayside groups of Negroes as a latter-day Moses chosen by God to lead his people out of the wilderness." The extravagant phrases were Abernathy's, to be sure, but *Newsweek* had already said as much when reporting this scene: "'Walk together, children, don't you get weary,'" the prophet King gently chided his people as the trek began, "'and it will lead you to the promised land.'" Along the way, however, symbolism had to be squared with mundane reality. King found it necessary to leave the march to deliver a speech in Ohio. It was the sort of chore—speech making, fund raising, generally showing the flag—that had clogged his calendar since Montgomery, and such activities never stopped, not even during a major campaign, because money had to be raised and support gathered at the most propitious time. But the scurrying about smacked more of the busy executive than of a new Moses. Not content to

38. Lewis, *King: A Biography*, 286; Fager, *Selma*, 147; Bishop, *The Days of Martin Luther King*, 386.

39. See Garrow, *Protest at Selma*, 116–18; and Lewis, *King: A Biography*, 289–90.

explain King's absence, *Newsweek* deftly converted it into evidence of his "mystical presence"—"a presence as real when he took a day and a half off to keep a speaking date in Cleveland as when he marched at the head of the column. His line officers handled the details; King instead was a living icon, to reassure the marchers that they were making history."[40]

Newsweek thought it necessary to demonstrate, as well, that the marchers were not alone as they made history, that America was with them. A week earlier, the magazine used Johnson's address to Congress to show that the nation was firmly united behind the cause in Selma. Johnson was pressed into service as the chief epistler of the secular religion of the Constitution, proclaiming to believers that "'I speak tonight for the dignity of man and the destiny of democracy.'" *Newsweek* sharpened the symbolism of that declaration by pointing out that as "the first Southern president in a century" Johnson "had ranked the bloodied ground of Selma . . . with Lexington and Concord and Appomattox among the great landmarks of the American quest for freedom."[41]

America was not just with blacks in spirit. There was, as well, the living testament of the Americans following King to Montgomery, to the Promised Land. Outsiders not usually found in the ranks of his foot soldiers, they had heard and answered King's call: "Clerics and nuns, pert coeds and hot-eyed student rebels. VIP's like the U.N.'s Ralph Bunche and anonymous farmhands from the Southwest Alabama cattle, corn, and cotton country. A blind man came from Atlanta, a one-legged man from Saginaw, Michigan. An Episcopal minister from Minneapolis got plane fare from a parishioner and took the gift to be a sign from God that he should make the pilgrimage. And a little Selma Negro girl tagged along 'for freedom and justice and so the troopers can't hit us no more.'"[42] *Newsweek* could have found no more compelling evidence of America on the march than this assemblage. The marchers were not actors, of course, but they were cast as carefully as any Hollywood war movie with the obligatory Texan, the kid from Brooklyn, and the all-American farm boy from the Midwest. In the panorama of a great social drama unwinding before it, *Newsweek* found no equivalent of the

40. "Selma, Civil Rights, and the Church Militant," 78; "Road From Selma: Hope—and Death," *Newsweek*, April 5, 1965, pp. 23, 25.

41. "The Starry Heavens—The Moral Law," *Newsweek*, March 29, 1965, p. 19. *Newsweek* also linked the campaign in Selma to the women's suffrage movement. "Where Are They Now?" March 29, 1965, p. 14.

42. "Road From Selma: Hope—and Death," 25.

clergy who went to Selma as the lame go to Lourdes and whose passion for
social justice, so it fretted a week earlier, might dissolve in the teacups passed
around middle-class parish houses.

One character cast by events was Mrs. Liuzzo, the Detroit housewife
murdered by a "night-riding lynch party." *Newsweek* had located its martyr.
To be sure, Mrs. Liuzzo had been savagely murdered, but that was only one
aspect of her martyrdom. She embodied a spirit that *Newsweek* distilled as the
essence of the march, the ordinary American who *had* to go—as indeed was
recollected by the husband she left behind. "'She asked me to understand,'
Liuzzo recalled last week. 'I tried to discourage her, but she said, "No, we've
got to go." I guess I had a premonition of trouble.'" The sense of sacrifice
gained further intensity from the poignant innocence of her young daughter's
question: "'Why couldn't Mommy have just died from being old?'"[43]

Despite the blood let, the tears shed, despite, even, the terrible questions of
a child, democracy's job remained to be done—so *Newsweek* reminded its
readers. If there were victories in hand, the "protest marchers would not stop";
no matter that the leaders of The Movement (the magazine's capitalization)
were unsure where to take it, "there was too much unfinished business—and,
after Selma, too much momentum—to stop. Not all the marches would be
wise or well-disciplined. But the march—and the outraged reaction to Viola
Liuzzo's death on the road from Selma—made plainer than ever the nation's
expanding commitment to the right of oppressed people to protest their lot."[44]
Thus King was not alone in exhorting his flock not to become weary. *Newsweek* was doing as much for the coalition that had made the civil rights cause
its own and that was now coming apart rapidly. The kind of national commitment cited by *Newsweek* did not happen as a matter of course. It had to be
stirred to reach live coals, as King did when he set his crisis in motion in
Selma. Whether the commitment was expanding, indeed whether it would
endure, would be determined by circumstances lacking the stark symbolism
of the march from Selma to Montgomery. Of the response, judging from self-
doubts one week and exhortations the next, *Newsweek* was by no means
confident, not even when employing a symbol as compelling as the messianic
Martin Luther King.

No such *angst* unsettled Luce's magazine. *Time* reconstituted the world

43. *Ibid.*, 23, 26.
44. *Ibid.*, 27.

once a week for readers in need of assurance that they learned not only the news but its meaning as well. The significance in this instance was national power and purpose.

Power and purpose had always fascinated Henry Luce. For a time he had even planned to christen his new business magazine "Power," but that was too naked, and he settled on *Fortune*.[45] But it was not simply the acquisition of power that moved Luce and, having moved Luce, moved his magazines. Rather, Luce had a will to use power in a manner that would satisfy the missionary in him. No better example of this could be found than in *Time*'s coverage of the week that encompassed the march.

Where *Newsweek* celebrated an outpouring of idealism, *Time* found initially little more than a mob of "marchers, marchers everywhere—and [only] a few who stopped to think." A strange lot, "bearded boys, girls in boots, and a surprising assortment of clergymen," they seemed all the more unsavory because many had heeded the call of the militant SNCC and because they were willing "to demonstrate anywhere, any time." The SCLC (thus King) fared little better. Through "Selma's patient Public Safety Director Wilson Baker," the SCLC was disparaged as the "Southern Stupid Leadership Conference" for staging demonstrations to keep up the spirits of touring civil rights buffs. All of this—not excepting the march itself—was a sideshow; "far more important were the sparks generated . . . in Washington—where last week the president of the U.S. demonstrated before Congress, as few others ever have, how a functioning democracy can meet its obligations."[46]

The time had come, *Time* declared, to assure "all American Negroes the right to vote." How this task was to be accomplished was another matter— certainly not by an odd-lot of bearded boys and booted girls. Wrongs would be set right, but with reason and order. Thus, *Time* invoked the rituals of the Republic. There were, for example, the trappings of a presidential address to the Congress, "old hat by now to many Americans, and yet insistently thrilling." Almost reverently, *Time* reported that the symbol in whose person national power and purpose were joined, President Johnson, spoke in a "cathedral-like hush," pricking "his country's conscience, uttering the unutterable."[47] This was the teleological vision that commanded the loyalties of Henry Luce, of America moved closer to her natural state of perfection by

45. Swanberg, *Luce and His Empire*, 82.
46. "Electric Charges," *Time*, March 26, 1965, pp. 19–20.
47. "'A Meeting of History and Fate,'" *Time*, March 26, 1965, pp. 20, 21.

men of good will and power, not by a sweating mob treading some dusty wayside.

The theme of confluent power and purpose was carried over into *Time*'s coverage of the Montgomery march. Now, however, its disdain for the mob was sharpened and transferred to the segregationists harrying the marchers. With its usual attention to telling details, *Time* listed the harassments: a man with one leg being cruelly heckled by whites; bitter Alabamians "yelping" obscenities like dogs from the safety of passing cars; a nun trudging grimly along under taunts questioning her chastity; the farcical indignity of the Alabama legislature gravely resolving that there was much evidence of fornication during the five days spent marching and camping along Highway 80. There was as well the atrocity, the murder of Mrs. Liuzzo by "the white racists of Alabama, [who] in characteristic fashion, shattered" the peace. Again, men of power and purpose would set matters right; in fact, they had already done so: "This act of moronic savagery once again outraged the national conscience" and "provoked the president of the United States into a nationwide television outburst, in which he announced the arrest of four Ku Klux Klansmen and demanded that Congress curb the Klan."[48]

Time accorded relatively little symbolic status to Mrs. Liuzzo, who became no more than an unlucky victim of segregationist savagery, and not a great deal more to King. He was "eloquent," but far from the messianic character of *Newsweek*. *Time*'s prophet, one seemingly sprung to life out of the Old Testament, was President Johnson. In *Time*'s juxtaposition, Governor Wallace peeked warily at the swelling crowd of marchers and attempted to excuse the inexcusable, the murder of Mrs. Liuzzo; the president promised stern retribution: "'Justice must be done, in the largest city as well as the smallest village, on the dirt road or on the interstate highway. We will not be intimidated by the terrorists of the Ku Klux Klan any more than we will be intimidated by the terrorists in North Vietnam.'"[49] Here *Time* found not merely fine words, as in the eloquence of King, but justice, swift and sure.

So far as it went, *Time* was not incorrect. In time, the long arm of the national government would reach into Selma, and the other Selmas, to ensure that blacks were not turned away from their rightful place in democratic elections. Although not always successfully, Klansmen would be brought to

48. "Protest on Route 80," *Time*, April 2, 1965, p. 21.
49. *Ibid.*, 22.

the bar of justice to answer for crimes against the peace and dignity of the people of Alabama, this also under federal authority when the state government shirked its duty to enforce its laws. Content with its symbols of good and evil, *Time* was ill-prepared to entertain another question. Would the symbolic chastisement of Jim Clark and George Wallace quiet the impatient voices in black America? By summer's end, *Time* would be shaken by the fury of those voices, raised in the first of the great urban explosions of the 1960s, in Watts.

A curious reversal marked the reports of *U.S. News* about the Selma march and related events. There was no change in the adamant opposition to the proposed voting rights law. On the other hand, there was the odd case of King—"arrogant and foolhardy," according to "some Negro leaders." There was more: "Some of his campaigns have failed, and brought Dr. King's strategy and administrative talents under fire." And finally, "It has been charged that he stirs up new racial trouble in the South whenever the SCLC needs funds, or when his image as the leading voice of the Southern Negro protest seems to be slipping."[50] The accusations were not new. As now used, however, they amounted to praising King by publishing fainter damns. On the whole, the article was complimentary rather than critical, the reason being evident in a more extensive story in the same issue that reported the emergence of "serious threats" to King's standing in the civil rights movement.

At another time, from another quarter, *U.S. News* would have welcomed a challenger to King. But for now, the magazine needed King; the disaffected members of SNCC appeared to be the greater threat. An impassioned speech by SNCC's director James Forman set in motion the reevaluation. Forman was angered by the cavalry charge into the demonstration in Montgomery. His anger was turned, however, against "crooks in the White House, . . . crooks in the Senate [and] . . . crooks in the House," and if those cited didn't do something, Forman threatened, "we're going up there to Washington, and we're going to stop traffic; we're going to stop every car, every truck; we're going to show them the biggest piece of civil disobedience the world has ever seen." Words of that tenor had even more impact because of the magazine's exquisite sensitivity to racial problems in Washington. Thus, it hastened to point out the moderate virtues of King, a move that explains the question concluding the article: "As Negroes press for further gains, who will lead

50. See *U.S. News & World Report*, "If Voting is the Problem—A Look Outside the South," 39, "An Immoral Law," 116, and "Martin Luther King: Who He Is . . . What He Believes," 18, all in the April 5, 1965, issue.

them—'moderates,' such as Dr. King, or those who threaten 'the biggest piece of civil disobedience the world has ever seen'?"[51]

Even more striking was the disposition of accusations against SNCC and the SCLC. SNCC was accused of deliberately trying to bring about a confrontation with police that would result in injury or death to white students; the SCLC, of turning a blind eye to sexual orgies during the march to Montgomery and of tolerating Communists who masterminded the demonstration. Rather transparently, *U.S. News* turned the accusations against SNCC rather than King, but that tack required the journal to ignore the practice of gauging newsworthiness in terms of prominence. The complaints about SNCC came from an obscure university chaplain who lacked the news value of King's accuser, not to mention that of King himself. Prominence was less important than was the opportunity to discredit the militants of SNCC, described by the clergyman as coldly calculating agitators who "'wanted dead bodies—our bodies.'"[52]

In sum, King, who created racial crises and was undermining the foundations of the Republic, was anointed as a "moderate" by *U.S. News*. It was a wondrous change, but *U.S. News* had managed the trick before and would do so again. Transformations by *Time* and *Newsweek* were no less rapid and not appreciably less dramatic. Their early finding that the true moderates were Selma's city fathers, caught between the relentless King and the violent buffoon Clark, was made untenable by Bloody Sunday. The two magazines hastily shifted to a new theme: America, outraged by the brutality in Selma, was determined to end the injustice of segregation. *Time* and *Newsweek* had to bring their symbols in line with the theme, matching them to audience expectations of good and evil. With one exception, the players in Selma were reordered symbolically. Above all, a new King emerged: in *Time*, as an eloquent spokesman for American ideals, even if overshadowed by President Johnson; in *Newsweek*, as a new Moses of such mystical power that his spirit hovered about the line of march when he tended to mundane business elsewhere.

51. "After Alabama . . . Negroes Next Battlegrounds," *U.S. News & World Report*, April 5, 1965, p. 38. *Newsweek* contraposed Forman as firebrand against King as peacemaker in "On to Montgomery," March 29, 1965, p. 22.

52. "Now, Charges of Orgies on Rights March," *U.S. News & World Report*, April 12, 1965, p. 11.

Henceforth, King would absent himself from the South more and more on business anything but mundane. With Jim Crow dying, he began taking up issues of race and poverty and the war in Vietnam. His Selma campaign symbolically reaffirmed his country and its determination to live up to its great ideals. In the future, King's undertakings would not be so unchallenging.

VI

A PROPHET NEW INSPIRED

Selma, the last great southern campaign, liberated King to take up two causes that had beckoned him for years. The first was to make nonviolence into a force for international peace. As early as 1959, King wrote that Gandhian principles would have to be extended to resolve power struggles among nations. Over the years, he followed up with statements registering dismay with the arms race and the growing arsenal of nuclear weapons. For the most part, however, his energies went into the civil rights struggle until the Nobel Peace Prize began to thrust upon him a sense of mission on the world stage. The second cause, poverty among black Americans, had concerned King as far back as the Montgomery bus boycott. Following the examples of a similar venture in Philadelphia and black boycotts of the 1920s and 1930s, the SCLC inaugurated Operation Breadbasket in Atlanta in 1962. The results (in five years the SCLC claimed the project had secured five thousand new jobs for blacks) were pitifully small measured against the need. King realized as much, and he proposed to the Democratic party in 1964 an economic bill of rights that would have required spending billions of dollars to relieve the misery of the poor.[1]

1. On King's early musings about nonviolence and international tensions, see Lewis, *King: A Biography*, 412. The impact of the Nobel Prize is described *ibid.*, 260. Gary Massoni, "Perspectives on Operation Breadbasket" (M.Div. thesis, Chicago Theological Seminary, 1971), 3–4. The proposal for an economic bill of rights is in *SCLC Newsletter*, July-August, 1964, p. 3.

If a sense of urgency was pushing King toward these causes, a sense of caution infected the SCLC board of directors, which gave his ideas a cool reception in 1965.[2] His belief that the principles of nonviolence ought to rule in international affairs, not especially controversial in itself, appeared in a different light after the escalation of the war in Vietnam. Stung by Viet Cong attacks on American outposts in South Vietnam and worried about the stability of the American-supported regime in Saigon, President Johnson began to Americanize the war with bombing raids, and in March the first contingent of American combat troops, 3,200 Marines, was ordered ashore. By June, more than 75,000 American troops were stationed in Vietnam. Speaking against the war would mean risking the displeasure of the Johnson administration, which had supported the southern campaigns, and would provide ammunition to those who stood ready to proclaim that King was giving aid and comfort to his country's enemies.

The situation was no more promising for shifting the movement from the South to the rest of the nation and changing the focus from segregation to poverty. King's concern for the poor might be taken merely as a sense of pastoral obligation writ large. It was not this simple. Almost from the beginning in Montgomery, King had believed that the poor needed to ally themselves along class lines, and he had not swerved greatly from the notion that some synthesis of Marxist thought and capitalist practice was the proper path to follow. In 1964, a journalist with close ties to King wrote that a class-oriented movement was the next direction the SCLC would take. "The practical necessity for an alliance exists on the white as well as the Negro side of the fence," Anne Braden wrote. The question was "how to convince enough whites that this is so." King subscribed to this view. In May of 1965, he preached that the plight of the American black was related to "what he called the world-wide class struggle." A similar point, couched in neo-Populist terms, was made in King's speech following the march from Selma. He called for demonstrations against segregated housing and schools and discriminatory voter registration, and spoke of the necessity of curing the problems of poverty. Standing in the Cradle of the Confederacy, King gave due attention to that symbol of segregation, Governor George Wallace. But King added this: Demonstration after demonstration should be conducted until "the Wallaces of our nation tremble away in silence."[3]

2. Lewis, *King: A Biography*, 295–96.
3. For the early economic thoughts of King, see *Stride Toward Freedom*, 94–95, 202–205.

Even if King had been making the point since Birmingham, it was still a sticky one indeed—the Wallaces of America, not only the South. Certainly there was work to be done outside the South. Blacks who already had access to the ballot and public accommodations were bent under other burdens: their schools often as segregated as any in the South; their housing, because of a quirk of Jim Crow, even more segregated; their livelihoods the urban equivalents of hewing wood and drawing water when they had work at all, being unemployed in greater numbers than whites. These were not the sort of grievances (unlike scenes of horsemen charging into ranks of orderly marchers) around which Americans, predisposed against claims of group or class disadvantages, would easily rally. Starting up campaigns outside the South would entail some risks. White backlash against the black movement could not be discounted as a possibility, even though that reaction had not materialized as a significant political effect in the 1964 presidential election. A campaign led by King in the North might push backlash to the surface again. Associated with this risk was another. The charismatic King would be able to enlist blacks in militant campaigns outside his native region, but there was no guarantee that the protests would remain nonviolent, given the occasions when the discipline slipped in Albany and Birmingham and the volatility of ghettos North and West.

The two courses King proposed to follow after Selma constituted a bigger gamble than he took in Birmingham. King was determined to press on, but judging from his shock at the criticism that would be heaped upon him, he was not as prepared for the trials that awaited him as a prophet new inspired.

The news magazines were required to make some marked editorial adjustments while covering King after the conclusion of the Selma campaign. A week after exalting King as a new Moses, *Newsweek*, for example, was confronted by his proposal (motivated by the murder of Mrs. Liuzzo) for an economic boycott of Alabama. King was promptly demoted from messianic leader to politician, who "floated a trial-balloon proposal" for the boycott, and advertising tout, who ran his "Alabama boycott proposal up the flagpole." But "not many people saluted," and the trial balloon was "promptly peppered by friends and foes alike." While accurate, the report contained a distinct chilli-

---

The SCLC's future direction was predicted by Anne Braden in *SCLC Newsletter*, October-November, 1964, p. 10. The class orientation of King's speeches in Alabama is cited by Bishop, *The Days of Martin Luther King*, 402. A copy of King's speech in Montgomery on March 25 is in Box 27, File 54, King Center Archives, Atlanta.

ness of tone, especially when measured against the effusiveness of the week before. A good part of the coolness could be ascribed to the fact that King was looking for new crises. "The big parade," as the magazine now described the epic march to Montgomery, was a tough act to follow, and the "SCLC's master strategy" was to venture out of the South. King promised to show up in a number of major cities. "'Selma . . . isn't right—but Baltimore isn't right either,'" he said, "'and New York City isn't right.'" However much *Newsweek* agreed with that sentiment, the magazine found the prospect of King "circuit-riding into the tindery black ghettos of the North" unsettling.[4]

Nevertheless, *Newsweek* stood ready to defend King, particularly when his enemies were at either extreme. From the right, "Dixie segregationists" were repeating the shopworn canard that Communists controlled King. Attacking him from the far left was the Mississippi Freedom Democratic party, which had aroused the magazine's enmity at the 1964 Democratic National Convention. Black moderates reported that "Fannie Lou Hamer, the Freedom Democrats' leading mouthpiece, is showing disturbing demagogic tendencies—attacking middle-class Negroes and whites, American policy in Vietnam, and Martin Luther King." *Newsweek* thus invited readers to take the measure of King by the enemies he made, segregationists and demagogic mouthpieces. By citing such attacks, *Newsweek* also could dispel anxiety about Communists in the civil rights movement that was appearing among staunch friends of the black cause, "some of them graying veterans of the traumatic wars with the Communists a generation ago." The left-of-center *Newsweek* had to heed those voices and reassure those anxious liberals. The story acknowledged that an occasional whisper was being heard from "government investigators . . . about one or another Communist ideologue supposedly close to King." However, the magazine added, "as one savvy Washington liberal said last week, 'As far as I can see, King faced up to his Communist problem and solved it.'" These references indicated that *Newsweek* had gotten more than a whiff of the FBI's campaign to destroy King and was underplaying it. Neither King nor the civil rights movement stood to benefit from a revelation that Hoover was still wrathy about King.[5]

4. "Summer Strategy," *Newsweek*, April 12, 1965, pp. 28, 29. *Time*'s milder response was that King failed to recognize a boycott might hurt the innocent as well as the guilty. "The Continuing Confrontation," April 9, 1965, pp. 24–25.

5. "Waving the Red Flag," *Newsweek*, April 12, 1965, pp. 30–31. In late 1964 and early 1965, the FBI approached a "substantial number of newsmen" with offers of material damaging

While smoothing away its subscribers' concern about King, *Newsweek* concluded that "the anxiety is less easy to dismiss" when it came to SNCC. SNCC's movement toward radicalism was being noted by liberals, and *Newsweek* was echoing what they were saying in other forums when it provided a catalog of SNCC's sins: an intensifying antipathy for the war, the stacks of Communist literature displayed in its offices, the retention of the leftist National Lawyers Guild to provide legal services. At this point, *Newsweek* spoke to, and on behalf of, liberals who bore the scars of internecine struggles with Communists. King had faced up to his Communist problem, it said, and bluntly, if indirectly, advised SNCC to follow his example and that of organizations that had to eject Communists "or take the bitter consequences."[6]

An attack from another quarter that spring was more difficult to counter. Former president Harry Truman delivered remarks critical of King. "'A troublemaker,' snorted Harry." Then Truman called "the Nobel Prize-winning Negro leader a 'rabble-rouser' who acted 'like a damn fool.' The march on Montgomery? All it did, snapped Truman, was disturb the peace."[7]

This was a tangled problem for *Newsweek*. Truman's standing as a symbol equaled or exceeded King's; moreover, he was a living part of the heritage of the Democratic party. Like other former presidents, however, Truman lived in the nether world of those who had passed from power to powerlessness, lingering beyond their time; that fact provided the way out of the dilemma. All of this talk of trouble making and rabble rousing, *Newsweek* said soothingly, and in so many words, was just what one had to expect. Harry simply was out of touch, as was demonstrated by the fact that Chief Justice Harlan Fiske Stone, who swore Truman in as president, was dead—"and so are so many others in the yellowing photograph of the swearing-in." But Truman lived on, informing his listeners softly, "'You don't know how difficult it is to be present at your own funeral and still be able to walk around.'" The same problem, if less intense, confronted *Time*, which met it by blaming the fuss on television newsmen who milked Truman "for every jaunty, testy word." Besides, *Time* observed with a sniff, Truman's remarks weren't even news.

---

to King and was "extremely disappointed and surprised" that none of it had surfaced in the press. Garrow, *The FBI and King*, 169–70.

6. "Waving the Red Flag," 30–31. On the estrangement of liberals and SNCC, see Viorst, *Fire in the Streets*, 251–52, 269–70.

7. "Chip Off the Chippendale," *Newsweek*, April 26, 1965, pp. 28–29.

He "has said the same sort of thing many times before. But either the reporters had not read their newspapers or they wanted to goad him on."[8]

No such subtlety was necessary when *Time* and *Newsweek* blunted attempts by southerners in Congress determined to destroy the Montgomery march's image as a crusade and King's image as a moral crusader. The politicians' campaign was part of a larger movement in the South. The direction of the campaign appeared in a polemic, published with the cooperation of state authorities in Alabama, that breathlessly advised: "The public will gaze upon never before published photographs which substantiate reports of the debauchery and indecency" during the march. Neither magazine was impressed by the evidence offered by a Republican representative from Alabama, William L. Dickinson, to back up his claim that the march was a "drunken debauch." They pointed out that Dickinson spoke from the sanctuary of the House of Representatives, thus claiming congressional immunity to lawsuits for slander; both quoted testimony from unfriendly witnesses, such as the southern editor who snooped around and found "'the orgy stories were invented 'to cover up the basic fact that people cannot vote in Selma'"; and both ridiculed the reports of debauchery, *Newsweek* by appealing to common sense ("one SNCC official scoffed: 'Baby, everyone was too tired from all that marching'") and *Time* by quipping that a purported black witness to the sins of the flesh was a "veritable Uncle Peeping Tom."[9]

Rather more interesting than the question of whether there was debauchery was why it should matter, especially since *Newsweek* conceded that perhaps there was some sexual activity, and *Time* that "there was bound to be some hanky-panky." The answer was that the march, far more than the Selma campaign itself, became a symbolic event in which the nation had joined. That Dickinson would attempt to divert attention from oppression to orgies was as predictable as *Newsweek*'s dismissal of the photographs he offered as so tame that even a nun could—and did—view them without blushing. Middle-class readers wanted their crusades pristine; not for them the jaded shrug of, say, Frenchmen hearing that the archbishop of Paris had died in the

---

8. *Ibid.*, 29; "On the Avenue," *Time*, April 23, 1965, p. 73.
9. Bud Gordon, *Nightriders: The Inside Story of the Liuzzo Killing* (Birmingham, Ala., 1966), 3; "Kiss and Tell," *Newsweek*, May 10, 1965, p. 40. *Time* dismissed Dickinson with this observation: "Last week he splashed mud all over the House floor. But only Dickinson got dirty." "Mud in the House," May 7, 1965, p. 27.

arms of a mistress. It was one thing to leer. (*Time* and *Newsweek* did it often enough. The latter suggested, for example, that Selma's mayor was searching for a prostitute when he was gulled by the black con man, and two years hence *Time* would poke among the flotsam of an anti-war demonstration and find " 'nothing but bras and panties.' ")[10] It was quite another matter to besmirch the high idealism of those Americans marching from Selma to Montgomery in a crusade for freedom.

U.S. *News* did not share this regard for the march or the man who led it, despite the magazine's brief promotion of King as a moderate. U.S. *News* restarted its echo chamber within two weeks by reviving the dispute between Hoover and King. Apparently, "some Negro leaders"—by implication, King—wanted federal intervention that would create a police state in the South. Opposing them, the Horatio-like Hoover "again has made it clear that the Bureau he has run for more than forty years will not be involved in any action smacking of 'totalitarian tactics.' " The tocsin was sounded again the next week. A broadside against civil disobedience by David Lawrence complained of clergymen who "insisted that they are morally right as they urge disobedience whenever a citizen feels a law is 'unjust.' " Then Lawrence asked rhetorically, "Is a pastor right in encouraging anyone to disobey the laws of the land because of some alleged 'higher duty'?"[11] Even though King was not cited by name, his association with civil disobedience and the tide of publicity inundating the Selma campaign would have made it difficult not to have read King into Lawrence's words.

The theme of King as a radical threat was reiterated dramatically in the issue of May 10. One story echoed the idea that King was determined to establish a totalitarian state. A conspiratorial tone was sounded in reporting Dickinson's allegations that King and federal authorities hatched a plot to invade Selma. Federal officials knew in 1963 that a "civil rights riot 'of unheard-of proportions' was to take place in Selma," Dickinson complained. He added an extra twist: " 'It might make my story a little more believable . . . if you remember that a part of the high-level planning that went into the Bay of Pigs invasion (of Cuba) was also assisting in the Selma invasion.' " No real rebuttal was permitted to the implication that federal plotters had caused the

---

10. "$107 Misunderstanding," 27; "The Morning After," *Time*, November 3, 1967, p. 17.
11. "National Police Force? 'No,' Says FBI Chief Hoover," U.S. *News & World Report*, April 12, 1965, p. 20; David Lawrence, "Is the Clergyman Changing His Role?" U.S. *News & World Report*, April 19, 1965, p. 116.

failure of one invasion designed to destroy a Communist regime and fostered another invasion that could impose tyranny on the South. Instead, *U.S. News* supplied some supporting evidence: A Justice Department official had been forced to resign "after disclosure that he had provided transportation" for King "in a car rented at Government expense."[12]

In another article, Dickinson recited again his allegations of orgies during the march, accused "several civil rights leaders of links with Communists or 'Communist front' groups," and complained that he was not allowed access to the FBI's files on King. (Possibly he had been denied that access—though the FBI was freely passing around reports designed to discredit King in Washington.) But Dickinson's complaint supported the thesis that Hoover was a champion of individual rights because he kept King's file confidential. In any event, *U.S. News* made Dickinson's point for him; the juxtaposition of his two statements implied that King was a Communist or consorted with Communists. About this matter *U.S. News* permitted no debate in its pages. Its readers were advised to look elsewhere, specifically on "pages 8307 to 8321 of the *Congressional Record* for April 27." Nor was King permitted to answer the charges of immorality during the march as he had been given the chance to do when *U.S. News* promoted him as a moderate. Instead, persons lacking his prominence—unidentified clergymen, for the most part—were lined up to offer responses. The seeming objectivity was a guise. The principal respondent actually supported, albeit indirectly, the allegations of debauchery with this comment: "'He [Dickinson] is forever crying, "I have proof." But he has no proof.'"[13]

King's value as a symbol often rose because of the enemies he made, particularly when he staked out the crucial middle ground. When King attempted, in 1965, to serve as a peacemaker in the Vietnam War, he made plenty of enemies, but they helped his image not at all. Indeed, King encountered stiff resistance in his own camp. His board of directors instructed him in April that he could not make statements about the war in his capacity as president of the SCLC. The SCLC's national convention proved to be more generous in August, authorizing King to turn the SCLC's full attention to

12. Dickinson claimed that the Selma campaign was scheduled to begin in 1963 but was postponed because of the Kennedy assassination. "How the Army Got Set to Move into Selma," *U.S. News & World Report*, May 10, 1965, pp. 16, 17.

13. "What Really Happened on Alabama March?" *U.S. News & World Report*, May 10, 1965, p. 17.

Vietnam and world affairs if he believed the international situation justified this. By then, King was already sailing those troubled waters, though measured against his position two years later, what he said in 1965 about the war was rather mild. Basically, he argued that the American bombing should be halted, that all parties should go to the conference table, and that the Chinese and North Vietnamese should give a signal that they would soften their demand for unilateral withdrawal of American military forces.[14]

Moderate or no, his statements caused a storm—in the Johnson administration, in the black movement, and in the news media. President Johnson treated King with evident coolness at the signing of the Voting Rights Act in August, but persuaded King to meet with the U.S. ambassador to the United Nations, Arthur Goldberg, for a briefing on the diplomatic efforts to bring peace to Vietnam. Goldberg assured King that the Johnson administration was resolved to reach a negotiated settlement, and that one, indeed, was imminent. Most civil rights leaders believed King's actions to be unwise, and some said so publicly. His chief financial adviser warned King that the adverse reaction could shut down the flow of contributions and force the SCLC into bankruptcy. The criticism was particularly intense in the news media. His press secretary recalled that King was "just bombarded with criticism, both in the Negro press and the white press, . . . and it upset him very much." With the pressure building, King wavered, then backed away. Although he continued to deplore the war, he picked his way carefully. His caution was apparent during a visit to Paris in October, where he encountered an intense debate about the American war in the former French colony. King conducted himself, reported the Paris press, with " 'extreme discretion.' "[15]

So far as the American news magazines were concerned, King should have used discretion earlier and kept silent. Their reaction was due in part to their support of the war, in part to the belief that black leaders had no business speaking about such matters. The latter attitude appeared when *Time* reported

14. On King and the SCLC board, see Lewis, *King: A Biography*, 296. *Cf. Southern Courier*, July 30, 1965, p. 2. King outlined his position on the war in a speech to the SCLC convention in Birmingham on August 12, 1965, copy in Box 28, File 7, King Center Archives, Atlanta.
15. On the criticism of King, see Lewis, *King: A Biography*, 304. On the Johnson administration's response, see *ibid.*, 305–307; and Wofford, *Of Kennedys and Kings*, 221. The press criticism is cited in an interview with Thomas E. Offenburger, director of information for the SCLC, by Katherine Shannon, July 2, 1968 (Transcript of tape 227, in Moorland-Spingarn Research Center, Howard University), 56–57. On King's circumspection in Paris, see "Dr. King and the Paris Press," *America*, November 13, 1965, p. 560.

speeches delivered by King in New York and Boston even before he publicly took up the war issue. The prevailing tone was established in the opening statement that "things being rather quiet in the South, . . . King marched in the North," and reappeared in the summary. King "allowed as how he didn't mind having fellow civil rights leaders speak out against the U.S.'s try-to-win policy in Vietnam, spoke up against, of all things, nuclear bomb testing—an issue that, if he had read a newspaper since the test ban treaty was signed on August 5, 1963, he should have known to be passé. Said King: 'One cannot be just concerned with civil rights. What good does it do me to integrate a lunch counter if the milk I drink there is loaded with strontium 90?'" From that report emerged a picture of a drawling bumpkin, so ignorant that he had not read a newspaper in years, who had wandered out of his native haunts and away from his natural calling because things were quiet for the moment. Lest King's credentials detract from the theme, *Time* stripped him of his Nobel Peace Prize and his doctorate from Boston University.[16]

When King actually spoke directly to the war issue, *Time* was less condescending but no less fixed in its opinion. Uncharacteristically, the news weekly seemed to be striving in July for a balance of perspectives about the question whether civil rights organizations should "tend merely to their own cause" or take positions on issues "such as U.S. foreign policy?" While dutifully reporting the positions of King, James Farmer of CORE, and Roy Wilkins of the NAACP, *Time* again stripped King of his Nobel Prize and favored the position of Wilkins, who provided the crisp ending prized by news magazines: "'I don't believe civil rights groups have enough information on Vietnam . . . to make it their cause. I don't think you can run a country with 196 million Secretaries of State.'" Characteristically, *Time*'s wrath, denied unhindered outlet in one direction, burst forth in another. A different story in the same issue recorded the indictment of a black leader in Selma on a charge of embezzlement. *Time* went out of its way to establish the consanguinity of King and the accused man: "Throughout the civil rights struggle in Selma, . . . and on the march to Montgomery, there at Martin Luther King's side was the Reverend Frederick D. Reese." *Time* also seemed to find a parallel between what King's SCLC colleagues were saying in Selma and King's statements about the war. In both cases, the real issue was being clouded with

16. "King Moves North," *Time*, April 30, 1965, p. 32. The Nobel Prize was pertinent because of the war issue, the doctorate because King was speaking in Boston. According to *Time*, King "attended" Boston University for four years.

emotionalism. One example was provided by Ralph Abernathy, whom King sent to deal with the situation in Selma. Abernathy insisted "with more emotion than legal merit . . . that what Reese did with [the] funds was 'none of the business of the Dallas County grand jury.'" Another example was the defendant who "outdid Abernathy in his emotional approach" by arguing that the charges were the result of a plot by whites. Significantly, much of the sting of *Time*'s previous characterization of Selma was missing. Mayor Smitherman, for example, became simply the mayor rather than the segregationist rube of "Mr. Smitherman Goes to Washington."[17]

As a prophet of peace, King posed a more complex problem for *Newsweek*, which was no less hawkish than Luce's journal and about as unswerving in the belief that King should stick to his own affairs. Still, he was a particularly important symbol to the coalition of conscience, as *Newsweek* liked to style it, that formed around the civil rights movement. But the alliance was cracking, and King's entry into the war issue was one of the lines of fissure. Naturally, he could not be let off the hook altogether. As presented by *Newsweek*, he was opportunistic and meddling. King was, in fact, in about the same position on the war as was SNCC; both had been "making capital in the peace-minded student generation—King by talking up a pacificist storm and SNCC by co-sponsoring an April peace march on Washington." That said, the journal hastened to put as much distance as possible between King and the war and between King and SNCC. King's position on the war did not differ substantially from President Johnson's, *Newsweek* maintained, and in any event King's statement was just talk, nothing more. King was mindful, readers were reassured, of the danger of expending "the moral capital built up by The Movement on the single, black-and-white issue of civil rights." In contrast to the pragmatic King, the hotheads of SNCC habitually rushed into "controversies in which they are long on passion and short on expertise."[18] King could be counted on—and SNCC could not—to act sensibly, to follow the middle way, and to refuse to strike a bargain with the "peaceniks," a word coined by *Newsweek* to stigmatize the anti-war element.

Actually, SNCC was—aside from CORE—about the only black organization not heaping coals on King's head for taking up the war as an issue. If it

17. "Confusing the Cause," and "Various Forms of Embezzlement," both in *Time*, July 16, 1965, p. 20. The embezzlement story also supported the thesis that King ought to mind his own business rather than meddle in matters not his concern. Developing that thesis indirectly was "The Benevolent Dictator," *Time*, September 3, 1965, p. 71, which reported the troubles befalling "a top deputy" of King.

18. "One War at a Time," *Newsweek*, July 19, 1965, pp. 22, 25.

was embarrassing to find King venturing into the "briar patch of foreign affairs," it was disturbing to find him lining up with the radicals of SNCC. *Newsweek*'s suspicions about SNCC deepened almost issue by issue. In late May, for example, came the warning that too long had "complacent liberals" comforted themselves "with the illusion that the bearded, blue-jeaned young cadres of SNCC were sort of a domestic Peace Corps helping the most down-trodden of Southern Negroes into the mainstream of American life. . . . SNCC's real aim is anything but that"; its cadres were preaching revolution, not reform. *Newsweek*'s hope that "time and the miraculous potential of America will blunt the harsh, alien edge of the New Left and make its radicals genuinely effective operatives within the traditional American consensus" was growing fainter. With its surer feel for the currents in the black movement and its exquisite sensitivity to the ideological disputes then raging between radicals and liberals, *Newsweek* was accurately charting the leftward move-ment of SNCC while *Time* was missing or ignoring the uncomfortable specta-cle of disillusioned idealists mocking their country's ideals as hollow.[19]

It became necessary to coin new terms of approbation for SNCC. *News-week* settled on "hypermilitant," which, perhaps coincidentally, served to underscore the difference between SNCC and King. The nomination of a former Mississippi governor to the federal bench, King said in the careful response quoted in July, "would be a 'great tragedy.'" By contrast, there was the "saber-rattling warning," delivered by John Lewis, chairman of the "hy-permilitant" SNCC, that the appointment "might set off 'mass social disloca-tion and civil disobedience throughout the South.'"[20]

There indeed was considerable distance between the radicalism of SNCC and the cautious pragmatism of King. Still, *Newsweek* did not simply report those differences but used them to reassure readers that King would return to the fold. The surest and simplest way of demonstrating this was to use the fire-eaters of SNCC as contraposed symbols, and to maintain that the coalition of conscience would endure despite the strains of radicalism and defection from the liberals' ranks.[21]

U.S. News maintained as fervently as did its competitors that King had no

---

19. "New Look on the Left: Solidarity Forever?" *Newsweek*, May 24, 1965, p. 31. *Newsweek* denounced Students for a Democratic Society as well as SNCC. "Inside Snick," *Time*, April 30, 1965, p. 74.
20. "Judgment on a Judge," *Newsweek*, July 26, 1965, p. 30.
21. See *Newsweek*, "That Summer," May 31, 1965, p. 22, "LBJ: Rights Are Not Enough," June 14, 1965, p. 37, and "Helping Hands," June 28, 1965, p. 24. The last article was about idealistic youth who symbolically took up the banner of liberalism flung down by SNCC.

business meddling in foreign affairs. Initially, however, its comments were less biting than was *Time*'s characterization of King as bumpkin. Even the finding by *U.S. News* that "some observers profess to see an attempt by Dr. King to 'escalate' his status as a national figure—perhaps with political goals in view" was mild in comparison.[22]

U.S. News surpassed *Time* when the echo chamber campaign was restarted within a month. A series of articles painted King as an opportunist trying desperately to maintain his leadership of the civil rights movement and as one of the reckless black leaders "exploiting dissatisfaction" in black America. In mid-May, a Republican congressman, H. Allen Smith, complained of Communist infiltration of peace groups. (Smith knew whereof he spoke, the magazine implied, citing his service as a former FBI agent.) *U.S. News* sounded a conspiratorial tone with the headline "How U.S. Reds Campaign for a Vietnam Pullout," and the political gossip column in the same issue echoed the suspicions: "Increased Communist penetration and influence inside some sections of the Negro movement . . . likewise is a subject of growing concern to the FBI and White House." By the end of May, Hoover was testifying that Communists in the United States were unified, organized, and powerful exploiters of misguided opponents of the war.[23] King's name did not appear in these stories, but his well-publicized statements about the war provided the necessary linkages between communism, the black movement, and the growing disaffection with the war.

In July, *U.S. News* published the full text of an address delivered by a retired Supreme Court justice, Charles E. Whittaker, who found that much of "the current rash and rapid spread of lawlessness in our land has been, at least, fostered and inflamed by the preachments of self-appointed leaders of minority groups to 'obey the good laws, but to violate the bad ones'—which, of course, simply advocates violation of the laws they do not like, or, in other words, the taking of the law into their own hands." (Mentioning King's name would have been redundant; a reference to a foreign body that awarded "him a

22. "New Tack for Dr. King: Broader Issues, Wider Goals," *U.S. News & World Report*, May 3, 1965, p. 18.

23. See *U.S. News & World Report*, "The Changing Mood of America: What a Nationwide Survey Shows," May 31, 1965, p. 42, "Washington Whispers," June 7, 1965, p. 32, "How U.S. Reds Campaign for a Vietnam Pullout," May 17, 1965, p. 22, "Washington Whispers," May 17, 1965, p. 27, and "From J. Edgar Hoover: A Report on Campus Reds," May 31, 1965, p. 84. Warnings delivered by Hoover and Allen were echoed in shorter versions in "Where Reds Are Busy on the Campuses," June 7, 1965, p. 54.

prize, of all things, for his contributions to peace" contextually established identity.) Whittaker's broadside was striking, as well, because it recapitulated articles of published warnings by the president of Howard University about the spread of lawlessness and Communists on campus; reports that the FBI and White House were disturbed by the increasing influence of Communists in the civil rights movement and their fomenting of unrest on the nation's campuses; and morsels of political gossip about King's "apparently insatiable appetite for power."[24]

The attack continued the following week. One article reported the complaint by Mayor Richard Daley of Chicago that Communists were working in the movement to force the removal of the superintendent of schools, Benjamin Willis. King was not named in that story, but his intention to mount a campaign in Chicago had been cited at least twice previously in the journal. The headline "Communists and Civil Rights—How Closely Linked?" coupled Daley's allegation to a report issued by a legislative commission in Alabama that "pinned a Communist label on several civil rights organizations working in the South." Placement and emphasis signaled that King was the quarry. His supposed misdeeds were reported first and in greater detail than those of SNCC, which U.S. News conceded was the commission's major target. Quoting the commission, the article said that King "'has been for ten years . . . closely advised by Communists, if not actually controlled by them'" and "'had received some sixty pro-Communist citations—a near record-breaking performance by this false prophet of the far left.'" Because of the headline, the two stories supported each other. The most damaging accusations appeared in the commission's report, which cited King by name. Given the campaigns in Montgomery, Birmingham, and Selma, however, fairness was not to be expected from the authorities in Alabama. Juxtaposed with the remarks of the presumably less prejudiced Daley, the commission's report was made to appear less motivated by malice. In turn, the weaker and vaguer bill of complaints issued by Daley was strengthened by the detailed assertions of the commission.[25]

24. "Lawlessness in U.S.—Warning from a Top Jurist," U.S. News & World Report, July 5, 1965, pp. 60–62. The interview with Howard president James M. Narbit, Jr., is "More Campus Unrest—Are Reds to Blame?" U.S. News & World Report, May 10, 1965, p. 14. Narbit made, and apparently intended, no reference to King, but Whittaker used his remarks as part of the background of developing radicalism.

25. "Communists and Civil Rights—How Closely Linked?" U.S. News & World Report, July 12, 1965, p. 12.

The reverberations continued relentlessly in the same issue. Whittaker's attack was echoed by Lawrence, who wrote that "even some clergymen are proclaiming that citizens need not obey laws which they consider 'unjust.'" There were other echoes in Lawrence's column: "The Mayor of Chicago declares he has evidence that Communists have infiltrated some of the Negro organizations engaged in street demonstrations in that city. Investigating committees of the legislatures of the states of Alabama and California say the same thing about outbursts in their areas." A week later, *U.S. News* revived the theme of King and communism. The journal noted snidely that King "has branched out as a spokesman on foreign policy. He urges negotiation with the Communist-supported Viet Cong to stop the war." To demonstrate the extent of King's radicalism, the magazine maintained that even other black leaders could not stomach his position. And two weeks thereafter, *U.S. News* returned to Whittaker and what had by now become an echo of an echo of an echo. Lawrence republished an editorial from the Chicago *Tribune* that quoted Whittaker's diatribe against "certain self-appointed racial leaders" and their "techniques of civil disobedience [used] in fomenting and waging their lawless campaigns which they have called 'demonstrations.'"[26] *U.S. News* was in full cry after King, raising the alarm about the danger posed by this "false prophet of the far left."

Another danger presented itself in August, summed up, then and later, in a single word: Watts. Aside from an unsuccessful attempt to bring peace to Watts, King had little to do directly and immediately with the situation in that district of Los Angeles. But he was at the center of the symbolic processes associated with the rebellion. King's victories signified almost nothing for the objective conditions of black life outside the South. Many whites assumed, however, that lifting the yoke from the shoulders of the black southerner—especially after the symbolically charged events in Birmingham and Selma, which gave rise to the great civil rights acts—would inspire gratitude among all black Americans, or at least lessen their impatience, and there would be peace. Watts shattered that assumption. Not only was there no peace; King failed to turn Watts residents away from violence. Watts, the first of the major urban insurrections, was a symbolic shock of the first magnitude echoing in American society.

26. David Lawrence, "Is This the 'Land of the Free'?" *U.S. News & World Report*, July 12, 1965, p. 108. See *U.S. News & World Report*, "Is Vietnam to Become a Civil Rights Issue?" July 19, 1965, p. 12, and "Example of the Cloth," August 2, 1965, p. 84.

The rioting was precipitated by an arrest on the night of August 11. A young black man who had been drinking was being taken into custody; a crowd gathered, and a woman spat at the officers. She also was arrested and, still struggling, was taken away. Distrust of the police ran high in Watts, and when rumors quickly spread that the arresting officers had manhandled a pregnant black woman, the rioting was on. It continued for six days until police and fourteen thousand National Guardsmen restored order. The casualty list was huge: thirty-four persons, almost all of them black, were dead; almost nine hundred persons had been injured; almost four thousand persons had been arrested; and property damage eventually reached more than $200 million.[27]

Another casualty of the Watts rioting was the notion that disorders could not happen here—here being wherever the doubters were situated. The anguished question was raised: "Why Watts?"

Any number of explanations were offered for the Watts explosion on the night of August 11. One of the more persuasive was provided by a young Watts resident who recalled that when the civil rights bill was signed in 1964, "nobody even thought about it in Watts. . . . It had nothing to do with us." Watts was untouched by the struggles in the South—untouched but not unmoved. King had said as much two years before. The black southerner could see change coming; not so his brethren in the North and the West. The blacks who fled the South for Los Angeles and Chicago and New York and Detroit found political rights and, in many cases, bettered themselves economically—but not without a price. If there was opportunity outside the South, there was also discrimination, more subtle, to be sure, but still degrading, and they learned the harsh lesson that the right to vote can exist side by side with political powerlessness. Furthermore, those two great social anchors of black life in the South, church and family, began dragging because of the strain of migration and the crime, the unemployment, and the drugs encountered in the cities. As Milton Viorst observed, the wretchedness of the ghetto was due not only to the power of whites but also to the insecurity and confusion and pain of strangers in a strange land "they could not master."[28]

The price of migration from rural South to urban West having been extracted from Watts residents, the gains from that migration having fallen short of anticipation, the victories of the southern movement having been arrayed

27. Viorst, *Fire in the Streets*, 310–20; Bishop, *The Days of Martin Luther King*, 414.
28. Viorst, *Fire in the Streets*, 310, 321.

before them, it was not so surprising that thousands began rioting in the streets of Watts. Despite its nihilism, there was a measure of truth to what a young man told King and Bayard Rustin after the rioting. Watts, he said, was a victory for the black man. Rustin questioned that, gesturing to the scenes of destruction about them. The young man was not persuaded. "'We won,'" he told Rustin, "'because we made the whole world pay attention to us.'"[29]

Other events had portended Watts: the rioting in Birmingham in 1963 when some of King's followers briefly shook off the discipline of nonviolence; the increasingly militant temper of the black movement spreading across the nation after Birmingham; the rioting that had caused hundreds of injuries and several deaths in Harlem and Rochester in 1964; other flare-ups in 1965. But the sheer scale of the bloodshed and destruction in Watts appalled America. Perhaps most unsettled were whites who counted themselves sympathetic to black aspirations. The March on Washington had reverberated against the struggle in Birmingham in 1963, a fulfilling contrapuntal symbolism of good and evil. Likewise Watts reverberated against Selma and the signing of the 1965 Voting Rights Act in August, but symbolism was turned upside down. In spirit, the nation had joined in a great crusade at Selma to secure the black man's right to vote. But black men residing where that right already was assured had risen in fire and blood to say that what had been accomplished was not enough, that much more would be demanded. What had seemed so simple before Birmingham and had appeared so again briefly in Selma was terribly complex and no longer so comfortably distant. Thus "Why Watts?" was not merely an inquiry into the causes of insurrection in Los Angeles. Posed in hurt bewilderment or anger or fear by men of good will, the question could as well have been "Why us?"

Sensitive barometers of middle America, *Time* and *Newsweek* were shaken by the scenes from the riot zone. Watts seemed to signal that American society was sheering rapidly toward racial war. *Time* reported Watts as a cacophony of hate: "Savagery replaced harmony with nightmarish suddenness . . . marauding mobs . . . burned and killed. . . . 'Here comes Whitey—get him!' . . . rioters surged through the streets screaming imprecations at 'whitey,' 'blue-eyed devils,' 'Okies,' and 'Crackers.' One rallying cry never failed: 'We're paying Whitey back!' . . . One of the riot leaders, a biochemistry

29. On unmet expectations, see Wills, *The Second Civil War*, 130. Viorst, *Fire in the Streets*, 341.

graduate . . . said . . . : 'I'm a fanatic for riots, I just love them.'" Only slightly more restrained was *Newsweek*'s account: "Night upon howling night, Negro mobs swirled through the streets of the nation's third largest city in a raging, bloodletting fury that paled the 1964 rioting by comparison."[30]

The shock was intensified by the contrast between the rioting in Watts and the successful struggle to bring justice to Selma. Only the week before, both magazines had invoked the symbols of the Republic when covering the signing of the 1965 Voting Rights Act in order to demonstrate that black Americans were climbing out of what *Newsweek* called the "dark Negro past." Now, with Watts, that past "engulfed the brightening Negro present." The contrast was drawn by *Newsweek*: "In Selma, . . . a Negro woman walked out of a Federal vote examiner's office, her voting certificate firmly in hand, and told a friend, 'Those white folks sure are nice.' And in Los Angeles, an 18-year-old girl, still caught up in the exultation of aimless, pointless, riotous anger told a white reporter: 'I threw anything I could get my hands on to hurt them. We were throwing at anything white. Why not do it to your guys? You're doing it to us.'"[31]

Some of that outrage spilled over onto King when he visited the scenes of the rioting on August 15. Many residents of Watts had never heard of him, and "almost all were hostile to his attempts at mediation."[32]

Newsweek and *Time* were almost as disenchanted with King. The latter concluded that King had "little standing among the slum dwellers" and supplied a quote to demonstrate it: "'Martin Luther Who?' they asked." *Newsweek* carped at King for delivering a "brief, platitudinous speech" and for canceling a tour of the riot zone "for 'security reasons.'" What shook the journal most, however, was his failure to persuade Watts. The language of *Newsweek*'s report, so different from that used for the March on Washington, imparted the sense that the black man of Watts differed greatly from King's new Negro of Montgomery. As King "drove into Watts under heavy guard, a Negro teen-ager said dourly: 'Aw, they're just sending another nigger down

30. "Trigger of Hate," *Time*, August 20, 1965, pp. 13–19. The technique of deleting intervening phrases to bring tone words into bold relief was borrowed from Swanberg, *Luce and His Empire*, especially 315–16. "Los Angeles: The Fire This Time," *Newsweek*, August 23, 1965, p. 15.

31. For the signing of the Voting Rights Act, see "A Barrier Falls: The U.S. Negro Moves to Vote," *Newsweek*, August 16, 1965, p. 15; and "'Your Future Depends on It,'" *Time*, August 13, 1965, p. 15. "Los Angeles: The Fire This Time," 17.

32. Lewis, *King: A Biography*, 306.

here to tell us what we need' ''; and "his welcome was a mocking jeer from an onlooker: '"I had a dream, I had a dream"—hell, we don't need no damn dreams. We want jobs.'" For all the good he had done, the magazine grumbled, King "might as well stayed home."[33]

Certainly King had strayed into a situation in which neither eloquence nor nonviolence was effective. But there was more to this matter. To begin with, if King had failed in Watts, so had the orthodox civil rights movement, and so had the orthodoxy of *Time* and *Newsweek*. Fine phrases about the great day coming when the black masses joined the American mainstream succeeded in Watts no more than had King. Still, some sense had to be made of Watts. *Time* and *Newsweek* could have begun by examining the symbol embodying the black rage that set Watts afire for six days—Malcolm X, who had articulated the discreetly unspoken hostility toward whites that "ghetto blacks carried in the recesses of their minds."[34] Acknowledging him as an icon of Watts would have required too much of *Time* and *Newsweek* (probably their middle-class readers as well). Malcolm X was too firmly established as a devil figure at the time.

Searching for signs of hope, *Newsweek*, not surprisingly, turned to the reformers, Farmer of CORE, Wilkins of the NAACP, Young of the Urban League. Their answers—more jobs, better schools, better homes—differed little from those King doubtless would have offered, but he had failed while they, not having ventured into Watts, had not had the opportunity to fail.[35]

While *Newsweek* consulted the oracles of reform, *Time* published its familiar paean to the American Dream. *Time* located two groups of blacks. The first resembled its own readers, prospering, committed to integration, having a stake in American society. But there was another group, a "slum level, mired in deepening ignorance, immorality, and irresponsibility, and growingly enamored of a chauvinistic, equal-but-separate kind of segregation." According to Lucean doctrine, all would be well if the black man would but seize the opportunities that had been and would be made available. Whites would continue to help, "but the Negro himself must do as much." This was the

---

33. "The Negro After Watts," *Time*, August 27, 1965, p. 17. See the *Newsweek* issue of August 30, 1965, for "Tough Years Ahead," 19, and "Mopping Up," 15.

34. Viorst, *Fire in the Streets*, 323. Malcolm X had repudiated hatred of whites before his death, but Viorst's point is valid about the symbolism attached to Malcolm X.

35. "Tough Years Ahead," 19.

quintessential Luce, the quintessential *Time*, down to the obligatory listing of black millionaires ("at least thirty-five"), eight black federal judges, one hundred blacks on other benches, an ambassador, a solicitor general, an attorney general, and so on. *Time* wrote with more puzzlement and impatience than ire that "the Negro . . . angrily [refuses] to look back over his shoulder to see how far he has come."[36] King himself, as "Man of the Year" in 1964, had provided the peg on which *Time* had hung another story celebrating the American Dream. Then, King had been fresh from the victory over Bull Connor. Now he was a failure among his own people, *Time* asserted.

Yet none of this explained the uneasiness with King demonstrated by *Time* and *Newsweek* before he was derided as "Martin Luther Who?" by the militants of Watts. Part of their disquiet was due to King's statements about the war. Troubling *Time* as well was this business of civil disobedience. A week before Watts, *Time* proclaimed it was time "for the revolution to move off the streets." If intended to apply generally, the statement nevertheless followed on the heels of another that in "Washington and Philadelphia, Martin Luther King led more marchers." Elsewhere, *Time* implied that King had encouraged the less polite forms of civil disobedience. "Under the umbrella of this idea that civil disobedience is O.K. when it is done in the name of civil rights, demonstrators have dumped garbage in New York's City Hall Plaza, urinated in a Montgomery, Alabama, public square, staged a sit-in in a White House corridor, and stopped traffic on scores of streets and highways by lying down on the pavement." "Civil righteousness" was the label *Time* attached to such conduct, borrowing the words from a ruling by a federal judge in Alabama.[37] The notion was as much *Time*'s as the judge's. These examples, far from the only types of civil disobedience that could have been cited, seemed calculated to arouse revulsion and indignation among middle-class readers with an appreciation for public order and a distaste for unseemly public conduct. According to *Time*, civil disruption and civil disobedience no longer served a purpose, not when the nation had legally guaranteed the black man his rights. And those who were stiff-necked enough to continue practicing civil

36. "The Negro After Watts," 16, 17.
37. "'Your Future Depends on It,'" 15; "'No Immunity,'" *Time*, August 13, 1965, pp. 15–15A. The phrase "civil righteousness" could be read as an indirect reference to King because he advocated civil disobedience, was associated with the civil rights movement, and was a minister. See also "Hot and Dry," *Time*, June 18, 1965, p. 26; and "Trigger of Hate," 19.

righteousness—King, for one, because he was prepared to move into the volatile northern ghettos and had already entered the war controversy—could expect some rough handling from Luce's magazine.

Newsweek also had begun reexamining its support for King before his failure in Watts. The evidence appears in the form of strained silence in three articles. One story reported the activities of armed black vigilantes known as the Deacons for Defense and Justice; despite his eminence as an advocate of nonviolence, King was not mentioned. Another article printed the conclusion of a government-sponsored study that the black family was disintegrating. *Newsweek* passed up the opportunity to seek the views of King, which would have been pertinent because of the intimate relationship of black church and black family and because of King's scholarly credentials. (A year before, the magazine had trotted him out as a symbol or spokesman even when his role was farfetched; now it all but ignored him.) The silence was even more strained in the report of the signing of the 1965 Voting Rights Act. Naturally, President Johnson symbolically dominated the ceremony and the story. But *Newsweek* did not even mention that King was present, an omission all the more striking because of references to the Selma campaign and the previous portrayal of King as a new Moses.[38] King indeed was a powerful embarrassment if *Newsweek* was treating him as no better than a gate-crasher at an event that he had done so much to bring about.

U.S. News provides a study in contrasts to the other magazines. Where *Newsweek* denied King a place at the ceremonial signing of the Voting Rights Act and *Time*, going even further, had him off on yet more marches, *U.S. News* reported that King "watched Mr. Johnson sign the bill . . . [and] predicted that, by September 1, nearly a million Negroes will be added to the South's voting rolls." King's presence was necessary to the editorial line; on this of all days, when the political subjugation of the South was accomplished, the chief collaborator with tyrannical federal authority could not be absent. Other considerations made it necessary to remove him from Watts. Reporting his inability to pacify Watts would have cast him as a peacemaker, even if a

---

38. "The Deacons," *Newsweek*, August 2, 1965, pp. 28–29. Wilkins of the NAACP and Young of the Urban League were chosen to comment on the study of the black family, in "New Crisis: The Negro Family," *Newsweek*, August 9, 1965, p. 35. Nor did *Newsweek* seek out King in a later treatment of the study and its attendant controversy. "The Negro Family: Visceral Reaction," December 6, 1965, pp. 38–40. King conditionally endorsed the report's findings in October. Lewis, *King: A Biography*, 309. The signing of the Voting Rights Act is treated *ibid.*, 303; and reported in "A Barrier Falls: The U.S. Negro Moves to Vote," 15.

failed one, thus contradicting the theme that he was bent on making trouble across the nation.[39]

One of the potential trouble spots in 1965 was Chicago, where blacks had been unsuccessfully campaigning for more than a year to force the removal of Superintendent of Schools Willis. There were other grievances related to housing and jobs. A number of civil rights and liberal organizations had formed a coalition in order to wrest concessions from city hall, and at their invitation King agreed to lead a campaign in 1966. In a dress rehearsal for the campaign, King spent three days in Chicago in July, 1965, delivering at least thirty speeches and, on July 26, leading thirty thousand persons on a march to City Hall to protest the administration of the schools by Willis. It was one of the largest demonstrations in the history of Chicago.[40]

Although *Time* and *Newsweek* had covered the campaign to unseat Willis, they all but ignored King's activities in Chicago and paid little attention to his announcements that he would start campaigning in the North. Those details were available in *U.S. News*, which fitted them into an overarching theme, the gist of which was caught by these rhetorical questions: With all that had been done for blacks, "What more can Negro leaders demand? What else do they want?"[41]

Quite a lot, according to *U.S. News*, whose evidence was that King, the troublemaker, was flitting from crisis to crisis and broadening the objectives of the SCLC "to include almost every demand raised by Negroes anywhere." There followed a cause-by-cause listing. "In Chicago, Dr. King led demon-

39. See *U.S. News & World Report*, "A Million New Negro Voters?" August 16, 1965, p. 8; and, for a restatement of the theme, "Now a March of Tribute, Not Protest," August 16, 1965, p. 12. *U.S. News* did report the wounding in Watts of the black social activist Dick Gregory. "Shifting Patterns in Race Problem," August 23, 1965, p. 37. This story used King to warn of the dangers presented by groups such as the Deacons for Defense.
40. Lewis, *King: A Biography*, 303; Oates, *Let the Trumpet Sound*, 368–69.
41. *Time*'s report on the anti-Willis campaign in Chicago, "Hot and Dry," 26, appeared before King's visit in July, but he had already begun a tour of northern cities designed, in part, to encourage black voter registration. Nor was King mentioned in an article on rising black political power in northern cities, "The Negro's New Force," *Time*, November 12, 1965, pp. 33–34. *Newsweek* published several articles about the nascent Chicago movement and the attempts to oust Willis: "Time Runs Out for Big Ben," June 7, 1965, p. 52; "The Gadfly of the Poverty War," September 13, 1965, p. 30; "Segregation in the North," September 20, 1965, p. 58; " 'Discrimination' in Chicago," October 11, 1965, p. 94; and "Leaning on HEW," October 18, 1965, p. 98. Two brief references by *Newsweek* to the SCLC's new focus were found: "The Periscope," September 6, 1965, p. 9, and "The Periscope," September 27, 1965, p. 20. See *U.S. News*, "Shifting Patterns in Race Problem," 32. The theme was previously expressed by *U.S. News* in "Tomorrow," August 16, 1965, p. 26, and was reiterated in "What Government Already Has Done for Negroes" and "101 Suits to Enforce Negro Rights," August 23, 1965, pp. 33, 34.

strations backing local Negroes' demands for ouster of the school superintendent. In Washington, D.C.—where Negro residents outnumber whites and
Congress governs the city—he spoke out for 'home rule.' In Philadelphia he
demanded admission of Negroes to a private school set up by a rich man's will
for 'poor, white, male orphans.' In Cleveland, he spurred a voter registration
drive among Negroes."[42]

The echo chamber was operating again. As always, it relied on the reitera-
tion of themes. A week after stating that King was exploiting almost any cause
anywhere, *U.S. News* reported that George Weaver, a black assistant secretary of labor, had chastised King for entering into the war controversy. While
welcoming that rebuke to King, the magazine was less happy that Johnson had
sent Goldberg to convince King that the administration was seeking peace in
Vietnam, regarding this as another example of the fallacy of "catering to
Negro demands." Some other echoes resumed in mid-September when *U.S.
News* foresaw a new wave of racial troubles. Part of the threat was traced to
King's announcement that "he will carry his crusade into the North, with
Chicago and Los Angeles—scenes of recent race riots—as his primary tar-
gets."[43] By juxtaposing King's announcement with the details of racial
disturbances in Mississippi and North Carolina, the magazine made it appear
that King was an active agent in those conflicts.

U.S. News also laid the blame at King's door for racial unrest in the North,
specifically in Springfield, Massachusetts, which had "taken pride in its record of harmony between Negroes and whites" for more than a century. The
harmony was shattered by "Negro agitators . . . crying 'police brutality' " and
dictating "shock tactics" that created "bitterness of a kind that 329-year-old
Springfield had never known before." Who were these troublemakers? They
appeared to be King or his disciples. Three quoted or paraphrased statements
maintained that the outsiders intended to make Springfield the "Selma of the
North." A fourth statement by a policeman linked Selma (thus King) to the
turmoil in Springfield. " 'At the time of the trouble in Selma last March,' " he
said, " 'my sympathies were with the Negroes who wanted to be voters. I was
inclined to scoff at the complaints the Alabama authorities were making about

42. "Shifting Patterns in Race Problem," 33.
43. "Negro Official Speaks Out: A Rebuke to Dr. King?" *U.S. News & World Report*, August
30, 1965, p. 16. *U.S. News* echoed it in "Washington Whispers," September 27, 1965, p. 29, and
in slightly different thematic form in "Tomorrow," September 6, 1965, p. 24. "Threat Across the
Nation: New Wave of Racial Troubles," *U.S. News & World Report*, September 13, 1965, p. 8.

"outside agitators." But now I believe I know what those Alabama officials were talking about. North or South, it's a nasty thing when outsiders come in and stir up trouble.'" Not until the last paragraph of a three-page story were the "outsiders" identified as "two national leaders of CORE."[44] Even then it was unclear whether the SCLC had joined CORE agitators in the Springfield campaign.

Two issues later, *U.S. News* proceeded to the ultimate denunciation of King as a radical agitator. Covering Watts, the magazine had not mentioned that King attempted to serve as a peacemaker. In early October, it blamed King for the rioting itself. *U.S. News* published excerpts from a speech made by James S. Kemper, Jr., an insurance executive, who said this:

> More than any other single man, . . . King is responsible for the devel-
> opment of mass crime in the civil rights movement. . . . The spectacle of
> a Nobel Peace Prize winner, supported by thousands of white and Negro
> clergymen, endorsing the breaking of any law is an open invitation to
> lawbreaking by anyone who chooses to do so. . . . Whatever may be the
> intentions of Dr. King and those who follow his philosophy, they have
> led the way to exactly the kind of violence that took place this summer in
> Los Angeles and other cities. . . . We start out with something called
> "nonviolent protest," and we end up by providing a haven for Black
> Muslims, Black Nationalists, Communists, Trotskyites, and the worst
> criminals of the Negro underworld leading the citizenry into organized
> violence and mass destruction.[45]

All in all, this was a fairly serious collection of sins for a man proclaimed a "moderate" by *U.S. News* shortly after Selma, when King looked to be less threatening than the radicals of SNCC. The words were uttered by Kemper; the ideas were those of *U.S. News*. This much was clear simply from the fact that the magazine quoted at unusual length a speaker whose credentials to comment about either King or nonviolence were almost nonexistent from a journalist's perspective. Furthermore, *U.S. News* strengthened the point. After Kemper blamed King for the violence in Los Angeles and elsewhere, *U.S. News* added a bland notation that the speaker had "quoted statements by several Negro leaders advocating violence" during the disorders in Watts. Inasmuch as no culprit was identified by name, there seemed to be a deliberate

44. "When Negroes Tried to Shock a Friendly City—," *U.S. News & World Report*, September 13, 1965, pp. 46–48.
45. "Dr. King's Policy: Invitation to Racial Violence?" *U.S. News & World Report*, October
4, 1965, p. 22.

implication that King encouraged or sanctioned the rioting. Not surprisingly, *U.S. News* published no rebuttal of the accusations; Kemper had merely sounded the themes in the echo chamber. While far from the last word *U.S. News* would say on the subject, the article distilled to the essence the alarming message the magazine wished to convey.[46]

The other news magazines were seeing radicalism afoot as well, but only *U.S. News* constantly attacked King. *Time*'s waspish scolding and *Newsweek*'s strained silence demonstrated that they were irked with King. But they simply wanted him to stay out of other controversies—especially the war— and get back into the mopping-up action against Jim Crow. King obliged on one count. By the final quarter of 1965, he had backed away from public positions on the war. That suited *Newsweek*: It chose to ignore his previous transgression in stories about the anti-war movement. *Time* thought the lesson needed to be driven home. Its chosen vehicle was an essay that mused, "To know the Vietnik is not necessarily to love him. At his best, he is inspired by the U.S. civil rights revolution and the practical results of nonviolent protest as applied to that Gandhian principle by the Rev. Martin Luther King, Jr. He has a rather irritating habit of claiming a monopoly on humanitarianism." While a source of inspiration to the Vietniks, King was not one of them, a small detail but an important distinction. King was spared the onus of a term coined to question the loyalty of war protesters. Nevertheless, the line be- tween King and the Vietniks was not so clearly drawn as to preclude the recognition that he could be smug or foolish or both. The Vietniks, and the man who inspired them, could be seen as fools unable to read the motives of the Communists in Vietnam and so blinded by ideological pretensions that they could not see that their movement would encourage "the Communist hope and expectation that the U.S. does not have the stomach to fight it out in Vietnam."[47]

46. *Ibid*. For other coverage in *U.S. News*, see David Lawrence's columns "The Wrong Way," August 30, 1965, p. 88, and "The Right to Loot?" September 6, 1965, p. 100. Much fainter is the echo of Whittaker's remarks in "Ex-Justice Severs Supreme Court Ties," November 1, 1965, p. 14. The conspiratorial tone sounded by Whittaker about King and Communists is included in "Communist Gains Among Youths—J. Edgar Hoover Reports," *U.S. News & World Report*, November 1, 1965, p. 46. Identification of King was contextual.

47. See, for example, *Newsweek*, "The Demonstrators: Why? How Many?" November 1, 1965, pp. 25–26, and "Battle of Conscience," November 15, 1965, p. 78. "The Vietniks: Self- Defeating Dissent," *Time*, October 29, 1965, pp. 44, 45. *Newsweek* made a similar distinction without associating King with either Vietniks or pacifists. "The Demonstrators: Why? How Many?" 25–26.

On another score, *Time* and *Newsweek* took similar tacks. King was neglecting his duty to the long-suffering black southerner, they said in effect, and the work was left undone or had to be done by others.

Time put the case most cuttingly in a story that bore the headline "The Law and De Lawd," the latter being King's nickname, used affectionately in the SCLC, derisively in SNCC. *Time* used it to take him down a peg. King had "trumpeted" an estimate that nine hundred thousand to a million new Negro voters would be registered within a year. But results fell short of those figures, and *Time* blamed King, in part, for the failure; he was "the most conspicuous absentee" from the registration campaign even though he had "raised Negro suffrage as his battle cry" for years. He was getting above himself since winning the Nobel Prize. "'De Lawd,' as his followers call King, has been so preoccupied with global affairs, such as the war in Vietnam, that he has had little time for the cotton-picker vote."[48]

Although less condescending, *Newsweek* was biting enough when King neglected his chores in the South. It made that point when reporting the acquittal of one of the Klansmen accused of murdering Mrs. Liuzzo after the Selma march. The verdict caused King to "cut short a trip to Europe" so as to mount a campaign against injustice in southern courts. "'All the progress we have made' was on the line, cried King." *Newsweek*, unimpressed, observed that "a quieter drive to reform Southern justice had [already] begun under the stewardship of Charles Morgan, Jr. . . . For months, Morgan has been papering the Deep South with lawsuits demanding an end to the systematic exclusion of Negroes from Southern juries." King had lost touch with his cause—indeed, with common sense. He proposed federal legislation directed against lynching, but Morgan (and *Newsweek*) had "no more than an impatient shrug" for this notion. "'You've still got the same white men on the grand jury. What difference would it make?'"[49]

Newsweek's dwindling patience was almost exhausted by year's end. In two articles, King, stripped of messianic trappings, began to resemble a hustler in search of "headline-catching gimmicks." First, SCLC strategists were spotted in the act of working up some "theatrical touches" for upcoming demonstrations in Alabama. They planned "to parade symbolic coffins, carried in horse-drawn hearses and accompanied by muffled drums, to sites

48. "The Law and De Lawd," *Time*, November 5, 1965, p. 38. Essentially the same tone was sounded later in "New Wave of Challengers," *Time*, December 3, 1965, p. 68.
49. "Opening a Second Front," *Newsweek*, November 8, 1965, p. 33.

where civil rights workers have died." Then *Newsweek* turned its attention again to King's penchant for creating crises. There was evident displeasure with his flitting from one cause to another. His "cause for the moment" was "righting the scales of justice in the courthouses of Deep Dixie," his motive for taking it up was the need to strike a spark that would lead to "another Selma," because the old magic was absent during his peregrinations in the black South.[50]

If that was the case, *Newsweek* asked in effect, what better location than Selma, what better symbolic angle to play than the trial of three men accused of killing the Reverend James Reeb? Here, King did not seek justice but a "quick acquittal [that] might be precisely the sort of shock effect his drive needed." King got the verdict he wanted, but, like the old King magic, it was not the same; "the softness of the prosecution's evidence drained it of much of its symbolic content. King's men made their pro forma attacks on the pro forma acquittal and vowed to go on with the drive—charged up, perhaps, with such headline-catching gimmicks as sit-ins in Southern jury boxes. But the spark that could fire the nation to action remained to be struck. Selma had not quite turned into another Selma."[51]

From what *Newsweek* reported, the crusaders for justice had adopted a strategy of cynicism that relied upon cheap tricks as tactics. To be sure, King and his associates had demonstrated a flair for gimmickery and a propensity for overblown rhetoric on more than one occasion. Still, this does not account for the withering scorn accorded symbolic gestures hardly any more frothy than the notion of marching five days in order to lay before a segregationist governor of Alabama a recitation of grievances from blacks denied the right to vote. The most likely explanation for *Newsweek*'s biting tones was that the magazine was reacting to the strain of containing King as a symbol after Selma. Certainly *Newsweek* seemed harder pressed than its competitors when trying to make sense of King. *U.S. News* had no great difficulty with the task; after Selma, its echo chamber resounded with attacks, direct and indirect, on the radical King. The campaign against King had never been conducted more relentlessly—or more effectively. Even *Time* was less distressed than was *Newsweek*. *Time* was outraged by a "civil rights parson" who presumed to interfere with the American struggle against the Communist menace in Viet-

50. *Newsweek*, "The Periscope," November 29, 1965, p. 15, and "Search for a New Selma," December 20, 1965, pp. 29–30.
51. "Search for a New Selma," 30.

nam, it was irked by King's bent for creating crises, and it was strident in its denunciation of civil disobedience. Yet *Time* fervently hoped that King would go away and sin no more and its mutterings would die away in silence if he would do this. *Time*'s implicit wish that King return to the good fight in the South was shared by *Newsweek*, which was, however, less sanguine that hope would be realized. There was reason to be dubious. King had already shown his determination to leave the reservation by plunging into the war issue, even though he soon extricated himself from that quagmire. Furthermore, King was preparing for yet another major campaign. And this campaign would be outside his native South, in the North's toughest city—Chicago.

VII

MARCHING SOUTH, MARCHING NORTH

A season of doubt followed the year of Selma, the Voting Rights Act, and the Watts riot. With the legal basis of segregation demolished, with the reformist force of the old civil rights movement almost spent, racial problems now appeared more complex and threatening as media reports of domestic turmoil, racial confrontations and anti-war demonstrations, became "almost a part of everyday life in the United States."[1] No less unsettled was the black movement; indeed, 1966 was the last year that convenient label "the movement" could be accurately used. The jostling for position by various black organizations and leaders had usually produced no more than the occasional roil on the surface harmony during the struggle against Jim Crow. By midsummer of 1966, however, the movement started breaking apart in a startlingly public fashion after the appearance of the Black Power controversy, becoming an alliance of convenience, then a quarrelsome league of clashing interests and colliding ideologies that no center could hold together.

As Black Power, more slogan than ideology, thrust itself into public consciousness in 1966, the news weeklies found King useful as a symbol to counter SNCC, which was then completing its passage from reform to radicalism. But the situation was muddied because King was marching outside, as

1. U.S. President's Commission on CIA Activities Within the United States, *Report to the President* (1975), 285.

well as inside, the South, and in neither instance—as the leader of the Chicago Freedom Movement and at the forefront of a march through Mississippi—was his symbolism clearly drawn. Nevertheless, *Time*, *Newsweek*, and *U.S. News* sought to spin seamless webs of meaning that matched the expectations of their audiences. They were often unsuccessful, but the events of the year unfolded so swiftly and chaotically and the symbols were so riddled with contradictions as to defy attempts to arrange them into neat patterns.

There were, for example, the frayed edges and missing threads of the early coverage of King by *Newsweek* and *Time*. When dividing the black movement into "old-liners" and "militants," *Newsweek* put King with SNCC and CORE in the latter category and assigned the NAACP and the Urban League to the former. However, it became necessary to demonstrate in the following weeks that there was militancy and ultramilitancy, the latter represented by SNCC, which announced its opposition to the war and counseled civil rights workers to avoid the draft by any legal means. For the moment, *Newsweek* (and *Time*, which labeled SNCC the "most militant of all U.S. civil rights organizations" and its statement as "typically intemperate") chose to regard this as a rash outburst rather than as disloyalty. Their concerns were that aid and comfort were being given to segregationists in the Georgia legislature and that SNCC had detracted from a black triumph. Seven of the eight blacks elected to the Georgia legislature in 1965 were seated in January, 1966. The eighth, Julian Bond, then SNCC's director of information, was denied his seat because he endorsed the statement opposing the war. *Newsweek* and *Time* mourned the loss of a pointed bit of symbolism. Had Bond learned the valuable political lesson of "knowing when to keep his mouth shut," as *Time* put it, he would have symbolized black progress by taking his seat in the same House from which he was once ejected following the command of a legislator to "'get those niggers out of the white section of the [visitors'] gallery.'"[2]

While displaying a strained tolerance for SNCC's rashness, the magazines displayed a marked shortness of memory when it came to King. He led a demonstration in Atlanta protesting the refusal to seat Bond. *Newsweek* du-

2. See *Newsweek*, "Larger Battleground," January 10, 1966, p. 23, "SNCC's 'Dissent,'" January 17, 1966, p. 26, and "Two-Time Loser," January 24, 1966, pp. 26, 29. "One Word Too Many," *Time*, January 21, 1966, p. 20. On the Bond controversy, see Garrow, *Bearing the Cross*, 458–59; Morgan, *One Man, One Voice*, 155; and Marshall Frady, *Southerners: A Journalist's Odyssey* (New York, 1980), 169–73.

tifully reported this fact but omitted the usual background details of King's entry into, and retreat from, the war issue, citing instead the constitutional issues of free speech and prohibition of nonjudicial punishment. For its part, *Time* ignored King's role in the protest. The net effect was to put as much distance as possible between King and the war, a matter the magazines regarded as best forgotten.

King did not fare as well with *Time* after he launched the Chicago Freedom Movement in January. The SCLC was invited in by the Coordinated Council of Community Organizations, under whose umbrella were assembled local affiliates of SNCC, CORE, the NAACP, and the Urban League, as well as other white and biracial groups. King set his campaign in motion by moving into a slum dwelling. If there was a studied element to the gesture, it nevertheless reflected more than symbolism; King's wife and children lived with him until the rigors of ghetto life made the children hostile and sullen, and they were "shipped back home to the fresh air of black middle-class America." Neither the symbolic gesture nor the grimness of ghetto life won *Time* over. Two stories labeled King, in effect, as an opportunist, as not much better than a thief, and as a rustic mimicking the worldly ways of the big city into which he had wandered. Mockingly, *Time* recounted the adventures of a preacher turned pool shark: "We got trouble! Right here in Windy City! The very reverend himself had taken up a cue. . . . Cracked the preacher, who had hustled in from a civil rights walking tour of the city for a game: 'I'm just shooting my best stick.' "[3]

Possibly this was no more than badinage. But *Time* followed up a month later with an article asserting more sharply that King was out of his element in Chicago. The SCLC staged a rent strike in the building in which King was living, and used the money, which would have gone to the landlord, to rehabilitate the structure. As an organ of the middle class, *Time* could not condone such high-handedness with private property. A federal judge (carefully introduced as the "first Negro ever appointed to a federal bench in the continental U.S.") delivered the magazine's first lecture, that the laws against theft were as important to blacks as to anyone else. He also relieved *Time* of the task of characterizing an American symbol as a criminal whose "trustee-

3. Lomax, "When 'Nonviolence' Meets 'Black Power,' " 168; "People," *Time*, February 25, 1966, p. 42.

ship" of property amounted to "theft." Another lecture was given for *Time* by Chicago's Committee of 100, an interracial civic organization. Flouting laws in a just cause might be excused "in those parts of the South where the law has two faces, one black and one white. . . . But in the North, particularly in Chicago, . . . no one is above the law here."[4] *Time*'s unblinking defense of the rule of law would have been more persuasive had Chicago been noted for its devotion to legal niceties.

By contrast, *Newsweek* added a dash of realism to its concoction of symbolism. Doors in the ghetto seemed to spring open at the very mention of King's name, it reported, but the people behind them remained to be convinced that nonviolence would work. That was far from King's only problem. *Newsweek* analyzed accurately the difficulty King would have when his enemy declined to oblige with the savage violence that made the way easier in Birmingham and Selma. By moving into a slum apartment, King had hoped to dramatize the failure of the city government to enforce its building standards in the ghetto. One of King's aides leased the apartment in his own name to avoid alerting the landlords to the prominence of their tenant. At the last minute, the landlords got wind of King's forthcoming occupancy, and the aide found eight men frantically repairing and redecorating the dilapidated apartment. This was the kind of yielding resistance *Newsweek* had predicted: "Unlike the Clarks and the Connors of the South, the Daleys of the North are . . . accustomed to balancing the conflicting demands of ethnic blocs by piecemeal accommodation. Jim Clark greeted King with a Never button; Daley with a cheery 'welcome' to the city (even as his ghetto precinct captains infiltrated King's block meetings to keep themselves, and presumably the boss, posted)."[5] *Newsweek* had located the central fact of Chicago public life, the cozy mingling of politics and law.

The article was fortuitously timed, appearing before other events that would have done King's image no particular good. One was the rent strike. Even *Newsweek*'s liberal (but affluent) readers might object to that assault on property rights. Another was the meeting of King and Elijah Muhammad, the chief prophet of the Black Muslims, who announced that they would under-

---

4. On the rent strike, see Lewis, *King: A Biography*, 317–18. "Render Unto King," *Time*, March 25, 1966, pp. 18–19.
5. Lewis, *King: A Biography*, 315; "Gamble in the Ghetto," *Newsweek*, January 31, 1966, p. 25.

take a "collaborative effort to end discrimination" in Chicago.[6] While the collaboration went no further than talk, even mentioning such an alliance might cause distress to *Newsweek*'s readers.

Rather than recapitulate the rent strike or the announcement with Elijah Muhammad, later stories promoted King as an alternative to a strain of radicalism moving from South to North. The doctrine was armed self-defense, its advocates the Deacons for Defense and Justice. The Deacons, organized in Louisiana to protect black communities against raiding parties of armed segregationists, lately had dispatched agents to the North in search of recruits and money, *Newsweek* reported in a tone that stopped just short of ominousness. The Deacons provided "a beguilingly tough alternative" for blacks dubious about the efficacy of appeals to white consciences. Should King's strategy fail and rioting occur, *Newsweek* warned through an intermediary, a "militant black preacher," the result would be "a thousand Deacons overnight." In fact, the Deacons served mostly to make King a beguilingly nonviolent alternative for *Newsweek* readers. As even the magazine conceded, the Deacons had gathered few converts in Chicago. By casting around a bit, *Newsweek* could have easily found radical organizations commanding more support in the ghetto. The Black Muslims, whose headquarters were in Chicago, would have served quite nicely had there been some way around the awkward point that King and Elijah Muhammad had announced they would be working together. In a pinch, the Deacons would have to do, they having not been seen lately in King's company.[7]

While *Time* and *Newsweek* celebrated, respectively, the rule of law and the nonviolent moderation of King, *U.S. News* was strangely silent. The echo chamber had resounded in 1965 with reports of the radical King shuttling about the country in the service of almost every cause anywhere. Now *U.S. News* seemed to regret showering publicity on him. Not until May, four months after King took up residence in Chicago, did *U.S. News* note his presence in the city. At the end of March, *U.S. News* adopted the theme that Chicago was a city that was "trying—perhaps a bit harder than others—to

6. On the meeting with Elijah Muhammad, see Lewis, *King: A Biography*, 317. *Newsweek* reported in passing that rent strikes would be used in Chicago, but King was only indirectly associated with the tactic.

7. "The Deacons Go North," *Newsweek*, May 2, 1966, p. 20. The Deacons also were useful in another way. Armed self-defense might be appropriate to "the Klan-ridden Louisiana outback," *Newsweek* asserted. "But the North is quite another matter: Racial discrimination there goes in many guises, but bedsheets are not among them." *Ibid.*

solve its problems," whatever they might be. The omission of King's activities was particularly glaring because of what the article identified as Chicago's "most difficult problems—race relations and the plight of the Negroes." Predictably, the magazine lined up with the Chicago establishment. It accorded respectful attention to the director of the Chicago Urban League, who declared that the "decision-makers in the city's power structure" recognized the problems of blacks and were determined to try to solve them. But there was something incongruous in the way a right-wing Republican magazine gingerly handled the boast of Daley, the boss of the country's leading Democratic machine, that "in the next two years we will eliminate every slum and blighted building in Chicago."[8] Neither statement rested on any foundation firmer than words, but they served the same purpose: to demonstrate that Chicago, the city that worked, had no need of King.

U.S. News restarted the echo chamber near the end of April. It revived the controversial matter of civil disobedience by reprinting the full text of a speech delivered by retired Supreme Court justice Whittaker. Whittaker's speech was a broadside against social change, but *U.S. News* emphasized the portion devoted to civil disobedience. While King was not cited by name, contextual identification was provided by references to "racial leaders" who massed followers "on the sidewalks, streets, and highways" of the South and, after being appeased, did the same in "one Northern city after another, and eventually pretty generally throughout the land." Thereafter, Whittaker sounded the requisite tone of conspiracy: " 'The philosophy of "obeying only the laws you like," and of attempting to rule by force, has given rise to mobs and mob actions that have proved, as certainly we should have expected, to be tailor-made for infiltration, take-over, and use by rabble-rousers and radicals who are avowedly bent on the breakdown of law, order, and morality in our society, and hence on its destruction.' " After an unusually lengthy hiatus of two months, David Lawrence repeated the warning. "Our Republic," Lawrence muttered, "cannot function effectively under the duress of a mob spirit."[9]

There were other ominous signs on the horizon that, *U.S. News* and Mr.

8. See *U.S. News & World Report*, "Long, Hot Summer of Race Trouble Ahead?" May 23, 1966, p. 36, and "Chicago: A Big City Meets Its Problems," March 28, 1966, pp. 74–75, 78.
9. "A Former Justice Warns: Return to Law, or Face Anarchy," *U.S. News & World Report*, April 25, 1966, pp. 60, 62; David Lawrence, "Are Provocative Demonstrations Really Necessary?" *U.S. News & World Report*, June 20, 1966, p. 112.

Justice Whittaker notwithstanding, had little to do with King or civil disobedience and everything to do with SNCC and its estrangement from liberals. The process had begun long before. Contributing to the process were the failure of the Kennedy and Johnson administrations to protect SNCC field workers from segregationists, the refusal of the Democrats to seat the Mississippi Freedom Democratic party delegation in 1964, and the shift in the Johnson administration's priorities from social problems to the war in Vietnam. The sum of these and other grievances was taken by SNCC as proof of the perfidy of whites generally and of white liberals specifically. [10]

Relentlessly, SNCC moved away from nonviolence, reform, and integration and toward black separatism and a revolutionary posture. First, despite its precarious financial situation, SNCC boldly declared its opposition to the war; its leaders risked shutting down completely the already dwindling flow of contributions from unions, churches, and other institutions. Then SNCC started establishing all-black political organizations in Alabama. The man responsible was Stokely Carmichael, whose election in May as chairman would drive another wedge between SNCC and the liberals. What remained of liberal good will all but vanished in the summer when Carmichael captured the nation's attention with the Black Power cry. Along with good will went the desperately needed donations. In July, a SNCC field worker wrote that "the national SNCC office is not supporting us at all at this point—not even subsistence, as funds have stopped coming in there since Stokely's advent into power!"[11]

Well before Carmichael came to power, the sense was flowering in *Newsweek* that there was an urgent need to do something to prevent a situation that threatened to come apart. All about were ominous signs: in the anti-war movement; on the nation's restive campuses; among the poor, who might become the tinder of revolution; in the black movement; above all, in SNCC. Its "hypermilitants" were opting for the "panther-style politics of racial hostility" of Carmichael and his political organizations in Alabama, which selected as their emblem the black panther. Some countering symbol was needed. Luckily, King was available. The contrast was starkly drawn in a report of a meeting called by King's "coalitionist-minded" SCLC. Carmichael (not yet elected as SNCC's chairman) declared: "'We pull no

10. Viorst, *Fire in the Streets*, 347.
11. Gloria Larry to Slater King, July 26, 1966, in Box 2, File 6, Slater King Papers, Fisk University.

punches—we don't trust white folks.'" Then he asked a menacing rhetorical question: "'You ever see a panther? He can't be tamed, and once he gets going, ain't nothing going to stop him. He's a mean cat.'" Responding, as a surrogate for King, was the "SCLC's Hosea Williams: 'We don't want no part of it. . . . Will Negroes treat white folks like the white folks treated them? We may mess around here and create a monster in Alabama. . . . We can't go pitting race against race.'"[12]

Matters had taken an alarming turn since the Freedom Democrats caused *Newsweek* to sputter about "moralistic obstinance." Now Carmichael was proclaiming, "We're not going to work from within the Democratic Party— we're going to wreak havoc from without." It could not have happened at a worse time. Wallace was preparing to campaign for reelection as governor, and, said *Newsweek*, almost wistfully, as if some golden opportunity was slipping away, "the stunning reality was that the Negro vote could conceivably decide an Alabama election." A measure of its wistfulness was the revival in modern dress of southern populism, which seemed to be the antithesis of the extremist preachments of Carmichael and Wallace. Political opponents of Wallace were speculating about some future Democratic party in Alabama that would reach across racial lines and unite workingmen into "a permanent alliance of the farmer, the millhand, the people in the chili cafes—and the Negro."[13]

This is not to say that *Newsweek* was adopting anything like a Marxist theory of class struggle—not as a magazine of the middle class, not as a supporter of a war against communism in Southeast Asia, definitely not as a magazine that had internalized the bitter depression-era struggles between liberals and Communists. *Newsweek* held no brief for the "cultivation of class conflict" or for actions designed to "'rub raw the sores of discontent'"; the sores of discontent were raw enough as it was in 1966. No doubt populism seemed safe to *Newsweek*: It was nativist rather than alien, the vestige of an American political movement with deep roots in the South and other regions, and it was essentially reformist rather than revolutionary. But *Newsweek* missed some ironies as it went about the business of promoting the notion of

12. See *Newsweek*, "Larger Battleground," 23, "Crusade Against Gringos," January 3, 1966, pp. 17–18, "DP's in the Delta," February 14, 1966, pp. 28, 30, "'Secret' Crisis in the Delta," March 7, 1966, pp. 28–29, "U.S. Latins on the March," May 23, 1966, pp. 32–36, and "Panther on the Prowl," February 7, 1966, pp. 20–21.
13. "Panther on the Prowl," 20–21.

populism reborn. Southern populism did produce some examples of cooperation by blacks and whites. By the turn of the century, however, populism in
the region had become rabidly racist. And perhaps the most delicious irony of
all: *Newsweek* proposed, in effect, that this new populism be used against
Wallace, who was suckled on the Populist politics of Alabama.[14]

Newsweek also located some historical examples that demonstrated the
American system was working and would continue to work. One lesson was
found in the 1963 March on Washington, from which scenes were extracted
for a report about a government film. Foreign audiences (the qualification was
necessary because the film was produced for exhibition abroad) "can only be
favorably impressed by discovering some Negroes and whites working together in the American civil rights movement." Presumably, *Newsweek*
readers would be no less impressed by scenes—rare in these hard times—of
black and white together. While King made his great speech, *Newsweek*
pointed out, a District of Columbia policeman stood alongside him, "white
and vigilant and protecting the Negro leader." The film served another purpose as well. It showed Americans finding fault with their democracy and the
grand spectacle of free men and women, hundreds of thousands of them, free
to demonstrate even at the symbols of nationhood, "at the foot of the Washington Monument, at the feet of a brooding Lincoln." Here indeed was a
democracy that worked. Still, *Newsweek* seemed less intent on proving it
worked in the Washington of 1963 than that it would work in 1966—in, say,
Alabama, where Carmichael was proclaiming his distrust of whites, apparently with as much conviction as King once proclaimed his faith in America.[15]

It seemed that democracy was about to start working in Alabama, the
symbol of segregation at its worst. A year after Bloody Sunday, two of King's
former adversaries, Sheriff Jim Clark and Al Lingo, the director of the Alabama state police, were nervously trying to adjust to the political realities
created by the 1965 Voting Rights Act. Lingo, running for sheriff in the
county in which Birmingham was located, found it necessary to venture

---

14. See, for example, *Newsweek*, "The Gadfly of the Poverty War," 30, and "Close to Home,"
May 16, 1966, p. 35. On southern populism, see C. Vann Woodward, *Origins of the New South,
1877–1913* (Baton Rouge, 1951), 254–63, 345–49. Interestingly, Marshall Frady, who covered
the 1966 gubernatorial campaign in Alabama for *Newsweek*, later wrote a sensitive appraisal of
Wallace and his Populist mentor, Governor James Folsom. Marshall Frady, *Wallace* (New York,
1968), 98–117, 125–27.

15. "Films from Uncle Sam," *Newsweek*, April 18, 1966, p. 110. On Carmichael, see Carson,
In Struggle, 199–200.

"before a meet-the-candidates session convened" by the SCLC "and, with a forced but photogenic smile, dropped a bill into the collection plate." The crux of the matter was stated bluntly by *Newsweek*. The Voting Rights Act had "handed the black man the ballot and told him it was his ticket to freedom"—here was attached the caveat—"if he learned to use it wisely and well."[16] The scene of Lingo rendering tribute was an object lesson: It was King who had brought Lingo to heel—not Stokely Carmichael, who distrusted whites and wanted to wreak havoc on the Democratic party.

As a matter of fact, a similar position was taken by SNCC chairman John Lewis, who was having his own troubles with Carmichael. A native of Alabama, Lewis knew that rural blacks regarded the Democratic primary as the only election that mattered, the general election simply ratifying results of that primary. Without power in the state Democratic party, Lewis believed, blacks would be condemned to political impotence. Although often painted as a firebrand, Lewis was about the only member of SNCC's top echelon willing to keep up contacts with liberals. But Lewis was becoming increasingly isolated in SNCC. On May 8, the situation came to a head. At the annual staff meeting, Lewis at first won reelection easily; ideological differences aside, SNCC members respected his courage and determination, and there was some reluctance to introduce additional divisions. The ballot was challenged, however, and Lewis was persuaded to resign to clear the way for a new vote. By then, many of Lewis' supporters had left, and Carmichael was elected. SNCC started down a new road.[17]

Carmichael's victory caused consternation at *Newsweek*, which finally reported the "persistent tensions" in SNCC between moderates and radicals "dating at least to 1961." Adjectives had to be reshuffled as well. With Lewis out, *Newsweek* had to downgrade him to "militant" in order to upgrade Carmichael to the more dangerous "hypermilitant." Predictably, with SNCC "taking one more giant step out of the mainstream of the civil rights movement," *Newsweek* turned to King. *He* at least was rock solid, preaching a "black-and-white coalition as the only real hope for Dixie's Negro minority." The magazine had good reason to cling to King. Shock followed shock. At a White House conference on civil rights, to take one example, those militants who did not actually boycott the meeting sparred furiously with moderates. In

---

16. "Selma Revisited," *Newsweek*, April 25, 1966, pp. 25–26.
17. Carson, *In Struggle*, 200–204.

the Mississippi Delta, for another, even the benign National Council of Churches had to stop one of its social projects from organizing separate social, economic, and political entities for blacks and to prod it toward integrationist activities. By now, *Newsweek*, perhaps mirroring the attitude of its more enlightened readers, seemed to feel the sting of rejection. The magazine's reports became laced with testiness after finding its good works valued so slightly or scornfully dismissed altogether. *Newsweek* imparted the sense of being under fire—whether reporting SNCC's curt refusal to talk to a reporter because he was white, or recounting a flare-up in Watts during which the magazine's Los Angeles bureau chief, who had escaped white mobs in the South without major injury, was set upon and savagely beaten by a black gang.[18]

The movement toward Black Power was denounced by *Time* with less urgency and with no sense of institutional rejection. *Time*'s certitude was difficult to prick. If, for example, there was a war to be fought, then it would be won, whether in Vietnam or against poverty, such being the American spirit. Like *Newsweek*, *Time* demonstrated that the system was working. It did not, however, use King extensively as a symbol. For *Time*'s purposes, no better examples existed than the Voting Rights Act and "Dallas County's bully-boy sheriff" James Clark, whose "cattle-prodding tactics" helped to assure the passage of the act. America was putting its house in order by humbling the Jim Clarks. The next step was correcting housing discrimination. Here, too, was progress: President Johnson sent to Congress "his third civil rights bill in as many years" and proclaimed the "discriminatory practices that 'deny the Negro his rights as a citizen'" must be ended.[19]

Underlying this panegyric was the notion that rights had been given to blacks rather than won at considerable cost in suffering and blood. Along with this idea ran the implicit question: What would blacks do with their new freedom? *Time* was less certain of the answer. After all that the nation had

18. "Growl of the Panther," *Newsweek*, May 30, 1966, pp. 33, 36. The White House conference was reported by *Newsweek* in "Moderate vs. Militant," June 13, 1966, p. 38, the Delta project in "Showdown in the Delta," June 6, 1966, p. 67. The attack on the newsman was reported by *Newsweek* on the contents page, p. 15, and in "Flashpoint in Watts," May 30, 1966, p. 33, and the magazine's editor recounted the incident more than a decade later in Elliott, *The World of Oz*, 81.

19. "Challenge in Alabama," *Time*, March 18, 1966, p. 29A. See also "Big Jim's Comeuppance," *Time*, June 3, 1966, p. 19, reporting Clark's electoral defeat and a federal court's rejection of his complaint of election fraud; and "A Corner Turned," *Time*, May 13, 1966, p. 23. Johnson's remarks appear in "Round Three," *Time*, May 6, 1966, p. 24.

done for blacks (the unspoken attitude), it was poor recompense to have some turn away in scorn. Among them was Carmichael, who was attempting to persuade blacks to boycott Alabama's primary "even if it means the defeat of Negro candidates or sympathetic whites." Then Carmichael in effect equated the American political system with the ultimate evil in modern history. In the Alabama of 1966, taking part in politics meant joining in Democratic politics. " 'To ask Negroes to get in the Democratic Party,' he says, 'is like asking Jews to join the Nazi Party.' "[20]

The heresy of CORE followed the heresy of SNCC. CORE had a new director, Floyd McKissick, and "almost all white members and most Negro moderates have either resigned or been nudged out of national policy-making positions. Opposition to the war in Vietnam has reached hysteria, and CORE leaders have come close to damning any cooperation with whites." McKissick even went a step further than did Carmichael. " 'Join the white man?' " he asked. . . . " 'How can we? How can we have respect for a race that has no respect for itself—not even for its God?' " *Time* correctly asserted that CORE had made "a chilling alteration in its basic principles," and could as easily have said the same of SNCC. Still, the elegiac cry of moderation lost rang a bit hollow. The "old" CORE, whose passing *Time* now mourned, had been described by the magazine a few years before as an assemblage of misfits and peaceniks. Similarly, John Lewis had raised *Time*'s hackles earlier in 1966 with a "typically intemperate statement" attacking the war. Now, Lewis seemed not so intemperate after all; he at least "welcomed white members and ventured some cooperation with less militant civil rights organizations."[21] Moderation being both a relative and a mutable virtue for *Time*, Lewis' stock would rise even higher in the future.

While revising its militancy scale, *Time* found King less useful as a contraposing symbol.[22] In fact, *Time* expressed suspicions that King's strategy of translating law into political reality in Alabama differed little in effect, if not intent, from Carmichael's. In the 1966 Democratic primary, George Wallace, barred by law from succeeding himself as governor, used his wife, Lurline, as a surrogate candidate. Wallace's major opponent, state attorney general Rich-

20. "The Divided Negro Vote," *Time*, April 29, 1966, p. 30.
21. "Chilling Shift," *Time*, June 10, 1966, p. 36. For *Time*'s disparagement of CORE in 1961, see "Trouble in Alabama," 16. *Time*'s reevaluation of Lewis as a moderate started in "Thinking Big," May 27, 1966, p. 22.
22. A possible exception is a passing reference in "Thinking Big," 22.

mond Flowers, eagerly courted black voters, and King campaigned energet-
ically on behalf of Flowers. But Flowers and several other candidates, segregationists and moderates alike, were inundated by the white vote for the
Wallaces. King analyzed the result as a "protest vote against the tide of
inevitable progress." With its customary disdain for losers, *Time* brushed
aside his explanation: King himself "helped solidify the white vote by stump-
ing" for Flowers. While most blacks cast their ballots for Flowers, "the
specter of a black bloc vote effectively polarized" the white vote that otherwise might have been "sufficiently fragmented among other candidates to
force a runoff election."[23]

Time's glib analysis did not go very far. Even if King had been politically
inept, it would have mattered little; a runoff election almost certainly would
have ended as a victory for the Wallaces. By rebuking King, *Time* glossed
over a major embarrassment. *Time*'s vision of America the perfectible came
out of the Alabama primary frayed around the edges. So far as could be seen
from the governor's race, the system had not changed one whit, despite what
Time (and *Newsweek* as well) had proclaimed as a political revolution. Blacks
had registered, had voted in significant numbers in Alabama; for all of that,
Wallace remained firmly in control of the state government and was ideally
positioned to administer another series of political shocks by running for
president. Someone had to bear the burden of failure; luckily for *Time*, King
was at hand.

Politics would change in Alabama, were already changing, in fact, as *Time*
and *Newsweek* hastened to point out, reporting the defeat of Jim Clark. In
another year, the failure of black voters to swing an election in Alabama
would have been of little importance. The outcome of that election mattered
very much indeed in 1966, when Carmichael and McKissick were urging
blacks to drop out of the system and were implying that this was only the first
step toward separatism—or worse. And in the remainder of 1966, the flow of
events and the flowering of black radicalism would force the news magazines
to reevaluate King as a symbol, most dramatically when King led his marches
in Chicago and points south, and Stokely Carmichael found a Rubicon to
cross in Mississippi.

Black Power swept out of Mississippi as a slogan in the summer and took up

23. "A Corner Turned," 23. The gist of the criticism was repeated in "Let George Do It,"
Time, May 13, 1966, p. 24.

position as an ominous presence on the national stage. Like other great rallying cries, it signified a great deal and, leaving at least as much unsaid, invited
the hearer to interpret what it meant. There were numerous interpretations,
each unsettling or menacing in greater or lesser degree to white America. At
its least exceptionable, mustering pride in heritage, Black Power challenged
white attitudes and Western ethnocentrism by asserting the greatness of the
ancient black African civilizations and exhorting black Americans to look to
Africa rather than to Europe for their identity. A more immediate and frightening reading was as a summons to race war or revolution in a society shaken
by several summers of rioting and entertaining no realistic hope the disorders
would not recur. Falling somewhere between cultural challenge and insurrection was the idea that Black Power was a demand that blacks write off
integration as beyond achievement, or white society as beyond redemption,
and concentrate on developing black social institutions and, insofar as possible, independent economic and political power.

However interpreted, Black Power thrust itself onto center stage with an
impact that could not have been foreseen, not even by Carmichael, the man
who carefully chose the moment to utter those words in Mississippi. Black
Power at once gathered strength from, and contributed to, the sense of turbulence in American society. Still, the reason it burst on the scene at this
particular moment requires some unraveling. The phrase itself was not original: Marcus Garvey had used it; so had Richard Wright. No more than six
weeks before Carmichael demanded Black Power, Harlem congressman
Adam Clayton Powell raised the same cry—and went unheard.[24] Symbolism
and circumstances made the difference, the symbolism being attached to
Carmichael, who became identified with the plunge into radicalism by some
elements of the black movement. His professions of distrust of whites were
the strongest since Malcolm X was winning converts for the Black Muslims
by denouncing whites as evil, corrupt, and doomed to extinction. But Carmichael's words probably would have passed unnoticed had he not had the
perfect symbolic stage from which to utter them: the Meredith March.

The march was started as an unorthodox demonstration by James Meredith,
who went down in the history books as the man who broke the color line at Ole
Miss, a milestone reached at the cost of two lives and scores of serious injuries

24. Bishop, *The Days of Martin Luther King*, 432. For Powell's use of the term, see "Negro
Leader's Advice to Members of His Race," *U.S. News & World Report*, June 13, 1966, p. 14.

when Mississippi authorities permitted an insurrection against federal authority to develop. One of the most enigmatic figures in the black movement, Meredith had a sense of personal destiny; a federal judge described him as a "man with a mission and a nervous stomach" before the ordeal at Ole Miss.[25] He also was something of a loner; he set off on his march to Jackson, the capital of Mississippi, having neither solicited nor received any support from black organizations.

Meredith walked only a few miles into Mississippi before he was wounded on June 6 by a white man waiting in ambush with a shotgun. By the following day, King and other black leaders were in Memphis, where Meredith was recovering, attempting to persuade him to permit them to carry on his march. They were more successful in this than in settling their own disagreements about the relative merits of nonviolence and self-defense and the question of whether white sympathizers could join the march, once resumed. Indeed, Carmichael recalled that he promoted the wrangling in order to anger the conservative leaders of the NAACP and the Urban League sufficiently that they would refuse to participate.[26] As it happened, King, Carmichael, and McKissick of CORE formed an alliance of convenience to carry out the demonstration.

The strange bedfellows leading the march and the "clangor of the competing ambitions and ideologies" produced the perfect symbolic setting. Over the miles there continued a running debate between the moderate and the radical wings of the black movement, King on one side, Carmichael and McKissick on the other, with print and broadcast journalists in constant attendance.[27] Carmichael had the attention of the news media; what he needed to do was pick his moment.

Tensions of a different sort also were getting the attention of reporters covering the march. Hostility toward journalists rarely surfaced in the old civil rights movement; many reporters were regarded as allies or welcomed

25. Jack Bass, *Unlikely Heroes* (New York, 1981), 179.

26. For the beginning of Meredith's march, see Viorst, *Fire in the Streets*, 371. On the ideological dispute, see Garrow, *Bearing the Cross*, 480–89; and Morgan, *One Man, One Voice*, 73–75; cf. James Lawson, "The Meredith March . . . And Tomorrow," *Concern*, July 15, 1966, p. 1. Carmichael recalled that he wanted to drive King to the left by depriving him of his usual position in the middle between two factions. Viorst, *Fire in the Streets*, 371–72.

27. "The March Meredith Began," *Newsweek*, June 20, 1966, p. 31. On press and television coverage, see Renata Adler, "Mississippi," in Leon Friedman (comp.), *The Civil Rights Reader: Basic Documents of the Civil Rights Movement* (New York, 1967), 100, 106.

because their presence sometimes kept segregationists in check, lest acts of violence be reported. In the past year or so, cordiality had given way to mistrust, even to physical attacks on the reporters covering the rioting in the cities. On the Meredith March, reporters were getting it from both sides—enduring the jeers of white segregationists and the disdain of the marchers.[28] Some reporters responded in kind, filing dispatches filled with tones of impatience and irritation.

For whatever reason, irritation was laced throughout the reports in *Time*. It scorned as opportunists "the entire hierarchy of Negro civil rights movement leaders [that] swooped down on Memphis" determined to dedicate "the shooting of Meredith . . . to something—somehow." *Time* was not entranced with Meredith himself, whose plan seemed "neither divinely inspired nor notably responsible," but he had to be handled gingerly. Meredith was useful for making the point that the black leaders were self-serving and irresponsible; they ignored his protests that a major demonstration would put "a burden upon the Negroes in the area" because it was the season for planting crops. King particularly irked *Time*, which regarded the march as a publicity gimmick from which King was determined to wring the last drop of advantage by ascribing every turn of events to racism, justified or no. For example, King complained that the routine release of Meredith from a hospital in Memphis—where he had undergone treatment for "multiple superficial abrasions"—had "overtones of injustice." Likewise, King whipped up "an instant sermon against Mississippi bigotry," the key passage of which was that a marcher's death by heart attack " 'meant, in a sense, that he was probably underfed and undernourished, overworked and underpaid.' " To buttress its point, *Time* quoted the scathing comments of a black Mississippian with impeccable civil rights credentials, Charles Evers of the NAACP: " 'I don't want this to turn into another Selma, where everyone goes home with the cameramen and leaves us holding the bag." Evers complained further of exploitation of the situation "by the Negroes and whites who want to raise money and get publicity" and added: "I don't see how walking up and down a hot highway helps.' "[29] Nor did *Time*, which concluded its article with that sentence.

28. On hostility toward reporters, see Adler, "Mississippi," 100–101. A marcher noted that the demonstrators "all got the lesson early of not trusting any of the radio, TV, newspapermen." Stanley Plona Diary, June 22, 1966, n.p., and "Memo to Marchers," n.d., both in Box 9, File 73, Mississippi Valley Collection, Memphis State University.

29. "Heat on Highway 51," *Time*, June 17, 1966, pp. 26, 27.

Newsweek used some of the same elements, albeit with a different emphasis and with less certitude. Casting about for the meaning of it all, the magazine found contradictory scenarios. The shooting sounded "an echo of Oxford and Birmingham and Selma," providing another ugly reminder that "there were still places in America where a black man takes his life in his hands by asserting his right to live." The listing of the milestones of the old movement—"Oxford and Birmingham and Selma"—was an incantation as well. If those cities-as-symbols represented the worst of times, they also evoked the best of times, when the goal was unmistakable, the way clear. Finding, in Meredith's injury, a sign of renewal, *Newsweek* said, in effect, it could happen again, the old liberal spirit could be revived. Birmingham produced the Civil Rights Act of 1964, Selma the Voting Rights Act, and history might repeat itself: "Once again, a president of the U.S. was moved to speak the nation's anger at an 'awful act of violence.' Once again, a fresh charge of adrenaline surged through a Congress that had been considering a civil rights bill with more deliberation than speed. And once again, the civil rights movement was galvanized."[30]

Fine words about righteous anger and surges of adrenaline skirted a question. For what was the movement galvanized? The question was underscored by the contradictions that *Newsweek* reporters found when leaders of the movement addressed a rally. First to speak were the conservatives, Wilkins of the NAACP and Young of the Urban League. "'If you start hating all white men, you're going to waste your energies,'" Wilkins said. "*And he was applauded.* 'Let us be mad at people who don't register and vote, . . .' Young counseled. *And he was applauded.*" Then the militants: "McKissick paraphrased the inscription on the base of the Statue of Liberty, [and] suggested that they 'break that young lady's leg and throw her into the Mississippi.'" *And he was applauded.* "'We got to tell the Federal government about all those lies they have been telling us,' cried Carmichael. . . . 'We need power!'" *He was applauded.* Finally, there was King, intoning, "'We have power, and it isn't in bricks and guns. We have another weapon—nonviolence.' He was applauded, too."[31]

Here was the ultimate frustration of the news magazine reporter—news that defied interpretation. To make it worse, even King was drifting toward

30. "The March Meredith Began," 27.
31. *Ibid.*, 29–30.

the rhetoric of the "radical left," copying it from—of all persons—McKissick: "'In Africa they say *Uhuru*,' McKissick called. 'That means freedom! In Mississippi, it's *Uhuru* too.' It was the new rhetoric; it struck a spark, and King—ever attuned to a crowd—tried it on for size. 'We want some black sheriffs in Mississippi,' he cried. The crowd whooped and clapped, and, off to one side, Stokely Carmichael, the apostle of vote-black politics, smiled a knowing smile." In other circumstances, King might have earned a sharp rebuke. *Newsweek* needed him too much now. He represented the middle way "between the fire-eaters and the moderates." The magazine therefore brushed aside what King said as no more than trying out a crowd-pleasing gimmick. It also discounted Carmichael's boast that "'we've got all the cards.'" *Newsweek* was confident that King, not Carmichael, would set the dominant tone "if only because he attracts the most attention."[32] That was another matter passed over by *Newsweek*. King's presence guaranteed media coverage; whether his voice would drown out the voices of Carmichael and the other militants was something else entirely.

Gloomily contemplating these events, *U.S. News* posed its familiar question: "Can more racial violence be avoided?" It provided a familiar answer. Enraged blacks were out marching by the hundreds, some were talking ominously "of striking back at white violence," and whites "remembering the Negro riots of recent years in Northern cities, voiced fears of a new wave of rioting." While the chief threat was Carmichael ("'I'm not going to beg the white man for what I deserve,' . . . he said, "'I'm going to take it.'"), the journal chose to bury the differences between King and Carmichael on the last page of a three-page article. It would not do to make King appear moderate just because he spoke of nonviolence while Carmichael acted the fire-eater. There was, indeed, an implied threat in a quotation seized upon by *U.S. News*. "'We are going to put President Johnson on the spot,' said Dr. King. 'We are demanding immediate action by the federal government.'"[33]

Here was another in the unending stream of black demands to which *U.S. News* objected. The magazine found impatience that mirrored its own in Congress. On one side, Senate Republican leader Everett Dirksen, a key figure in the passage of the civil rights bills, rumbled about events that "open the wells of mischief all over again." On the other side, a Democratic liberal,

32. *Ibid.*, 31.
33. "Race Issue Inflamed Again: Aftermath of Shooting," *U.S. News & World Report*, June 20, 1966, pp. 36, 37–38.

Representative Emanuel Cellar, complained that Carmichael "and others of the same ilk" would make passage of civil rights legislation all but impossible if they "accentuate the theory of blacks for blacks and the devil take the whites." (Interestingly enough, Cellar obliged *Newsweek* with a different message; the wounding of Meredith might prove that the "civil rights movement has no greater friend than its enemy," which neatly made the journal's point about the assistance provided the civil rights movement by such unwitting allies as Jim Clark and Bull Connor.) Politicians have been known to issue statements more contradictory than Cellar's, but journalists also have been known to choose and discard statements on the basis of how they matched a particular theme. *Newsweek* and *U.S. News* could therefore quote Emanuel Cellar toward different ends.[34]

With his own ends in mind, Carmichael picked his moment on June 17. He was arrested during the day in Greenwood, Mississippi. An audience at a rally that night was harangued by one of his aides about the injustice of the arrest. Then Carmichael, out of jail on bond, appeared dramatically on the platform. " 'The only way we gonna stop them white men from whuppin' us is to take over,' he cried. 'We been saying freedom for six years and we ain't got nothin'. What we gonna start saying now is'—and then he shouted, 'Black Power.' "[35]

The news weeklies failed initially to catch the impact of the slogan—perhaps because the circumstances seemed so removed from the rest of the country. *Newsweek* came closest with the observation that SNCC's young radicals at times "seemed to be carrying the day with their new battle cry of racial alienation." It remained fascinated, however, by the possibility that the moderates and the militants would smooth over their differences in order to undertake concerted action against racial injustice. *Newsweek* was hopeful in another way, regarding Carmichael as a will-o'-the-wisp that could not prevail against the immense popularity of King.[36]

Time treated Carmichael's speech as little more than a diversion from the campaign to get black voters registered in Mississippi, and it now depicted the march almost as a reprise of Selma. Only segregationist villains and an incident that would galvanize Congress to quickly pass the new Johnson civil

34. *Ibid.*, 37; "The March Meredith Began," 29.
35. Viorst, *Fire in the Streets*, 373–74.
36. " 'Black Power!' " *Newsweek*, June 27, 1966, p. 36.

rights bill were missing from the scenario. The racists, *Time* reflected almost mournfully, had become wiser in the ways of publicity and image building. Mississippi's governor, Paul Johnson, for one, "realizes that blatant oppression merely helps the civil rights cause." As a result, "the atmosphere could hardly have seemed more unreal if the Ku Klux Klan had plied" black marchers with doughnuts and coffee.[37]

While regretting the paucity of villains, *Time* betrayed, strangely enough, an impatience with heroes. It had created enough in the past and would make more in the near future, but as it had during the Selma march, *Time* turned to the myth that it continually recreated: America the perfectible. For the magazine, the "ultimate hero" became "the democratic process itself."[38] Thus the meaning of the march was democracy and the courage of free men—Americans!—who were "succeeding in James Meredith's original task of showing Negroes that they could walk through Mississippi with dignity." Against such a vision, the angry cries of a Stokely Carmichael seemed to be mere carping; the machinations of a Mississippi governor, feeble thrusts against the inevitable; and those strung out in line of march along Highway 51, no more than bit players in the drama of America coming to terms with its greatness.

U.S. News had a different vision. The march was a "strange" demonstration for reasons hastily made clear. Discrimination against blacks had vanished; indeed, little in the report indicated discrimination had ever existed. The march meandered through the Mississippi Delta, "where Negroes outnumber whites in many communities—but" (the magazine did not inquire into the reasons for this state of affairs) "where Negro voters do not outnumber white voters." Seldom had cause and effect been so blandly separated. Nor did *U.S. News* inquire into the southern hospitality extended even to such firebrands as Carmichael, who was muttering threats to burn down every courthouse in the state. Blacks who wished to register "found no obstacle." Indeed, "Mississippi officials went out of their way to accommodate them"—even when (*U.S. News* could be counted on to include such episodes) blacks responded to courtesy with rudeness. As in the reports from Chicago earlier in the year, the effect was to demonstrate that the march was unnecessary. In the words of one

37. "Br'er Fox," *Time*, June 24, 1966, p. 31.
38. "On the Difficulty of Being a Contemporary Hero," *Time*, June 24, 1966, p. 33.

registration supervisor, "'The Negroes know all they had to do was come in here and tell me they want to register'" because "'the registration books are open six days a week the year around.'" Not for long: The books were slammed shut once the march had passed.[39]

With equal alacrity, the news weeklies began scrambling to catch up with the Black Power phenomenon. They were less concerned with the slogan's impact in Mississippi than with the effect it might have, as *Time* said, "on the mass of America's twenty million Negroes." *Time* was fretting because of scenes of violence from the Meredith March. The black leaders had picked out a schoolyard in Canton as a camping ground for the demonstrators. The authorities countered with offers of other sites, which were rejected as unsatisfactory. The negotiations broke down, and policemen moved in, firing tear gas cartridges and clubbing the marchers.[40]

Years past, Luce's journal would have damned the club-swinging policemen as savages, pressed the nation's leaders to set things right, then dropped the matter. No longer was it this simple. Blacks were edgier about the proposition that a whack from a policeman's billy club was a necessary rite of passage to citizenship. *Time* sensed this. Crowds along the march route were fickle, ready to cheer any speaker, applaud any philosophy from Black Power to nonviolence, and flare-ups such as the one in Canton might tip the balance toward the militants by providing "proof that Negroes can hardly expect much in the way of help from whites." *Time* took what comfort it could from an unpromising situation. Certain that most blacks wanted only good jobs, housing, education, and so on, *Time* was now willing that they get a "more generous slice" of the prosperity promised by the American dream without the waiting and the bootstraps effort on which it once insisted. Indeed, it feared that the pace of change might be too slow, that the summer would end with "well-meant moderation choked in Mississippi dust."[41]

With "black Jacobinism" rampant, *Time* turned to King, who, luckily, was a mutable symbol able to survive the transformation from publicity-seeking exploiter of causes to prophet of moderation. Against King's voice, the voices

39. "The Strange March Through Mississippi," *U.S. News & World Report*, June 27, 1966, p. 48. On closing the registration books, see Lewis, *King: A Biography*, 324.

40. Lewis, *King: A Biography*, 327–28; Adler, "Mississippi," 105. On the campsite, compare "The Last Three Days of the Memphis to Jackson March," a report by observers from the Birmingham Police Department, uncataloged, in William C. Hamilton Papers, Birmingham Public Library. "The New Racism," *Time*, July 1, 1966, p. 13.

41. "The New Racism," 13.

of Carmichael and McKissick sounded shrill, even unpatriotic. Carmichael decried integration as irrelevant and demanded Black Power. McKissick symbolically assaulted the Statue of Liberty, proclaiming, "We ought to break the young lady's legs and point her to Mississippi." King, by contrast, reaffirmed America and the democratic process as the hope of the black man and rebutted "the evangelists of Black Power. 'It is absolutely necessary for the Negro to gain power,' he said, 'but . . . we must never seek power exclusively for the Negro but the sharing of power with the white people.'" That was *Time*'s notion no less than King's. It had another one: The Carmichaels and the McKissicks resembled white supremacists more than right-thinking Americans. King was a useful symbol here as well. *Time* therefore sketched a dramatic encounter in Neshoba County, where the three civil rights workers were murdered in 1964. At a memorial service in the street, King said: "'And I believe in my heart that the murderers are somewhere around me at this moment.' 'They're right behind you,' chuckled a white onlooker, to roars of delight from fellow townsmen. Said King, 'I'm not afraid of any man. Before I will be a slave, I will be dead in my grave.' Shouted a chorus of whites: 'We'll help you' [into it]."[42] King was back in *Time*'s good graces, but it had taken Stokely Carmichael and Floyd McKissick to get him there.

U.S. News was the last to catch up with the Black Power phenomenon and to rediscover King's usefulness as a symbol. By mid-July, *U.S. News* had realigned its symbols. On one side were Carmichael and McKissick, equally radical, equally threatening. To McKissick, nonviolence was a "dying philosophy"; to Carmichael (in a statement that probably struck *U.S. News* as both presumptuous and close to treason), the closed subject of nonviolence would be reopened only when President Johnson was "ready to talk nonviolence with the Viet Cong." McKissick and Carmichael were given space to deny that Black Power meant black supremacy or hatred of whites, but their statements did not dispel the magazine's suspicions, which were supported by a newly anointed moderate:

> "It was only with the coming of the term Black Power that these problems in the civil rights movement came into being," Dr. King [said]. . . . "I think the phrase is unfortunate because it gives the wrong impressions. It can give the impression that we are preaching a doctrine of black supremacy, that we are concerned with power for power's sake, and will

42. *Ibid.*, 11, 12.

use any method to gain that power, that we are advocating power exclusively for Negroes in a pluralistic society where power should be shared, and that we can go it alone without whites. These are all negative and wrong impressions. The cry for Black Power can incite bitter antiwhite feelings among Negroes and it can intensify white prejudices and resistance."[43]

When King was permitted to make such a lengthy statement without rejoinder or qualification, it was a sign that he had indeed risen in the magazine's regard. There was more. King criticized CORE and SNCC for moving to a position of defensive violence that might lead to " 'an armed camp all over the South and in parts of the rest of the nation' " and insisted that he had retained his faith in nonviolence.[44]

The faith of Newsweek was ebbing. It was not disillusioned with King as an advocate of nonviolence, but the magazine's confidence that King could beat back the challenge to his leadership was much weaker. Once again, Newsweek was leading its two competitors in following the main current of events. The implications were dismaying. Nonviolence was taking a beating, figuratively and literally. When white policemen attacked demonstrators in Canton, some marchers responded in kind. There was a disturbing development. The savagery of the police assault made it seem that the "eye-for-an-eyewing" of the Meredith March—not King—"might have the larger hold on reality." To make matters worse, there appeared another crack in the liberal coalition, whose fragile condition obsessed Newsweek. The Johnson administration picked this moment to become difficult. It "embarrassed" the march leaders by "noting that they had been offered three campsites other than the schoolyard; by insisting on that spot, the marchers had forced the confrontation—if not the raw form it took." The magazine papered over the crack as best it could. Following the clash, King had sent a telegram asking Johnson to send federal marshals to protect the marchers. It was not answered. Newsweek did not report this cold snub.[45]

43. See *U.S. News & World Report*, "Around the Nation, Racial Violence Erupts," July 4, 1966, p. 8, and "Negro Leaders Dividing—The Effect," July 18, 1966, p. 32. Wilkins was used by *U.S. News* in the same fashion as King in "NAACP Head Warns 'Black Power Means Black Death,'" July 18, 1966, p. 34.

44. "Negro Leaders Dividing—The Effect," 32, 34. In this, though not in later articles, the Deacons for Defense and the Revolutionary Action Movement were depicted as even more threatening than CORE or SNCC.

45. "The March—in Step and Out," *Newsweek*, July 4, 1966, p. 14. Lewis ascribed Johnson's coldness to King's anti-war activities. *King: A Biography*, 329. Whatever Johnson's

While Carmichael's cry of Black Power split the black movement into hostile camps, it produced a remarkable unanimity among the news weeklies. Earlier in 1966, only *Newsweek* had designated King as an alternative to radical forces. The most *U.S. News* could manage to say was that King was slightly less objectionable than was Carmichael, while *Time* had savaged King as an exploiter of causes in Chicago and Mississippi. Now the slightly left-of-center *Newsweek*, the centrist *Time*, and the rightist *U.S. News* agreed: King was a prophet of moderation.

The unanimity of opinion lasted one week. It was shattered by the Chicago Freedom Movement, which had started six months before the marchers began trudging along Highway 51 in Mississippi.

For various reasons, King had been unable to devote full energy to the Chicago campaign. In the beginning, he insisted on spending three days a week fulfilling pastoral obligations in Atlanta. Then as the Chicago movement was gearing up for more demonstrations, Meredith was wounded; thereafter King shuttled between Chicago and Mississippi. The movement compiled a lengthy list of demands, including improvements in jobs and schools for minorities, reform of the welfare system, and creation of a civilian board to review complaints about police misconduct, but its focus was housing. While the disputes within the Chicago Freedom Movement were as lively as any seen in the black movement, lack of adequate housing was one issue that could command something close to unanimity among blacks in Chicago, one of the nation's most segregated cities.[46]

Of Chicago's 3.5 million residents in 1966, almost 1 million were black, and almost half of them were impoverished and crowded into slums on the South and the West sides. Pressure for black housing had been growing for more than a decade in Chicago and surrounding areas. There were a series of

---

motivation, it would have been appropriate to report that he did not answer the telegram. Perhaps *Newsweek* was unaware of King's message to Johnson, but even Birmingham police observers knew of it. "The Last Three Days of the Memphis to Jackson March," 2. In other ways, *Newsweek* sent out conflicting signals. It began to back away from a "certain strand of wishful thinking" that the Meredith March would unite the rival wings of the black movement. By July 4, its wryly accurate assessment was that "there were times when what the different organizations seemed to be hunting was one another." Nevertheless, it continued to promote King as the man most likely to bring peace to the black movement. See "The March—in Step and Out," 14, and reports in the issue of August 22, 1966, on King's standing in the movement, "Black Power: Road to Disaster?" 32, 34, 36, and "How Negroes Rank Their Leaders," 34.

46. Lewis, *King: A Biography*, 314, 319, 344–45; "Program of the Chicago Freedom Movement," July, 1966, in Box 1, File 16, King Center Archives, Atlanta.

riots and other racial incidents when black families moved into all-white enclaves in the late 1940s and early 1950s. In the most infamous incident, a mob of several thousand persons launched an assault against an apartment building in Cicero into which a black family had moved in 1951. National Guardsmen and police managed to restore order after several days of arson and looting. While the most publicized, the Cicero riot was by no means the worst of the outbreaks of mob violence accompanying attempts to integrate neighborhoods in or near Chicago.[47]

Cicero would eventually figure in King's plans, but he began his campaign with three objectives: to educate people about slum conditions; to organize ghetto residents into a union to force landlords to keep their buildings in good repair; and to mobilize those people into an army of nonviolent demonstrators. However, Mayor Daley's facade of affability proved difficult to puncture. The Daley machine countered with an announcement in February that fifty housing inspectors would be hired and a promise to prosecute vigorously any landlords found guilty of housing code violations. Thereafter, the campaign settled into move and countermove, with Daley winning most of the points, thwarting "King's efforts to undermine the black community's allegiance to his political machine."[48]

The situation started heating up on June 12. Rioting erupted in a Puerto Rican district after a youngster was shot by police. The following day, seven persons were injured during exchanges of gunfire between rioters and police.[49]

Possibly those disorders caught the attention of the leaders of the Chicago Freedom Movement; possibly they had in mind all along to find allies who shared "with Negroes common problems of slum housing, welfare dependency, inferior education, police brutality, and color discrimination." In any event, the movement's program, issued the month after the rioting, included some demands important to Hispanics and announced that the movement was "seeking ways to join in a united effort with its Latin American brothers."[50] It

47. Arnold Hirsch, "Making the Second Ghetto: Race and Housing in Chicago, 1940–1960" (Ph.D. dissertation, University of Illinois-Chicago Circle, 1978), 77–78, 80.
48. Viorst, *Fire in the Streets*, 366. See also Lewis, *King: A Biography*, 316.
49. Lewis, *King: A Biography*, 325; interview with Robert Lucas, chairman of the Chicago chapter of CORE, by John Britton, February 20, 1968 (Transcript of tape 155, in Moorland-Spingarn Research Center, Howard University), 15.
50. "Program of the Chicago Freedom Movement."

was a step toward the class-structured Poor People's Campaign, which King would assemble two years hence.

At the moment, however, King had his hands full trying to get the Chicago movement going. The SCLC conducted a rally at Soldier Field on July 10. Even its gate-count of 65,000 persons fell far short of the 100,000 anticipated. King proclaimed to those attending that "we must decide to fill up the jails of Chicago, if necessary, in order to end slums," issued a call for black political power, and led a march of about 5,000 persons to City Hall, where, emulating Luther, he attached a list of demands to the doors. A day later, King and Daley met, but the mayor was politely noncommittal.[51]

A month after the violence in the Puerto Rican section of the city, rioting erupted in the black ghetto. It was set in motion on July 12 when children turned on a fire hydrant to wash away the steamy heat of a Chicago summer, and police turned it off. The riot eventually spread to 140 square blocks. On the third night, a "prolonged period of sniper fire" was answered by volleys from some of the 4,000 National Guardsmen sent into Chicago.[52]

The events in Chicago caused U.S. News to break ranks with the other news magazines. After acting in haste in anointing King a moderate, it repented as hastily. In late July, turning from the South and Black Power to Chicago and Black Power, U.S. News found King sharing the speakers' platform during a rally in Chicago with Floyd McKissick—in brief, consorting with the enemy. Other matters were no less troubling. U.S. News conceded that King and his aides had attempted to curb outbreaks of rioting, but it spurned his argument that the rioting was caused by the intransigence of the Daley machine. The magazine favored the position taken by Joseph Le Febour, president of a police association in Chicago, who complained that wherever King "'goes and preaches nonviolence, violence erupts.'" Another (though unnamed) "Chicago official" explained further: "'You simply can't get together crowds of people in sweltering heat, many of them illiterate, tell them how bad off they are, work them up, and then expect them to do nothing. You can't control them—and he can't.'"[53]

51. Lewis, *King: A Biography*, 331–33; Paul Good, "Chicago Summer: Bossism, Racism, and Dr. King," *Nation*, September 19, 1966, p. 240.

52. Lewis, *King: A Biography*, 335.

53. "As Negro Unrest Continues to Spread," *U.S. News & World Report*, July 25, 1966, p. 30.

Some matters were ignored or passed over hastily. One was King's statement praising the conduct of Illinois National Guardsmen dispatched to control the rioting. Making King out to be a law-and-order man was not on the agenda then. Nor did the magazine dwell on the rioting by Puerto Ricans or the tentative steps by the Freedom Movement toward an alliance with Hispanics. Starting in 1965, *U.S. News* published several stories that asked, in effect, why blacks were rioting when other impoverished minority groups remained orderly. Its intent was to establish that blacks were relentlessly grabbing all that they could through violence or threats of violence. Associating the rioting by Hispanics with disorders involving blacks would have punctured the editorial line that the latter were not as bad off in Chicago as King claimed. King no longer seemed "safe," as he had when *U.S. News* made him a symbolic alternative to Black Power. By August 1, King was dropped from the list of the black leaders who advocated nonviolence; his replacement was Wilkins of the NAACP.[54]

After reversing course, *U.S. News* put the echo chamber back in operation, depicting King, with few exceptions, as a radical, a troublemaker, or subversive. In most cases, the identification was contextual. On August 1, for example, David Lawrence associated King with "the wave of discontent" sweeping the country. Clearly, Lawrence had King in mind because of the echo picked up from the previous week's story about the rioting in Chicago. His question was this: "Why, then, are the leaders of the civil rights movement preaching 'nonviolence,' but, in effect, arousing passions and inciting people to violence?" His ready answer took the form of questions implying conspiracies: "Are the outbreaks spontaneous or planned? Why the sudden appearance of firebombs and shotguns in the crowds? Why all the arson? What is the record and background of some of the top advisers who sit beside certain gullible leaders in the civil rights movement and plan 'targets' for the mobilization of demonstrators? Why has the information about subversive activities been withheld?"[55]

54. A copy of King's statement praising the guardsmen is in Box 3, File 13, King Center Archives, Atlanta. *U.S. News* reported the riot of Puerto Ricans in "New Problem—Puerto Rican Riots," June 27, 1966, p. 8, but did not associate the episodes of rioting by Hispanics and blacks. On the peaceful, nonblack poor, see, for example, "Tomorrow," September 6, 1965, p. 24. *U.S. News* listed advocates of nonviolence in "A 'Black Power' Advocate in a Powerful Post," August 1, 1966, p. 8.

55. David Lawrence, "Who is to Blame?" *U.S. News & World Report*, August 1, 1966, p. 84. See also "The Rising Threat of U.S. Communists," *U.S. News & World Report*, August 15, 1966, p. 9.

Perhaps some readers failed to decipher those references to preaching nonviolence and inciting the opposite and to subversives sitting at King's right hand. If so, they only had to wait a week for clarification. The next issue, King was identified as one of those who had "spread a riot mood." *U.S. News* published what amounted to a rogues' gallery—not using photographs but reprinting the statements of the troublemakers, allowing them, as it were, to convict themselves. Actually, the statements of King (and some others) were mild, measured against Carmichael's and McKissick's. But *U.S. News* condemned all of them equally, first by placing them in each other's company, then by declaring that such statements were denounced "as part of the climate that has fostered violence," and, finally, by linking the statements through juxtaposition to incendiary publications "flowing into Negro areas and openly inciting slum dwellers to guerrilla war." King was not singled out for especially harsh condemnation; he was, if anything, a lesser light in the company of President Johnson, Vice-President Humphrey, Senator Robert Kennedy, and Congressman Adam Clayton Powell. Still, King had an important place in the rogues' gallery as a promoter of the climate of fear and violence.[56]

Other articles did single out King for special treatment. For example, *U.S. News* eradicated its previous distinction between King and the Black Power advocates when reporting an incident during which King was struck by a rock hurled from a white mob; both article and headline implied that King had led a Black Power march. *U.S. News* also painted him as a dangerous leader. The best way of attaching this label was to maintain that King refused to heed the counsel even of his allies. One ally was Archbishop John P. Cody (carefully identified as "an advocate of civil rights for Negroes"), who asked black leaders to suspend their marches in order to avoid "'serious injury . . . and even the loss of lives.'" In response, "Negro leaders in the drive" headed by King "rejected the Archbishop's appeal and scheduled more marches." A different twist was used the following week. King denounced as unconstitutional an injunction obtained by Daley to limit demonstrations, then declared defiantly: "'We are prepared to put thousands in the streets if need be.'" He had already put hundreds of protesters in the streets, and *U.S. News* marshaled some statistics that portended the demise of law and order in Chicago. "Offi-

---

56. "'Rouse the Masses,'" *U.S. News & World Report*, August 8, 1966, pp. 40–41. The theme was echoed in "If Mob Rule Takes Hold in U.S.—A Warning from Richard Nixon," *U.S. News & World Report*, August 15, 1966, pp. 64–65; and with more explicit venom in "A Down-to-Earth Look at a Growing Problem," *U.S. News & World Report*, August 22, 1966, p. 53.

cial figures," *U.S. News* reported, "showed that 699 Chicago policemen were injured in the last two months and 134 resigned this year." Juxtaposition made it appear that the injuries and the resignations were due solely to the marches led by King.[57]

The coverage of King was effectively wrapped up on a familiar note from a familiar source, retired justice Whittaker. His attrited message cited, as usual, "the irresponsible and inflammatory preachments of some self-appointed leaders of minority groups 'to obey the good laws, but to violate the bad ones'—which, of course, simply advocates violation of laws they do not like, or, in other words, the taking of the law into their own hands." And, in other words, the source of the danger was the false prophet King. *U.S. News* had come full circle, deviating from its usual course only when Carmichael and Black Power seemed more dangerous, and King was useful to counter them. Well before year's end, King was back in his familiar role again, consorting with the enemy and refusing to repudiate Black Power after doing so earlier.[58]

In what *U.S. News* reported there was a grain or two of truth. After the rioting subsided, King started escalating the marches and demonstrations in order to bring pressure to bear on Daley. Daley was difficult to pin down. Even when he overreached by complaining that anarchists, Communists, and the SCLC had provoked the rioting on July 12, he quickly modified his statement to exempt King from any blame. Subsequently, Daley and King announced an agreement of sorts, but the points covered were almost mean-

57. "Riots, Battles, Power Marches—It's Still a Hot Summer," *U.S. News & World Report*, August 15, 1966, p. 36. "Power Marches" is a form of "Black Power Marches" shortened to fit the space allotted for the headline. King was the only person identified as having led a protest march. A photograph and caption accompanying an article about Carmichael linked Black Power to a "Chicago civil rights rally" without further explanation, thus placing Black Power indirectly in the context of the well-publicized Chicago movement. "Inside Story of 'Black Power' and Stokely Carmichael," *U.S. News & World Report*, August 15, 1966, p. 12. A week later, King, Carmichael, and Adam Clayton Powell were grouped as critics of the housing section of a proposed civil rights bill. Significantly, their statements were variations on a theme. Theirs were the only statements published, though *U.S. News* noted that another critic was Roy Wilkins. "The Policing Job Washington Now is Trying to Get," August 22, 1966, p. 38. For the stories in *U.S. News* on King and Cody, see "Mounting Concern over Racial Violence," August 22, 1966, p. 6; and on statistics about police who resigned or were injured, see "A City Cracks Down on Demonstrations," August 29, 1966, p. 10.

58. Charles E. Whittaker, "Planned Lawlessness Threatens to Get Out of Hand," *U.S. News & World Report*, September 19, 1966, p. 37 (echoed the next year in "Blamed in Crime Rise: Civil Rights Excesses," February 27, 1967, p. 15). See also "Now, Negro Attack on 'Black Power,'" *U.S. News & World Report*, October 24, 1966, p. 14, in which King did not denounce Black Power. An exception is "How to Solve Racial Problems—Varying Views of Negro Leaders," *U.S. News & World Report*, September 5, 1966, p. 14.

ingless. Thereafter, waves of marches were sent into white enclaves. Chicago police recorded at least twenty-four marches near the end of July and the first two weeks of August. On August 14, three groups marched simultaneously into three separate areas. The atmosphere was becoming explosive as large crowds "varying in size from several hundred to several thousand people, gathered along the line of the march carrying signs, hooting, [and] throwing rocks, firecrackers, and other missiles at the marchers."[59]

The Daley machine was now feeling the pressure. Daley secured an injunction on August 19 limiting the number of demonstrations and demonstrators and prohibiting night marches. King considered disobeying the injunction, but the SCLC lacked the money and the number of volunteers willing to go to jail that would have been necessary for massive civil disobedience. He did have a trump card that he and his aides had hinted previously would be played—a march through Cicero. King's announcement that such a march would be held on August 28 pulled a number of militants into his camp and sent shivers through the Chicago establishment. No one had forgotten the riot of 1951, and the prospect of a bloody repetition forced Daley to make a deal two days before the march was scheduled to enter hostile Cicero.[60] King had won, so it appeared, by following his Birmingham strategy of escalating demonstrations until the opposition cracked. Unlike Birmingham, the taste of victory in Chicago would be short-lived.

Before and after King played his Cicero card, *Time* continued to portray him as a prophet of moderation and reason when compared with the radicals of Black Power. Few opportunities were missed to damn the doctrine or its advocates, whether this required the rehabilitation of John Lewis, former chairman of SNCC, or the painting of SNCC as a deadbeat organization that skipped town without paying its bills. CORE was treated in like manner. CORE ignored the call of reason sent out by "the best known and most popular of the rights leaders"—King, of course—who "felt obliged to warn that the movement is 'very, very close' to a permanent split over the issue of Black Power, [and] urged civil rights leaders to patch up their differences before it is too late." Transmogrified, CORE became the "Congress of Racial Superi-

59. Lewis, *King: A Biography*, 335–36. On the marches, see *Chicago* v. *King*, bill of complaint, in Box 2, File 1, King Center Archives, Atlanta.

60. On the injunction, see Lewis, *King: A Biography*, 342. The SCLC's weaknesses are cited in McGraw, "An Interview with Andrew J. Young," 2. On the strategy of a march through Cicero, see Lewis, *King: A Biography*, 340, 344, 345; and Lucas interview, 16.

ority." The annual convention of CORE, *Time* carefully noted, was boycotted by King and the conservatives (described as moderates by *Time*) of the NAACP and the Urban League. It was bad enough that CORE ignored the opinions of King and *Time* magazine about Black Power; but CORE went further. To begin with, it described the conduct of the American war in Vietnam as "filled with conscious racism"—stronger language than the cautious words King had used in 1965 and, of course, far stronger than his statements now in the rare instances when he said anything publicly about the war.[61]

CORE took another line guaranteed to enrage Luce's journal by scorning the middle class, black or white. In fact, CORE derided—*Time*'s disbelieving word—the black middle class, which "has borne most of the leadership burden of the civil rights struggle and has the technical and professional know-how that is indispensable in preparing other Negroes to pass through the doors now opening." This indeed was heresy. Opposing the war was a grievous sin, but *Time* had managed to forgive King his lapse. CORE was debunking the American center, and doing it in the rudest possible way. At CORE's convention, *Time* reported, no doubt with some confusion about the precise meaning of the term, moderates "like Dr. King were called 'chicken-eating preachers.'" At another time, the magazine might have relished that wickedly deflating phrase. Not, however, when alarms were echoing in the streets and King was a useful, if not always consistent, symbol of opposition to the "racism in reverse" of Black Power.[62]

Time's newfound regard for King appeared as well in its reports from Chicago. A few months earlier, it believed Chicago could manage quite well without a southern Baptist preacher insufficiently reverent about private property. Black Power and the rioting in July changed that attitude. To be sure, *Time* had to swallow hard on occasion, as, for example, when King and McKissick linked arms on a speakers' platform. Even worse, when King and McKissick agreed publicly that black problems could be solved peaceably, the accord made no difference: rioting still erupted. Significantly, whatever

---

61. "Black Power in the Red," *Time*, July 8, 1966, p. 21; "At the Breaking Point," *Time*, July 15, 1966, p. 15. King believed it politic to emphasize that his statements about the war were not made as a civil rights leader. He apparently did not make that distinction during a press conference in Paris in the spring of 1966, but hastened to do so in a subsequent encounter with the press in Stockholm. William Gordon, U.S. public affairs officer in Stockholm, to U.S. Information Agency, Washington, D.C., April 6, 1966, in Box 2, File 6, King Center Archives, Atlanta.

62. "At the Breaking Point," 16. *Time* also used a similar statement about reverse racism from Roy Wilkins.

his shortcomings and inconsistencies, King continued to receive support from *Time*. The blame for the unrest in Chicago was assigned not to King, not even to McKissick, but to Daley. His police provided the spark that ignited the riot by cutting off a fire hydrant on a scorching day, and at times the police "matched the rioters in reckless violence with club and gun." As for Daley, he had "consistently fumbled his dealings with the Negro population that makes up nearly one-third of his constituency." *Time* dismissed Daley's attempt to shift the responsibility for the rioting onto King's shoulders, reporting that King had tried to persuade rioters to disperse. *Time* was being persuaded by King that the riots were a sign of desperation; that much more than sprinklers would be needed to relieve the wretchedness of the ghetto and to defuse its explosiveness, and that it would require a great deal of effort to improve housing, sanitation, and schools, and to make more jobs available to impoverished blacks.[63]

Although it had preached this message for years, *Newsweek* of late was plagued by doubts, especially doubts about the effectiveness of King as a symbol. His magic was diminishing among young volunteers for whom "protesting the war in Vietnam has replaced civil rights as the top-priority issue." Doubts lingered as well from the Meredith March. Black Power had created "a crisis of allegiance among Negroes and" (here *Newsweek*'s dismay registered most clearly) "of confidence among sympathetic whites." King, "dreaming his eloquent dreams of nonviolence and integration," could not be abandoned; there was no other symbol to replace him. But hard facts had to be faced. King had been outpointed by Carmichael; indeed, Carmichael had used King to get Black Power the kind of media attention only King's presence could deliver. Most disturbing was the implicit question that haunted *Newsweek*: Of what efficacy was King's eloquent dream against the bleak reality of life in the ghetto or the rural South? Viewed in that harsh light, integration became "mere pie in the sky to be portioned out by whites to those few middle-class Negroes they find acceptable. A 'subterfuge for white supremacy,' SNCC's Carmichael calls it." A militant from Washington elaborated: " 'King is not raising serious issues, he's talking about integrated cups of coffee.' "[64]

63. See *Time*, "Battle of Roosevelt Road," July 22, 1966, pp. 18–19; "The Jungle and the City," July 29, 1966, p. 12; and "What the Negro Has—and Has Not—Gained," October 28, 1966, pp. 32–33.

64. See *Newsweek*, "Summertime," June 27, 1966, p. 60, and " 'Black Power': Politics of Frustration," July 11, 1966, p. 26.

Bleakness was piled on top of bleakness the next week. Everywhere there appeared to be a scramble to capitalize on the Black Power phenomenon: by CORE, which adopted Black Power as its policy; by SNCC, which "one-upped CORE" with the slogan on the Meredith March; by the NAACP, whose executive secretary, Roy Wilkins, was grabbing headlines by denouncing Black Power as a "reverse Mississippi, a reverse Hitler, a reverse Ku Klux Klan." Although King occupied the middle ground, *Newsweek* recognized sadly that this position now conferred little advantage because of the "mounting pressure on one hand to break finally with the Black Power advocates—and, on the other, to step up his own militancy" in order to compete with them. Once King had been the honest broker of the black movement; now *Newsweek* doubted the factions could even be persuaded to sit down together at the same table, King or no King. *Newsweek* was correct about King's inability to bring the warring sides together. The analysis went no deeper. *Newsweek* did not, for example, entertain the disconcerting possibility that King might move, or be pushed further, toward radicalism, or that he might use civil disobedience immoderately, yet remain within the Gandhian tradition.[65] Better a failing symbol than one turned on its head.

The doubts recurred during the rioting in July. *Newsweek* willingly defended King against Daley's canard that King or the SCLC bore some responsibility for the uprising; this "seemed eminently unfair" because King had attempted to draw youth gangs into civil rights work, and he had sped around the riot area trying to restore order. The problem was that he had failed. Few listened to him during the rioting; few had heeded King's "plaintive" (therefore ineffectual) "plea for nonviolence" beforehand.[66]

Along with doubts about King's effectiveness, an edginess of tone found its way into the magazine. It could be ascribed to King's penchant for creating crises. The point was made most forcefully by Raymond Moley, a columnist, who complained that King (and Wilkins) were letting things get out of hand: "While preaching nonviolence, they so forcefully remind their followers of injustices that they excited emotional and nonrational reactions which they may not have anticipated. And so they found their movements out of control." *Newsweek*'s columnists tended to march to the beat of their own drums, but a week later the same sentiment emerged from a report that stated that "King's

65. "Line in the Dust," *Newsweek*, July 18, 1966, pp. 23, 24. More radical direct action was being contemplated within the SCLC. See Lawson, "The Meredith March," 3.
66. "West Side Story," *Newsweek*, July 25, 1966, pp. 17, 18.

scenario" for nonviolent demonstrations "has always included a strand of provocation—he calls it 'creative tension.'"[67] The same tone had been sounded before when King appeared determined to press the matter in Birmingham and Selma. *Newsweek* came around when King won smashing victories in those cities. It would do so again in Chicago—but first King would have to win.

Soon after, he seemed to be winning, relentlessly applying pressure through marches into white neighborhoods. The response was as violent as in the campaigns in Dixie. *Newsweek* reported scenes of "white mobs pelting King's integrated columns with bricks and bottles, waving placards ('We Want Wallace'), howling threats ('We'll kill you niggers if you don't get out')," and warbling this racist ditty:

> "I wish I were an Alabama trooper,
> That is what I would truly like to be;
> I wish I were an Alabama trooper
> 'Cause then I could kill the niggers legally."[68]

Grumblings about provocative demonstrations and questions about the judgment of a leader willing to put himself and his followers in jeopardy would matter little—so long as King was winning. Although his marches provoked violence, he remained committed to nonviolence when others were renouncing it; he was leading integrated demonstrations when the sight of blacks and whites marching in common cause was becoming rare, when the very idea of integration was being derided by the disciples of Black Power. (At about this time, in fact, SNCC was attempting to persuade blacks in Atlanta to forgo the well-meant assistance of a white volunteer whom SNCC scornfully characterized as a "white Jesus.") Only if King faltered could *Newsweek* abandon him without signaling abandonment of the cause that it had made its own and that it now presented as the alternative to Black Power or revolution.[69]

Newsweek's problem was complicated by the necessity of showing dissatisfied blacks that moderation produced results beyond the symbolic while reas-

67. Raymond Moley, "Pattern of Revolution," *Newsweek*, August 8, 1966, p. 84; "The Touchiest Target," *Newsweek*, August 15, 1966, p. 29.

68. "The Touchiest Target," 29.

69. The SNCC campaign was reported by *Newsweek* in "'White Jesus,'" July 25, 1966, p. 29. On *Newsweek*'s use of King as a symbol of moderation, see, for example, "Black Power: Road to Disaster?" 32, and "The Longest, Hottest Summer," August 22, 1966, p. 57.

suring whites who (if *Newsweek*'s polling was accurate) were more and more resentful of the bill of demands presented by the black movement. The situation in Chicago was particularly delicate because, a survey found, "any demonstration looks to whites like an incitement to trouble." By that standard, King and his allies were out looking for trouble almost every day in late July and early August. Open-housing marches provoked much hostility. Most blacks wanted to live in integrated neighborhoods, *Newsweek* reported, but "roughly half the whites bridle at the prospect. And even those who assent, more often than not, impose their own conditions: the Negro next door must be a Negro of the right sort. Demands for housing integration touch the white man's most sensitive nerve." Chicago, it added unnecessarily, "was only a casebook example of what can happen when Negro demonstrators rub it raw."[70]

The nerve would be rubbed raw—and more—if King carried out the march into Cicero. Although the police chief of Cicero made encouraging noises to the effect that there would be no violence, the sheriff of Cook County expressed a grimmer view. He warned King that the demonstration would be suicidal. The governor of Illinois, alarmed by the possibility of bloody clashes, put National Guardsmen and state police on alert. Two days before the Cicero march, however, Daley and the Chicago establishment were forced to conclude an agreement with King.[71]

What came to be known as the Summit Agreement covered ten points, including several open-housing issues, such as mortgages, and reform of the welfare system. The agreement angered some militants, who objected to vague clauses and opposed King's decision to cancel the Cicero march. Many of the militants, in fact, did not support open housing, believing that it would not help most black families or would dilute black political power. The Chicago chapter of CORE had supported King at the outset out of the belief that he had a hidden agenda: to show "how racist Chicago or the North is."[72]

There were similarities and differences in the readings of these events by

70. *Newsweek*, seeking examples of integrated situations, located one, ironically, in that most conservative of institutions, the military, where "the color of a man's uniform counts more than the color of his skin." "The Great Society—in Uniform," August 22, 1966, pp. 46, 48. For *Newsweek*'s reports about white attitudes, see "White Consensus: 'They're Trying to Go Too Fast,'" August 22, 1966, p. 24, and "The Longest, Hottest Summer," 57.

71. Lewis, *King: A Biography*, 343–44. That overused term, *establishment*, is appropriate because many of Chicago's civic and business organizations and governmental agencies were represented in the bargaining process.

72. The Summit Agreement's terms, open housing, and the unhappiness of the militants are treated *ibid.*, 344–47. See also Good, "Chicago Summer," 238; and Lucas interview, 17, 27–28.

Time and *Newsweek*. King impressed *Time* with his threat to march through Cicero, "a Selma without the Southern drawl," thus forcing the powers-that-be to take "positive action" to open up housing for blacks. In effect, *Time* applauded King's version of brinkmanship—particularly since he stepped back from the edge—"until the Chicago leadership had had a chance to demonstrate its good intent with action." The hostility of the militants earned King *Time*'s approbation. Their complaint about cancellation of the Cicero march was dismissed with the cutting note that "they, too, backed down at week's end" from a threat to proceed without King. King demonstrated the Christian spirit by averting bloodshed, but—a Lucean twist—King was a "practical Christian" who pledged "'to watch to see, day by day, week by week, that it is being carried out.'" If the agreement wasn't honored, "he plans again to march on Cicero."[73]

Seldom had *Time* written so glowingly of King, and it continued for several weeks to reiterate his credentials as a moderate. Then it maintained a studied silence for almost all of the last quarter of the year, probably because it had dawned on *Time* that King had failed disastrously in Chicago.[74]

As evidence of his failure, there was a Cicero march—one King did not lead. The march was orchestrated by dissidents from the Chicago Freedom Movement, chief among them Robert Lucas of CORE. On September 4, a white mob assembled along the march route, but a show of force by police and National Guardsmen prevented serious violence. Other signs of failure appeared in King's speeches, where pessimism mingled with the bleak recognition that the task in Chicago was much greater than he had expected. Very likely King also had begun to realize what became undeniable within a few months: The Summit Agreement was worthless, and the Chicago Freedom Movement would be written off as a disaster.[75]

73. "Crossing the Red Sea," *Time*, September 2, 1966, p. 19. See also "Pharaoh's Lesson," *Time*, September 9, 1966, p. 22.

74. *Time* employed King as a symbol in opposition to Black Power ("Stokely's Spark," September 16, 1966, p. 37) or as a symbol of the reconciliation of whites and blacks ("Intruders in the Dust," September 23, 1966, p. 26; and "Ahead of Its Time," September 30, 1966, p. 21). King was conspicuously absent from *Time*'s later stories about the Black Power controversy. See, for example, "The Turning Point," October 7, 1966, pp. 29–30; "Herald of the Dream," October 7, 1966, pp. 36–37; and "From Toehold to Foothold," November 18, 1966, pp. 29–30.

75. On the march in Cicero, see Good, "Chicago Summer," 241–42; *cf.* Lucas interview, 27. On the fate of the Summit Agreement, see Good, "Chicago Summer," 238; and Lewis, *King: A Biography*, 351. Two reports concluded that little had been done to achieve open housing: William H. Moyer, Chicago Freedom Movement Follow-up Committee, to CCCO delegates retreat, October 23, 1966, Box 2, File 4, and statement by CCCO chairman Albert A. Raby *et al.*, March 28, 1967, Box 1, File 17, both in King Center Archives, Atlanta.

Newsweek proclaimed the Summit Agreement to be a "Victory in the North" for King. Buried in its report, however, was this cautionary note: "Whether the package would or even could be enforced remained to be seen."[76] The Byzantine twists of Chicago politics made that an understatement of the first order.

While celebrating King's victory, *Newsweek* gave signs of being disturbed by King and his crises. As evidence, there was the word *provocation*, which *Newsweek* said was the essence of his strategy of "parading into precisely those Middle and East European 'ethnic' neighborhoods where anti-Negro feelings run closest to the surface." And there was Cicero: "The mere thought of hundreds of Negroes marching through Cicero sent shivers through Chicagoans who remembered the bitter race riot that erupted there when a lone Negro family tried to move in fifteen years ago." The magazine returned again and again to the staging of confrontations. "King and his nonviolent legions," it now reported, "consciously escalated tensions to the point where the Chicago establishment would have no choice but to negotiate their demands." King created a crisis—this fact appeared in his own remark—and he went "right on turning up the heat" until "Daley at last had no choice but to talk turkey with King."[77]

There was more to such phrases than admiration for the way that King forced the canny Daley to the bargaining table. *Newsweek* dropped the exculpatory adjective "creative" when summarizing the tensions produced by King's tactics. Then the magazine turned to those whom King had summoned to his side in the past. "Even some civil rights leaders," it said, even "Northern liberals who had approved similar civil rights campaigns in the distant South" were troubled when King escalated tensions in order to win in Chicago.[78]

—Which is not to say that King had changed his strategy or, in the main, his tactics. He had tried them out, somewhat clumsily, in Albany. He had honed them in Birmingham and in St. Augustine; he had defeated Jim Crow in Selma with the same weapons of nonviolence. In Chicago, he did what any other successful general would have done: use what had brought victory in the past. The times were more volatile, of course; Watts and Black Power testified to that. Place was no less important a consideration. The prospect of hundreds of blacks provoking violence by marching into Cicero was frightening, but

76. "Victory in the North," *Newsweek*, September 5, 1966, p. 21.
77. *Ibid.*, 20, 21.
78. *Ibid.*

Cicero was no more hostile territory than was Birmingham or Selma. The fact of the matter was that King was alarming those who at once professed sympathy for the black man and cautioned that change should come with deliberate speed. *Newsweek*'s audience was perhaps a notch or two to the left, but its members were anything but radical, and if they were disturbed by the Chicago campaign's "deep implications for cities across the urban North," so was *Newsweek*.[79]

Doubts hardened into certainty: King was not the man for the job in Chicago. That thesis took shape in the last quarter of 1966 and reappeared early in 1967. While exploring the possibility of a new strategy promoted by "mainstream" black leaders, an alliance of interests between the poor, black and white, *Newsweek* relegated King and his mass demonstrations to the dustbin. There would be "a longer, subtler twilight struggle with issues that cannot be settled in the streets. 'Circuses are no longer needed in this movement,' says Bayard Rustin, gangly, chain-smoking ringmaster of the 1963 March on Washington." *Newsweek* had in mind one particular circus. Little more than a month after proclaiming King victorious, *Newsweek* twitted him for causing "a wave of white anger without placing a single Negro family in a white neighborhood." There remained work for King to do, but not in the North; a reference to King's "Southern-style mass-marching campaign" was no accident. "Some wish, in fact," *Newsweek* reported, undoubtedly counting itself among them, "that King would pack up his charisma, go back South, and become, as one put it, the 'pied piper' in a massive voter registration campaign." The reproach was all the more cutting because King was becoming realistic. The magazine noted, accurately enough, that the SCLC went into Chicago overly optimistic about a quick victory. Now King was speaking of organizing the ghetto as a five-year task: "'We know we're not going to accomplish all these things overnight or in a matter of a few months.'"[80]

If King had awakened to realism, why, then, did *Newsweek* want him to get out of Chicago and return to the South? It was not a simple matter of defeat snatched from the jaws of victory. True enough, King presided over a first-class debacle in Chicago. But King was no stranger to failure; his defeat at the

79. *Ibid.*, 20.

80. "What's Ahead for the Negro," *Newsweek*, November 28, 1966, pp. 30, 31. King's somber analysis actually came almost on the heels of the Summit Agreement, about six weeks before this article was published. Good, "Chicago Summer," 239–40. The SCLC allowed eighteen months in which to achieve success in Chicago. Bishop, *The Days of Martin Luther King*, 422.

hands of Laurie Pritchett had been almost as crushing, and King had applied the lessons learned, winning a spectacular victory a year later when his opponent was Bull Connor. The difference was that when the disaster in Albany could not be denied, *Newsweek* wrote him out of its history, while in Chicago it acted as if he had never lost a campaign before—or learned from his mistakes. Possibly, *Newsweek* may have simply recognized that because of the SCLC's deficiencies, the job was unlikely to get done. Probably other factors were more important, particularly the political problems that white backlash would cause for Democrats. Another answer might be located in the problems of opposing Daley. Given the machine's hold on the city, community organization would require an alliance of blacks and other impoverished minority groups. That logic had struck the Chicago Freedom Movement at least as early as July, and the SCLC followed through by making an occasional gesture toward Hispanics, though there is little evidence to suggest an alliance was brought to fruition.[81]

Earlier, *Newsweek* had suggested a coalition of blacks and Hispanics. Later in 1966 the suggestion was reiterated, but with a different twist. The goal was the same: solving the problems of the poor, whatever their racial background. As translated by *Newsweek*, this meant "an alliance of self-interest with labor and liberal whites."[82] However, *Newsweek*, a liberal but far-from-radical journal, wanted that alliance situated within a revived civil rights coalition dominated by those with power and organizational skills who would dampen any class conflict.

By most standards of logic, *Newsweek* should have been first in line to enlist King in any coalition formed to rebuild the ghettos of the North. Certainly King had been edging toward economic issues for years, and the movement he led in Chicago had made the first halting steps toward an alliance across racial lines. Furthermore, King had begun talking soberly of five years

---

81. On the SCLC's shortcomings in Chicago, see Lewis, *King: A Biography*, 314–15; and, in a general context, Charles Fager, *Uncertain Resurrection: The Poor People's Washington Campaign* (Grand Rapids, Mich., 1969), 14. *Newsweek*, in "How Much of the Way with LBJ?" September 26, 1966, p. 26, and "Colorful Campaign," October 17, 1966, p. 29, cited the political implications of the white backlash produced by the Chicago movement. On attempts to bring Hispanics into the Chicago movement, see speech by Albert A. Raby, CCCO head, n.d. [*ca*. July, 1966], in Box 4, File 21. One gesture toward Hispanics is recorded in Robert Hostetter to Albert Raby, July 15, 1966, in Box 2, File 3. Both documents are in the King Center Archives, Atlanta.

82. See *Newsweek*, "Crusade Against Gringos," 17–18, "U.S. Latins on the March," 32–36, and "What's Ahead for the Negro," 30.

or more being required to do community organizing in the North. Another development could only have been welcomed by *Newsweek*. Lately, King seemed to be moving away from reliance on mass demonstrations, the tactic declared passé by the magazine (just as it had done before King got his campaign off the ground in Selma a year earlier). Nevertheless, there was to be no place for King in this multiracial coalition promoted by *Newsweek*, in part because King had not delivered results in Chicago. There was another factor. *Newsweek* seemed to labor under the delusion that King could do no more than prick the conscience of the nation, and open-housing marches through hostile ethnic neighborhoods—such as he led in Chicago—obviously would enrage whites rather than win sympathy. Actually, two strains ran through Gandhian nonviolence—persuasion and coercion, the latter taking the form of civil disruption escalated until major civic functions ground to a standstill. Just such a result was in the minds of members of the maverick chapter of CORE that threatened to stall automobiles on roads leading to the 1964 New York World's Fair. While King recognized the opportunity two years later, he did not seize it. As Lerone Bennett wrote, in Chicago, King "never went as far as his mentor, Gandhi." The question was, would King continue to draw back from the brink? From the reports of *Newsweek*, it appeared he would—or that the magazine desperately hoped he would. In any event, *Newsweek* wanted King out of Chicago, out of the North, and back on his home ground.[83] If King was to be a pied piper, let the tune that he piped be a summons to black southerners to register to vote. Thus defining King as a prophet, *Newsweek* was attempting to keep him a symbol that threatened no one except deluded bigots clinging to a dying system of segregation. For other uses, he was no longer safe.

King did return to the South, where, brooding over the failure of the Chicago campaign, perhaps came to his mind Gandhi's dictum that freedom had to be won, nonviolently if possible, but won in any event. King did not abandon nonviolence because of the failure in Chicago, but in 1967 he would set out on radical courses, taking up the anti-war cause once more and laying the foundation for a new march on Washington differing radically from the one he led in 1963.

83. Lewis, *King: A Biography*, 334. *Newsweek*'s thesis that King should stick to his affairs in the South was restated in allegorical form in "Homesick in Freedomland," February 13, 1967, pp. 37, 38.

VIII

PROPHET OF PEACE

After retreating from the issue in 1965, King continued to oppose
the war, but did it "as quietly as possible." Departing from that
policy entailed some weighty risks. King risked, first of all, a final break with
Lyndon Johnson, a politician notorious for nursing political grudges. The loss
of badly needed contributions to the SCLC was another consideration, as was
the likelihood of exacerbating the tensions within the black movement. Nevertheless, self-interest and conscience pushed him back into the anti-war
movement. His standing had been damaged by Black Power and the disastrous Chicago campaign. But King was also motivated by the concern that the
war was diverting billions of dollars that could be better spent relieving the
misery of the poor. His commitment to nonviolence was genuine, and he
regarded the prospect of war, especially nuclear war, with abhorrence. And
the Nobel Prize had encouraged him in the belief that he ought to strike out
onto the world stage.[1]

1. On King's quiet opposition to the war, see Charles E. Fager, "Dilemma for Dr. King,"
Christian Century, XVI (March, 1966), 332. On the SCLC's financial losses, see Andrew
Young, SCLC executive director, to Chris Folcker, July 7, 1967, in Box 39, File 4, King Center
Archives, Atlanta. Earlier, the SCLC believed it necessary to enclose a defense of King's right to
speak against the war in a fund-raising solicitation. Southern Christian Leadership Conference,
*Does Martin Luther King, Jr., Have the Right? The Qualifications? The Duty? to Speak Out on
Peace?* (Atlanta, n.d. [*ca.* April-May, 1967]), copy in SCLC Pamphlet File, Labadie Collection,
University of Michigan Library. *Cf.* Lewis, *King: A Biography*, 357. On the considera-
tions weighing on King, see Fager, "Dilemma for Dr. King," 13–14; and Viorst, *Fire in the
Streets*, 383.

236

On April 4, a year before keeping another appointment with destiny in Memphis, King crossed the Rubicon. (Actually, he had done so earlier, but Rubicon crossings in modern times require the undivided attention of journalists, which, on that earlier occasion, King did not have.) King delivered an address, at the Riverside Church in New York City, in which his objections to the war transcended its economic and human cost: He damned it as immoral. The most vitriolic passage of his speech was a comparison of America's war in Vietnam to the genocidal practices of the Third Reich: "We have destroyed their two most cherished institutions: the family and the village. We have destroyed their land and their crops. We have cooperated in the crushing of the nation's only non-Communist revolutionary force—the Unified Buddhist Church. We have supported the enemies of the peasants of Saigon. We have corrupted their women and children and killed their men. What liberators! . . . What do they think as we test out our latest weapons on them, just as the Germans tested out new medicine and new tortures in the concentration camps of Europe?" That condemnation of the war was all the more powerful because King was a symbol of the nation's resolve to live up to its principles. His critique would not go unanswered.[2]

It did not go unanswered by the new magazines, which were haunted in 1967 by fears of radicalism and violence. Those specters were manifestations of the turbulence of the times but also were grounded in specific events that included the resumption of King's public opposition to the war, the summer rioting that left almost one hundred cities scarred by some of the worst disorders in American history, and the first stirrings of the Poor People's Campaign. As always, King was a mutable symbol. The events of the year and King's role in them required such striking alterations in the magazines' portraits of King that he would have been justified in repeating an observation of some years back in which, after reading some journalistic accounts of his activities, he confessed that he was a wonder to himself. Readers of the news magazines would not necessarily have agreed. The journals they read made sense of the world week by week. However contradictory when read over time, the presentations of King were matched to the flow of news in a given

<hr>

2. See King's speech to The Nation Institute, Los Angeles, February 25, 1967, copy in Box 28, File 33; and *Speeches by the Rev. Dr. Martin Luther King, Jr., About the War in Vietnam* (New York, n.d.), 6, copy in Box 28, File 43. Both documents are in the King Center Archives, Atlanta. On the reaction to King's speech, see Garrow, *Bearing the Cross*, 553–54; and Carl T. Rowan, "The Consequences of Decision," in C. Eric Lincoln (ed.), *Martin Luther King, Jr.: A Profile* (New York, 1970), 213.

week and to the necessity of the moment to use him as a symbol, whether moderate or radical.

Certainly symbolism weighed heavily in the initial report by *Newsweek*, which provided the first intimation that King would take up the war as an issue. Initially, the magazine regarded him as a moderating influence. He had decided to join the Spring Mobilization protest against the war, *Newsweek* reported, because he was "convinced he can moderate the tone of the protest through his presence." Two weeks later, the best face possible was put on King's new cause. His motivation, the magazine emphasized, was that the war was siphoning off money needed for social programs, a far less controversial position than comparisons of America's and Hitler's war tactics such as King would draw at Riverside Church. *Newsweek* may have handled King gingerly because he was sharing the anti-war platform with John Kenneth Galbraith, a Harvard professor with impeccable liberal credentials. Galbraith, "one of America's best-known intellectuals," was more difficult to dismiss than a Baptist preacher, even one with a Nobel Peace Prize. Still, *Newsweek* might not always be so diplomatic; this possibility was implied by the statement that King dismayed "some of his best liberal and moderate friends" by planning to lend his prestige to a campaign run by "political extremists."[3]

Agreeing with Galbraith was one thing, consorting with political extremists another; mentioning America's war and Hitler's death camps in the same breath was leaping out of bounds altogether. Certainly King went beyond the limits set by *Newsweek*, and its coverage of the Riverside Church speech reflected as much. For one thing, his Nobel Prize vanished; it would not do to include credentials indicating King might know whereof he spoke. For another, *Newsweek* expressed embarrassment—there is no other way to put it— for King. Certainly he had the right to complain of the war's impact on domestic social programs, but he was, after all, no John Kenneth Galbraith. When King "plunged into geopolitics, he seemed to be in over his head," and the reaction of "the elders of the civil rights movement, hawks and doves alike" was "mainly embarrassed silence." The elders, it seemed, held to the belief that King "ought to stick to the unfinished business of the Negro revolt." No doubt many of them did believe that—but *Newsweek* had been saying the same thing for months, adding the specification that he ought to stay with the

3. See *Newsweek*, "The Periscope," March 27, 1967, p. 21, and "Signs of Erosion," April 10, 1967, p. 32.

southern branch of the revolt. Some of the same points were made more strongly by columnist Kenneth Crawford after King made two anti-war speeches in which he counseled blacks to resist the draft. Those statements, wrote Crawford, amounted to "demagoguery" and "reckless distortions of fact." The columnist complained bitterly that King "seemed to have abandoned his dream—of an America in which people of all races and kinds would stand equal—in favor of a nation in which a race-conscious minority dictated foreign policy."[4]

Newsweek would return to this theme, and its tones would become harsher. Yet the magazine betrayed the wistful hope that this latest problem created by King would pass. *Newsweek* wanted King back in the South, it wanted the issues of war and race kept apart, and it wanted the anti-war protests to fade away before radicals converted them into a serious threat. For the moment, *Newsweek* found reassurance in the beliefs that there would be no alliance between the black movement and the anti-war movement and that the extremists would be contained. If there was no alliance, the war protesters who remained, earnest but misguided, would be about as effectual as one of their zany demonstrations, from which *Newsweek* extracted a parable of misplaced idealism. It seemed that a "protesting parachutist in San Francisco" took aim at his target, bailed out, and came "floating down under a chute lettered with the word 'love'—but he missed his mark and ended up in an anticlimactic heap in the parking lot."[5] Still, *Newsweek* could not be certain the peaceniks would continue to miss their mark—not with King's prestige behind their cause.

If *Newsweek* was dismayed, *Time* was outraged. Here was another example of King's providing aid and comfort to the enemy, in this case George Wallace, who was poised to make another race for the presidency. *Time* observed gloomily that Wallace might do even better than he had in 1964 if there were more riots in the summer, more "rabble-rousing Black Power speeches by Stokely Carmichael," and more statements from "King comparing the U.S. role in Vietnam to Hitler's in Europe." These remarks were just for openers. A week later, *Time* argued that, as a black leader, King had no business protesting the war. It accused him (despite the qualifying word "possibly") of reneging on his commitment to "the entire cause of nonviolent Negro advance-

---

4. "Lord of the Doves," and Kenneth Crawford, "The Non-Debate," both in *Newsweek*, April 17, 1967, p, 46.
5. "The Peace Marchers," *Newsweek*, April 24, 1967, p. 28.

ment." Lacking better material to drive home the point about abandoning a cause, *Time* drafted a rather awkward scenario featuring another Nobel laureate, Ralph Bunche, under secretary of the United Nations, to whom King delivered a statement accusing the United States of violating the UN charter. Bunche responded: "'I saw you crossing the street. It was a shorter walk than we had in Selma, Martin.'" The remark, said *Time*, captured the "concern that many Americans felt in seeing King diverting his attention from the civil rights movement to the anti-war campaign." Another article made clear *Time*'s distaste for clergymen who, having pushed the social gospel too far, "may become involved in complicated situations they do not understand."[6] Obviously it had King in mind—even if he was not specifically cited as one of those meddling ministers.

Time's condescension did not cover up the bind in which the journal found itself. *Time* supported America's war with all of the fervor it had mustered for a decade and a half in the service of Stemming the Red Tide in Asia. It could not deny that cause without denying Henry Luce, who loved China and despised Communists with approximately equal passion. Even though Luce had been in the grave for almost two months, his vision still dominated *Time*. Nor could *Time* deny Luce's notion that America was divinely inspired and would realize its greatness in the process of realizing its ideals. Inasmuch as one of these ideals was the right to dissent, *Time* was tugged in different directions. Surely it would have been easier had the dissenters been radicals such as Carmichael, whose embittered speeches painted him in villainous shades onto which only a bit of tinting needed to be dabbed. Under the banner of the anti-war movement, however, had gathered many men and women who had risen to the top, writers, intellectuals, even a few politicians—yet they failed to recognize what was so evident to *Time*: the justice of America's war. Worst of all, in a way, was King. *Time* had done its share to make him a symbol of American greatness, and now it was stuck with a symbol turned upside down. *Time* picked its way carefully, defending, as it had to, the right to dissent; this abstract ideal was "democracy's great self-corrective," and the nation would rise to the challenge of the dissidents as it had risen to other challenges. Then *Time* denounced anti-war demonstrators as participants in

6. See "The Temper of the Times," *Time*, April 14, 1967, p. 32; and "The Dilemma of Dissent," 21, and "The Churches' Influence on Secular Society," 27, both in *Time*, April 21, 1967.

"a mindless happening devoid of rational ideas."[7] Celebrating one of the glories of America and simultaneously accusing those who practiced dissent with perverting dissent, *Time* ate its cake, then disgorged it.

The Lucean dilemma was not shared by *U.S. News*. Lawrence's magazine had thundered often enough against tolerating dissent that bordered on treason; in King's case, *U.S. News* said that the treason was recurring inasmuch as he was "'almost lining up with Hanoi.'" Its response was otherwise much the same as that of the other news weeklies: King was ignorant of the best course to follow in settling the war; he was a source of discomfiture to his "liberal" allies (not so great a transgression in the eyes of the conservative *U.S. News*); and he was an ingrate, unappreciative of rights won for him by other Americans willing to nourish the Tree of Liberty with their blood. The last lesson was embedded in a parable borrowed from the chaplain of the Senate. "In America, a man stood up in a free pulpit to preach," he wrote. "Rhetorically, he asked, 'What has a sword ever accomplished worthwhile?'" A worshiper responded: "'The sword in the hand of those who have resisted militant evil has given you the right to stand here today and to proclaim your convictions without fear of being liquidated.'"[8]

Another complaint of *U.S. News*: King had allied himself with the disciples of Black Power. The editorial tactic of establishing guilt consanguineously was, in fact, being used by all of the news weeklies, which usually associated King with Carmichael of SNCC and McKissick of CORE. *Time*, not *U.S. News*, was the first to use the technique. It accused King of being a liar who consorted with "such demagogic 'Black Power'" advocates as Carmichael and McKissick, despite the vow "never to stand on the same platform with Carmichael as long as he spouted an anti-white line." *Time* founded the firm of "King, Carmichael & Co.," the better to associate those radicals-in-arms. Neither idea nor phrase was to be soon discarded. The idea was picked up by *Newsweek* columnist Emmet John Hughes, who used phrases even stronger:

7. "The Right to Dissent and the Duty to Answer," *Time*, May 12, 1967, p. 23.

8. "Washington Whispers," *U.S. News & World Report*. April 24, 1967, p. 29. *U.S. News* associated King with Carmichael and McKissick and reported the distress of King's "liberal" allies in ". . . And a Round of War Protests, Too," April 24, 1967, pp. 10, 12. For the parable, see Frederick Brown Harris, "'The Blade of a Righteous Sword,'" April 24, 1967, p. 120. Whether Harris intended specifically to refer to King, Lawrence did. An editor's note attached to Harris' article stated that King "has been saying that the United States is 'the greatest purveyor of violence in the world today.'" *Ibid*.

Bad enough that King had launched an "extravagantly vituperative attack on his government" and urged a coalition of civil rights and anti-war activists; worse was the company he was keeping, "the smirking Adam Clayton Powell" and "the snarling Stokely Carmichael," whose "eyes have bulged with hate for all white 'honkies.' . . . And this has been the time chosen by Dr. King to reverse his stand of all years past and join Mr. Carmichael in proclaiming that the fate of the Negro in America and of the war in Vietnam is but one cause."[9] How King had "reversed his stand of all years past" by opposing the war was not explained.

Another tactic required the news magazines to turn to the military. There they found evidence of black advancement or located blacks willing to criticize King for neglecting his proper cause and for speaking against the war without understanding what was at stake. One example was *Time*'s caustic response to "the charge—first proclaimed by Stokely Carmichael and now echoed by the likes of Martin Luther King—that Vietnam is a 'race war' in which the white U.S. Establishment is using colored mercenaries to murder brown-skinned freedom fighters. . . . Most incomprehensible to men who have seen their buddies maimed by [Viet Cong] steel and booby traps is Carmichael's statement that it's better to shoot a white cop than a Vietnamese." *Time* found a "Negro Army major" to complain that King should see for himself " 'the savage butchery that the Viet Cong have wrought in the name of liberty' " before speaking out. Then it located a black military officer in Vietnam who began by denouncing King for "preaching sedition," then added that "King was unqualified 'to open his mouth on American policy in Vietnam.' " To assure readers that such "harsh words" were not motivated by pique, the officer, Lieutenant Colonel Warren P. Kynard, was introduced as the former fiancé of King's wife and as "still a close friend of the couple."[10]

U.S. News gave its story a different spin. King and other black leaders were criticizing the war for "interfering with the drive for racial equality." Actually, they themselves were standing in the way of the advancement of the race, the conservative journal said in so many words, because the war was "channeling Negroes into the middle class." King's neglect of his proper cause was emphasized in *Newsweek* by columnist Kenneth Crawford, who maintained

9. "The Dilemma of Dissent," 21, 22; Emmet John Hughes, "A Curse of Confusion," *Newsweek*, May 1, 1967, p. 17.
10. "Democracy in the Foxhole," *Time*, May 26, 1967, pp. 18, 19.

that blacks soldiering in Vietnam were "probably accomplishing more for the just cause of civil rights" than was King.[11]

Still, it pained *Newsweek* greatly that King had to be scourged, contradictory editorial lines being characteristic of the magazine. King was described as a "headline-catching spokesman" for the anti-war movement and as an opportunist who took up his new cause in order to tap the rich coffers of white angels when financial support for the SCLC dried up. But he was also as much victim as villain: a naïve tool of moneyed whites who wanted blacks to do their fighting for them in opposing the war, and a potential tool for Communists who were infiltrating the peace movement. As a leader, King was deficient, his followers abandoning him because he was abandoning their cause—" 'the war isn't King's problem. . . , but the Negro problem is,' " said a source in one of the news weekly's polls, " 'and he ought to stick to it.' " He did not choose his way purposefully but "wandered at least part-time into the peace movement"; and he had taken up with bad, which is to say radical, company.[12]

In short, King, his nonviolent philosophy, his doctorate, and his Nobel Prize notwithstanding, was a bit of a fool and more of an embarrassment. *Newsweek* fervently wished that he would go away, preferably into the southern hinterland. The wish being father to the act, *Newsweek* caused King to go away, at least as far as the war was concerned. A special issue on the war dissenters in July maintained that King's status was falling among blacks because of his position on the war, but otherwise was silent about his critical role in the anti-war movement. Not even when *Newsweek* heard the voices of

11. Crawford, "The Non-Debate," 46. "Growing Success of Negroes in the U.S.: The Story That's Being Overlooked," *U.S. News & World Report*, July 3, 1967, p. 54. This was part of an exploration in the same issue of the rise of the black middle class. See "Negroes Move Up in Government," *U.S. News & World Report*, 57–58. The articles appeared to be at least partially motivated by King's complaint that the war was draining federal support from social programs. "Dr. King's Crusade: How He Hopes to End the War," *U.S. News & World Report*, May 8, 1967, p. 14. *Newsweek* columnist Hughes offered the military as an example of integration at work in "A Curse of Confusion," 17.

12. See the *Newsweek* issue of May 8, 1967, for "The Home-Front War," 31, 34, and Kenneth Crawford, "Let the Negro Do It," 46. The argument that King was being abandoned by his followers required juggling statistics. *Newsweek* suggested a dramatic decline in King's popularity because only 15 percent of blacks would vote for him for president, implying that the cause was that his anti-war activity was clouding his previous role as a champion of the black cause. The magazine was comparing apples and oranges. See *Newsweek*, "The Negro View: A Special Anguish," 34, "LBJ's Supporters: Varying Plumage," pp. 23–24, both in the issue of July 10, 1967, and "Which Way for the Negro?" May 15, 1967, p. 27.

respectable dissenters ringing in the land—clergymen, professors, doctors, lawyers, and congressmen—did King appear. The lengthiest reference to him had nothing to do with war or dissent; rather, it cast King in a limited role, receiving, in the South, a bequest from a white benefactor with deep sympathy for black rights.[13]

A tone tolerably close to despair crept into *Newsweek*'s reportage during the summer. The old "triumphs over Southern segregation now seemed pale." Carmichael was scorning Washington and Lincoln as honkies and Lyndon Johnson as a buffoon, and he and McKissick were advising blacks to remove themselves from "the System." King, "wavering" between the camp of the moderates and the camp of Black Power, no longer was a potential bridge between the two factions but was drifting "in the process a shade closer to the Carmichael view of the world." (When *Newsweek* could bring itself to confess this, its view of the crisis must have been bleak indeed.) All about were heard the ominous rumblings of revolution. Small wonder that *Newsweek* turned to black moderates and conservatives, who, even if disillusioned, "recognize that they need the System more than ever before."[14]

Thus *Newsweek* turned to Thurgood Marshall, the quintessential symbol of the System working through the agency of the courts. As the first black elevated to the Supreme Court, he was useful to a magazine worried about revolution and revolutionaries. For blacks whose failed search for the American dream had left a bitter aftertaste, Marshall's rise was "a chapter by a black Horatio Alger" who traced his roots to "a nineteenth century Congolese slave . . . so pawky that his bemused owner set him free"; his father was a Pullman car waiter and later a steward at a posh club, his mother a teacher in the segregated schools of Baltimore.[15] The chapter could have been titled "Up from Slavery."

Marshall's work for the black cause was as hazardous as leading a march, his achievements fully as great as King's, said *Newsweek*. "As the NAACP's chief attorney, Marshall barnstormed Dixie—showing his face in places

13. "Dissenters: Rebels with Many Causes," *Newsweek*, July 10, 1967, p. 29. *Newsweek* again discouraged King from resuming his campaign in Chicago, in "Which Way for the Negro?" 33. The bequest was reported by *Newsweek* in "News and Newsmakers," July 10, 1967, p. 92.

14. "Which Way for the Negro?" 27, 33. *Newsweek* treats black conservatives *ibid.*, 30, and in "Whitney Young, Power Player," May 15, 1967, p. 29. Radical and revolutionary movements were cited by *Newsweek* in "The Man from SNCC," May 22, 1967, p. 45, "Tijerina Brass," June 19, 1967, pp. 37–38, and "Equality Defined," July 3, 1967, p. 30.

15. "Mr. Justice Marshall," *Newsweek*, June 26, 1967, p. 35.

where it was dangerous to be a Negro, much less a Negro lawyer committed to convulsing the Southern Way of Life." Then followed a listing of battle ribbons: the University of Alabama in 1956; Central High School in Little Rock a year later; and Birmingham, where Marshall showed up "before Martin Luther King." Furthermore, though a crusader "for first-class citizenship" for blacks, Marshall "vigorously pounded the law books, not the picket line pavements." Marshall was, in sum, evidence that "America may romanticize its radicals, but it more often rewards its reformers."[16]

Although not gripped by the same bleak mood, *Time*, no less than *Newsweek*, needed to demonstrate that the System was working. It found a symbol, as compelling as Marshall, two rungs down in the federal judiciary. On its cover appeared Frank Johnson, a federal district judge in Alabama who personified not "civil rights but the law." Now another symbol loomed in retrospect over the civil rights crusades once dominated by King:

> It was Frank Johnson who applied the school desegregation decision to the Montgomery bus system. . . . It was Frank Johnson who ordered both marchers and police to halt their confrontation at Selma, and then— although he disapproves of most demonstrations—gave the marchers permission to go ahead. It was Frank Johnson who sat as a member of the three-judge court that abolished the Alabama poll tax; that handed down the first order requiring a state to reapportion its voting districts; that produced the first reapportionment plan devised by judges. It was Frank Johnson who so inspired an Alabama jury . . . that it was able to convict the three Ku Klux Klansmen who gunned down Viola Liuzzo on the road back to Montgomery from Selma.[17]

The remainder of the cover story lauded Johnson as a judge of uncommon rectitude. The praises were not misplaced. Johnson was one of the most remarkable of the extraordinary class of Republican judges appointed by President Eisenhower to district and circuit court benches in the South. However, the cover story was, by journalistic standards, mistimed, appearing a decade after the Montgomery bus boycott, two years after Selma, and, most important, when the southern civil rights struggle was all but eclipsed by the war, Black Power, and rioting in the nation's cities. Johnson represented

16. *Ibid.*, 34, 35.

17. "Interpreter in the Front Line," *Time*, May 12, 1967, p. 72. Actually, Johnson was one of two federal judges who voted to strike down the bus segregation ordinance as unconstitutional. The third member of the judicial panel voted to uphold it. Such details would have detracted, however, from the symbolism *Time* wished to attach to Johnson.

something beyond the legal rulings that altered the folkways of the South. He personified the law in a turbulent period when *Time* missed few opportunities to proclaim the need for the supremacy of law. Johnson was useful to make another point. King succeeded in Montgomery and in Selma because of the law (and the society it represented), not despite it; Johnson put flesh upon that abstraction. To make Selma better fit its thesis, *Time* stripped layers of symbolism from the campaign. "Militant civil rights leaders"—meaning King, of course—"descended on the Dallas County city of Selma in March, 1965." A certain tawdriness was affixed to their delight in "the reflex anger of Dallas County Sheriff Jim Clark and his mounted posse men, his electric-shock cattle prods, and forced marches of Negro children."[18]

Indeed, the SCLC rejoiced when Clark fell into the trap, but Clark was no less mutable a symbol than King. Before Bloody Sunday, *Time* portrayed Clark as a buffoon; afterward, he was converted as rapidly as possible into a brutal symbol of segregation. Now *Time* swung back partially to an earlier interpretation because of something it wanted to demonstrate—not about Clark but about King. What King did to bring freedom to black southerners faded almost to insignificance beside the majesty of the law as personified by Johnson. If there was considerable truth to that theme, it was truth established at a particular time in order to make a particular point.[19]

Unlike its competitors, *U.S. News* needed no substitute symbols. King again was the target of its echo chamber campaign. Forces were conspiring against the Republic, and somewhere in the scheme, it implied, was the hand of King. A conspiracy existed, for example, to cause riots; this thesis could be read in the notion that those who predicted where riots would break out had more than a little to do with bringing them about. *U.S. News* gave its theme an extra nudge by associating King with the radicals. " 'Black Power' advocates such as Stokely Carmichael are accused of stirring Negro youth to anger," *U.S. News* first reported. Then another Black Power disciple, Floyd McKissick, "called the turn last spring by naming in advance eight cities where riots occurred and predict[ed] the likelihood of trouble in as many as forty cities in the coming summer." Thereafter, King "warned on April 16 that

18. *Ibid.*, 77.

19. Compare *Time*'s description of Clark in 1966 when it was attempting to counter the enticements of Black Power: "Challenge in Alabama," 29A, and "Big Jim's Comeuppance," 19. See also "Court v. King," *Time*, June 23, 1967, p. 20. *Time*'s chronology made it appear the Selma campaign did little to bring about the 1965 Voting Rights Act.

at least ten cities are 'powder kegs' that could 'explode' in racial violence this summer." Space was allotted for King to preach nonviolence "with all my might" and for his disclaimer that what he said probably would fall on deaf ears because the "intolerable conditions which brought about racial violence last summer still exist." *U.S. News* turned a deaf ear, noting, as it had in the past, that there was a difference between preaching and practicing: "King talks of leading new Negro marches into white neighborhoods of Chicago and Cicero . . . where similar marches drew white attacks last year."[20]

U.S. News found unexpected support for its theme in the unlikeliest of places, the Supreme Court, which dismissed King's appeal of a conviction during the Birmingham campaign. Here at last was official recognition (albeit in weaker phrases) of what Mr. Justice Whittaker had been fulminating against. No longer would King and others like him be "'free to ignore all the procedures of law and carry their battle to the streets. . . . Respect for judicial process is a small price to pay for the civilizing hand of law, which alone can give abiding meaning to constitutional freedom.'"[21]

Whatever smug satisfaction *U.S. News* took from the Supreme Court's ruling was short-lived. *U.S. News* soon would be forced to remake King as a symbol. In fact, *Time* and *Newsweek* would find themselves in as much need of King because of the riots of the summer of 1967, the most serious of which were in Newark and Detroit.

Time started its reinterpretation before the Newark and Detroit disorders. Now and then, it rebuked King with stinging phrases. In one article, for example, *Time* pointed to a "sense of malaise . . . [that] was not helped by King's veiled hint of summer violence to come in Cleveland and nine other cities." Yet *Time* also found King's arguments compelling when they matched its own. When King complained, for example, that "'everyone is worrying about the long, hot summer' . . . [when] we had a long cold winter when little was done about the conditions that create riots,'" he voiced *Time*'s own criticism. Only lately had *Time* taken up the cry that something must be done about the bleakness of ghetto life, but it now pitched in with a will, castigating mayoral administrations for not taking action that would remove the causes of rioting. In the act of complaint was an act of faith—the faith that

20. "U.S. Race Riot Outlook for '67—What Negro Leaders Predict," *U.S. News & World Report*, May 1, 1967, pp. 42–44.
21. "High Court Ruling that Went Against Dr. King," *U.S. News & World Report*, June 26, 1967, p. 10.

time remained to correct the social problems that produced the rioting and the welling hope that it would be done. When *Time* covered the Atlanta and Tampa riots in early summer it saw problems, of course, but it also took heart from the work of black volunteers to keep the peace; when it delved into the causes of urban unrest, *Time* was encouraged by corporate America's enlistment in programs to provide jobs and diversion for the poor.[22]

With summer came a time of trial for even so deeply rooted a faith as *Time*'s in the perfectibility of America. The riots of 1967 were the most widespread and destructive disorders in peacetime up to that date in American history. Beginning in June, riots broke out in Tampa, Boston, Chicago, Cincinnati, Atlanta, and Dayton; other disturbances soon flared up across the country, in cities large and small. By early August, *Time* was toting up casualties, a grim butcher's bill of more than eighty persons killed, more than two thousand injured, and more than eleven thousand arrested in more than thirty cities.[23]

The riots set the stage for the reemergence of King as a prophet of moderation. Converting King from radical to peacemaker was a tricky problem for *U.S. News* because of what it reported from the Black Power Conference. That meeting was held following the rioting, the worst since Watts, in Newark between July 12 and July 17. Neither *Time* nor *Newsweek* mentioned that at least one delegate from the SCLC attended; that omission by the latter was striking because it found among the delegates "zealous revolutionaries, hot-eyed U.S.-style Mau Maus, disciples of the late Malcolm X, CORE and SNCC activists—even delegates from the moderate NAACP and Urban League." *Time* separated King and other moderates from the Black Power Conference by statement as well as by omission. "Notably absent," it reported, were Roy Wilkins, Whitney Young, and King. *Time* also dropped from a caption the identification of one of King's aides, Jesse Jackson. *U.S. News* did identify Jackson, apparently wishing, as the other news weeklies patently did not, to place SCLC—thus King himself—in the Black Power camp. *U.S. News* reported that "Negroes gathered in a 'Black Power' conference and talked about 'black revolution,'" ignoring pleas to move the meet-

22. *Time*'s rebuke to King appears in "Promise Denied," June 9, 1967, p. 34, its approving phrases in "Recipe for Riot," June 30, 1967, p. 21. See also "Mind Over Mayhem," *Time*, June 23, 1967, p. 19.

23. "Riot Toll: 1967 and Before," *Time*, August 11, 1967, p. 11. A congressional subcommittee some years later published this accounting: 83 persons killed; 1,397 persons injured; 16,389 arrested; 2,157 convicted; and property damages estimated at $664,500,000. President's Commission on CIA Activities, *Report*, 286.

ing to another city to avoid "the risk of stirring new violence" and indulging in "bitterly anti-white speeches." One address was by Ron Karenga, "a black nationalist from the Watts area of Los Angeles, [who] said: 'Everybody knows whitey is a devil. The question is, what are you going to do about it?'"[24]

A new King emerged the following week after he joined Wilkins, Young, and A. Philip Randolph in issuing a statement condemning the wave of violence and rioting. They echoed the call of *U.S. News*: "'Mob Law—Let's End It Now.'" The irony of using King to signify law and order escaped *U.S. News* because it urgently needed him. The Newark riot was just past; the ghettos remained volatile; and King, a powerful symbol for blacks, was in good (that is, *conservative*) company with Wilkins, Young, and Randolph. With Carmichael and his successor as SNCC chairman, H. Rap Brown, preaching revolutionary doctrines, *U.S. News* choked back its inclination to castigate King; he and his co-signers became "among the most responsible of the civil rights leaders." What they said could only strike the magazine as responsible: "'Killing, arson, looting are criminal acts, and should be dealt with as such. Equally guilty are those who incite, provoke, and call specifically for such action. There is no injustice which justifies the present destruction of the Negro community and its people. . . . Riots have proved ineffective, disruptive, and highly damaging to the Negro population, to the civil rights cause, and to the entire nation.'"[25]

If King was so responsible, however, why would a delegate from the SCLC attend the Black Power Conference? *U.S. News* dealt with the awkwardness as best it could, explaining, as it had not done in its first report, that King, Wilkins, and Young did not attend, thus disassociating them from the "avowed goal" of the Black Power Conference: "to split the U.S. into two separate nations—one white, the other black."[26]

No such defense of "responsible" black leaders was necessary for *Time* and *Newsweek*, but they shared another demanding task—making sense of the

24. "Black Power Summit," *Newsweek*, July 31, 1967, p. 19; "Spreading Fire," *Time*, July 28, 1967, p. 10; "'Black Revolution'—Theme in Newark," *U.S. News & World Report*, July 31, 1967, p. 8. *Time* and *U.S. News* published the same photograph from the Black Power Conference. *U.S. News* also linked Black Power to Communist subversion in "'Black Power' Threatens a Leading Negro College," July 31, 1967, p. 39.

25. "'Mob Law—Let's End It Now,'" *U.S. News & World Report*, August 7, 1967, p. 11.

26. "What 'Black Power' Leaders are Demanding," *U.S. News & World Report*, August 7, 1967, p. 31.

bloody outbreak in Detroit in the last week of July. Detroit had seemed an unlikely city to experience major disorders. Although the unemployment rate, at 7 percent, was almost twice the national average, about 40 percent of the black population owned their own homes, a statistic taken as one of the indices of social stability. Detroit's administration had a reputation for enlightened governance, and the city had one of the most extensive poverty programs in the country. The violence was precipitated on July 23 by a police raid at an illegal after-hours drinking establishment and soon spread beyond the control of police and National Guardsmen. At the request of Governor George Romney, President Johnson federalized Michigan National Guardsmen and ordered a force of almost five thousand army paratroopers into Detroit to restore order. Not until July 30 were the regulars withdrawn. During almost a week of disorders, the casualty figures mounted rapidly until they reached 43 dead, more than 600 injured, and more than 3,800 arrested. Insurance claims were paid to the extent of about $32 million—about 75 percent of the reported losses.[27]

Poking through the ruins was painful to *Newsweek*. The old consensus was shattered, the old solutions seemed useless, the old leaders were leading no one, and the uprising in Detroit was "tragically far beyond the ken of most whites and many middle-class Negroes." King and the co-signers of the statement denouncing the riots were moderates, but *Newsweek* believed that "the cruel irony . . . was that the very victories they had won had only quickened Negro hopes—not satisfied them. Revolts are born of hope, not utter despair, and they quickly cast aside those leaders who seem unable to keep the pace. King recognized the point when someone suggested that he go to Detroit. 'I am not a fireman,' he said. 'My role is keeping fires from starting.'"[28]

Newsweek questioned whether King could even stop fires from starting if he and other moderates had been replaced by such "Jacobins of the ghetto" as Carmichael and Rap Brown, coiner of the nihilistic slogan Burn, baby, burn. The doubts about King were not new; now, there was a deeper malaise. *Newsweek* doubted even the president. "Mr. Johnson," it reported bleakly, "had in the end nothing new to offer except (1) a national day of prayer; (2) better riot training for National Guard troops; and (3) a bipartisan study

27. Willard A. Heaps, *Riots USA, 1765–1970* (Rev. ed.; New York, 1970), 147–54.
28. "An American Tragedy, 1967—Detroit," *Newsweek*, August 7, 1967, p. 25.

commission . . . to investigate causes and cures." A measure of the crisis was *Newsweek*'s muttering that money alone would not suffice, that the job would require "a good deal more presidential leadership as well." Prayers, riot training, and yet another government commission struck the magazine as woefully inadequate to meet the crisis (and ticking off Johnson's proposals, one, two, three, made them appear even more so). "The tragedy was that nobody knew how to stop" the rioting, reported *Newsweek*. Close to despair, it added: "—if, indeed, it could be stopped at all."[29]

Time found many of the same elements while sorting through the rubble. The nihilism and anarchy shook, but did not shatter, *Time*'s confidence that the crisis would be resolved through good will and good works, if only there was enough determination. No more potent symbol existed for making that point than King, preaching, in Luce's magazine, Luce's message of hope and faith. "'We've come a long, long way,'" was King's message; "'we've got a long, long way to go.'" Naturally, the signs of progress had to be listed: "long-ago philanthropies of Northern white idealists who financed many of the Negro colleges; the verve, bounce, and guts of Negro athletes and entertainers; the quieter achievements of Negro professional and business people; the great national economic surges that have pulled millions of Negroes into Northern industrial employment; and in the past thirteen years since *Brown v. Board of Education of Topeka* a whole train of new laws and judicial decisions." As even *Time* conceded, the list was inadequate, shopworn by repetition, and attractive primarily to aspirants to the middle class whose frustrations, so it believed, were being worked out in spasms of rioting and looting. Nevertheless, the list served to demonstrate "to the Negro that he can find justice and hope in America, and that he can find it soon."[30]

King served much the same symbolic purpose. No doubt *Time* would have preferred to promote Whitney Young, whose position on the war was better than King's "simplistic" ideas. *Time* recognized, however, that King was the more powerful symbol. However important the good work of Young's Urban League in opening up economic opportunities, those mundane activities paled beside the accomplishments of the symbolic King, who had awakened "the

29. *Ibid.*, 18, 25, 26.
30. "A Time of Violence and Tragedy," *Time*, August 4, 1967, p. 13. *Time* believed that the rioting was caused by dissatisfaction among blacks somewhat better off than the poorest of their brethren. *Ibid.*, 12–13. See also *Time*, "The Other Ninety-Seven Percent," 13, and "What Next?" 12, both in the issue of August 11, 1967.

nation's conscience" to the injustice of segregation. King signified to blacks that the nation had corrected injustice before and would do so again; to whites, his was a reassuring presence, no trifling consideration when "with every incendiary statement from the Black Power evangelists, the moderates find a more receptive audience among whites, who see them as constructive alternatives to the nihilists." Still, *Time* had to snip away some awkward matters relating to the war. Making King more like Young would make King more acceptable symbolically. Thus, this careful framing: Young, *Time* reported, "personally regrets the size and cost of the U.S. commitment" in Vietnam; King, by contrast, made the "simplistic argument . . . that an end to the war would instantly transfer billions of dollars to the cities."[31] More important was what *Time* did not say. Once King's likening of America's war to Hitler's genocide was bypassed, the controversy could be reduced to maneuvering based upon racial interests—no more objectionable than what other ethnic politicians did.

The same tactic was applied to domestic programs. Young was convinced of the necessity of providing "jobs, jobs, and more jobs." So was King. He started Operation Breadbasket in more than forty cities in order to get new or better jobs for blacks, and it was working: "King credits Breadbasket with getting jobs for twenty-two hundred Chicago Negroes, [and] hopes to open up as many as sixty thousand new jobs a year for Negroes in cities with populations exceeding one hundred thousand." What remained to be done would be accomplished by reformist measures such as the "massive WPA-style programs" sought by Wilkins of the conservative NAACP, sought by King as well.[32]

A week later, however, King the reformer set in motion his most radical social movement. It was the Poor People's Campaign, which King made public during a speech to the annual convention of the SCLC in Atlanta on August 15. He outlined tactics of civil disruption such as school boycotts, mass sit-ins at factories, and a march on Washington by the unemployed. There was a note of grimness. The weapons of nonviolence, he said, were the weapons of choice because they were more likely to produce earthquakes in society. Disrupting the "functioning of a city without destroying it can be

31. "The Other Ninety-Seven Percent," 12, 13, 17. *Time* also scourged Carmichael and Brown, but not King, for opposing the war in "Another Kind of Fighter," August 18, 1967, p. 22.
32. "The Other Ninety-Seven Percent," 16.

more effective than a riot because it can be longer-lasting, costly to the society but not wantonly destructive." As a practical matter, King argued, the government would find nonviolent disruption more difficult to counter since violence could be put down by superior force. Finally, there was the mingling of the pragmatic and the philosophical: Civil disobedience would channel the rage of the ghetto into "a constructive and creative force."[33] King, the good Gandhian who drew back from the brink in Chicago, now was preparing to press nonviolence to the limit.

The news magazines were aware of the potential effects of nonviolent disruption, as could be seen in their response to the plan to stall cars on the highway leading to the 1964 World's Fair. That plan had come to nothing, but it had no more weight behind it than could be mustered by one CORE chapter acting despite the disapproval of the civil rights establishment, including its parent organization, including, for that matter, King, who objected that the scheme was neither well planned nor directed at specific goals. Hazy though it was in August of 1967, King's plan was infinitely more radical than stalling a few automobiles on a busy highway, and with him at its head such a campaign might indeed produce severe shocks in American society.

Time and *Newsweek* dismissed the plan, however, as a desperate move by King to seize the initiative—from "extremists," as *Time* put it; from SNCC, said *Newsweek*. *Newsweek* registered its impatience with King's damn-the-consequences attitude. "Where and when?" it demanded curtly. "Neither King nor the SCLC had any battle plan. . . . But King nevertheless talked of starting the campaign before Congress adjourns"—adding even more curtly "—the likely backlash be damned." In truth, the magazines seemed more irritated than alarmed. Certainly *Newsweek* had cause for irritation. For a year, it had been urging King to go back South—with no sign that King would ever do so. Besides, *Newsweek* was fascinated at the moment by SNCC's Black Power rhetoric, and it buried King's statement deep in an article about the dispute then heating up between SNCC and some Jews over Zionism and Israel, giving his speech even less prominence than it accorded a notation that the SCLC celebrated its tenth anniversary. *Time* buried the announcement also (it doubted whether the SCLC "could actually organize such nonviolent

33. King's speech to SCLC convention, Atlanta, August 15, 1967, copy in Box 28, File 37, King Center Archives, Atlanta.

rebellion— or keep it nonviolent") and gloomily chalked it up as one more sign that "the responsible civil rights movement, which has accomplished much for the Negro in the 1960s, today faces a crisis of survival."[34]

Those readings of the situation contained a measure of truth. King's standing had slipped because of Black Power and the failure in Chicago; since Selma he had won no major victories, and victories were needed to keep his position intact. Yet beneath the cavalier dismissal ran a strain of wishful and wistful thinking. It was wistful inasmuch as Newsweek and Time retained due appreciation for King and the SCLC, which stayed, in Newsweek's phrase, "determinedly biracial" when biracialism was going out of fashion. It was wishful thinking because they were denying that he could be a symbol other than one of their choosing. But King had already demonstrated otherwise, becoming a powerfully effective critic of the war. He had moved perceptibly to the left and might go further still, if his vague plan for the Poor People's Campaign was any evidence. Their irritation betrayed the wish that King would go away. They stopped short of asking, What if he did not?

U.S. News suffered no such disability in covering King's speech. Three weeks after converting him into a symbol of law and order, the magazine transformed King back into a familiar devil figure. "Riot-torn cities of the North," it reported, were now confronted by a "new threat" with King "organizing what he calls 'civil disobedience on a massive scale.'" Then the magazine listed some of the elements of the new march on Washington. Thousands of unemployed blacks "would camp out in the capital city somewhat like the 'bonus marchers' of 1932." There would be a "'hungry people's sit-in' at the Department of Labor" and weekly school boycotts. "The idea, as Dr. King put it, is 'forcefully to cripple the operations of an oppressive society.'"[35]

U.S. News was as skittish as ever about racial demonstrations in Washington. That aside, it provided a far more realistic picture of what King planned to do than did the other news weeklies. In truth, King was becoming dangerous to the established order. He had not abandoned the dream of America as a truly integrated society, but neither was he sanguine about the misery of the poor being relieved because of appeals to conscience. White

34. "End of the Road?" Time, August 25, 1967, p. 18; "SNCC and the Jews," Newsweek, August 28, 1967, p. 22.
35. "New Negro Threat: Mass Disobedience," U.S. News & World Report, August 28, 1967, p. 10.

decisionmakers, said King in that speech in Atlanta, would have to be *forced* to improve the lot of the poor, the force being applied by massive disruption of the cities where most production was carried out, where most Americans lived, and without which the suburbs would die.[36]

The echo chamber went back into operation. The theme was familiar, as were the phrases: "Being accepted rather widely, as a result of racial demonstrations in recent years, is the view that people are entitled to disobey laws they don't like. [The] result is rioting that has neared civil war in some cities." Then King was brought into the picture. "The idea grows that rioters are entitled to shoot, burn, and loot. On August 15, the Rev. Dr. Martin Luther King, Jr., civil rights leader who preaches nonviolence, blamed the widespread destruction and bloodshed in the cities this summer not on the rioters, but on 'the policy-makers of the white society.'"[37] Thus was a transformation worked in a man who was depicted as one of the "most responsible" black leaders because he denounced mobs.

The radicalism of King was part of a mosaic of radicalism being constructed by *U.S. News* as it reviewed the various threats to society. Values were being undermined by welfare and pornography; domestic security was being threatened by crime and violence; and American radicals were receiving aid and comfort from such sources as the Castro regime in Cuba. Even worse, *U.S. News* hinted (not for the first time), subversion had reached into the government itself. It found evidence of subversion in the denials issued by high officials that a conspiracy touched off the riots, despite testimony in "city after city where . . . officials spoke of patterns indicating a nationwide guerrilla warfare plot."[38]

Nevertheless, King's radicalism was not diminished. With few exceptions, *U.S. News* depicted him as a threatening presence for the remainder of the year. That theme was brought center stage on October 30, when the magazine reprinted an article by Lewis F. Powell, a former president of the American Bar Association. (Powell later served on the Supreme Court.) Powell de-

36. King's speech to SCLC convention, August 15, 1967.
37. "Is There a 'Sick' Society in the U.S.?" *U.S. News & World Report*, August 28, 1967, pp. 49–50.
38. The breakdown of values in American society was cited *ibid.*; and in "Militant Clergy—Critics Fire Back," *U.S. News & World Report*, November 27, 1967, pp. 66–68. Conspiratorial tones were sounded by *U.S. News* in "Is Castro Behind Guerrilla War in U.S. Cities?" August 14, 1967, p. 24. See also "Search Starts for Cause of Riots in U.S. Cities," *U.S. News & World Report*, November 13, 1967, pp. 53–54.

nounced civil disobedience as heresy and King as the chief heretic. By juxtaposing King with other radicals, Powell also tainted King symbolically. He
conceded that their ideas and roles differed; nevertheless, each of those with
whom King kept company was "determined to remake America—not by the
democratic processes . . . but by varying forms and degrees of coercion."[39]
And Powell provided both echoes and summaries of themes featured in previous issues:

> Dr. King seems bewildered at times by the escalation of his own
> doctrine. On occasion he has joined moderate Negro leaders in criticizing
> riots. But he is arm-in-arm with Mr. Stokely Carmichael and Mr. Floyd
> McKissick . . . in slandering his own government and in inciting viola-
> tion of draft laws. He has said: "America is the greatest purveyor of
> violence in the world today." And he has compared the use of new
> American weapons in Vietnam to the Nazi testing of "new tortures in the
> concentration camps of Europe."
> Dr. King's favorite role is organizing disruptive demonstrations. He is
> now urging "massive civil disobedience" for the purpose of "dislocating"
> Northern cities. He is planning such "nonviolent" tactics as weekly
> school boycotts, blocking plant gates with unemployed Negroes, and
> disrupting governmental operations with sit-in demonstrations in federal
> buildings.[40]

Powell also splattered King with red paint. King, he wrote, took part in
such anti-war activities as Vietnam Week in April, the initial planning for
which "took place at a Chicago conference, instigated and dominated by
Communists and fellow travelers." Similarly, guilt by association was proven
in the case of the Vietnam Summer protest organization—"a coalition [that]
includes well-known Communist allies"—and a New Left conference in
which "the Communist Party, as in the case of Vietnam Week, was active in
the planning and manipulation." What Powell said was, of course, only the
latest in a chain of echoes extending back to 1964.[41]

The final echo of 1967 was sounded in late December. The Poor People's
Campaign was tinged with radicalism as *U.S. News* integrated it into an
extensive interview about parallels between insurrections abroad and riots and
disorders in the United States. Interestingly, King himself was less a menace

---

39. Lewis F. Powell, Jr., "'Civil Disobedience: Prelude to Revolution'?" *U.S. News &
World Report*, October 30, 1967, pp. 66, 67.
40. *Ibid.*, 67.
41. *Ibid.*, 67, 68; "Search Starts for Cause of Riots in U.S. Cities," 53.

than a tool of radicals waiting for the opportunity to provoke greater violence. Yet the theme stretched far enough—as it had in the past—to encompass King as an unwitting dupe of radicals and Communists. The full dimensions of his plan were no doubt unknown to *U.S. News*, in part because the campaign was still being developed, in part because the SCLC's public relations apparatus was carefully keeping some elements from view.[42] But *U.S. News* had heard more than enough (it would have taken precious little in any event) to conclude that King was a false prophet.

From the coverage in *Newsweek* and *Time*, it would be difficult to conclude that King was any kind of threat. In *Newsweek*, he was a symbol out of the past, what was already the *old* southern movement. In contrast, *Time* anointed King a vital symbol in the troubled present.

The most striking feature of *Newsweek*'s coverage was that it published little about King in the last quarter of 1967. Five articles referred briefly to King. Except for two references—King's speech (bereft of bitter criticism of the war) to the New Left conference, and a notation that King was supporting a proposed boycott of the 1968 Olympics by black athletes—King was presented as a prophet from the old movement or as an icon that could lead blacks to register as voters. In this case, however, the black voters were in Cleveland, where Carl Stokes was poised to become the first elected black mayor of a major city. *Newsweek* reported tersely that "King led the drive to get out the vote in Negro wards" in Cleveland. His work rated only the briefest reference possible in the report of the primary election and none at all in the article summarizing the general election. This was curious, considering that King was doing what *Newsweek* had advised him to do, persuading blacks to register and cast ballots, and doing it exceedingly well.[43] *Newsweek* almost ignored King, perhaps because he was once again out of the South, perhaps

---

42. "Is Insurrection Brewing in U.S.?" *U.S. News & World Report*, December 25, 1967, p. 33. King believed that nothing less than "the restructuring of American society" was required because a society with forty million poor was fundamentally flawed. Details on how this was to be accomplished were hazy, then and later. The remark was made during a session at the SCLC's Ministers Leadership Conference in Miami, February 23, 1967. A remark that garbage might be dumped on the steps of an unresponsive Congress apparently was deleted from a segment broadcast by the SCLC. Transcripts in Box 28, Files 51 and 33, King Center Archives, Atlanta.

43. See *Newsweek*, "First Things First," September 11, 1967, p. 24, and "The Periscope," December 11, 1967, p. 20. The quotation is from "Black Breakthrough," *Newsweek*, October 16, 1967, p. 30; the report on the general election is "Cleveland and Gary," *Newsweek*, November 20, 1967, pp. 66–67. On the Cleveland undertaking, see Garrow, *Bearing the Cross*, 560, 568, 580.

because his position on the war had gotten King out of the good graces of the Democratic party, or both.

King was interpreted, in late November, as a voice from the past in a special "advocacy issue" analyzing the nation's failure to live up to its promises to the black man. *Newsweek* proposed no radical alterations in the System, arguing instead that steps should be taken to provide what the black man "deserved and what he has always wanted: decent homes, jobs, and schools, a piece of America's plenty." Who would lead him to that Promised Land? From indications in *Newsweek*, it would not be King. He was one of the "old leaders" neutralized by the movement they had set in motion; "so despondent" was King (and Wilkins of the NAACP and Young of the Urban League) that he "quite seriously contemplated announcing this autumn that" he would quit as a civil rights leader "in six months unless something is done." King had endured an extended period of *angst* after his campaign in Chicago, but *Newsweek*'s representation was King the symbol, not the man. Along with Wilkins and Young, King served as a warning of the fire coming unless white America delivered victories to the responsible black leaders, thus denying the radicals the opportunity for which they were waiting.[44]

The rub was that King was becoming a radical himself. However, *Newsweek* used another contraposed symbol to make King (and others in the moderate wing of the black movement) appear all the more reasonable. The framing was of King the assimilationist versus Malcolm X the "radical separatist" who mercilessly excoriated white America and whose demand for a separate state for blacks *Newsweek* spurned as "improbable." *Newsweek* bypassed some elements that would have clouded its pristine comparison. For one, Malcolm X, greatly influenced by Islam, had started moving away from separatism before his murder in 1965—as *Newsweek* itself had reported previously. For another, King had, since 1965, been drifting—perhaps, more precisely, had been pushed by events—closer to the militancy of Malcolm X. The changes went unrecorded now because *Newsweek* needed the starkly contrasting symbolism of Malcolm X and King.[45]

In the last four months of 1967, King was a far more powerful and vital

44. See *Newsweek*'s issue of November 20, 1967, for "What Must Be Done," pp. 33–37, and "Thinking Black," pp. 38, 40. On King's *angst*, see Lomax, "When 'Nonviolence' Meets 'Black Power,'" 170–72.

45. "Thinking Black," 40. The changes in Malcolm X are difficult to isolate even decades after his death, but all in all, *Newsweek* did a good journalistic job in "Death of a Desperado," March 8, 1965, pp. 24–25, and "Satan in the Ghetto," November 15, 1965, p. 132.

symbol to *Time*. King personified the glorious past of the old southern movement, of course, but he also was a living reminder that American ideals were
being put into practice in 1967. Preoccupying *Time* during this period of crisis
was its self-assigned mission of struggling against the doubts about the America that Luce never doubted. As an antidote for the afflictions of race, *Time*
offered to blacks the promise that they, too, could rise. The proof existed in
the person of Thurgood Marshall, the "son of a sleeping-car porter and great-
grandson of a slave," now the newest Supreme Court justice. The same
process was evident in Cleveland, where voters, black and white, had chosen
the "great-grandson of a slave" over (*Time* carefully established) "the grandson of a president."[46]

In events great and small, *Time* was finding evidence of America rising to
greatness. Even in Mississippi examples were found: a confirmed segregationist presiding with "scrupulous fairness" over the trial of white men accused of murdering three civil rights workers in 1964, and a jury of Mississip-
pians convicting white defendants for the first time in a civil rights murder
case. Even the anti-war movement produced a useful example, a huge demonstration at the Pentagon. Not that *Time* approved; the protest was "ill-
conceived." Nevertheless, it reminded "the world of America's cherished
right of dissent."[47]

King became a major symbolic figure in *Time*'s land of free men and
unhindered opportunity. There were awkward moments in the late summer
and the early autumn when King spoke against the war, but the references
were brief and, aside from some sotto voce remarks about ambitious men and
opportunism, nowhere near as scathing as the attacks against others in the
anti-war movement. Likely as not, *Time* considered King to be an "un-
sophisticated pacifist"; people of that category were "suckered into the hard-
line camp and end up unwittingly propagandizing as activists."[48]

Even if *Time* harbored murkier suspicions, it put them away rather than

46. "People," *Time*, October 13, 1967, p. 42, briefly reports the seating of Marshall on the
Supreme Court. The Cleveland election was covered by *Time* in "The Real Black Power,"
November 17, 1967, p. 23; and it developed a similar theme—though more to encourage whites
to support opportunities for blacks—in "The James Gang Rides Again," October 13, 1967, p. 31.

47. On the trial in Mississippi, see "Reckoning in Meridian," *Time*, October 27, 1967, pp.
32–33. The Pentagon demonstration was reported in "The Banners of Dissent," *Time*, October
27, 1967, p. 24.

48. *Time*'s subtle complaints about ambition appear in "A Question of Priorities," September
8, 1967, p. 14, and "Chaos on the Left," September 15, 1967, p. 23. For its characterization of
anti-war activists, see "The Banners of Dissent," 25.

discard a useful symbol. King came to be, in fact, *Time*'s favored source (as once he had been *Newsweek*'s) for commentary on race and on the black man's progress. Among the events indicating racial progress were a "marriage of enlightenment" and the election of black mayors in Cleveland and Gary. The marriage was a sign of how far the country had come when "Dean Rusk, Secretary of State of the U.S., native of . . . Georgia, and grandson of two Confederate soldiers, had given his only daughter's hand to a Negro." *Time* took care of the carping of white bigots; it chose King to deal with the nattering of black bigots. " 'Individuals marry,' " said King, " 'not races.' " To explicate the meaning of the elections in Cleveland and Gary—as well as the defeat of a candidate in Boston who opposed school integration—*Time* turned to King. He obliged: The elections were a " 'one-two-three punch against backlash and bigotry.' " In contrast to *Newsweek*, *Time* made much of King's efforts to bring about the election of Stokes as Cleveland's mayor. The outcome vindicated the candidate's (and *Time*'s) " 'faith in American democracy' " and was an object lesson to any who had doubted or had lost that faith.[49]

King also was a reminder of the glory days of the old movement. Thus, *Time* restored some of the symbolism stripped from reports published earlier in 1967. When, for example, King and three associates returned to Birmingham to serve a sentence imposed in 1963, Bull Connor was absent from the story, but other facets of the Birmingham of old were brought out. The incarceration "stemmed from a Good Friday march in 1963, led by King against Birmingham's lunch counter and restroom segregation." King's symbolic attributes were emphasized by mentioning how often he had gone to jail for his beliefs. First, he was identified as "one of the few winners of the Nobel Peace Prize to admit to even a single incarceration." Then, he marched off to jail "for at least the fifteenth time." Making the point inescapable, *Time* said that King had been arrested so often that he kept handy a "Bastille Day uniform—denim shirt, sweater, and blue work pants." These compelling details sketched a satisfying symbolic portrait of King as the self-sacrificing leader. There was another lesson. King accepted his punishment even though he complained that the Supreme Court, by refusing to hear his appeal, failed in its duty to uphold individual rights. Thus he accepted the rule of law and the

49. *Time*, "A Marriage of Enlightenment," September 29, 1967, pp. 28, 29, and "The Real Black Power," 23. On the Cleveland primary, see "Vindicative Victory," *Time*, October 13, 1967, p. 29.

consequences of disobedience. That lesson *Time* had taught more than once—sometimes by using King as a rather different symbol.[50]

Near year's end, *Time* dissolved the firm of King, Carmichael & Co. It had become essential to distinguish the nuances of ideology among adherents of Black Power, the "fanatical" leadership of Carmichael versus the "responsible" element represented by King. Unlike Carmichael, King counseled "his people 'to love your enemies, bless them that curse you, and pray for them that despitefully use you,'" and he embraced "the new Negro ethic in its most reasonable application," as a call to blacks to amass "'political and economic strength to achieve their legitimate goals. No one can deny that the Negro is in dire need of this kind of legitimate power.'"[51]

A few days after the story was published, King formally announced that the Poor People's Campaign would begin in the spring of 1968. This most reasonable King, it appeared, was not so reasonable after all.

The symbolic King underwent some striking transformations in 1967. *U.S. News* began the year by sounding the warning that King was a radical who preached nonviolence but sowed trouble, and the reverberations intensified once King delivered his pronouncements on the war. The riots led to a symbolic transformation when he, like *U.S. News*, decried "mob law." This theme soon faded and was replaced by depictions of King consorting with Communists and threatening to cripple cities with civil disruption. *U.S. News* was fairly accurate in portraying King as a dangerous man—though not as a promoter of violence. But it had defined King as a radical even when he was a reformer. Now the man had caught up with the definition.

To *Newsweek*, King was a source of embarrassment—and no little unease. *Newsweek* wanted him to abandon the war issue; he would not. *Newsweek* wanted him to become an icon of civil rights; instead, he began planning the radical Poor People's Campaign. Once, King had been the bridge between the radicals and the conservatives. By 1967, with the old consensus of conscience shattered beyond repair, with radicals and revolutionaries all about, with violence spilling into the streets, *Newsweek* would have settled for King differentiating between friends, the moderates, and enemies, the Black Power firebrands. Instead, he made common cause in the anti-war movement with

---

50. "Birmingham Revisited," *Time*, November 10, 1967, pp. 28–29. *Time* was not incorrect. Gandhian philosophy holds that those who violate unjust laws must accept penalties willingly, thus demonstrating respect for the rule of law.

51. "Black Power and Black Pride," *Time*, December 1, 1967, p. 21.

men who spat the name of their country from their lips while agitating for rebellion or revolution. *Newsweek*'s uneasiness sometimes appeared between the lines. King's essentially reformist work of registering black voters in Cleveland was all but ignored. An American symbol had been turned on its head, and *Newsweek* averted its gaze from that distressing spectacle.

Editorial silence was a tool of the trade for *Time* as well; it published little about King for the first quarter. In April, however, he burst onto the public stage with a bitter attack on a war that was close to a holy crusade for Luce's magazine. Predictably, there were cutting denunciations: King was ignorant of the war and its meaning; he had abandoned his proper cause; he was associating with radicals such as Carmichael. Furthermore, *Time* stripped away symbolic trappings from his civil rights campaigns. The government and the law—thus the society—had brought freedom to black southerners, and now King was attacking that government and that society. In short, King knew neither his place nor his friends. King returned to his place when he denounced violence and rioting. Thereafter he was a useful symbol as *Time* sought to prove to the black American that he, too, would enjoy the blessings of liberty and prosperity. King was also useful as a counterpoint in the last few months of 1967. King was a reasonable man; the prophets of black violence and black revolution were fanatical—a neatly framed comparison not lacking in truth but requiring editorial silence and filing down of some rough edges to sustain. King was in his proper place at year's end, so far as *Time* was concerned. Keeping him there would be a considerable problem in the year to come.

IX

PROPHET WITH A SWORD

Before his death in April, King had journeyed a far distance from Montgomery, Birmingham, and Selma, those triumphant milestones of the old southern movement to *Newsweek* and *Time*, those exercises in trouble making to *U.S. News*. In 1968, the actual King resembled more closely the symbol sketched by *U.S. News*. He began the year as a reformer-turned-radical. As a critic of the war in Vietnam, he not only questioned the wisdom of expending so much money on the war when the poor were in misery, but challenged the morality of American military tactics. King was moving toward radicalism in another way, by organizing the Poor People's Campaign as a movement of the underclass. Gathering beneath his banner in Washington would be blacks, impoverished whites, Hispanic Americans, and American Indians, each grouping with its special grievances but bound together by the common bond of poverty. Structuring a movement along class lines would have been controversial enough—class interests and coalitions were at best suspect; at worst, they smacked of communism. But there was more to King's radicalism. He did not expect poor people to succeed by appealing to conscience. There would have to be an escalation of the campaign of civil disobedience until America's leaders had to heed the cries of the poor lest the cities of the nation be crippled by nonviolent disruption.

King was a grimmer prophet in 1968. Certainly grimmer than he had been in 1965 when he turned back the march across the Edmund Pettus Bridge, trusting that the nation would intervene to secure the rights enshrined in the

Constitution. He was more determined and more realistic than he was in 1966 when he accepted a Chicago politician's promises, worth as much writ on air as on paper without the force of compulsion behind them, and called off the confrontation in Cicero. In the year of his death, King set forth to bring not peace but a sword to the America that honored him as a prophet.

U.S. News made sense of this grim prophet simply: King was a sower of the seeds of trouble and violence, and firm measures should be employed to meet all such threats. In one case, King provided a useful example. Radicals had threatened to disrupt the Democratic National Convention. *U.S. News* reached back to King's 1966 campaign in Chicago, where it unearthed the injunction used by the Daley machine to counter protests. Inasmuch as the injunction had been an effective tactic against one troublemaker, King, it could be used to good effect against others bent on the same type of mischief.[1] The echo chamber was operating again.

Over the next eight weeks, echoes warned of King's upcoming "campaign of massive civil disobedience." An example was an article about new weapons and tactics being readied for the coming summer riots. Missing no opportunity to sound the tocsin about King, the journal advised that Washington, "facing a massive demonstration" led by King in April, "will have the help of both National Guardsmen and Regular Army troops if needed. Plans call for a quick show of strength at the first sign of serious trouble. . . . Rioters are going to find this country more prepared than it was last year to meet force with force." In three weeks, another echo followed. *U.S. News* foresaw a "siege of Congress and the White House" by "thousands of Negroes vowing to camp . . . until their demands for 'jobs or income' are met—and threatening 'massive civil disobedience' if their demands are rejected." Their demands were to be placed before the Congress and the president. That, *U.S. News* warned, was only the first step: "If no satisfactory response is forthcoming— and Dr. King concedes that he expects none—then thousands of marchers will start moving on Washington. The first big wave—estimated at three thousand or more—is expected to be in the capital by the end of April. . . . It is predicted that 'tens of thousands' of marchers might eventually gather in Washington. Mass demonstrations are also to be held in other big cities."[2]

1. "Will Violence Upset '68 Campaign?" *U.S. News & World Report*, January 22, 1968, p. 47.

2. See *U.S. News & World Report*, "A 'Liberal' Group Speaks Out Against Draft Violation, Rioting," February 12, 1968, p. 68, "As Cities Prepare for Riots—New Weapons, New Tactics," February 26, 1968, p. 37, and "March on Washington—What to Expect," March 18, 1968, p. 44.

The prospect of having thousands of disgruntled blacks camping on its doorstep for months shook the magazine, but not only because of the number of demonstrators, their race, and how long they would spend in Washington. It was disturbed by the term *aggressive nonviolence* bandied about by King and his men. Since the SCLC was more reticent now about its tactics, *U.S. News* combed through past statements for clues to what the Poor People's Campaign might do. What it found were these possibilities: picketing government offices; holding a "lobby-in" in Congress, perhaps even at the White House itself; staging "sit-ins" in federal buildings; constructing shanties "among Washington's famous cherry trees" and in other public places; and, most important, disrupting "the functioning of municipal and federal governments, and blocking bridges and highways." King's assurances that traffic would not be disrupted and that demonstrations would remain nonviolent failed to convince *U.S. News.* Its suspicions were not unfounded. Striking from the list the blocking of bridges and highways did not materially alter the potential for disruption. And the magazine took little comfort from the fact that King had secured a promise from Stokely Carmichael not to interfere with his campaign. King's confidence that there would be no violence was not shared by "some Washington officials and lawmakers," the magazine claimed, its tone suggesting that dubious attitude was entirely realistic.[3]

Time and *Newsweek* were also among the doubters. These magazines, however, were much less concerned with the Poor People's Campaign. Only one brief reference to it in the first quarter of 1968 was located in *Time.* It cast King as a failed alternative to black violence. King described his venture as a "'last desperate try at nonviolence,'" but *Time* doubted that "King or anyone else can provide what he calls 'an alternative to a long, hot summer.'. . . Police forces around the nation are operating on the assumption that the summer will be a sizzler."[4]

The way out of the ghetto was not through Black Power or a massive demonstration such as King's, argued *Time*, but through "green power." This assertion was included in a reexamination of the 1966 Chicago campaign published in the issue of March 1. King had won no victory; instead, whites had fooled him "with a hatful of vapid promises." Victories were being won instead by using the "black pocketbook power" developed in Chicago by "Jesse Jackson, 26, a burly, apothegmatizing King lieutenant who praises the Lord and believes in the might of economics." In contrast to King, Jack-

3. "March on Washington—What to Expect," 44.
4. "The Crucible," *Time*, January 26, 1968, p. 12.

son had "wrested work from ghetto businessmen for three thousand of his flock and boosted South Side Negroes' annual income by twenty-two million dollars."[5]

The point—*Time* almost always had one to make—seemed to bear less on what was happening in Chicago than on what King planned for Washington. The moral was simple: King had failed in Chicago, Jackson had succeeded. And Jackson had done so by bringing the constructive force of the marketplace to bear on a situation requiring correction. Furthermore, Jackson's plans to put pickets in several southern cities were emphasized over the national economic boycott intended to be one feature of the Poor People's Campaign. As national journalism, this was odd indeed—the part greater than the whole, the follower achieving where the leader had failed—and it ran contrary to *Time*'s insistence in the past that the SCLC was no more than King's lengthened shadow. No doubt it helped, as *Time* said, that Jackson both praised the Lord and believed in the might of economics; so did King, but his notions about economics were more radical than were those being put into effect in Chicago.[6]

Newsweek's initial response to the campaign in January was favorable, but too much can be made of this reaction. *Newsweek* had a blind spot: its hope that the civil rights coalition somehow could be put back together again. At first, the campaign was presented as a reprise (in spirit, if not organization) of the 1963 March on Washington, possibly serving as a rallying point for a new coalition "of all strategic shadings, from the Urban League to Carmichael's own hard-lining SNCC." A month later, with hopes for a coalition dashed, optimism yielded to a decidedly pessimistic expectation that mirrored the judgments of urban specialists studying "Negro unrest." Their bleak conclusions: that the "poverty march on Washington may signal the start of the rioting," and even if it didn't, something else would "detonate the street fighting"; that violence would spread from city to city and that nothing could be done to stop the tragedy; and finally, that "the nation is 'building toward organized insurrection within the next few years.'"[7]

5. "Black Pocketbook Power," *Time*, March 1, 1968, p. 17.

6. Massoni, "Perspectives on Operation Breadbasket," 4. On the national economic boycott, see Fager, *Uncertain Resurrection*, 18; and Viorst, *Fire in the Streets*, 432–33. *Time* did acknowledge, however, the symbolic force of King's name. "Off and On," January 26, 1968, p. 17.

7. See *Newsweek*, "Back in Circulation," January 22, 1968, p. 28, and "The Periscope," February 19, 1968, p. 17.

Thereafter, *Newsweek* delegitimized King's venture. What had been a "massive civil rights drive" in late January became, in mid-February, a "shantytown demonstration city" and, a week later, King's "spring squat-in." In another two weeks, the campaign became a measure of the volatility of the racial climate. Washington had never been considered "a major racial tinderbox" because most of its black workers held federal jobs and were "insulated by civil service security from the worst chills of black despair." Now even Washington was nervous: "Gun possession is growing, and in April, Martin Luther King is due in town with three thousand demonstrators to begin a summer-long campaign of picketing and marching for jobs and income." Unflattering labels were attached to King. He was one of the "Visigoths" expected to descend on the Democratic National Convention in Chicago and was inducted into *Newsweek*'s "Who's Who of alienated America," along with others such as "self-styled 'professional radical' Saul Alinsky" and "Timothy Leary, the guru of the LSD set."[8]

Curiously, as King's stock fell with *Newsweek* because he would not abandon his new movement, it also rose because he opposed the war. The meddling in foreign affairs that earned him sharp denunciations from *Newsweek* was put in a different light by the Tet offensive in the spring of 1968. (On January 30, almost seventy thousand North Vietnamese regulars and Viet Cong insurgents launched an offensive that smashed into more than a hundred cities and towns. While a military disaster for Communist forces, Tet was a strategic victory for them, hastening the grinding process, already under way, whereby many Americans came to believe that the war was folly.) *Newsweek* gave space to a "stalwart hawk" to raise this disbelieving question: "'My God, supposing the doves are right and we're wrong?'" *Newsweek* was not quite ready to concede the point, but merely entertaining the question revealed the magazine's doubts. Thus it was not surprising to find the journal lending a receptive ear to King's pronouncements. The former meddler now "planned to deliver a stirring call for an end to the war" at Arlington National Cemetery. As it happened, the federal courts prevented him from doing so because special pleadings were not permitted in the cemetery. *Newsweek* nevertheless placed King at the head of a ceremony of silence at Arlington, during which prayers for peace gained impact as they were contrasted to the military commands of the honor guard at the Tomb of the Unknown Soldier. "'In this

8. See *Newsweek*, "Rendezvous with History," February 19, 1968, p. 23, "Vigilantes and Visigoths," February 26, 1968, p. 26, and "Surveying Summer '68," March 11, 1968, p. 45.

period of absolute silence,' intoned the Rev. Dr. Martin Luther King, Jr., 'let us pray.' . . . Then Rabbi Abraham Heschel dramatically repeated the words of Jesus on the cross, " 'Eli, Eli, lama sabachthani' " (My God, my God, why hast Thou forsaken me) to which Roman Catholic Bishop James P. Shannon concluded, 'Let us go in peace.' "[9]

With the Tet offensive still under way, peace seemed as elusive as ever in Vietnam—and the situation was not much more promising in the United States. The riot season of 1968 was only a few months off. After four summers of disorders ranging in seriousness from minor skirmishes to appalling carnage, riots were regarded as almost as inevitable as July heat. Already, major demonstrations such as the Poor People's Campaign were being prepared. The summer gave every sign it would be what *Time* had forecast: a sizzler.

About this time, one of those volatile situations was developing in an unlikely place and in an unlikely form. The place was Memphis, and it was unlikely because Memphis seemed to be a placid outpost of racial harmony. Memphis had escaped the major protests and racial incidents that made Birmingham a byword for racism. Its reputation was such that the Southern Regional Council, a biracial organization noted for exposing racism, once observed that Memphis had "begun to shine as a beacon of reason and decency for the Deep South."[10]

Published in 1964, that observation was at once accurate and dated. Memphis was an anomaly in the South. Blacks there had voted since the turn of the century as a subordinate but important element of Boss Crump's machine. Black political power, put to effective use in a coalition style of political maneuvering, had grown because of the vacuum in local political and civic leadership that was created by Crump's death in 1954. Some progress had been made toward dismantling Jim Crow over the years. Black policemen had been employed in Memphis for a number of years; public accommodations, such as restaurants, and public facilities, such as schools, parks, and playgrounds, had been quietly desegregated, though often in token fashion and only because of federal court decrees. Politically, the results were, if not overwhelming, at least reasonable. By the beginning of 1968, blacks held

9. The hawk's question appears in "Rendezvous with History," 24. The Tet offensive marked a turning point in *Newsweek*'s support of the war. Elliott, *The World of Oz*, 100. For the ceremony at Arlington, see "Silent March," *Newsweek*, February 19, 1968, p. 58.

10. Benjamin Muse, *Memphis* (Atlanta, 1964), 48.

three of the thirteen seats on the city council, one of the eleven seats on the county board of supervisors, one of five cabinet offices in the mayor's administration, and a criminal court bench. If Memphis was no paradise for blacks, racial conditions there were far better than they were in the small towns and rural districts of Mississippi, west Tennessee, and eastern Arkansas whence many of the city's residents, black or white, had moved. Memphis had its own brand of racism, but it was a diluted, more genteel variant of the cultural values brought to the city by the migrants.[11]

By 1968, Memphis had arrived at a point in race relations—as the term was applied during the old southern movement—that made it closer to contemporary American society than to the Jim Crow South.[12] But this was 1968, not 1964, and rights secured in Selma and Birmingham were not enough anymore, whether in Memphis or in the rest of America.

The unlikely cause of the racial crisis in Memphis was a strike by public works employees, members of Local 1733 of the American Federation of State, County, and Municipal Employees. The cause was unlikely because trade unionism never had been established as firmly in Memphis—or anywhere else in Dixie, for that matter—as in the rest of the nation, and the spillover of organized labor into the public sector was a fairly recent phenomenon in the South. Furthermore, the striking public works employees, most of whom were black, had failed three times previously to wrest a contract from the city government. The most unlikely element of all was that the strike came to be equated with the lot of blacks in Memphis. As responsible as anyone for that symbolic identification was Mayor Henry Loeb. A reformer early in his political career, Loeb enjoyed the support of blacks, but he lost it by declaring himself a segregationist in the early 1960s. In 1967, Memphis voters—including blacks, who supplied the margin of victory—approved the formation of a new mayor-council form of government. Loeb won his subsequent

11. On black politics in Memphis, see Harry Holloway, "Negro Political Strategy: Coalition or Independent Power Politics?" *Social Science Quarterly*, XLIX (1968), 534–47. Black voters in Memphis numbered 19,608 of 104,671 registered voters in 1951 and 80,033 of 235,505 by 1967. Thomas Beebe Ripy, Jr., "Changes in the Formal Structure of Municipal Government and Their Effect on Selected Aspects of the Legislative Process: A Case Study of Memphis, Tennessee" (Ph.D. dissertation, University of Kentucky, 1973), 96. On desegregation in Memphis, see Muse, *Memphis*, 2, 31–42. The cultural affinity of Memphis and surrounding areas is described by Shields McIlwaine, *Memphis Down in Dixie* (New York, 1949), 15; and William D. Miller, *Memphis During the Progressive Era, 1900–1917* (Memphis, 1957), 5.

12. Pat Watters, "Beale Street and Points North: Memphis is Also America," *Nation*, April 22, 1968, pp. 529–31.

mayoral campaign even though he went against the grain of Memphis politics by neither seeking nor receiving black support. During the garbage strike, Loeb became a symbol of paternalistic racism.[13]

The strike was begun by Local 1733 on February 12. It started as a simple labor dispute; the parent union had no desire to interject racial issues into a strike it regarded as ill-timed and ill-conceived. The union's demands were modest: Essentially, it wanted the city government to sign a contract with the local and to arrange to deduct union dues from the paychecks of union members. Within two weeks, the strike evolved into a racial issue, in part because of a brief skirmish between police and demonstrators, in part because of the intense symbolism attached to the strike.

The events heading toward tragedy in Memphis generally escaped the attention of the news weeklies. This was to be expected: Memphis was off the beaten path during the old southern movement and was even more so in 1968, when journalists were directing their attention to weightier matters of war and peace, the probability of another summer of disorders, and demonstrations such as the Poor People's Campaign, then about six weeks from its scheduled commencement.

Newsweek ignored the strike. For its part, *U.S. News* harrumphed that Loeb's refusal to bargain with the union was a welcome example after New York City's abject surrender to union demands during a garbage strike. While not extensive, *Time*'s coverage was an exception to the pattern. *Time* cited the strike as another failure to sort out grievances between public employees and management, but it was more thoughtful than was *U.S. News* about the issues involved and more sympathetic to the workers' grievances.[14]

By mid-March, however, *Time* regarded the strike as "a premonition in microcosm of next summer's national threat." Memphis was portrayed as a "passable paradigm of racial harmony" with integrated schools, black citizens who "have voted since the early 1900s," and a climate so amicable that "Memphis police have never faced a serious charge of brutality." To be sure, the city had its problems; its "two hundred thousand Negroes have discovered not only that they are poor, but also, even by honky standards, undeservedly

13. Richard Lentz, *Sixty-Five Days in Memphis: A Study of Culture, Symbols, and the Press, Journalism Monographs*, XCVIII (August, 1986), 12, 18–19.

14. See *U.S. News & World Report*, "Militant Public Employees—More Trouble for the Cities," and "A Warning Against City Workers' Strikes," both in the issue of February 26, 1968, p. 78. "The Worker's Rights and the Public Weal," *Time*, March 1, 1968, pp. 34, 35.

so." In most respects, however, Memphis resembled other American cities confronted by racial crisis. Several passages in *Time* made that point: Black Power militants were gathering in Memphis; police, "for the most part, in keeping with Memphis tradition, . . . have kept their cool," and the best elements were attempting to set matters right—in this instance, "fashionably dressed white housewives," weary of "Mayor Loeb's intransigence," who urged him to give in, and members of the city council who issued statements supporting recognition of the union and adoption of a policy by the city that workers would be treated equally when hired or promoted.[15]

Despite those efforts cited by *Time*, the strike was far from a settlement, and by the middle of March, King was about to become involved in the dispute. He was persuaded by James Lawson to make a speech in Memphis. Lawson was the SCLC's leading theoretician of Gandhian nonviolence and pastor of a black Methodist church in Memphis, and he led a coalition dominated by black clergymen. Their organization, Community on the Move to Equality, assumed effective control of the strike after it became a racial issue.

King undoubtedly intended to do no more than make one or two speeches to rally flagging enthusiasm and to generate national media coverage for a cause hitherto ignored. Little more could have been expected by Lawson, because King was preoccupied with his troubled Washington campaign. King had lost the support of some old allies, including Bayard Rustin, the tactical organizer of the 1963 March on Washington, who believed the atmosphere was too volatile for what King had in mind. Others in the black movement less sympathetic than Rustin were maintaining a studied, even hostile, silence. Circulating within the SCLC itself were doubts about the wisdom of the project when tensions were so high, as well as pragmatic questions related to problems in recruiting and logistics.[16]

15. "Memphis: Pre-Summer Blues," *Time*, March 15, 1968, pp. 19, 20. See also "Studying the Study," *Time*, March 15, 1968, p. 17.

16. On Rustin's opposition, see Viorst, *Fire in the Streets*, 437–38. The disapproval of the NAACP and the Urban League is cited by Lewis, *King: A Biography*, 369. On objections within the SCLC, see Marian Logan to King, March 8, 1968, provided by David Garrow from his files; and Offenburger interview, 32–33. King planned to send three thousand demonstrators to Washington initially. SCLC files show approximately eleven hundred had signed up by late March. The records are probably incomplete but, along with related correspondence, point to serious recruiting problems. King Center Archives, Atlanta, contains reports on recruitment, various dates, in Box 178, Files 1–20, Albert Turner to Hosea Williams, April 3, 1968, in Box 177, File 44, and Hosea Williams to Bernard Lafayette, February 11, 1968, in Box 177, File 7. See also Garrow, *Bearing the Cross*, 589–94, 606–607.

The problems were so pressing, the arguments against continuing so compelling (including the notions that King did not wish to embarrass the Democratic party or to jeopardize the chances of a liberal or a moderate winning the presidency) as to convince some authors that King planned to cancel the Washington movement.[17] To be sure, King had pulled back from the brink before, but that did not mean necessarily that he would do so again in 1968.

For one thing, King had become more radical and more open about it. His speeches on Vietnam indicated as much, as did the thousands of miles he traveled in the early months of 1968 recruiting Hispanics, Indians, and poor whites for the campaign. Representatives of those groups assembled at the SCLC's headquarters in Atlanta on March 15. "Delegates repeatedly pointed out," said an SCLC press release, "that the established powers of rich America have deliberately exploited poor people by isolating them in ethnic, nationality, religious, and racial groups. As one poor white person explained, 'It is not really the poor people who are responsible for hatred in our country, but the powerful economic and political managers who want to keep us down. We will no longer permit them to divide us.'" The same rhetoric of class interests and class conflicts had appeared earlier among the SCLC staff, but when the staffers responsible for press and public relations felt free to use such radical phrases, the project had to be coming to a head. And there was more here than hype. The implications of the Poor People's Campaign struck a spark in one of King's allies, Myles Horton of the Highlander Folk Center in Tennessee, who caught a "glimpse of the future" in Atlanta: "We had there . . . authentic spokesmen for poor Mexican-Americans, American Indians, blacks and whites, the making of a bottom-up coalition."[18]

If King was preparing to scuttle the Poor People's Campaign, he had a risk to consider. A campaign develops a momentum of its own and after a given date becomes all but impossible to call off. For the Washington campaign, the date was March 15. Had King dropped the project, he would have had to make an accounting to the more than seventy representatives of various ethnic groups attending the Atlanta conference—not to mention Stokely Carmichael, with

17. See, for example, Viorst, *Fire in the Streets*, 438; Lewis, *King: A Biography*, 385; Bishop, *The Days of Martin Luther King*, 29.

18. King Center Archives, Atlanta, contains SCLC press release, March 15, 1968, in Box 179, File 25, confidential memorandum to SCLC staff, January, 1968, in Box 179, File 18, Myles Horton to Andrew J. Young, April 5, 1968, in Box 177, File 20. Horton's letter was intended for King, but King was killed before it could be mailed; it was rewritten and sent to Young.

whom King had reached an agreement for support of the venture.[19] Backing down after March 15 would have been embarrassing. Probably the cost would have been much stiffer: additional damage to King's leadership, already undermined by Black Power and the failure in Chicago. In short, the problems besetting the campaign were great, but even greater were the pressures to continue.

Those problems most likely were preying on King's mind when he flew to Memphis to deliver the speech that Lawson requested. He was surprised by the large (approximately thirteen thousand persons, a Memphis newspaper reckoned) and enthusiastic crowd that greeted him on March 18. A general work stoppage should be used as a weapon, King said, if the city government refused to settle the key issue, establishing a system to collect union dues. With an eye cocked to a greater concern, King "asked the rally to 'make this the beginning of the Washington movement.'" He also promised to return to Memphis to lead a major protest march as a gesture of support for the strikers.[20]

A massive snowstorm forced the postponement of that demonstration until March 28. In the interim, the Loeb administration agreed to accept the services of a mediator in the strike. It was a ploy; Loeb had no intention of signing any agreement with the union.[21] Sensing there would be no good-faith bargaining and wishing to dramatize the march that King would lead, the union broke off negotiations on the eve of the demonstration.

Approximately five thousand persons assembled for the march. It was organized by the ministers of COME. They botched the job. Placards attached to heavy sticks were issued to marchers and became weapons when trouble broke out. Parade marshals issued conflicting instructions through bullhorns. Rumors that a black student had been killed by police swept through the milling crowd awaiting King's arrival. When King finally appeared, the demonstrators swarmed around the automobile that brought him from the airport, and it took some time to sort everyone out and begin the march. Trouble

19. On whether Carmichael pledged not to interfere with the campaign or promised material aid, cf. Paul Good, "No Man Can Fill Dr. King's Shoes—But Abernathy Tries"; and Jose Yglesias, "Dr. King's March on Washington, Part II," in August Meier and Elliott Rudwick (eds.), *Black Protest in the Sixties* (Chicago, 1970), 288 and 278.

20. Memphis *Commercial Appeal*, March 19, 1968, p. 1; Offenburger interview, 33.

21. Interview with James Manire, a lawyer who advised Loeb, by Anne Trotter and David Yellin, August 7, 1968 (Transcript of tape 43, in Mississippi Valley Collection, Memphis State University), 47–48.

started after the march went a few blocks. Black youngsters began breaking windows and looting the stores along the march route. Memphis police officers used force indiscriminately against the marchers (more than sixty persons were injured during and after the violence), and they arrested more than two hundred persons. A black youth was killed by officers whose story, disputed by some witnesses, was that he attacked them with a knife. Still, the affray, while a nasty skirmish, was minor by the grim standards established by Watts, Detroit, and Newark.

The effect upon King was anything but minor. He was accused of cowardice because his aides had spirited him away from the march after the violence and the looting started. More important, he was forced into a situation of proving that he could lead a peaceful march in Memphis; otherwise, there would be no Poor People's Campaign. Although shaken by the aborted demonstration, he gave a flat analysis: "No Memphis, no Washington."[22]

King read the situation realistically. The white establishment, ranging from the New York *Times* to President Johnson (who appeared on national television to denounce "mindless violence"), was hostile. Black conservatives were no more encouraging. Breaking its silence, the NAACP expressed doubts, a signal that the NAACP wanted the campaign shelved. From the left, Harlem congressman Adam Clayton Powell scorned King as Martin *Loser* King. The controversy shook even the SCLC. After meeting all day on March 30, the executive committee believed it necessary to reassure the SCLC staff that King was no coward, that he had been physically forced to leave the line of march against his wishes, and that the violence was caused by young people who "felt ignored by some adult community leaders."[23]

Even more telling was another part of the confidential message from the executive committee to the staff. If ever there was a time to drop the Poor People's Campaign, it was at that moment, when relentless pressure was coming from all directions. But the staff members who were responsible for putting the campaign together, and who would have to pick up the pieces if it were canceled, were informed privately that "OUR PLANS FOR WASHINGTON HAVE NOT CHANGED. . . . We are going to Washington as planned. . . . Our

22. Gerold Frank, *An American Death* (Garden City, N.Y., 1972), 28. See also Garrow, *Bearing the Cross*, 611–15.

23. Lewis, *King: A Biography*, 383; Watters, "Beale Street," 530; New York *Times*, March 30, 1968, p. 32; Wofford, *Of Kennedys and Kings*, 210. Thomas Offenburger on behalf of the executive committee, to SCLC staff, April 1, 1968, in Box 122, File 10, King Center Archives, Atlanta.

action in Memphis will be a prelude to Washington, and should not detract from the Poor People's Campaign. . . . Memphis is a smaller version of what we're going to Washington for."[24] All things considered, it was a ringing declaration of determination.

Some of the pressure was coming from the news magazines, which had awakened abruptly to the situation in Memphis. Although emphases varied, they shared a common interpretation: The violence and the looting in Memphis signaled what could easily occur in Washington—except in the nation's capital, the disorders might be a hundred times worse.

Newsweek, for one, found an "ominously disturbing" lesson. "For the first time in a decade of nonviolent agitation, Nobel Laureate King lost control of a demonstration as it swept through the streets—a portent of what could happen in Washington, D.C., later this month when he plans to mass thousands of poor blacks to pressure Congress for more anti-poverty funds. In Memphis, King's peaceful march was catalyzed by the most volatile and most dangerous force in the ghetto: restive young blacks turned on to violence almost as an end in itself. Their soul brothers live in every city, and they are talking tougher every day." The black radicals, *Newsweek* asserted, wished King consigned to the "dustbin of history." In its own way, so did *Newsweek*. Herein was a slightly reworked version of its recurring theme that King should limit himself to pursuits in the South. "Only a few years ago," it maintained, "such a march would have been a prayerful, tuneful, and probably uneventful parade past gawking whites. But in the tindery atmosphere of post-Watts America, it was riskier than King imagined."[25]

Granted that social conditions were more volatile, *Newsweek* was stretching for a point. Its recollection made the marches of the old movement seem placid. Certainly civil rights marches had not always been observed only by peacefully gawking whites; St. Augustine proved the contrary, as did Birmingham and Selma. Certainly, as well, the discipline of nonviolence had slipped before—in Albany and in Birmingham, for example. And in Memphis, King had done little more than step from a car and start marching at the head of a demonstration that neither he nor his men had organized. Holding King responsible for what happened next, window smashing and looting, was not much more than a canard on *Newsweek*'s part.

24. Offenburger to SCLC staff, April 1, 1968, in King Center Archives.
25. "Memphis: An Ugly New Portent," *Newsweek*, April 8, 1968, p. 33.

King, of course, was not completely innocent of courting risks, present or past. One theme appeared in *Newsweek*'s reports from Birmingham, Selma, and Chicago: King was determined to create a crisis. Birmingham, to take one example, did not just happen. King and his lieutenants stoked the fires there, expecting Bull Connor would react violently, hoping—but prepared to run the risk—that blacks would not respond in kind. As Wyatt Tee Walker once observed, the SCLC needed a crisis to get results, and the Poor People's Campaign was intended to produce just such a crisis. (That matter, far more important than anything King did or did not do in Memphis, was ignored by *Newsweek*.) King could hardly be unaware that nonviolence might fail in the Washington campaign; he had, as *Newsweek* admitted, struck a bargain with Carmichael and "other Washington-based militants" precisely for the purpose of reducing the possibility of violence.[26] Furthermore, King stood ready to gamble more than once that his movement of the poor would remain peaceful. If a crisis in Washington did not accomplish his purpose, he was ready to bring about other crises in other major cities.

Planned crises and massive disruption of cities did not fit the image of an icon from another era, which was what *Newsweek* fervently wished King to become. In that role he would be safe, as removed from the tumult of the times as any other icon trotted out and hoisted aloft as the multitudes gathered to celebrate their faith. *Newsweek* had described King as "a black icon," fearing that should he lose that status, it would be "a damaging and perhaps irreparable blow to hopes for peaceful social change in America." Wanting to preserve King's value as a symbol, *Newsweek* felt compelled to show that he was worthy, that he had not, as *Time* said, "beat a prudent retreat," that he had not, as *U.S. News* claimed, "slipped down a side street to a waiting car and sped away" after the trouble started during the march in Memphis. Instead, in *Newsweek*'s version, "aides closed around King and hustled him . . . to safety."[27]

The theme pieced together by *U.S. News* after the Memphis demonstration also was not new. Year by year in the echo chamber, King was denounced as a preacher of nonviolence, an agitator who produced the opposite. Senator Robert Byrd of West Virginia now came forward to reiterate that assertion. Byrd regarded "Memphis [as] a 'preview of what may be in store' for Wash-

26. *Ibid.*, 34.
27. *Ibid*; "Memphis Blues," *Time*, April 5, 1968, p. 25; "'Bloody Memphis'— And More to Come?" *U.S. News & World Report*, April 8, 1968, p. 8.

ington 'if this self-seeking rabble-rouser is allowed to go through with his plans.'" Thus was sounded the tocsin. The Washington campaign would escalate if the demands of the poor were not met by the national government; King himself had "said he could not guarantee that there would be no violence in future Memphis demonstrations or in Washington," only that "our demonstrations will be nonviolent." *U.S. News* preferred the reassurances of President Johnson—"'We will not let violence or lawlessness take over this country.'"[28]

Time alternated between criticizing King and condemning Memphis authorities for producing a racial crisis. Memphis police were chastised for losing "their cherished reputation for restraint," the authorities for panicking at a minor outbreak of violence and looting, and Loeb for "stoking the Negroes' discontent." King was treated quite as roughly. His "prudent retreat" was hardly a good example, *Time* said implicitly—the leader skipping out at the first sign of trouble, leaving "local civil rights leaders to herd the marchers" away from the scene. Worse still, King provided an opening for the black militants of Memphis, and there were black militants awaiting as well in the nation's capital. Yet King was so reckless—"undismayed" was *Time*'s word—that he planned to bull ahead with the Washington campaign even though "his nonviolent mantle was in shreds."[29]

In one way or another, King was depicted as a threat because what occurred in Memphis could be repeated in Washington. Yet the news magazines did not plumb the depths of his radicalism, especially the class orientation of the Poor People's Campaign. Possibly, they simply followed the practice in American journalism of eschewing "even non-Marxist notions of class conflict." Still, denying the legitimacy of class conflict would not preclude denunciations of a social movement organized along class lines.[30] Most curious of all, *U.S. News* did not use the Poor People's Campaign to paint King with the red brush, even though since 1964 it had missed few opportunities to do that. The missed opportunity probably can be attributed to the coming siege in which *U.S. News* would be among those besieged. The prospect of hordes of black demonstrators pouring into a city with a majority black population and staying not for a day but possibly for months preoccupied *U.S. News*. What King

28. "'Bloody Memphis'—And More to Come?" 8.
29. "Memphis Blues," 25.
30. See, for example, "The Gadfly of the Poverty War," 30. On class and journalists, see Gans, *Deciding What's News*, 24.

proposed to do in Washington threatened *U.S. News* immediately and directly—and it was not surprising that the journal took them one threat at a time.

By contrast, *Newsweek* and *Time* were confronted by the dilemma of a reformer-become-radical. As a reformer, they had honored him; as a radical, they had ignored him or counseled him to place his feet on the right path again—each response reflecting the power that King exerted as a symbol. *Time* and *Newsweek* could not ignore the campaign that King proposed to begin in Washington. But they could criticize him for recklessness without calling into question the symbolism that made him the embodiment of the American way of moderate reform. It was a variation of what they had done in the past—damning his judgment, his tactics, or his timing, but not attacking his value as a symbol.

That symbolism would have been difficult to maintain had *Time* and *Newsweek* reported the disruptive and coercive nature of his new march on Washington, the proposed construction of his coalition along class lines, and his notion that the time had come for a radical transformation of American society. What sort of radical transformation King had in mind was deliberately hazy in outline, and perhaps was missed by the news magazines. Other facets of the campaign—in particular, its organization as a class coalition—were becoming clear before King's death, indeed before the March 28 demonstration in Memphis.[31] A free-lance writer caught the crux of the situation in a story published by the *New York Times Magazine* at the end of March: "They are not going to Washington, as in 1963, to support proposed legislation; they are not speaking for blacks alone, but for all poor people, and they will not be following a line of march benevolently set out for them and protected by a

---

31. On various occasions, King mentioned the nationalization of certain industries, a guaranteed annual wage, a comprehensive review of foreign investments, and attempts to inject new life into the decaying urban centers. David Halberstam, "When 'Civil Rights' and 'Peace' Join Forces," in C. Eric Lincoln (ed.), *Martin Luther King, Jr.: A Profile* (New York, 1970), 201–202. The core demand of the Washington campaign "was a twelve billion dollar 'economic bill of rights,' guaranteeing employment to all the able-bodied, viable incomes to those unable to work, an end to housing discrimination, and the vigorous enforcement of integrated education." The demands were deliberately left vague. Lewis, *King: A Biography*, 373. Although the evidence suggests that the news weeklies should have been aware of King's ideas, the case for this is weaker than is the case for the factors of disruption, coercive force, and class structure of the campaign. Some evidence of the recruitment of nonblacks was available in the New York *Times*, February 18, 1968, p. 61, March 5, 1968, p. 28, March 15, 1968, p. 36, and March 20, 1968, p. 4. *Time* and *Newsweek* customarily paid respectful attention to stories in the *Times*.

generally approving administration. . . . The tactics are nonviolent and the tone of the language, in SCLC literature, is moral, but the substance of the demands is revolutionary for America: class demands dramatically expressed through other than the orderly democratic process."[32]

Time and Newsweek responded to the dilemma with editorial silence. Their articles about Hispanic protest movements in which poverty was the central concern cited neither King nor the Poor People's Campaign, even though the linkages should have been easy enough to establish and despite the fact that the articles appeared incomplete symbolically because of the omissions. Newsweek's story, the better illustration, described César Chavez, then a relatively obscure Hispanic leader, leading a farm workers' strike and conducting a fast. King's absence from the article was conspicuous because of the references to Chavez, his philosophy of nonviolence, and his "Gandhiesque" qualities. Chavez could have been labeled the Hispanic Martin Luther King, the sort of device cherished by journalists, including those who labored for the news magazines, because it clarified a political position without the necessity of an involved explanation. That trick of the trade was used to identify Chavez's contraposed symbol, Reis Lopez Tijerina, as "the middle-aged equivalent of Stokely Carmichael." (Ironically, King was trying to persuade both Chavez and Tijerina to lead their followers into the Poor People's Campaign.)[33]

In short, Time and Newsweek spared their readers the spectacle of an American prophet preparing to assault, even if nonviolently, the society that honored him. Having a symbolic investment in King (as did, of course, the

32. Yglesias, "Dr. King's March on Washington, Part II." The article, originally published in the New York Times Magazine, March 31, 1968, was presumably researched in February or early March and demonstrates the ease with which reporters were able to secure information about the campaign. Yglesias undoubtedly was more sensitive to issues of class than most reporters; he researched a book in Cuba in 1967, In the Fist of the Revolution: Life in a Cuban Country Town (New York, 1968). It is doubtful, however, that he had any advantage over news magazine correspondents. Expecting queries from journalists about such matters as disruption, communism, and the like, the SCLC provided its staffers with suggested responses that were reasonably frank. See confidential memorandum to SCLC staff, in King Center Archives.

33. "Brown Power," Newsweek, March 25, 1968, p. 37. The same general point can be made, though not as strongly, for "César's War," Time, March 22, 1968, p. 23. Chavez was unable to attend the conference in Atlanta but sent a message of support and scheduled a meeting with King. SCLC press release, March 15, 1968, in King Center Archives. Tijerina later led the campaign's Southwest contingent. Judging from its press release, the SCLC publicized its dealings with Hispanic groups.

middle-class culture they served), the two magazines acted once more to preserve his value as a symbol by omitting some disquieting elements of his latest campaign.

Before that campaign could get under way, another engagement required King's attention and energies. As he said, no Memphis, no Washington. Thus, King returned to Tennessee, arriving in Memphis five days before he was scheduled to lead a second march. This demonstration had to be peaceful. The task would not be easy. Loeb's lawyers filed a lawsuit requesting the federal court to enjoin the demonstration, and the judge assigned to the case issued a temporary restraining order until the legal issues could be heard. There was a more vexing problem with the young militants. Members of his staff were already attempting to convince the suspicious, hard-to-handle youngsters that the way of nonviolence from which they had strayed on March 28 was just as militant and more effective than violence. But the staffers needed King—his enormous prestige, of course, but also his singular ability to get people of disputatious personalities to work on the same team. He had managed the feat before under circumstances equally as trying, and if anyone could do it in Memphis, that person would be King.

His skill as an orator was also needed to keep enthusiasm for the cause alive, and he provided it in full measure. On the night of April 3, King delivered one of his finest speeches. He seemed to foretell his own death, evoking the biblical image of a prophet ascending to the mountaintop: "And I've looked over and I've seen the Promised Land. I may not get there with you, but I want you to know tonight that we as a people will get to the Promised Land." And then the passage that brought the audience cheering and weeping to its feet: "So I'm happy tonight, I'm not worried about anything, I'm not fearing any man. Mine eyes have seen the glory of the coming of the Lord!"[34]

His prophecy, if such it was, was correct. He would not live to pass over into the Promised Land.

34. Frank, *An American Death*, 52–53.

X

THE RESURRECTION OF THE PROPHET

There was to the death of Martin Luther King a haunting sense of inevitability, almost as if King were a player in some Greek tragedy and the motel balcony onto which he strode to meet his fate a dimly lit theater. With one shattering stroke, his time on the public stage was ended. But more than the fact of his passing made his death high drama; there was a rightness to how and where he died, as if he of all men was fated to perish as he did on April 4, symbolically leading the ranks of faithful, anonymous black men, women, and children on yet another march toward justice and the realization of American ideals in that heart of darkness, that country-within-a-country, the American South.

The sense of drama, as that of inevitability, must be taken into account in any analysis of the news magazine stories. The journals could not have ignored the drama of King's last speech when he told the garbage collectors of Memphis that he had been to the mountaintop, that he had seen his own death—not even if he had foretold his death on other occasions. Simple and moving, this and other scenes lent themselves to the sketches that ordered the actors' movements so as to create a complete and fulfilling denouement. The craft of the writers and editors of the news magazines created anew the life of a prophet, the course of which could be summarized as (with intervening stops) Montgomery to Memphis. The prophet had arisen in the South, his death in Memphis confirmed his symbolic role in the larger culture, and to the

South, symbolically as well as actually, his body could now be returned. With the passing of the corporeal King, his spirit, like John Brown's, was free to march on, an affirmation of the best of America: its belief in equality and brotherhood.

Yet the truth of King was not self-evident. It demanded of the news magazines the ability and the willingness to smooth away an awkward connotation here, to silence an embarrassing outcry there. Such was required if the dream and the dreamer were to be reunited; in order that the radical could once more be the reformer; so that the man who had made common cause with radicals and militants could take on the mantle of moderation; and to make it possible that the man who had preached that his country's war was little removed from genocide could be resurrected as a symbol of faith in America.

Of necessity did the magazines preserve King as a pristine symbol. American symbols of all sorts were toppled or roughly handled in the 1960s. Students were running amok on campus, causing convulsions in the institution hitherto insulated from the pressures of American society; armed blacks were crying for revolution, and other ethnic groups were showing signs of becoming as militant. Middle-class values, of which the news weeklies were protective in degrees ranging from the vigorous to the fanatical, were being derided by a vocal segment of young Americans that included the sons and daughters of privilege. The year of King's death was especially unsettling, symbolically and otherwise. After the Tet offensive of late January and February, American military prowess seemed ineffectual against Vietnamese peasants. Black militants, such as H. Rap Brown of SNCC, were scorning Lincoln, the Great Emancipator, as just another honky. Lyndon Johnson, who as president embodied the virtues and the greatness of the Republic, had been emasculated politically by the conflict that had become LBJ's War. Other shocks followed: the assassinations, first of King, then of Senator Robert Kennedy, a political leader with a good chance of becoming the next president, and a national symbol since the assassination of his brother. Even *Time*, in which faith in America welled so readily, seemed bewildered by the events of the year. With 1968 three-quarters completed, *Time* paused to reflect upon what had transpired. History, it came close to conceding, "is one damned thing after another."[1]

As a year, 1968 indeed was one damned thing after another. The most

1. "What a Year!" *Time*, August 30, 1968, p. 21.

pressing domestic crisis early in the year was the rioting that began on the evening of King's death. The riots spread to more than 130 cities in 29 states, "a scale never before experienced in the United States." Casualties mounted rapidly, eventually numbering 46 deaths, more than 7,000 injuries, and more than 20,000 arrests. Property damages rose to an estimated $100 million. Ironically, Memphis escaped serious disorders, though 1 man was killed and a number of persons were injured.[2]

The crisis demanded action on the part of the federal government, aside from the use of troops to put down the disorders. A period of mourning was declared for King; the obsequies were a state funeral in all but name. A week after the assassination, Congress passed, and President Johnson later signed into law, a civil rights bill prohibiting discrimination in housing. One of the most intense manhunts in recent memory was conducted by the FBI. The search for the sniper who fired the fatal shot from a shabby rooming house across the street from the motel where King was staying would continue for more than two months before the arrest of James Earl Ray in London. It also became imperative to settle the garbage strike, and Johnson sent an assistant secretary of labor to Memphis as a mediator.

In the midst of this crisis posed by the disorders, the news magazines had another crisis on their hands. It was a crisis of symbols that was produced by the radicalization of King. They met the crisis by constructing three major themes. In the first theme, King appeared as a heroic moderate contraposed to extremists; in the second, King was limited essentially to his role as a prophet from the South, the leader who brought down Jim Crow; finally, the theme of national symbolism portrayed King at one with all Americans—other than segregationists and black radicals and extremists—and as a martyr-in-common with President Kennedy.

The theme of moderation required the magazines to dispose of several problems. Perhaps the most critical was bound up in King's genius as a speaker. Any summary of his public life would be unacceptably incomplete if it lacked excerpts from his most memorable speeches. Some addresses, especially the "I have a dream" speech from the March on Washington, represented no problem because they were resounding endorsements of America's good will and high ideals. Not so King's utterances against the war and his

2. Heaps, *Riots, USA*, 167–68. On Memphis casualties, see Memphis *Commercial Appeal*, April 7, 1968, p. 8.

speeches delivered while organizing the Poor People's Campaign. Editorial silence greeted the later speeches. Particularly striking was a *Newsweek* article that sought to convey King's "impassioned lyricism." From that account, it appeared King had been struck dumb between the Selma march of 1965 and March 31, 1968, the period during which King moved from reform to radicalism.[3] The gap of approximately three years and the absence of references by King to the war, class and class interests, and urban problems argue against the idea that *Newsweek* was merely hitting the oratorical high points.

Time arranged the "soul-stirring resonances" of King's addresses thematically, rather than chronologically, and published one excerpt from the period of King's radicalism. The gist of the statement was that the black man could not separate himself from American society, a sentiment with which *Time* heartily agreed. In fact, the magazine had once described the idea as "the most reasonable application" of Black Power. Other sentiments were not so acceptable. The Poor People's Campaign implicitly represented a class-structured movement—and had been presented fairly explicitly as such by the SCLC. However, *Time* chose to run an innocuous observation made by King in 1965 that it did little "'good to be able to sit at a lunch counter if you can't buy a hamburger.'" And King's indictment of the war—"We have supported the enemies of the peasants of Saigon. We have corrupted their women and children and killed their men. What liberators!"—yielded to a paean to peace with which few readers could quarrel: "'Sooner or later all the people of the world will have to discover a way to live together in peace, and thereby transform this pending cosmic elegy into a creative psalm of brotherhood.'"[4]

U.S. News incorporated a few excerpts into stories that transformed King astoundingly. No longer was he the familiar devil figure who consorted with Communists, the false prophet of civil disobedience, or the relentless black leader preparing to besiege Washington. Instead, King preached "not revolution but brotherhood," and it appeared he had never espoused any other gospel: "His dedication was to a struggle, which he preached . . . must be waged without violence. It was devotion to this idea which had won Dr. King, at 35, the Nobel Peace Prize. . . . His crusade in the South stressed 'passive disobedience' of segregation laws. . . . Dr. King led a series of 'marches' on which world attention was focused when police turned dogs on Negro

3. "'I've Been to the Mountaintop,'" *Newsweek*, April 15, 1968, p. 38.
4. "Visions of the Promised Land," *Time*, April 12, 1968, p. 20.

marchers. Dr. King, urging restraint, was credited with preventing a major battle between Negroes and police." *U.S. News* even cast new light on the March on Washington. In 1963, it had anointed A. Philip Randolph as the leader of the demonstration and, rebuking King for militancy that "momentarily stirred" the crowd, had not permitted the sacred phrases of the Declaration of Independence to pass his lips. After his death, King was transformed into the leader of the March and was allowed to mingle his phrases with Jefferson's in order to express faith in his country: "'I have a dream that one day this nation will rise up and live out the true meaning of its creed: "We hold these truths to be self-evident, that all men are created equal."'"[5]

Had there been nothing more, the silence of *Newsweek* and *Time* and the reinterpretation by *U.S. News* would have shown remarkable unanimity among the three news magazines about the meaning of King's life and his value as a symbol. But another awkward problem required smoothing over. *Time* and *U.S. News* had to dispose of their earlier implication that King scurried away like a coward from the march in Memphis after trouble started. The episode was ignored and King was praised for his courage. *Time*'s publisher, for example, recalled that previous cover stories warned of "the danger to Dr. King" and one "commented on how he 'unflinchingly faced the possibility of violent death.'" King's own words were used toward the same end. "'Maybe I've got the advantage over most people,' he mused. 'I've conquered the fear of death.'" Still, he was no fool; he was "well aware of his vulnerability." Similarly, *U.S. News* selected telling details that established that King lived with danger. "He had been struck, kicked, spat upon, and shot at. His home had been bombed, his life threatened repeatedly. Once he was stabbed, almost fatally, by a deranged Negro woman." Even *Newsweek*, which had not questioned King's courage in the first place, cleared away any doubts by publishing the passage foretelling his death.[6]

It bears repeating: King was no coward. As he said when refusing to join the Freedom Rides in 1961, a man had a right to pick his own Golgotha, King

5. See *U.S. News & World Report*, "'Even If I Die in the Struggle—,'" April 15, 1968, p. 33, and "As 200,000 Marched in Washington—," 40.

6. James R. Shepley, "A Letter From the Publisher," *Time*, April 12, 1968, p. 15; "The Assassination," *Time*, April 12, 1968, p. 18; "Dr. King's Prophetic Words—," *U.S. News & World Report*, April 15, 1968, p. 34. Slightly different versions of King's speech were published in "'I've Been to the Mountaintop,'" 38, and "Visions of the Promised Land," 20. Similar prophetic statements from 1962 were reported in the stories of *Newsweek* and *U.S. News* just cited.

arriving at his after spending more than a decade going in harm's way. Still, the issue is not King's bravery but the way the news weeklies emphasized it. In part, their motivation was the drama of his prophecy of his own death. There was more: He had been to the mountaintop, had seen the Promised Land, had feared he would be turned back before he could cross over into it, yet had remained strong in faith and courage. The stories fixed King more firmly as a symbol fit for the American pantheon; they accomplished this by removing any doubts—without referring to them—that lingered after his hasty departure from the march in Memphis. The stories also served another, similar purpose. Nonviolent courage fitted awkwardly with American images of heroism. Back in 1957, *Time* had anticipated just such raised eyebrows among readers; a decade later, a man who prophesied his own death and yet persisted in his hazardous cause clarified matters greatly.

King had demonstrated courage, less acceptably, as a prophet of peace. The news magazines had generally taken the line that he was ill-equipped to comment on the war and should remain silent. Now *Newsweek* and *Time* disposed of the awkwardness crisply. According to the former, King's "digression" into the anti-war movement "irritated the [black] movement's moderate elders." (*Newsweek* had been no less irked.) For its part, *Time* passed over the force of King's moral fervor with the statement that he opposed the war because "it hamstrung the civil rights drive and the war on poverty."[7] *U.S. News* ignored King's role in the peace movement altogether. While perpetuating his value as a symbol, those strategies required a sharp break with the journalistic standards that reckon news value in terms of the prominence of the subject and the timing of the event reported. King was one of the most well-known critics of the war. Because of the patently obvious association of time and theme (memories of the Tet offensive were still vivid), journalists normally would have developed fully his activities against the war. Silence from one magazine and a sentence in each of the two others fell short of that standard.

Why so little attention was paid to King's struggle against the war probably comes down to the matter of respectability. It was not particularly disreputable to call the war a blunder at this late date because Tet had legitimated the anti-war movement. Still, King's struggle against the war demanded careful

7. " 'King Is the Man, Oh Lord,' " *Newsweek*, April 15, 1968, p. 37; "Transcendent Symbol," *Time*, April 12, 1968, p. 21.

handling. For one thing, King had been most intemperate. Americans might be confused about their government and dubious about its promises; whether they were willing to accept King's comparison of America's soldiers and Hitler's *Schutzstaffel*—"we test out our latest weapons" on the Vietnamese, King had said, "just as the Germans tested out new medicine and new tortures in the concentration camps of Europe"—was something else entirely. The situation became more complicated. King had joined Carmichael of SNCC in counseling young Americans to defy the draft rather than serve in the military. Having King and Carmichael share a cause would be embarrassing when the news magazines were putting as much distance as possible between them. Off and on since 1966, the news weeklies had juxtaposed the two, generally with King symbolically contraposed to Carmichael. When King became a prophet of peace in 1967, they were joined (to use *Time*'s phrase, but the idea common to all three journals) in the radical firm of King, Carmichael & Co. Now with King dead, the news weeklies were striving for this exemplification: on one side, violence and radicalism—in a word, Carmichael; on the other, non-violence, moderation, and reform—King.

Oddly enough, the contraposing of King and Carmichael was strongest in *U.S. News*, which had previously exerted itself to make it known that they were radicals-in-arms. King's marches "sometimes ended in trouble," it reported, but he nevertheless "had exercised a restraining influence with his preaching of 'nonviolence.' Now, with Dr. King gone, the Negro masses are seen as open to incitement by more radical leaders." The leading radical was Carmichael, who "called on Negroes to 'get guns, and retaliate'" for the murder. The article concluded with a sociologist's dire analysis that Carmichael had become "'the man of the hour among Negroes, and I see no way for the country to avoid being plunged into racial war.'" The theme was subsequently extended. In late April, *U.S. News* reported that Carmichael had raised his fist in the Black Power salute at King's funeral and had declared on Radio Havana that "'the United States of America must fall in order for humanity to live.'" A week later, the magazine reiterated Carmichael's connections to the Communist bloc, including North Vietnam. By contrast, the same article contraposed King as a moderate not only to Carmichael but to "Negro extremists" who were "rabble-rousers."[8]

8. See *U.S. News & World Report*, "More Violence and Race War?" April 15, 1968, pp. 31, 34, and "Negro Leaders—More Militant Now?" 19, and "Washington Whispers," 22, both in the issue of April 22, 1968. "Insurrection: Outlook in U.S.," *U.S. News & World Report*, April 29,

To *Time* and *Newsweek*, it appeared that a fierce struggle was under way to seize control of King the symbol. The militants, they maintained, had scoffed at King, before his death, as worn-out and useless but now wished to exalt him for their own pernicious ends.[9] Determined to resurrect King as a symbol in their own image, the two magazines found "Black Power-monger" Carmichael almost as useful as King himself.

In *Newsweek*'s account, for example, Carmichael spouted incendiary rhetoric and dishonored the memory of the prophet of nonviolence by brandishing a gun during a memorial service. *Newsweek*'s King was sketched by the mayor of New York City, who urged "'the young men of this city to respect our laws and the teachings of the martyr.'" The message was reiterated the next week. The death of King, one of "the nationally known Negro moderates," left the field "more open than ever to the black militants." Chief among them was Carmichael, who "confidently proclaimed" that America "'must be burned down in order for us to survive.'" *Time* deployed its symbols similarly but, as had *U.S. News*, denounced Carmichael as a Communist lackey. After getting marching orders from the Communists, in this case "the Cuban press agency, Prensa Latina," Carmichael appeared on the streets of Washington "waving a pistol and urging blacks to arm. 'A lot of people who were afraid to pick up guns will now pick up guns,' he said later. 'They clearly made a mistake when they killed Dr. King. It would have been far better if they killed Rap Brown or myself. Then they could have said that "they lived by the sword and they died by the sword."'"[10]

The funeral provided other opportunities to contrast the two symbols. Carmichael was portrayed as a discordant and unwelcome interloper. On what *U.S. News* described as a "day of perfect order" in Atlanta, Carmichael not only made an inappropriate gesture—the clenched-fist Black Power salute—but arrived with a "personal bodyguard" in tow. *Newsweek* added the implication that Carmichael was an unwanted gate-crasher; he and his bodyguards, "a half-dozen SNCC janizaries, argued their way inside." Most compelling,

---

1968, pp. 38, 39; and David Lawrence, "What's Wrong with America?" *U.S. News & World Report*, April 22, 1968, p. 108, also vilify Carmichael as an insurrectionist. The former refers to King as a moderate, as does "Now a New Shift in '68 Politics," April 22, 1968, p. 58. For comparisons of King and Carmichael, see "Racial Problems Ahead," *U.S. News & World Report*, April 22, 1968, p. 45.

9. "'King Is the Man, Oh Lord,'" 34; "Transcendent Symbol," 19.

10. See *Newsweek*, "'Take Everything You Need, Baby,'" April 15, 1968, pp. 31, 34, and "'It May Be a Bell Tolling for Me,'" April 22, 1968, p. 24. See *Time*'s issue of April 19, 1968, for "Rampage and Restraint," 17, and "The Moderates' Predicament," 19.

however, were the details supplied by *Time*. Carmichael lacked the proper sense of decorum and occasion. At the funeral of a national symbol, he wore a "dark suit, dark blue Mao shirt, shades and zippered suede diddybop boots," then "darted down to Coretta King and began a whispered conversation. Mrs. King listened for several minutes, and, after sipping briefly from a Coca-Cola glass of iced water, dismissed him."[11] Conduct and dress demonstrated that Carmichael was an intruder; that was one point. He had been properly dismissed, with no untoward scene to mar the dignity of the day; that was another. Finally, if Carmichael had no rightful place at the funeral, he could not lay claim to King as either a symbol or a fellow radical. The facts were selected judiciously. However true that King was wedded to nonviolence and Carmichael to the opposite, the pragmatic King unblinkingly had made his peace with Carmichael when it suited King's purposes to do so.

The Poor People's Campaign represented another difficulty. The disruption would be so massive, King believed, that it would force the government to relieve the misery of the poor and would, eventually, lead to a radical transformation of society. Only the element of disruption was developed to any extent by the news magazines. *Time* outlined it most clearly: "He threatened national boycotts and spoke of disrupting entire cities by nonviolent but obstructive camp-ins. . . . Late last year he added: 'We have learned from bitter experience that our government does not move to correct a problem involving race until it is confronted directly and dramatically.'" Finally, *Time* noted that King was organizing a "massive march of the poor on Washington—and if Congress proved recalcitrant, he threatened to obstruct the national political conventions." Certainly the passage painted King as something of a radical, but it did not stand alone. Previously, he had been introduced as a leader "dangerously close to slipping from prophet to patsy" of the black militants. In effect, *Time* said, King had been manipulated by militants in the same way that extremists in Memphis had cozened him, laying their plans for violence and waiting for him to show up and turn out a crowd.[12]

The true King was, by contrast, the leader who did not threaten white America but pricked its conscience with the promise to "'wear you down by our capacity to suffer.'" Thus the radicalism of King was diluted in a message

11. "As 150,000 Said Farewell to Dr. King," *U.S. News & World Report*, April 22, 1968, pp. 38, 39; "King's Last March: 'We Lost Somebody,'" *Newsweek*, April 22, 1968, p. 26; "King's Last March," *Time*, April 19, 1968, p. 19.

12. "Transcendent Symbol," 19, 21.

that—couched as it was "in the language of the prophets and the revivalists—never directly threatened, probably never really disconcerted."[13]

The radicalism of his last campaign was thinned almost to the point of invisibility. Except for the most veiled references, there was no indication that it was class structured. Nor did *Time* refer to King's encounter with Marxist thought as a theology student. *Newsweek* did report that King had studied Marx. King remained untainted by the association, however, because he merely "dabbled in the literature of social conscience and social change: Thoreau, Gandhi, Marx, Hegel." And *Newsweek* made no connection between class and the campaign; it did note that blacks and whites would take part in a "squat-in." Essentially, the Washington campaign was presented as a legitimate exercise of King's "ministry to the poor" as a Baptist preacher.[14]

Newsweek obscured King's plans for the disruption of Washington. It evoked the tactics of the old southern campaigns in which the "guiding principle was nonviolence, a holy order for King," which some black militants misunderstood as submissiveness and some whites mistook as the promise of comfort. Instead, "King and his men were conscious provocateurs, stretching a community's racist nerves up to and sometimes past the breaking point. 'Nonviolent direct action,' King wrote in a celebrated letter from a Birmingham jail cell, 'seeks to create such a crisis and . . . tension that a community . . . is forced to confront the issue. It seeks so to dramatize the issue that it can no longer be ignored.' "[15] In fact, King planned to do this much and more in the nation's capital. He had expected to mount a nonviolent campaign, as *Newsweek* said; as it did not say, he also intended to raise hell nonviolently in Washington.

The point did not escape *U.S. News*, located in the target city. Even with its newfound appreciation of King's value as a symbol, Lawrence's journal regarded the Poor People's Campaign as a threat. If the protesters' demands were not met, the campaign would "escalate until 'hundreds of thousands' would be besieging the capital by mid-June." In the same issue was one of the last notes in the echo chamber, a shopworn denunciation of "clergymen, who, while preaching nonviolence, have closed their eyes to the incitement to violence which results from street 'demonstrations' and, in some cases, from

13. *Ibid.*, 21; Lewis, *King: A Biography*, 394.

14. "Transcendent Symbol," 19; " 'King Is the Man, Oh Lord,' " 34, 36, and "King's Last March: 'We Lost Somebody,' " 31. On King's study of Marx, see Lewis, *King: A Biography*, 36.

15. " 'King Is the Man, Oh Lord,' " 37.

defiance of the law itself." This was probably an accident rather than a last assault on King's reputation; indeed, *U.S. News* now feared that King would be replaced by "firebrands [who] will repudiate and destroy" his legacy of nonviolence.[16]

The process of resurrecting King as a safe and effective symbol required an accounting of his Chicago campaign. For purposes of limiting him symbolically to the role of a prophet from the South, his inadequacies as a leader outside the region had to be established. But some explanation of why he failed would be necessary, and the failure could not be so great as to overshadow the earlier triumphs. The problem was easily handled. References to the Chicago Freedom Movement were few and brief. The editorial discretion exercised by *U.S. News* was particularly striking. During the old civil rights struggle, *U.S. News* had grumbled repeatedly about northern hypocrisy in matters racial and warned that the North's time was coming. Nevertheless, the magazine accounted for the failure of "the northward surge of Dr. King's movement" with the explanation that, in these changing times, "militant Negroes challenged Dr. King and extremists ridiculed Dr. King's nonviolence."[17]

Time and *Newsweek* agreed. King had failed outside the South because he had been bypassed by the very forces he had helped set in motion. *Time*'s didactic point was embedded in an incident from the Watts riot; "a young looter, asked if he thought Dr. King would approve, retorted: 'Martin Luther Who?'" The theme was extended the following week: "His real influence was largely limited to the South, where the Negro pastor had traditionally had a strong hold on his flock . . . and where King could point to concrete victories as legal segregation was abolished. In the North, where racial attitudes are subtler and the Negroes' plight is largely one of economic deprivation, he never achieved comparable success." Indeed, the magazine noted that King was sometimes ignored in the ghetto; even worse, "militants in Harlem showered him with rotten eggs in 1965."[18]

Newsweek offered the most complete account. By any measure of pragmatic gains, King lost more often than he won. Even in *Newsweek*, however,

16. "More Violence and Race War?" 32–33. For the last note in the echo chamber, see David Lawrence, "The Power of Reason," *U.S. News & World Report*, April 15, 1968, p. 108, which was first published in 1965.

17. "'Even If I Die in the Struggle—,'" 33. See also "Negro Leaders—More Militant Now?" 20.

18. "Transcendent Symbol," 20–21; "The Moderates' Predicament," 19.

his major disasters seemed to come when he ventured out of the South of Bull Connor, Jim Clark, and Jim Crow:

> But events tumbled past King; he seemed somehow to lose the pulse of history. The locus of the movement shifted from the South to the North, and King's style did not travel well. The focus changed, too, from issues of dignity to subtler questions of poverty and caste—the sort that cannot be dealt with by protest alone. King's Southern victories, moreover, quickened expectations in the Northern slums—and fed the fires of discontent that were to flare in Harlem, in Watts, in Detroit. . . . The young radicals of SNCC—King's spiritual godchildren only a few years before—stole the 1966 Meredith March from him and made it a showcase for the heresy called "Black Power." King for a time seemed adrift. His first Northern venture in Chicago fizzled.[19]

The assertions that King had lost the pulse of history or was frustrated by militants glossed over much else. The burden of failure in Chicago properly rests upon King's shoulders. Yet the story ignored the cause of King's failure. King and the Chicago establishment had signed the Summit Agreement, which covered open housing and other issues, but the politicians and businessmen had broken the pact with alacrity. An agreement cynically made and as cynically abandoned was no shining example of America in the process of perfecting itself. By omitting the fate of the agreement (so obvious as to require an effort to ignore it), the sense was preserved that reformism was the most productive way to achieve social change.

Nor did *Time* or *Newsweek* acknowledge that King had learned from his mistakes in Chicago. As both pointed out, King absorbed the lessons of Albany and went on to triumph in Birmingham in 1963. King had intended to apply what he had learned at equal cost in Chicago; one lesson from that defeat was, apparently, that a coalition of the poor was necessary. The failure contributed to King's plans in 1968 in another way. King came to realize that he had been taken by Chicago's powers-that-be and could expect little better elsewhere. The grimness of his thinking stands out in bold relief in a lecture delivered in 1967. "We must formulate a program and we must fashion the new tactics which do not count on government good will, but instead serve to compel unwilling authorities to yield to the mandates of justice," King said. "We in SCLC must work out programs to bring the social change movements through from their early and now inadequate protest phase to the stage of

19. "'King Is the Man, Oh Lord,'" 37.

massive, active, nonviolent resistance to the evils of the modern corporate society."[20] Clearly, King had traveled far, ideologically, from the struggle with Jim Crow.

The southern theme dominated *Time*'s and *Newsweek*'s reports of the death and the funeral of King. Considered as journalism, much of the coverage was neither contrived nor unexpected. King was murdered in a southern city while leading, albeit reluctantly, a strike by a predominantly black union local, his funeral was that of a black, southern Baptist, and his campaigns before 1966 had been confined to the South. Even those factors (which contributed, of course, to the symbolism attached to him) do not altogether account, however, for the theme's persistence and power. It was developed through emphasis, omission, and direct statements. An example of the last was *Newsweek*'s delimiting analysis: "King was first a Southerner and a preacher, and his great contributions were uniquely Southern and Christian." From the pulpits of "black churches named Shiloh and Siloam and Mt. Zion . . . his rolling baritones called up courage and hope and dignity out of the shame of blackness in the Jim Crow South." *Newsweek* consigned him to "the 'dignity period' of the movement—the days when the bull's-eye issue was Southern Jim Crow and the civil rights leadership was knitted in ecumenical unity." Similar was *Time*'s examination of King as black southern preacher and activist: The southern movement "has been led in great measure by men with 'the Rev.' before their names. . . . By comparison with King and other outspoken Southern pastors, the majority of Northern clergy have been much more passive in the struggle for equality—and have allowed the movement to fall into militant secular hands."[21]

As part of the southern theme, *Time* and *Newsweek* contraposed King to other symbols standing for the brutality of segregation. *Time* recalled, for example, when King traveled to Birmingham and "flayed that citadel of Dixie bigotry on national television." No story would have been complete without a reference to Bull Connor, "the white villain" waiting to attack "King's black heroes as they marched—clad in their Sunday clothes—to meet his trun-

---

20. The Albany and Birmingham campaigns are cited by *Time* ("Transcendent Symbol," 19–20) and are implicitly developed in *Newsweek*'s statement ("'King is the Man, Oh Lord,'" 37) that in Birmingham and Selma, King learned to pick his spots and his antagonists. For the impact of the Chicago disaster upon King, see Lomax, "When 'Nonviolence' Meets 'Black Power,'" 171. For King's lecture, see "A New Sense of Direction," *Drum Major*, I (August, 1971), 5, 8–9.

21. "'King Is the Man, Oh Lord,'" 37; "The Faith of Soul and Slavery," *Time*, April 19, 1968, p. 70.

cheons, hoses, and dogs." *Newsweek* invoked, as well, Jim Clark of Selma and his "billy-swinging posses."[22] Such statements (not reproduced in *U.S. News*) fixed King as a symbol of reform.

Superimposed on images of King during the March on Washington in 1963 were other images presented with something akin to nostalgia. The crusade had been pristine then—or so it seemed a half decade later. King had been the instrument of reconciliation of black and white; his clarion call for simple justice had awakened the conscience of the nation, and the nation had responded. Birmingham and the 1963 March on Washington now seemed inseparable, drawing strength each from the other as symbols contrasted. The dogs, the fire hoses, the flailing clubs in Birmingham had brought "whites flocking to the civil rights movement," bearing collective testimony to the vitality of their country's ideals. The huge crowd that had gathered before the Lincoln Memorial had done likewise, showing, even before King had uttered his words, that the dream was possible. Small wonder, then, *Time*'s half-wistful tone or *Newsweek*'s recollection, almost a keening, not for King alone but for a time, those "romantic days," when much seemed possible, even that the "dream of a beloved society might one day come true."[23]

The images from the struggle in the South were reduced to the simplest level. Before Birmingham, for example, it had been possible to believe that the black movement would remain confined to the South. But Birmingham produced a wave of demonstrations, as well as considerable white backlash, across the nation, showing conclusively that the black revolt had burst its bounds, showing also that Birmingham was the pivotal event of the black movement. (In 1968, *Time* and *Newsweek* passed over what they had recognized five years earlier—that Birmingham signaled a new phase of the black struggle—because of the demands of symbolism.) Such was the paucity, in 1968, of useful symbols that *Newsweek* and *Time* scrutinized the rioting touched off by the assassination for any sign that the breach between black and white would be healed, that, as the former put it, Americans would realize King's life and death "argued that it was time at long last to come home."[24] Thus were preserved King and Birmingham and the March—symbols ex-

---

22. "Transcendent Symbol," 20; "'King Is the Man, Oh Lord,'" 37. See also "The Bull and the Dogs," *Newsweek*, May 6, 1968, p. 20.

23. "Transcendent Symbol," 19; "'King Is the Man, Oh Lord,'" 37.

24. "'King Is the Man, Oh Lord,'" 38. See also "Rampage and Restraint," 17; and "Hot and Cool," *Newsweek*, April 22, 1968, p. 26.

tracted from an age when national unity seemed in retrospect a given, when the moral greatness of America was reaffirmed in the process of bringing justice to the black southerner. In such a year as 1968, symbols of such magnitude were not to be discarded by magazines that had to make sense of a world regarded, no doubt, as mad by many of their readers.

Another strain of the southern theme was provided by Memphis, which, along with its mayor and the garbage strike, was symbolically recreated in *Time*'s and *Newsweek*'s reports as a contemporary parallel to the old movement. The process was begun immediately by *Time*, which mingled Faulknerian images of "a Southern backwater" and the strike. The plight of the sanitation workers "first attracted and finally eradicated Dr. King, the conqueror of Montgomery, Birmingham, and Selma." Nor was there merely irony: King's death was a "tragic finale to an American drama fraught with classic hints of inevitability," and it was in a long line of such tragedies in the South—the twelfth major assassination since 1963. Not so deft in its manipulation of symbols, *Newsweek* simply set Memphis apart from almost any other American city: "It would have been hard to imagine a similar labor dispute—a major municipality taking a stand against recognizing an established municipal union. But it was precisely this issue that locked the city of Memphis in conflict with its sanitation workers—a dispute that first led to a bloody riot and ultimately set the stage" for the assassination. Memphis was set apart in another way. Throughout the nation, the "common reaction was shock and grief" when the assassination was reported. Not, however, where King was struck down: "A grocery store in a well-off white Memphis suburb hung out a sign that said, 'Martin Luther Coon is dead.' "[25]

No matter how compelling, such stories required a personification of the evil against which King had struggled. Mayor Henry Loeb served that purpose. *Time* limited itself initially to the accurate observation that Loeb's refusal to meet the demands of the strikers produced the crisis. Later, however, Loeb was transformed into a "wealthy Southern patrician-turned-politician," a phrase that evoked the southern planter aristocracy and that fixed Loeb as a symbol against the black Everyman of Memphis, represented collectively by the black strikers. The symbolism attached to Loeb by *Newsweek* was similar. He was depicted as a hypocrite, if not a coward, who

25. "The Assassination," 18. See also "Transcendent Symbol," 19. "The Mess in Memphis," *Newsweek*, April 22, 1968, p. 33. A similar statement appears in "'You're Such a Brave Lady . . . !'" *Newsweek*, April 22, 1968, p. 32. See also "'King Is the Man, Oh Lord,'" 38.

"called on all his seven hundred thousand townspeople to be without fear" while hiding "a sawed-off shotgun under his desk." Even more than *Time*, *Newsweek* laid the responsibility for the "Mess in Memphis" at Loeb's door, ascribing his actions to "his segregationist politics [derived] from the traditional white paternalism that still permeates Memphis at every level." After the settlement of the labor dispute, *Newsweek* became less acerbic about Loeb, but the strike remained the cause of King's death. "The price of victory," *Newsweek* mourned, would "not easily be forgotten. 'We won,' said one old garbage man, 'but we lost a good man along the way.'"[26]

Some discordant elements were omitted. An example was the Jim Crow label affixed to Memphis. Memphis had its share of racism, but there were other complex and contradictory factors that *Time*, to take the more noticeable illustration, stripped from its post-assassination articles because those elements would not fit so readily into the southern theme. Whatever its failure to deal justly with the black man, the Memphis of 1968 bore more resemblance to other American cities than to the Birmingham of 1963 or the Selma of 1965. (As Pat Watters argued after the assassination, Memphis' "racial crisis of 1968, and its murderous failure were those of all America.")[27] Loeb was another case in point. Neither *Time* nor *Newsweek* overstated his responsibility for the evolution of a minor strike into a racial crisis. Nevertheless, the two magazines' creation of a "Southern patrician-turned-politician" who took "his segregationist politics from the traditional white paternalism [of] Memphis" was as much symbolic as actual. Paternalistic, stubborn, sensitive to white public opinion and to the possibility of losing face—all of this was Loeb. Still, Loeb was hardly a southern aristocrat; his family's money was made in the laundry business. And practicing segregationist politics in a city with an old and dynamic tradition of black political power was not something Loeb could expect to bring off—as he tacitly acknowledged by appointing a black man to his cabinet. That sort of public act would be unimaginable for a Bull Connor, but Loeb was the only forceful symbol of racism at hand, and *Time* and *Newsweek* made do with what they had.

26. "The Assassination," 18; "Posthumous Victory," *Time*, April 26, 1968, p. 19; "'King Is the Man, Oh Lord,'" 36; "The Mess in Memphis," 33; "Price of Victory," *Newsweek*, April 29, 1968, p. 22. Loeb did keep a weapon beneath his desk, possibly at the insistence of his police bodyguards.

27. For *Time*'s restatement of its earlier interpretation of Memphis, see "Hurt Pride in Memphis," April 26, 1968, p. 44. Watters, "Beale Street," 529.

Equally compelling was the presentation of the strike as a revolt by oppressed blacks against oppressive whites. That sketch was accurate but incomplete. The journals ignored the parent union's role in the strike. When reporting the settlement, for example, *Time* anointed as the strike leader T. O. Jones, the black president of Local 1733. Jones did lead the local into the strike, but within a day or two the American Federation of State, County, and Municipal Employees sent its staffers to Memphis and they took control of the strike from Jones. If Jones was a symbol, he also was a cipher.[28] After the strike became a racial issue, effective control was assumed by black clergymen of the Community on the Move to Equality. The working coalition of the ministers and the national union went unrecorded by *Newsweek*—an odd omission, given its propensity for seizing upon every sign that the old civil rights coalition might be revitalized. In Memphis, where such an alliance was so visible it could hardly escape notice, *Newsweek* did not record its existence. By designating Jones as the strike leader and passing over the important part played by the AFSCME, *Time* and *Newsweek* enhanced the symbolism. The presence of the national union would have detracted from an essential part of the southern theme, oppressed blacks rising up against white oppressors, and lessened the symbolism attached to King. While leading downtrodden sanitation workers, King also would have had to be portrayed as an ally of a large, powerful, and aggressive national union.

By contrast, *U.S. News* attached little significance to the strike or to the city in which King was murdered. It reported only that "Dr. King had returned to Memphis to prepare for another march in support of a strike by city garbage collectors, most of whom are Negroes." Nor did it regard the strike as the proximate cause of his death.[29] Naturally, the conservative *U.S. News* would find no significance in King's death in a southern city. There was another

28. On the beginning of the strike, see interview with T. O. Jones, by Joan Beifuss and David Yellin, January 30, 1968 (Transcript of tape 228), 30, 39. The national union regarded the strike as ill-timed. Interview with David Caywood, by Anne Trotter and David Yellin, May 20, 1968 (Transcript of tape 141), 25. Jerry Wurf, AFSCME president, described his role in the strike in an interview conducted by Carol Yellin and David Yellin, February 3, 1972 (Transcript of tape 305), 28. These interviews are in the Mississippi Valley Collection, Memphis State University. The two Memphis newspapers fed the cultural paranoia and siege mentality of Memphis by emphasizing the role of the national union. Lentz, *Sixty-Five Days in Memphis*.

29. "More Violence and Race War?" 34; "What Union Won in Garbage Strike," *U.S. News & World Report*, April 29, 1968, p. 82. *U.S. News* was the only news weekly to identify the parent union.

reason not to emphasize where King perished. It would have undercut the theory, offered by David Lawrence in late April, that a Communist conspiracy was afoot. Was the assassin "hired and directed by some organization? We know that a few Communists have been covertly involving themselves in the civil rights movement. Their purpose, of course, is to hurt the image of America before the world and turn our attention away from the Vietnam war to a domestic crisis." Naturally, Lawrence did have someone in mind: Stokely Carmichael, not named but identified contextually as one of the "militant" travelers to Communist countries who, upon return to America, urged the populace "to rise, to burn property, to obtain guns, to defy the agencies of government." Lawrence added, "This isn't an American concept" (as King's version of Gandhian nonviolence once was un-American). "It is a Communist tactic aimed at undermining government" (as civil disobedience once threatened to undermine the rule of law).[30] A month or so earlier, *U.S. News* had used phrases with similar venom to attack King. Now, the magazine was doing its part to resurrect him as the martyr.

The theory of a Communist conspiracy held no appeal for *Time* and *Newsweek*. Racism, their motive of choice, meshed smoothly with the southern theme. *Time* reported, for example, that "amateur assassinologists" believed that "King's death had been engineered by a group of white Southern racists." Further strengthening the implication was its description of the fugitive assassin James Earl Ray as a follower of George Wallace and as one who "loved hillbilly music and spoke in Southern-accented ungrammatical speech."[31] (While reporting similar elements, *Newsweek* brushed aside the notion that a cabal of white supremacists plotted the assassination.) It was logical to throw a net in the midst of the segregationists. Many were violent men, some no doubt were capable of murder, and the threats against King's life during the old movement made that a possibility worth pursuing. But the net was too small. As King became more radical, the list of his enemies encompassed more than cross-burners (J. Edgar Hoover, for example). And there was another matter, suggested by *Newsweek*'s handling of a theory then "under investigation by G-men in California"; method and motive were described as a "hired-gun killing arranged by a Negro with a personal animus against King." In fact, FBI agents were investigating the possibility that King was

30. Lawrence, "What's Wrong with America?" 108. See also "Were Riots Organized?" *U.S. News & World Report*, April 22, 1968, p. 12; and "Insurrection: Outlook in U.S.," 38–41.
31. "Who Killed King?" *Time*, April 26, 1968, p. 20.

slain at the instigation of a cuckold. Whether aware or not of the reason for the personal animus, *Newsweek* cast doubt on the theory as "farther-out."[32]

The southern theme was most intense in reports of the funeral. The strength of the theme can be explained partially by the circumstances, including the intense media coverage, and by the necessity of explaining the rituals and passions of black Christianity to white readers. Nevertheless, the news magazines also manipulated powerful symbols to limit King to the status of a prophet from the South. Predictably, the theme was weakest in *U.S. News*, though traces of it emerged even in the magazine hostile to King's war against Jim Crow. Perhaps most striking was the closing of the story that used (as did *Time* and *Newsweek*) the conclusion of King's speech during the 1963 March on Washington: "Dr. King's . . . marble crypt bore the words of an old slave song: 'Free at last, free at last, thank God Almighty, I'm free at last.'"[33]

In *Time*, the southern theme was stronger, in part because of its detailed explanation of black religious rites. The black church, King, and the civil rights movement were associated through small but significant details. His activism was demonstrated even in the description of the garb of Ralph David Abernathy, the new president of the SCLC, who wore beneath his minister's robes "scuffed, thong-laced 'marching boots,'" and the point was buttressed by the label attached to the trip from church to cemetery: "King's Last March."[34]

The theme was strongest by far in *Newsweek*. One article offered King's widow, Coretta Scott King, as an exemplar of a black wife and mother whose serenity was honed by adversity and by the insults and the injuries visited upon her race in the South. "In a hundred painful explanations to her four children over the years—why whites called them 'nigger,' why they couldn't go to a segregated amusement park called 'Fun Town,' why God made some people colored—she had renewed her faith in her husband's gospel of tolerance." She continued to share her husband's burden; a day before he was buried, "she kept one more engagement he couldn't fill," leading a demon-

---

32. "Where is James Earl Ray?" *Newsweek*, April 29, 1968, p. 22. The evidence suggests, though not conclusively, that *Newsweek* decided to omit the specific nature of the animus. There is little reason to believe that the FBI would have hesitated to leak the information; it had actively attempted, with little success, to leak to reporters derogatory material about King before his death. Garrow, *The FBI and King*, 123–28. On the FBI theory, see Bishop, *The Days of Martin Luther King*, 83.

33. "As 150,000 Said Farewell to Dr. King," 38.

34. "The Faith of Soul and Slavery," 70; "King's Last March," 18, 19.

stration for the strikers whose cause "had brought King to his fateful rendezvous in Memphis."[35]

Not acknowledged were other burdens Mrs. King had shared. Perhaps the most telling service in her husband's cause occurred when she and their children lived with King for a time in a slum apartment in Chicago. That episode was well publicized in 1966, but two years later, *Newsweek* rushed past this phase of King's career. Nor was Mrs. King permitted to hoist another banner fallen with her husband, his opposition to the war. *Newsweek* managed to find a smidgen of space, however, to record the fact that she substituted for her late husband as the commencement speaker at Harvard.[36]

First to last, *Newsweek* suffered by comparison with the more polished *Time*. On this one occasion, however, *Newsweek*'s writers and editors rose to the challenge and outdid Luce's magazine in sheer power of prose. From the rituals of the day, *Newsweek* extracted images that re-created the religiosity of the old movement: elderly people filing "past the casket in the dim light of an electric cross," and the crowd appearing on streets and porches and rooftops "when a sultry morning broke through the freshly blossoming dogwoods. These were the ordinary people, men in floppy, double-breasted Sunday suits, women in weeds impossibly heavy for the heat of the day," and among them an old lady who grieved: "'We lost somebody, didn't we? I'm hoping Easter Sunday he'll rise again!'"[37] Services complete, the crowds outside the church parted to make way for King one final time. The casket was placed in a wagon drawn by two mules for "King's last parade":

> And then the marchers. They were funereally silent at first, and so, as they passed the rows of spectators lining the sidewalk, there was only the low rumble of footsteps, the slow clip-clop and an occasional outcry: "Oh Lord . . . Oh King Jesus, King Jesus." But then, as they flowed into the shuttered streets of downtown Atlanta, the old songs welled up—and mostly, in measured cadence, "We Shall Overcome."
>
> All that was left was the ride to the slope in South View Cemetery, founded a century ago by black men grown tired of burying their dead through the back gate at the municipal graveyard.[38]

35. "'You're Such a Brave Lady . . . !'" 32. The examples appear to be taken from King's Letter from the Birmingham Jail but were not so credited, possibly because they would clash with readers' expectations of a loftier tone.

36. On the King family in Chicago, see Lewis, *King: A Biography*, 317. On Mrs. King's speech at Harvard, see "Newsmakers," *Newsweek*, June 24, 1968, p. 59.

37. "King's Last March: 'We Lost Somebody,'" 26.

38. *Ibid.*, 31.

With such scenes were mingled—in *Time* as well—images of Jim Crow, represented this day in Atlanta by Georgia's Governor Lester Maddox, he of the ax handles and the racist mutterings. Past the gold-domed Georgia capitol marched the mourners, past Maddox who "cowered under heavy state police guard. . . . 'If they start coming in here,' Maddox solemnly told his troopers, 'we're gonna stack them up.' They didn't; they marched past singing 'The Battle Hymn of the Republic'"—America's anthem, not Dixie's—"while the cordon of hardhatted troopers stared balefully out at them."[39]

Such scenes evoked both the recent past and the glory days of the old movement. As George Wallace had peeked furtively and fearfully through the blinds of his office at the swelling tide of marchers arriving from Selma in 1965, as Henry Loeb had told whites in Memphis not to give way to fear after the death of King, then hid a shotgun under his desk, so also did Lester Maddox cower behind the ranks of police guards. As the sign with the racist epitaph went up in a Memphis store, so also did some of Maddox's underlings, peering down through the blinds at the procession, cheer one another with gibes: "'Hey, y'hear they caught the fella that killed King. Yeah, fined him $15 for killin' coons out of season.'"[40]

King had come almost full circle as a symbol. He was born in the South, had risen to greatness there when good and evil had seemed so clear—indeed, were clear in most respects—and, in any event, could be packaged as such by journalists. Clarity having become considerably muddied of late, more and more packaging was required, not excepting the packaging of the prophet King. Returning King symbolically to his native soil diminished the later, radical King by obscuring his move North, by silencing his bitter outcries against the war. And his preparations to lead America's poor into a siege of Washington were lost in the symbolic brilliance, the sheer *rightness*, of King's death while he led black southerners in yet another struggle against an intransigent white oppressor. The crude jeering of bigots as his body was borne past was no indignity but testimony to his place in history as the conqueror of Jim Crow. His epitaph, fittingly, was the exuberant shout of faith—"Free at last, free at last, thank God Almighty, I'm free at last"—not only in God but in America, and its great principles, and its people.

Completing the circle was the theme of national symbolism. It included a number of interrelated elements, not all of which were present in equal mea-

39. *Ibid.* See *Time*, "King's Last March," 19, for a similar message.
40. "King's Last March: 'We Lost Somebody,'" 31.

sure or appeared with equal intensity in each of the news magazines; indeed, the theme was muted in *U.S. News*. Although some of their reports were reasonably straightforward news magazine journalism, they nevertheless emphasized some matters and maintained a studied silence about others.

The theme was reproduced most tellingly in the reports of the funeral. For example, *Newsweek*'s account of marchers, black and white together, striding past the cowering governor of Georgia served a powerful symbolic purpose as a reminder that the nation had revitalized its ideals in the South.

The funeral had most of the trappings of an affair of state. Flags flew at half-staff, messages of sympathy were dispatched, and national and international dignitaries traveled to Atlanta to take part in the ceremony. The nation was represented symbolically by President Johnson, calling for peace in the streets as a memorial to King, seeking a "nation united, a nation caring, a nation concerned." He also offered condolences by telephone to the widow on behalf of the nation. *Newsweek* reported the call and Mrs. King's response: "'I'm glad I live in a country where the president takes time to make a call like this. Thank you, Mr. President.'" Similar in tone was the succinct observation by *U.S. News*: "The nation staged a funeral such as no American private citizen had ever received."[41]

As managers of the symbolic stage, the news magazines maintained a discreet silence about something of more than passing moment: Where was the chief symbol of the Republic? Johnson had ordered the flags flown at half-staff and had proclaimed a day of national mourning, but he could not quite bring himself to attend the funeral of the man "who had done so much to turn opinion against the war in Vietnam and thus bring down his presidency."[42] *Time* and *U.S. News* merely noted that Vice-President Humphrey was sent as the president's special representative; *Newsweek* did no more than record Humphrey's attendance. Passing over the absence of the president, the magazines were free to pass over as well the enmity aroused at the White House by King's resumption of the campaign against the war in 1967. Harmony was thus preserved, as was the symbolism of King.

Contributing to the theme was the notion of a nation at one in its grief. Television was the instrument whereby Americans were brought together. The magazines referred to the millions of viewers who watched the services,

41. "'King is the Man, Oh Lord,'" 36; "The Periscope," *Newsweek*, April 22, 1968, p. 19; "As 150,000 Said Farewell to Dr. King," 38.

42. Wofford, *Of Kennedys and Kings*, 203.

but the numbers were less important than was the sense of vicarious community. *Time* found usually busy streets "echoed eerily and emptily under sunny
skies; banks and department stores, their windows unlit, were closed all or
most of the day; schools in many cities were shuttered in tribute." *Newsweek*
listed similar details about the postponements of various rituals, such as the
annual motion picture awards and the opening of the baseball season, explaining that "in the shock of the assassination and its aftermath, there seemed little
doubt that Americans wanted to do something."[43]

If there was a community of shared grief, there had to be a leveling of the
barriers of race and class. Each journal observed that the funeral occasioned
grief among blacks and whites. The obsequies were described as democratic.
Time recounted the "humbling experience for some of the sixty U.S. Congressmen who attended the funeral and found themselves forced to wait
outside," while *U.S. News* reported that "mourners [were] of every degree
and station, laborers mingling with governors, and welfare mothers with
millionaires." *Newsweek* combined both points, writing of "the stunning
impact, for plain Negroes, of seeing whites of power mourn a protestant
black."[44]

Not all Americans mourned King. To maintain otherwise would have been
nonsensical—and not as useful to make manifest King's status as a symbol.
Among the deviants were the southerners who had fought King so long and so
violently to prop up segregation. *Newsweek* reported, for example, that
"George Wallace managed the word 'regrettable' when informed of the death
of King." By contrast, Chicago's Mayor Richard Daley, who had fought King
as vigorously and with far more cunning and success than had Wallace,
"pleaded for peace on TV after King's murder," even though his words "fell
on deaf ears."[45]

Black radicals served much the same purpose as white segregationists. The
news magazines erected King as a symbol in opposition to the rioting and the
looting touched off across the nation by his death. *Newsweek* put it most
directly: Even as King "made his last journey, the black pall of arson and the

---

43. "King's Last March," 18; " 'It May Be a Bell Tolling for Me,' " 23.
44. "King's Last March," 18; "As 150,000 Said Farewell to Dr. King," 38; "King's Last
March: 'We Lost Somebody,' " 26.
45. " 'Take Everything You Need, Baby,' " 33. *Newsweek* did report that some white southerners joined blacks in honoring King. Daley was also omitted as an adversary of King's by
Newsweek in "Reading the Riot Act," April 29, 1968, p. 22, and by *Time* in "Should Looters Be
Shot?" April 26, 1968, p. 18.

crack of snipers' rifles dishonored his memory in cities across America."
Similarly, *Time* and *U.S. News* excoriated those engaged in the violence and
the looting as exploiters of the prophet's memory. *Time* summed it up in a
headline, "Avenging What's-His-Name," and a lead paragraph that proclaimed that if the rioters "demeaned the cause of nonviolence, that was not in
most cases their intent. The majority of plunderers and burners in American
cities last week was about as ideologically motivated as soldier ants." Sputter-
ing with rage, *U.S. News* denounced "Negro mobs [that] terrorized the nation's capital, burning, looting, beating whites, attacking police and firemen,
and threatening wholesale slaughter."[46] And this, of course, was almost
precisely the outcome *U.S. News* had predicted because of the appeasement of
the insatiable demands of blacks—except, of course, the warnings had often
cited King's pernicious doctrine of civil disobedience as the cause that would
produce bloody anarchy. Now, however, King was a moderate, useful as a
symbol to be contrasted to all manner of radicals, thugs, and looters.

Strategically positioned with the scenes played out by black rioters and
white bigots were other scenes that had the effect of making King at one with
the nation. His death had stirred well-to-do Americans. *Time*, naturally,
compiled another of its lists, this one of gestures that exemplified the "pro-
found effect" on the white conscience: "Some girls from . . . a private college outside riot-torn Baltimore, loaded cars . . . with cartons of food and
relayed them to the city's burned-out core, racing against a four p.m. curfew";
women in the Washington area contributed food, clothing, and shelter to
victims of the rioting; and suburbanites in New York "signed up for a massive
'clean-in' this week in the city's slums. Indeed, most white Americans were
moved by conscience and events to seek means of cementing racial amity
rather than further polarizing black and white animosities." Some San Fran-
ciscans even "moved to rename the Bay Bridge for King, reasoning that 'he
himself spanned the gap between black and white.'"[47]

The point is not the accuracy of the reports—other contemporary sources
document a number of similar actions—but the *uniformity* of the responses
cited by *Time* (and *Newsweek*). Not for the first time had they found unanimity

46. "'It May Be a Bell Tolling for Me,'" 23; "Avenging What's-His-Name," *Time*, April 19,
1968, p. 16; "Mobs Run Wild in the Nation's Capital," *U.S. News & World Report*, April 15,
1968, pp. 8, 10. See also "The Looted Merchants Tell Their Story," *U.S. News & World Report*,
April 29, 1968, p. 42.

47. "Rampage and Restraint," 17. It should be noted, however, that *Time* and *Newsweek*
praised some black militants for helping keep the peace in some cities.

of opinion about King. Reporting King's activities against the war, for example, neither magazine managed to locate one black American (other than clearly identified radicals) who did not consider it odd that a winner of the Nobel Peace Prize should oppose the war.[48]

Another strain of the theme of national symbolism was the association of King and John Kennedy as American martyrs. *Newsweek*, already busily creating the myth of a latter-day Camelot as its dissatisfaction with Lyndon Johnson grew, found in the murder of King an analogy to the assassination of Kennedy that "was hard to escape. 'I weep for Mrs. King and for her children for this senseless, senseless act of hate which took away a man who preached love and hope,' Jacqueline Kennedy wrote," and the late president's brother, Robert Kennedy, standing hunched and wan on an Indianapolis ghetto street corner, told his listeners: " 'For those of you who are black and are tempted to be filled with hatred . . . I can only say that I feel in my heart the same kind of feeling. I had a member of my family killed.' " The association was weakly drawn in *Time*'s initial report, which noted only that King's "death demands expiation, as did that of John F. Kennedy."[49]

The strain was developed most intensely when the news magazines covered King's funeral, which was attended by various members of the Kennedy family. *Newsweek* associated the two men most strongly through depictions of their widows and through the evoking of "an old and remembered anguish." As had been the case during another tragedy, the nation "found itself drawing strength from the calm grandeur of the victim's widow." On the day of the funeral, Jacqueline Kennedy and Coretta Scott King met and spoke, "leaning toward each other like parentheses around the tragic half-decade of national turbulence."[50]

Time implicitly united the two widows in grief. In a caption, it observed that Mrs. Kennedy "brought with her memories of another assassination, paid a sympathy call on Mrs. King before the funeral, [and] braved jostling crowds to attend the services." King and Kennedy also were symbolically conjoined through *Time*'s comparison of the rituals of mourning, the difference being essentially that "between black and white, Baptist and Catholic, soul and

48. Curiously, only *U.S. News* had managed to find a nonradical black who approved of King's anti-war stand.

49. " 'King Is the Man, Oh Lord,' " 38. See also *Newsweek*, "Not Since Dallas . . . ," April 15, 1968, p. 91. "An Hour of Need," *Time*, April 12, 1968, p. 17.

50. " 'You're Such a Brave Lady . . . !' " 32.

suzerainty," and through two cities-as-symbols, Dallas and Memphis. In an essay about violence, *Time* recorded the comment of a sympathetic Japanese diplomat: " 'Your poor country. I had thought that after Dallas this could not happen again.' "[51]

Even *U.S. News*, less interested in promoting a Democratic president, printed some references to the Kennedys who attended the funeral. And the magazine chose to illustrate its thesis about anarchy in the streets by quoting an adversary of King's and an ally of Kennedy's. " 'Men poised with Molotov cocktails, incendiaries, or fire bombs of any kind,' " said Mayor Daley, " 'are the same as the assassins who pulled the triggers on the guns that killed' " King and Kennedy.[52]

Some statements ran counter to the pattern. *Newsweek* reported, for example, that King had forced Kennedy to introduce a civil rights bill in 1963 by pressing his campaign in Birmingham to the crisis point. And some of the thematic development can be attributed to the celebritization of the Kennedy family then under way in American journalism. Even so, the news magazines trimmed the material at their disposal to bring it into line with audience expectations. The principal point of association was not King's or Kennedy's respective role in dismantling segregation; rather, it was that both had been murdered by snipers firing from ambush. A shared martyrdom for Kennedy and King would have been difficult to sustain except in superficialities. Changes in the black movement between the assassinations in 1963 and 1968 were too wrenching to support the thesis that Kennedy's and King's perspectives on racial matters were similar. After the stories in *Time* and *Newsweek*, King's analysis that "no president has really done very much for the American Negro" though Kennedy and Johnson "have received much undeserved credit for helping us," comes as a bit of a shock. A better case could be made for an analogy between the deaths of King and Malcolm X, who had been contraposed often enough by *Time* and *Newsweek*. Their perspectives were coming closer together at their deaths, certainly closer than were King's and Kennedy's. Malcolm X had changed considerably. In 1963, he criticized

51. "They Came to Mourn," *Time*, April 19, 1968, a photographic essay; "King's Last March," 18; "Violence and History," *Time*, April 19, 1968, p. 44. In the last article, *Time* observed that the murder of King and the subsequent rioting "reinforced a world image of America the Violent: a vast, driving, brutal land that napalms Vietnamese peasants and murders its visionaries along with its presidents." It neglected to add that King had contributed to that image by accusing the American military of using genocidal tactics.

52. "Any Answer to Riots?" *U.S. News & World Report*, April 29, 1968, pp. 34, 36.

King for using the tactics of "an Uncle Tom." In June, 1964, after his break with the Black Muslims, Malcolm X reportedly offered to help King "in the racial struggle down South if the United States Government fails to take decisive action." For his part, King seemed to have developed an appreciation for Malcolm X, judging from his telegram to the latter's widow in 1965: Malcolm X "had the great ability to put his finger on the existence and root of the problem. He was an eloquent spokesman for his point of view, and no one can honestly doubt that Malcolm had a great concern for the problems that we face as a race."[53]

With the theme of national symbolism complete, so also was the symbolic resurrection of King. It was, of course, not simply a whim of the news magazines. His death touched something deep in the American psyche—because, among other factors, of the unhappy fate of American symbols in the late 1960s—and *U.S. News* was on the mark when it observed that the nation had given King a funeral such as no other private citizen had ever received. But the news magazines played their part as well. Hewing the available material to fit the three major themes of King as a moderate, as a prophet from the South, and as a national symbol, they made sense of something that made none: an American prophet who transformed himself from reformer to radical.

King was resurrected as a gentle prophet from a simpler time when right-thinking Americans could see the way of justice stretching before them, and no need to ponder the complexities that bedevil men of conscience. The process was accomplished in a remarkably short period of time, encompassing King's death and funeral, and perhaps a week or two in addition. When the process ended, King was risen, his symbolic force directed in channels considered right and proper for an American prophet.

But one test remained. Although King was dead, there approached his final campaign—not an insignificant labor strike but a national movement, which King had promised would visit plague after plague upon the government of the United States until the poor won justice for themselves.

53. For the assessment of Kennedy and Johnson, see Martin Luther King, Jr., "A Testament of Hope," *Playboy*, XVI (January, 1969), 232. For the statement of Malcolm X, see transcript of interview with Malcolm X on radio station WUST, and FBI Field Office File, January 20, 1965, both in FBI surveillance file on Malcolm X. King's telegram to the widow of Malcolm X in 1965 and a copy of his more cautiously worded public statement are in Box 27, File 57, King Center Archives, Atlanta.

XI

THE RADICAL VISION

As he looked down from the mountaintop before his death, Martin Luther King was possessed of a vision national in scope and radical in purpose, strategy, and tactics. From different parts of America, as he saw it, the marchers would arrive in Washington, and not blacks alone, though their numbers would dominate. From the West and the Southwest would come Indians and Hispanic Americans. The cities would contribute blacks, from the ghettos of New York and Chicago and eight or more other cities, but there would be Puerto Ricans as well. From the South would march the foot soldiers of King's triumphant campaigns in the old movement, a goodly number from Birmingham, but joining them would be southern whites, most of them making the trek from the bleak highland villages of Appalachia. Their grievances were disparate: Indians, to take one group, angered by the loss of fishing rights guaranteed by treaty; Mexican Americans, for another, attempting to regain holdings in the Southwest allotted by the ancient land grants of the Spanish crown. Uniting them, black, brown, white, and red, would be the common thread of poverty, and they would struggle for redress of their own group's grievances and those of the poor generally.

The strategy represented a departure for King in one sense; it was a tested element of his generalship in another. The poor would create a crisis that could be neither ignored nor put down by the superior might of what King chose to call Pharaoh. King had created crises before and he proposed to do so again in the spring of 1968. Now, however, the Pharaoh whose power King would try in battle was the national government, which had aided him in the struggle against Jim Crow.

The campaign would begin with three thousand of the poor settling into a shantytown in Washington. Thereafter would begin skirmishes testing the will and the capacity of Pharaoh to counter nonviolent demonstrations. Following a mass rally, the campaign would escalate into arrest-provoking incidents designed to disrupt the operations of government. Inevitably, many would be jailed, but the losses were expected to be made good by volunteers stepping forward by the hundreds, perhaps by the thousands. And the movement would be supported by a national boycott of certain industries and shopping areas and by demonstrations in other cities. Escalation was built into King's battle plan: "You don't deal with . . . Pharaoh's hardened heart with just one plague. You got to keep plaguing Pharaoh. And we want wave after wave . . . of people coming in, bringing their grievances to Washington. . . . And for thirty or sixty days, no American will be able to ignore the black man. He'll be on their television screens and . . . in their newspapers."[1]

That had been King's vision, grim and bleak and radical. But King was dead. He had been resurrected as a symbol, however, by *Time*, *Newsweek*, and *U.S. News*. Now, beginning in late April and early May of the crisis year of 1968, the magazines were confronted by the problem of achieving a concordance between King's most radical venture and the symbolism of a benign, reformist prophet they had created after the assassination.

If the problem was critical, the solution was simple in concept: The news weeklies separated King from the radicalism of his final campaign. In execution, it was not so simple, because of his association with "the spectacular King died planning," to use *Newsweek*'s phrase. Naturally, the magazines pursued different courses. *U.S. News*, for example, damned the Poor People's Campaign as a radical threat but maintained a strained silence about the author of that threat. By contrast, *Time* and *Newsweek* initially depicted the campaign as reformist, not radical. Almost immediately, however, they be-

---

1. See Fager, *Uncertain Resurrection*, 16–19. Most of the SCLC documents relating to the project were lost when Resurrection City was destroyed by the federal government. The statement occurred during the discussion of the campaign at a ministers' conference sponsored by the SCLC in Miami, Florida, February 23, 1968, transcript of recording in Box 28, File 33, King Center Archives, Atlanta. King probably tailored his remark about the visibility of "the black man" to his audience; all but one of the hundred clergymen at the conference were black. Lomax, "When 'Nonviolence' Meets 'Black Power,'" 165–66.

gan to put distance between King the symbol and the emerging radicalism that he had set in motion. The process started with *Newsweek*'s contrasting picture of marching on Washington in 1963 and in 1968:

> "In a sense," said SCLC staffer Andy Young, "this is to be a war—a war without violence. It isn't going to be a Sunday-school picnic like the '63 March on Washington. . . . Something is going to change or we'll all be in jail. This is do or die—not just for nonviolence but for the nation— and we'll do whatever is necessary to open the economic doors of this nation for the poor.". . . SCLC leaders envisioned a massive assembly roughly resembling the 1963 march, where King dreamed his eloquent dream. Should Congress still fail to act, Abernathy & Co. hinted that silent witnessing might turn to civil disobedience—and that the whole campaign might follow the pols out of Washington to the national party conventions in August.[2]

Then the twist. "And so," *Newsweek* reported, "to their own mild embarrass- ment, SCLC's nonviolent staffers found themselves talking the lingo of war and escalation." Why should they be embarrassed? Nothing in Gandhian philosophy precluded militancy; Gandhi himself ranked violence above cow- ardice. Certainly nothing in King's plan was at odds with the statements of Young and his associates. The embarrassment, therefore, was *Newsweek*'s, which had no taste for schemes to disrupt Washington or, for that matter, the Democratic and Republican conventions.[3] In that disapproving remark about warlike rhetoric was the beginning of the thesis that the disciples were stray- ing from the path of moderation trod by their late master.

Time published similar thematic elements, but not solely out of concern for King's image; they represented as well a characteristic (if not lately seen) reaction to crisis. The nation would respond to reformist tactics, in *Time*'s judgment; indeed "many whites . . . have contributed money and time" to the campaign. And even though poverty seemed "like the inescapable obverse of the American dream," *Time* insisted it was "ultimately curable." Further, the nation was responding to the crisis of race by asking "more insistently than ever, 'What can I do?'"[4]

2. "'Do or Die,'" *Newsweek*, May 6, 1968, p. 30.

3. *Ibid.* King planned to disrupt the political conventions, partly to protest the war. *News- week* continued to ignore this facet of King's activism. It reported that King's widow urged participants in peace rallies to "press on for peace 'until the last gun is silenced,'" but it did not add that King had said far more. See photo caption, May 6, 1968, p. 30.

4. See *Time*, "City of New Hope," May 3, 1968, p. 23, "A Nation Within a Nation," May 17, 1968, p. 32, and "What Can I Do?" May 17, 1968, p. 36. City of New Hope was renamed Resurrection City after King's death. To avoid confusion, the latter is used throughout.

There was at least a grain of truth in *Time*'s reaction, but it also signaled a momentary resurgence of Lucean faith in the perfectibility of America. Luce had died in 1967, but enough of his influence lingered that, for the moment, *Time* was making sense of the world by proclaiming Luce's vision to be whole.[5]

Not every American shared that vision of America's greatness and sense of justice. *Time* framed the issue by reporting this response to the Poor People's Campaign: "'When that bunch comes here,' bellowed Louisiana's Senator Russell Long, 'they can just burn the whole place down, and we can just move the capital to some place where they enforce the law.'" Long served as a reminder of enemies who had done more than bellow against King's campaigns in the South. And *Time* provided a number of images from the old southern movement as the "poverty pilgrims" made their way toward Washington, driving buses or battered cars or occupying farm wagons "drawn by mules named Stennis and Eastland, George Wallace and Jim Clark." The route took them past landmarks that stirred up memories of earlier civil rights struggles. Passing through Selma, for example, Abernathy paused beside the Edmund Pettus Bridge, scene "of a club-flailing confrontation between King's marchers and Sheriff Jim Clark's lawmen." Elsewhere, "wreaths were laid at the spots where Mrs. Viola Liuzzo and the Rev. James Reeb died." The cast of martyrs and villains was assembled, in part, because of the itinerary established by the SCLC, which wanted to wring publicity from a stopover in Selma. But *Time* did its part to limit the symbolism of King to that attached to his struggle against segregation. In Selma, for instance, it reported that "during a speech recalling King, Abernathy suddenly fell silent and let the tears roll down his cheeks. Then a huge Negro woman began singing: 'Jesus—got all the power.'"[6] King, Mrs. Liuzzo, and Reeb, juxtaposed with symbols from the South's racist past and bigoted present, Eastland and Stennis of Mississippi, Wallace and Clark of Alabama, were reminders that *Time*'s America had eliminated much of the gap between its ideals and the realities of Jim Crow.

Despite those fundamentally reassuring images, *Time* had belatedly discovered the militancy within the SCLC spotted earlier by *Newsweek*. *Time* arranged a comparison. On one side, a white editor argued that before the

---

5. An example of Lucean optimism is "Soul Brother Humphrey," *Time*, May 10, 1968, p. 29.

6. "City of New Hope," 23; "Challenging the Pharaoh," *Time*, May 17, 1968, p. 35. On the stop at Selma, see Fager, *Uncertain Resurrection*, 20.

white American passed judgment on the campaign, "he ought to understand what he is judging." For the other side, the SCLC, *Time* trotted out that familiar verb "cried" to disparage the SCLC's rhetoric as hysterical nonsense. "'By the time we're through in D.C.,' cried March Coordinator Hosea Williams, 'white folks gonna say, "Where's Dr. King? Wake up, Dr. King!" These white folks killed the dreamer, but we're gonna show these white folks what become of the dream. The poor people are marching to challenge the Pharaoh.'"[7] Clearly, *Time* accepted reluctantly, if at all, the possibility raised by Williams (by King, for that matter) of an oppressive Pharaoh in Washington and had no use for the notion that white America collectively shared the guilt for the death of King.

While *Time* was publishing optimistic essays, *U.S. News* kept its attention fixed on the coming siege. After a brief, even-handed report at the end of April, *U.S. News* launched an intense editorial attack on the Poor People's Campaign in early May. Several critical stories were published in one issue. Two senators raised the specter of radicalism and communism. Conspiratorial tones were sounded in what was almost a rhetorical question the journal posed to Senator John McClellan of Arkansas: "To what extent have your investigations found subversive influence playing a part in these riots?" Not surprisingly, McClellan was "'confident that subversive influences are present'" and advised that "'Communists are right now planning to get into this "poor people's march" on Washington.'" McClellan added other terms of disapprobation, declaring that Congress "must not yield to threats and blackmail, or pay tribute to criminals." Another article portrayed the campaign as a threat that would start on a small scale but would "grow to mammoth proportions. By the end of May, leaders of the march predict, there will be hundreds of thousands of poor people—most of them black—laying siege to the nation's capital and government."[8] Whether that wildly unrealistic estimate resulted from an editorial error or exaggerated predictions by the SCLC is almost beside the point. It fitted the needs of *U.S. News*: The bigger the number, the graver the threat.

Time and *Newsweek* had published articles about the problems of the poor. To *U.S. News* none of this was relevant. It observed instead that the dem-

7. "Challenging the Pharaoh," 35. The militancy of the SCLC may explain why *Time*'s cover story on poverty in the same issue included only one reference to the Poor People's Campaign. Had standard journalistic practices been followed, the tie-in would have been exploited.

8. "How Riots Are Stirred Up," 71. Senator Robert Byrd of West Virginia was quoted to the same effect in "What's Wrong With a 'Poor People's March,'" 72. "The Growing March on Washington," 73. All stories are in the May 6, 1968, issue of *U.S. News & World Report*.

onstrators would descend upon Washington in order to find places on the welfare rolls. That shot was followed by a salvo. In mid-May, *U.S. News* provided a taste of what was coming. A delegation of the poor arrived in Washington to lobby for their cause. As reported by *U.S. News*, the delegation, a hundred strong, filed "into the offices of cabinet members and high officials, delivering 'demands' on the government of the United States." This was not the usual sort of lobbying. "Their demands were high, their words blunt, their attitudes often angry"—and not only were they uppity, they were rude, being late for "most appointments, [and] keeping some cabinet members waiting." What they delivered were threats, not just demands; Abernathy was quoted as saying that the demonstrators would "back up our words with the most militant nonviolent direct action in the nation's history."[9]

U.S. News was no more won over by Abernathy's promise of nonviolence than it had been by King's. Its attitude appears in two questions: "Will the march in Washington result in violence in a city already rocked by one major riot?" and (in a headline) "Communist Influence in March on Washington?"[10] Punctuation notwithstanding, the magazine seemed certain of the answers.

The magazine's siege mentality intensified during the following week. A graphics device traced the routes to be taken by nine caravans of the Poor People's Campaign from various points across the nation and their convergence on what was labeled "TARGET: The Nation's Capital." (Another headline described Washington as "A City Braced for Trouble.") While dutifully reporting the belief of some members of Congress that an agreement between the government and the SCLC about a campsite might "materially improve the prospects for an orderly demonstration," *U.S. News* was not reassured. Its suspicions were recorded in a lengthier article about various plagues already visited upon Washington—crime, the rioting that followed the murder of King. And now, it said, "on top of all this, comes the 'march on Washington,' expected to bring tens of thousands of 'poor people'—mostly black—threatening to camp in the capital until their costly demands for jobs and aid are met."[11]

9. On demonstrators and welfare, see "Washington Whispers," *U.S. News & World Report*, May 13, 1968, p. 30. "The 'Poor People's March': Its Demands, the Prospects," *ibid.*, 44.
10. "The 'Poor People's March': Its Demands, the Prospects," 45. See also "The President Talks About 'Poor March,' Taxes, Unity," *U.S. News & World Report*, May 13, 1968, p. 55. Senator Jennings Randolph of West Virginia complained of Communists in the campaign; one of those so identified, David Dellinger, was permitted a weak reply in the same issue. "Communist Influence in March on Washington?" 45.
11. See pictogram, *U.S. News & World Report*, May 20, 1968, p. 11. Beneath the message

The article appeared beneath a headline that warned of a threat of anarchy, but the magazine considered it more likely that a conspiracy was at work. Senator McClellan was quoted to the effect that Abernathy—whom *U.S. News* regarded as bad enough—would be deposed and replaced by two unnamed but "very radical and extremist leaders."[12] The threat was amplified by this statement:

> "Certain militant leaders of marchers [McClellan said] have announced in secret meetings" their intention to:
> Build a "shantytown" on the Mall near the Capitol—"whether or not they have a permit to do it."
> Prevent Congressmen from reaching their offices by accosting them on the streets of Capitol Hill.
> Defy the laws which prohibit demonstrations and disorders in the vicinity of the Capitol.
> Put children in the forefront of demonstrations to gain publicity about "police brutality" if law enforcement officers are compelled to intervene.
> Carry weapons into Washington.
> Incite demonstrators to violence and rioting. . . . [and] there are threats to block Washington traffic and bridges.[13]

The article was almost devoid of references to King. King had intended, of course, neither to incite violence nor to encourage demonstrators to arm themselves, but most of the tactics listed by the magazine had been contemplated by him before his death or could be made to appear so.[14] However, *U.S. News* had no wish to link King with radicals and extremists supposedly plotting to wrench control of the campaign from Abernathy. To effect such a coup, the conspirators would have to be associated with the campaign in some capacity; the best evidence of this connection was the agreement reached by King and Stokely Carmichael before the assassination. By passing over that matter, the magazine also passed up the opportunity to introduce evidence both genuine and cut to fit its theme—a sacrifice never undertaken lightly, and even more unusual now, when *U.S. News* was casting about for any weapon to use against the invaders. *U.S. News* could make its case that anarchists,

---

was a bull's-eye. See also in the same issue " 'Poor March' on Washington: A City Braced for Trouble," 11, and "A Threat of Anarchy in Nation's Capital," 47.

12. "A Threat of Anarchy in Nation's Capital," 48.

13. *Ibid.*, 47. *U.S. News* quoted two members of Congress who decried the hysteria, but their voices were lost in the extensive reports about the approaching conflict.

14. Compare, for example, the list compiled by *U.S. News* in "March on Washington— What to Expect," 44.

radicals, and Communists were about to descend on Washington; and even though the case was weakened, the magazine avoided calling into question a symbol whose resurrection as a moderate made him too valuable to waste.

To *U.S. News*, braced for invasion, the symbolism of the Poor People's Campaign was almost beside the point, and thus it took only the briefest notice that the southern caravan had pushed off for Washington. To *Newsweek*, symbolism seemed almost the only thing that mattered about "King's last and grandest pageant." The marchers assembled at the Memphis motel where King had been killed and dedicated a memorial marker. "Then, in a spectral reprise of King's funeral, they formed ranks behind a creaky wagon drawn by a brace of mules and toiled off via Mississippi toward Washington—the first of nine columns in a nesters' army determined to bring down the Jericho walls of color and caste in the United States."[15] What they encountered—before and after the departure—had more to do with color than caste, as shown by the account of a confrontation that occurred while students were recruiting marchers in Mississippi:

> The lead trooper clubbed a girl sitting on the lawn with the butt of a carbine. Other students stumbled to their feet in a swirling, screaming eddy. Police flailed at them with billies and gun butts. Two troopers caught a youth against the jail wall and stomped him. The demonstrators fled through town, leaving a litter of shoes and purses behind them. Laughing, troopers broke ranks and chased them six blocks back to the other side of the tracks. Ambling along behind, a highway patrol inspector . . . growled, "This is the only thing these sons of bitches understand. The Memphis police department killed three during the riot. We haven't yet, but we will time [*sic*] this is over."[16]

The images in the following issue were almost as intense. In Edwards, Mississippi, state troopers "glowered in narrow-eyed silence" as Abernathy boarded a wagon. "Muttered one trooper: 'All we wanna do is get these niggers out of here.'"[17]

Vicariously, the readers of *Newsweek* encountered other reminders of Jim Crow. With the marchers, they found "irascible Jim Clark's walk-soft successor, Sheriff Wilson Baker, waiting to shepherd them through Selma and bridling only when Abernathy twittingly tried to get him to join a chorus of

15. "'We're on Our Way,'" *Newsweek*, May 13, 1968, p. 32.
16. *Ibid.*
17. "A Talk With the Lord," *Newsweek*, May 20, 1968, p. 45.

'We Shall Overcome.'" They made a pilgrimage in Montgomery to King's first church, then rolled on "through Birmingham without a ripple," finally reaching Atlanta, capital of *Newsweek*'s New South, the city that proclaimed itself too busy to hate, "where progressive Mayor Ivan Allen himself met them, beaming: 'Welcome . . . Good luck and Godspeed.'"[18]

Unlike *U.S. News*, *Newsweek* argued that the marchers represented no threat. Indeed, they were deeply religious, and their demeanor while awaiting the beginning of the march demonstrated "that deep patience of the Southern black poor." To be sure, one of their leaders, James Bevel, had folksily informed them of hearing from the Lord around 5:30 of a Mississippi morning—"'He told me to tell yawl He wasn't goin' to deliver yawl. . . . We have to deliver ourselves.'" But readers were assured that the marchers would do no more than camp in Washington "until some form of deliverance is legislated by Congress." Also in contrast to *U.S. News*, *Newsweek* raised the implicit question, Who could oppose the Poor People's Campaign? It happened that most of the opponents were southerners in Congress who could be depicted as unreconstructed racists. West Virginia's Senator Robert Byrd, for example, was labeled a "sometime Ku Klux kleagle." Otherwise, there was only "fusty old Karl Mundt of South Dakota," but all he did was advise "constituents to cancel trips to Washington."[19] The sketch reproduced the battle lines of the old movement, down to the drawl of Bevel who relayed the Lord's commandment to "yawl" and the Mississippi policeman's menacing southernism about killing more blacks "time this is over."

Certainly the marchers encountered brutal police and narrow-eyed racism, and the trek took them past the milestones of the old movement. Even so, much went unsaid or was shaded toward a particular emphasis. For example, the biblical image of Jericho's walls of color and caste was one word different but miles distant ideologically from the issues of race and class of which King spoke before his death. For another, there was the fixation on one of the nine caravans of the campaign. The Memphis caravan was important symbolically; the other eight caravans, which used transport more prosaic than mule-drawn wagons, lacked the journalistic "color" indispensable to *Newsweek* and *Time*. Still, *Newsweek*'s reportage was exceedingly restricted for a

18. *Ibid*. *Newsweek* had anointed Baker as a moderate during the Selma campaign, but a transformation was required for thematic purposes. *Walk-soft* designated an individual who accommodated himself to desegregation without acknowledging its morality or justice.

19. *Ibid*.

national journal. Blacks from the ghettos of New York, Chicago, and Boston also were on the move, as were Hispanic Americans from various parts of the country, including a contingent organized by Reis Tijerina, the middle-aged Stokely Carmichael, as *Newsweek* had labeled him earlier in the year. Whether blacks from the ghetto shared the deep patience of their southern brethren was far from certain, given the bloody riots of 1966 and 1967, and Tijerina's followers had demonstrated a willingness to go beyond the law in order to regain land they regarded as rightfully theirs.[20] All in all, it was strange to find a national magazine reporting a national movement—one that was giving the Congress and the president of the United States a lively case of nerves—essentially in terms of a mule train setting out from a forgotten hamlet in Mississippi. (Except, of course, the report matched the expectations of *Newsweek*'s audience, just as dire prophecies satisfied the siege mentality of readers of *U.S. News.*) Even odder was the tone that crept into the coverage. It imparted a peculiar sense—not of déjà vu but of a time warp. Watts had *not* exploded in bloody disorders. SNCC had *not* rushed pell-mell into radicalism. King *had* heeded *Newsweek*'s endless admonitions and had avoided radical causes such as he found in Chicago, in the anti-war movement, and in a campaign of the underclass definitely *not* designed to await passively the pleasure of the Congress of the United States.

Congress had evinced little pleasure when it came to the campaign, but the initial stiff resistance to providing land for a campsite dissipated after King's assassination. An agreement was reached to permit three thousand demonstrators to occupy the land for a month. By mid-May, the marchers were making their way toward the fifteen acres, in the park beside the Lincoln Memorial, that would become Resurrection City. King had speculated that the government might try to "run us out like they did with the bonus marchers of the Great Depression." He added, defiantly, "But if we go to jail, we'll stay there indefinitely, without putting up bail." No less defiant was Abernathy when he made a ceremony of driving in the first tent stake on May 13. The protesters would remain, Abernathy vowed, until the government did something about the plight of the poor.[21]

To make the campaign work, there would have to be more than defiance. But at the beginning, bad luck and poor management produced confusion and chaos, and the plagues of the sort that King had planned for Pharaoh settled

20. Fager, *Uncertain Resurrection*, 54.
21. See Viorst, *Fire in the Streets*, 434, 438.

upon Resurrection City instead. Frequent storms turned much of the site into a "barely passable stretch of viscous mire" four times in three weeks. Even without the rain, the logistics of operating what amounted to a small town for an extended period would have stretched to the limit—and probably would have snapped—the administrative capacity of the SCLC. By May 17, the SCLC already was being stretched: About five hundred demonstrators were living on the site; more than three hundred others were crowded into various churches in Washington; another eight hundred were to arrive that day in Maryland; and seventeen hundred more marchers were expected the day after.[22]

Resurrection City was also plagued with crime. While serious in numbers and types of offenses, the incidence of crime probably was not much greater than would be expected for any population of that size drawn from the poor. But there were differences. Resurrection City was a memorial of sorts to King. Furthermore, it was not some hamlet drowsing by a wayside but was situated in the nation's news center where hordes of reporters were on hand to record every misstep. Crime would have become an issue in any event, but the SCLC's dealings with the press suffered because some journalists fell victim to crimes such as robbery or were rudely treated by the camp's unofficial police force. As a writer commented wryly, "White reporters who are curious about what it must be like to be a young Negro constantly harassed by the police learn more than they want to know about the subject after a couple of days of being harassed by young Negro marshals in Resurrection City." Predictably, the SCLC won little sympathy with the defensive but not unreasonable explanation that "we didn't bring saints to Resurrection City."[23]

Strictly as a "sheer visual thing," conditions were about as terrible as the stories painted them to be. One SCLC staffer conceded that "the mud was thick and everything had . . . a polluted quality about it, and the shacks were sort of run down, . . . and food was all over the place." Still, the outcry over the conditions was ironical, as a media critic wrote at the time. "The poor in Resurrection City have come to Washington to show that the poor in America

22. Fager, *Uncertain Resurrection*, 42–43, 49, 52.

23. On crime, see interview with Katherine Shannon, chair of the SCLC's administrative services committee, by Claudia Rawles, August 12, 1968 (Transcript of tape 297, in Moorland-Spingarn Research Center, Howard University), 49. On the press, see Calvin Trillin, "U.S. Journal: Resurrection City," *New Yorker*, June 15, 1968, p. 78. *Southern Courier*, July 6–7, 1968, p. 4.

are sick, dirty, disorganized, and powerless—and they are criticized daily for being sick, dirty, disorganized, and powerless."[24]

While catching the irony of journalistic accounts, the writer missed something more important. It was not King's intent to show the powerlessness of the poor; that would have been restating the obvious. Nor had King expected Resurrection City (named City of New Hope while he was alive) to become the focal point of the campaign; at most, it was to be a place to house people and to make poverty visible in the midst of affluence. King intended to use the massed power of the poor, shaped and directed by Gandhian nonviolence. Resurrection City, therefore, was to be the beginning of the Washington campaign, not its *raison d'être*. Demonstrations were the reason for going to Washington—demonstrations growing in size and in degree of disruption and, if necessary, spreading to other cities.

King's plans did not precisely come to naught, but they came to far less than he had envisioned. Figuratively as well as literally, the SCLC became bogged down in the mire of Resurrection City. Its initial protest events were limited and uninspired. Nor did the SCLC prove equal to the critical task of forging working partnerships across ethnic lines. Particularly troublesome was Reis Tijerina, who complained constantly of slights and of the SCLC's failures. Probably Tijerina had signed onto the campaign only to get national publicity for the effort to regain or to secure compensation for the lost landholdings in the Southwest. His commitment to nonviolence was suspect, and he showed little interest in issues such as jobs and housing. But Tijerina was by no means the only disgruntled partner of the SCLC. The SCLC was ill-prepared for the onerous problems arising from a coalition of ethnic groups and probably even less ready to adjust its priorities to mollify its partners. Factions in black communities in the South had produced similar problems often enough in the old movement, but by inviting the SCLC in, local leaders had tacitly admitted that they could not handle the situation.[25] In Washington, the SCLC lacked that edge.

24. For the observations of the SCLC staffer, see Shannon interview, 36–37; the media criticism is in Trillin, "Resurrection City," 71.

25. Sources consulted include Fager, *Uncertain Resurrection*, 51, 54; Trillin, "Resurrection City," 74; Shannon interview, 46–47; and interview with Reis Tijerina, by James Mosby, June 12, 1968 (Transcript of tape 194, in Moorland-Spingarn Research Center, Howard University), 13–14. Some impoverished whites, fearing crime, refused to move into Resurrection City. Some blacks also were rebellious. Blacks from the Northeast, for example, refused at first to join the campaign but did so after King's murder. Their initial reluctance was attributed to fear of SCLC

The SCLC also lacked an edge that King could have provided. It was not administrative talent; on occasion, King had confessed his deficiencies and had promised to try to do better, but nuts-and-bolts administration was never his calling. What he could have supplied was more important: that great voice, the consummate power of a magnificent orator who spoke with authority across class and racial lines; his extraordinary moral presence, which might have directed attention away from the muck of Resurrection City and toward the ends for which it was founded; and his knack for recruiting people who disagreed with him and with each other, and getting them to work together. The clashing interests and disputatious personalities found in the Washington campaign would have severely tested King's diplomacy, but he had proven equal to the challenge before, and might have been so again.[26]

Instead of King, however, the SCLC had Ralph David Abernathy, whose misfortune it was to be measured against his old friend and colleague and found wanting, rather than to be judged on his own abilities.[27] The comparisons started almost immediately after the assassination and resumed in earnest once the marchers settled into Resurrection City.

What had been muted expressions of uncertainty about Abernathy after King's death were put on the record in late May by *Newsweek* in a way that required no speculation. Some SCLC staff members criticized Abernathy's "platform style and manner. 'He's just a small-town preacher,'" complained one of them. The preoccupation with style revealed as much about *Newsweek* as it did about the inevitable maneuvering for position within the SCLC. The roughhewn Abernathy, however effective from the pulpit of a black church, fell short of the image of King that the magazine was carefully cultivating.[28]

Newsweek also was putting something else on the record: New manage-

---

domination. Interview with Cornelius Givens, New York coordinator of the campaign, by Katherine Shannon, July 7, 1968 (Transcript of tape 223, in Moorland-Spingarn Research Center, Howard University), 5–6. The SCLC's capacity for dealing with its ethnic partners is critiqued by Fager, *Uncertain Resurrection*, 14. See also Myles Horton to Andrew J. Young, April 5, 1968, in Box 177, File 20, King Center Archives, Atlanta.

26. For examples of those challenges, see Lewis, *King: A Biography*, 336, 384; and Lomax, "When 'Nonviolence' Meets 'Black Power,'" 178.

27. Fager, *Uncertain Resurrection*, 27–28. See also Good, "No Man Can Fill Dr. King's Shoes—But Abernathy Tries," 284–301.

28. "The Periscope," *Newsweek*, May 27, 1968, p. 19. The assessment about style is borrowed from Fager, *Uncertain Resurrection*, 57, who argues more broadly that the press and the white liberals were unwilling to accept Abernathy as the SCLC's leader because of the differences between his style and King's.

ment was in charge. King's "last and grandest pageant" was handed over symbolically to Abernathy in late May. While *Newsweek* was burnishing King's image, establishing, for example, that he had donated to the black cause his considerable earnings as a writer and his $50,000 cash prize from the Nobel Foundation, it subtly eased him out of the Washington project. Its statement that " 'Resurrection City, U.S.A.' was little more than a gleam in Martin Luther King's eye when he was slain April 4" relieved him of the responsibility for what was transpiring on the campsite near the Lincoln Memorial.[29]

What was happening there distressed *Newsweek*, though this reading has to be pulled from between lines indicating otherwise. It dismissed, as the product of overheated imaginations, the near-panic in Washington. Resurrection City might be as chaotic as most other SCLC projects, *Newsweek* wrote soothingly, but it "still seemed a distinctly unmenacing place—except to Washington's white establishment." Some developments were reassuring, especially the engagement of certified moderate Bayard Rustin, the "master builder of the 1963 March on Washington, to stage-manage a reprise of that grand pageant on June 19." Still, *Newsweek* was having to cut its material quite a bit to support the notion that a "pragmatic lobbying campaign" was responsible for Washington's case of nerves. For one thing, *Newsweek* hastily qualified—with "nonviolent"—Abernathy's statement that "we're going to raise hell downtown during the day." For another, Washington's jitters were blamed on its heritage as a "provincial border town with a Southern exposure and an enduring apprehension about its burgeoning black majority." That description fitted; but *Newsweek* went a step beyond, emphasizing the less controversial factor of race over class with the assertion that the numbers of blacks in the campaign were matched by only a "symbolic smattering of whites, Indians, Puerto Ricans, and Mexican-Americans." The statement was incorrect, uncharacteristically vague for a news magazine, and should have been easy enough to check out. The emphasis on cultural paranoia tended to preclude another possibility, that the Washington establishment was apprehensive about the radicalism of the campaign as well as frightened by the

29. "Newsmakers," *Newsweek*, May 27, 1968, p. 56. *Newsweek* omitted two radical organizations, SNCC and CORE, while listing two respectable institutions, Morehouse College and Ebenezer Baptist Church, as recipients of King's largess. For the statement about Resurrection City, see " 'What Can You Do for Us?' " *Newsweek*, June 3, 1968, p. 22.

potential for racial violence.[30] Perhaps most worrisome of all was the fore-boding that the SCLC would ignore the counsel of moderates (Rustin being one, *Newsweek* another) to conclude the campaign with the mass rally sched-uled for June 19—a recommendation to fold the tents just when King had expected to lead his forces into nonviolent battle.

Aside from an obsession with the logistics of operating Resurrection City, *Time*'s reports differed little from *Newsweek*'s. *Time* tended to interpret Washington's nervousness in terms of the fear about crime, a code word for race. The magazine also welcomed any sign that the SCLC was tacking toward the middle way, whether in the form of an "emergency summons" to Rustin to manage the mass rally, or Abernathy's tempering his fiery rhetoric. The similarity was most marked when *Time* dealt with the leadership of the venture. During the early days of Resurrection City, King's name appeared only in passing references to the effect that he had set in motion the project now led by Abernathy. Furthermore, *Time* based its comparison of the two men on degrees of militancy. The comparison reiterated King's credentials as a moderate and called Abernathy's into question. Of late, *Time* reported, Abernathy had "shown an unhappy tendency to make inept remarks and to accept bad advice from ultramilitant SCLC officials whom King managed to keep in line."[31] Actually, King deserved the appellation "ultramilitant" more than did the aides to whom it was attached.

During this period, *U.S. News* preserved the aura of moderation surround-ing King while warning of the threat posed by the campaign and its new leaders. Where *Newsweek* characterized the marchers as patient, *U.S. News* maintained that radicalism ran through all ranks of the campaign, highest to lowest. Most graphic was the example of a black youngster whose rhetoric was as impassioned as his elders': "'Our enemy is not over there in Vietnam,' said the young boy, 'Our enemy is on Capitol Hill.'" He was chosen by the magazine to sum up "a sentiment expressed several times" during a meeting.

30. "'What Can You Do for Us?'" 22; "Washington's Racial Jitters," *Newsweek*, June 3, 1968, p. 27. Four hundred Hispanics and four hundred to five hundred whites from Appalachia made the trek to Washington. Interviews with Richard Romero, western coordinator, by James Mosby, June 11, 1968 (Transcript of tape 193), 15, and Ernest Austin, Appalachian coordinator, by Katherine Shannon, July 9, 1968 (Transcript of tape 264), 9, both in Moorland-Spingarn Research Center, Howard University. Inasmuch as the Hispanics, Indians, and Appalachian whites were housed separately, the numbers should have been easy to estimate.

31. See *Time*, "The Scene at ZIP Code 20013," May 24, 1968, p. 29, and "Ralph Abernathy: Out of the Shadow," May 31, 1968, p. 15.

"'If we don't get what we want, we are going to stay right here in Washington.'"[32]

With talk of that sort issuing from the mouths of babes, *U.S. News* was not about to soften Abernathy's promise to raise hell in Washington and, naturally, did not regard the nervousness of Washingtonians as the product of feverish imaginations or of southern-style racism. *U.S. News* did report, often in some detail, the complaints of the poor and, at least on one occasion, grudgingly conceded that the SCLC's professions of nonviolence might be sincere. Nevertheless, it published articles designed to discourage financial contributions to the SCLC and interjected information strengthening the arguments against the demands of the poor when Freeman did not make the case strongly enough.[33]

While this was going on, King was absent. In one instance the omission was ludicrous. *U.S. News* published a clumsy, half-humorous article designating the mules of the wagon train from the South as "a symbol of poverty" in the campaign. (True enough, but King was a far more important symbol.) When King did appear, he represented responsible dissent. One article reproduced a discussion by Supreme Court justice Abe Fortas about civil disobedience in its various forms, one of which was the poor people's march. "Said Justice Fortas: 'If the civil disobedience takes the form of disrupting traffic, preventing people from going to their offices, their buildings, perhaps even their homes—that is a violation of law that should not be called civil disobedience. It is simply lawbreaking on a large scale.'" For years, *U.S. News* had castigated King as the leading advocate of that type of disruption. He was not cited as such now. The following week, he was cited—as the exemplar of "the great tradition" of civil disobedience: motivated by high principle, carried out with discipline and intellectual integrity, and undertaken only by those prepared to "assume the legal penalties" for disobedience. As presented by *U.S. News*, as well as by the theologian supplying the assessment, "'This is what Martin Luther King stood for.'"[34]

32. "'Poor' vs. Freeman—How Many Hungry?" *U.S. News & World Report*, June 3, 1968, p. 24.

33. *U.S. News* reported that the SCLC had expelled some troublemakers in "For the 'Poor March': Detours," June 3, 1968, p. 47. *U.S. News* questioned the tax-exempt status of the campaign in "Is Gift to 'Poor March' Deductible?" May 27, 1968, p. 94, and interjected two paragraphs, taken from testimony by Freeman before a congressional panel, to rebut a statement made by Abernathy during a meeting with Freeman. "'Poor' vs. Freeman—How Many Hungry?" 22.

34. See *U.S. News & World Report*, "A Long Road for the Vanishing Mule," May 27, 1968,

Although their emphases differed somewhat, each of the magazines held, in effect, that others had taken over what King had begun and had pushed the movement into radicalism or irresponsible directions he had not intended. Ironically, the recurring theme was strongest when the campaign started to move haltingly along the radical path charted by King. An example was a demonstration at the Supreme Court building on May 29 on behalf of American Indians who claimed they had been unfairly deprived of fishing rights guaranteed by treaty, and whose grievance was that the Supreme Court had affirmed a lower court decision limiting those rights in certain rivers in Washington State. While dubious about the wisdom of the demonstration, Abernathy went ahead with it, in part as a gesture of solidarity, in part because pressure was being brought to bear on him by Tijerina, who complained, as *Time* put it, that "brown, red, and white Americans were being bossed around by the Negroes and shouted down at meetings."[35]

A few windows were broken and five demonstrators were arrested during the protest—a list normally not worth a second glance in those troubled times. The protest was a disaster, however, because it marred the dignity of the one governmental institution given unanimous consent to demand hushed voices and Tory demeanor of those who drew nigh. The point was made most tellingly by *Time*. It reported that the protesters ignored a law prohibiting demonstrations outside the Court, then sketched a scene of oafish disrespect for the Court itself. "Indian women let out war whoops. Others cried: 'Earl Warren, you better come out now.' Demonstrators defiantly sprawled over imposing marble statues, splashed in fountains, hauled down an American flag, and smashed five windows at the side of the building, though leaders of the march absurdly blamed the press and 'the CIA' for the breakage." *Newsweek* did not make as much of the episode—a "raggedy, window-smashing siege"—because, it twice assured its readers, few people were involved. (*U.S. News* paid even less attention; since it had never promoted the marchers as just another clutch of lobbyists, it regarded the noisy demonstration as business as usual.) Differences aside, *Time* and *Newsweek* were dismayed that the demonstrators singled out what the latter called the "unlikeliest target of all" and the former identified as the institution "whose decisions have done so much in the past decade and a half to secure the rights of all minorities."

p. 8, "Campus Riots: A Justice Speaks Out," June 3, 1968, p. 8, and "Is America Really 'Sick'?" June 10, 1968, p. 46. The last is an interview with theologian Robert E. Fitch.

35. "Turmoil in Shantytown," *Time*, June 7, 1968, p. 28. On Tijerina's complaints and Abernathy's response, see Fager, *Uncertain Resurrection*, 53, 55.

Not for the first time had *Time* and *Newsweek* mourned the failure of blacks to distinguish friends from enemies.[36]

A week later, *Time* and *Newsweek* were even more dismayed. Fueling their concern was the departure of Bayard Rustin from the campaign. Rustin had signed on at the behest of Abernathy, who had had to overcome some resistance within the SCLC before he could issue the invitation. Over the years, Rustin had drifted to the right of King and had, in fact, spoken out against the Poor People's Campaign before King's death. But there were good reasons to get Rustin on the team. He could serve as a bridge to white liberals disconcerted by the SCLC's movement away from the center. And whatever his politics, Rustin was a superb organizer, probably the best ever produced by the black movement, as shown by the almost flawless orchestration of the 1963 March on Washington. It was natural, therefore, to turn to him to organize the mass rally, now identified as Solidarity Day, scheduled for mid-June.

What Rustin brought to the campaign was considerable, but so was his price, which turned out to be higher than the SCLC was willing to pay. On June 2, Rustin released a revised list of demands that included the creation of a million jobs with funds to be supplied by the federal government, the passage of a housing bill, the repeal of certain restrictions on welfare, the restoration of federal financial assistance to various poverty programs, and other reformist measures. Abernathy and the SCLC disavowed the list as too limited. It lacked, for example, Hispanic land-grant claims and Indian fishing rights; nor did it include opposition to the war, one of King's causes that the SCLC staff was unwilling to jettison. Rustin quit the movement four days later, after Abernathy refused to endorse the revised program.[37]

Rustin's resignation crystallized the misgivings of *Time* and *Newsweek*. The latter wrote gloomily of a leadership vacuum that lingered after the death of King, making it clear Abernathy was unlikely to fill it. In private, "Abernathy was sounding more and more like a defeated man. 'I just have so many problems,' he moaned. 'Everybody is pulling on me. I need to get away.'" If

36. "Turmoil in Shantytown," 28; "Courting Trouble," *Newsweek*, June 10, 1968, p. 30; "Some Gains for 'Poor Marchers,' But Their Troubles Grow," *U.S. News & World Report*, June 10, 1968, p. 60. The last gave almost as much attention to an SCLC officer's refusal to pay a bill at a government cafeteria as it did to the demonstration.

37. Fager, *Uncertain Resurrection*, 62; *Southern Courier*, June 15–16, 1968, p. 1. Soon after Rustin resigned, Abernathy released a set of demands that differed little from Rustin's, suggesting that the SCLC was "considering ways of covering [its] tracks if the campaign" failed. Fager, *Uncertain Resurrection*, 66.

Time had its way, Abernathy would do just that—and not return. Abernathy's grip on the leadership, lax from the start, had been "steadily slipping away" until it had "relaxed to the point of paralysis," *Time* observed scornfully. Abernathy, "the pretender to the role of Martin Luther King," was allowing the prophet's final campaign "to wallow into disorder, disintegration, and self-defeat." What outraged *Time* was the "purge" of Rustin, who might have given the campaign "realistic direction." The phrase "realistic direction" and the characterization of Rustin's list as a "manifesto of reasoned, possibly attainable goals" tell the story. The final project of the moderate King was getting off track when Rustin's "measured moderation" was supplanted by people of the ilk of "Abernathy's fiery new demonstration director," Hosea Williams. First, Williams "sneered that Rustin's manifesto was an unauthorized 'bunch of foolishness,'" then "tried fecklessly to provoke mass arrests, bending the campaign toward civil disobedience." The following week, *Time* juxtaposed the SCLC with CORE and SNCC as partners in "a militant shift to the left."[38]

Undeniably, the SCLC had shifted to the left, but *Time* implied that the process had not started until after King was murdered. Actually, Abernathy had taken the SCLC no further toward civil disobedience than King intended, nor had Williams bent, thus altered, the course plotted by King. If anything, they were not pushing the campaign as fast or as far as he had envisioned.

U.S. News was not distressed by the resignation of Rustin. It merely noted that his resignation "appeared to imperil" the Solidarity Day rally and that several demands raised by the SCLC "have no chance of passage soon—if ever." The magazine was more impressed with Rustin's replacement, Sterling Tucker, the executive secretary of the Washington Urban League, a "moderate in the civil rights field," and (though this was not expressed) a known quantity in the tight little world of Washington. Certainly he appeared more restrained than did Abernathy. While Tucker "declared that there would be no 'acts of civil disobedience whatsoever,'" Abernathy issued threats, one of which was reported: Any attempt to throw the protesters out of Resurrection City would lead to violence in black ghettos across the nation.[39]

---

38. "Disarray in the Ranks," *Newsweek*, June 17, 1968, p. 53. See *Time*, "Insurrection City," June 14, 1968, pp. 24–25, and "Black Separatist," June 21, 1968, p. 24.

39. See *U.S. News & World Report*'s issue of June 24, 1968, for "Tough Job for New Leader of Big Protest: Trying to Avoid Violence," 16, and "'Poor March' Showdown Nears—Most Demands Still Unmet," 8.

It nevertheless was dawning upon *U.S. News* that there was desperation in Abernathy's voice, that, as one source said, "'the worst thing that could happen to the march leaders would be for the government to tell them, "Stay all summer if you want."'" Believing the campaign headed toward failure, *U.S. News* was loosening up a bit. It still framed as threats rhetoric such as this lecture delivered to Attorney General Ramsey Clark: "'We ain't got no money, man, but we got matches, man, [and] you better tell the police to get their guns ready because we're ready. For every one of us you kill in Resurrection City . . . ten cities are going to burn 'cause we ain't got nothing to lose.'" Nevertheless, *U.S. News* subtly betrayed its enjoyment of the spectacle of the liberal Clark squirming under tongue-lashings administered by the poor. *U.S. News* listed the attorney general's liberal credentials and recounted with relish that his unimpressed audience halted Clark's presentation with the curt declaration that the meeting was arranged "for us to present our demands to you—not for you to talk to us."[40]

U.S. News' reading that the campaign was on the ropes was reasonably accurate. Rather than a site where the marchers would live and dramatize the misery of poverty, Resurrection City itself occupied center stage—and there was plenty of unplanned misery. Hundreds of persons had been sent home for various reasons, and many more departed after finding the "lackluster demonstrations" insufficient compensation for the problems of mud, confusion, theft, and assault. Conditions were so bad that some militants staged a protest at the motel used as the SCLC headquarters, demanding the staffers abandon their comfortable rooms and move into Resurrection City. That embarrassing demonstration was only one in the litany of problems recited by news media. Even friendly journals found fault. The *Southern Courier* complained that SCLC staffers were often absent, and when leaders did appear, "it was often to promise things that weren't delivered, or to organize demonstrations that were unexpectedly canceled, leaving people to wait for hours at the gate."[41]

By mid-June, the SCLC had not much more than the hope that the Soli-

---

40. "'Poor March' Showdown Nears—Most Demands Still Unmet," 8, echoed in the same issue in "Washington Whispers," 24, and in "Tomorrow," 21. On the demonstrators and Clark, see "'Poor March': Threats, Disputes, and Confusion," *U.S. News & World Report*, June 17, 1968, p. 8.

41. *Southern Courier*, June 15–16, 1968, p. 1. There is disagreement whether Resurrection City's peak population was 2,500 or 3,000, and about how rapidly it dwindled. The best estimates are that the population was between 500 and 700 by June 6. Compare *ibid.*; and Fager, *Uncertain Resurrection*, 57. The demonstration at the SCLC headquarters is mentioned in Fager, *Uncertain Resurrection*, 61.

darity Day rally would salvage the project. It was a slim chance, to be sure, but an outpouring of support from tens of thousands of persons might rescue the movement from disaster. King and the SCLC had run that sort of gamble before. On this occasion, the SCLC would not have King, but it would have his symbolic presence, something that could hardly escape the notice of the nation when coupled to an event so closely resembling the 1963 March on Washington.

As it happened, King's name was appearing far more often in stories about the search for his killer and about the murder of Senator Robert Kennedy following his victory in the Democratic presidential primary in California. Kennedy's death led to an expansion of the theme uniting King and President Kennedy as cultural heroes. An illustration was *Time*'s apologue of lost innocence in the Class of 1968; the collegiates' "sober, even tragic view of life" was ascribed to the murders of John Kennedy, "a politician who gained their trust and inspired their ambitions" when they were high school seniors, and King, "the Negro leader who tapped their idealism and drew them into social protest" when they were college seniors. Similarly, *Newsweek* constructed confluent symbolism connecting King with Robert Kennedy, whose "special constituency" included the "impoverished and the oppressed" and whose murder was a devastating blow to a movement still "floundering in the leadership vacuum left by the death two months earlier" of King. *U.S. News* gave some attention to the trauma of the two assassinations as well, though passing it off blandly as "an emotional letdown."[42]

The theme required that the journals ignore a controversy. As attorney general, Kennedy had authorized the wiretapping of King's telephone. A column alleging that Kennedy had signed that order was circulated by syndicated columnists Drew Pearson and Jack Anderson shortly before Kennedy's murder. No accounts of the controversy were published by the news weeklies, not even by *U.S. News*, which had been grumbling for years about government spying and which, in early June, had dredged up an old dispute between J. Edgar Hoover and Kennedy about FBI wiretaps authorized while Kennedy was attorney general. Naturally, journalists would be reluctant to

42. "The Cynical Idealists of '68," *Time*, June 7, 1968, p. 78. See *Newsweek*, "Disarray in the Ranks," 48, 53, and "Understanding Violence," June 17, 1968, p. 43. See *U.S. News & World Report*, "Riot Outlook for '68," July 15, 1968, p. 32, and "Dirksen: 'We're Not Sick—We're Just Mismanaged,'" August 19, 1968, p. 34. *U.S. News* raised the specter of a conspiracy in "James Earl Ray: Manhunt Ends, but Mysteries Remain," 34–36, and "New Clues in RFK Death—Was There a Plot?" 36, both in the issue of June 24, 1968.

raise such an indelicate matter while the nation was mourning Kennedy. Yet audience expectations probably were taken into account in another way. Having been advised that the Kennedys and King were martyrs-in-common, readers might find it difficult to accept the contradiction of one martyr being spied upon at the behest of another.[43]

Most of the coverage at this time was devoted to the murder of King or to the search for James Earl Ray. In addition to publishing routine crime stories, the magazines speculated about the existence of a conspiracy. An old hand at unearthing sinister combinations, *U.S. News* reported the gossip that King's death was plotted in "Castro's Cuba and Red China," which, "hoping to foment widespread racial strife in the U.S., might have looked upon assassination of Dr. King as a trigger."[44] The article is significant for what it did not say. King had been pilloried by the magazine for years as a Communist dupe or collaborator whose organization was riddled with Communists or fellow travelers. By omitting such claims, *U.S. News* deprived itself of evidence supporting the theory of a Communist plot. The trade-off was that its silence kept a national symbol unbesmirched by radicalism.

Time exhibited some interest in a theory of a leftist conspiracy but was more convinced that the motive for the slaying was racial. The report of Scotland Yard's capture of Ray in London was unexceptionable. Ray was identified simply as an "Illinois-born . . . escaped convict." The next issue reintroduced the theme of racism. Ray was characterized as a "known racist" who was attempting to flee to "the white-supremacist breakaway state of Rhodesia." A week later, the theme was refined and redirected as southern racism, the exemplar being Ray's attorney, Arthur Hanes, the "former Birmingham mayor" whose "sympathies are no secret. In 1963, though just out of office as a bitterly anti-integration mayor, he continued to fight against" King's Birmingham campaign. The implication was that one racist killed King and another was defending the murderer.[45]

---

43. On the column, see New York *Times*, May 25, 1968, p. 17; and Robert Yoakum, "Drew Pearson and Jack Anderson and Martin Luther King and Robert Kennedy and . . . ," *Columbia Journalism Review*, VII (Summer, 1968), 18–19. "Some New Light on 'Spying' in the Kennedy Era," *U.S. News & World Report*, June 3, 1968, p. 16. On Kennedy and wiretapping, see Garrow, *The FBI and King*, 72–73, 91–100.

44. "Deepening Mystery of Dr. King's Assassination," *U.S. News & World Report*, May 27, 1968, p. 10.

45. "The Assassination According to Capote," *Time*, May 10, 1968, p. 65, recounted the theory of author Truman Capote that King's murder was carried out by leftists for political gain. *Time* reiterated Capote's theory in "Ray's Odd Odyssey," June 21, 1968, p. 23. Ray's arrest is

With few exceptions, the theme was developed for the remainder of the summer. The most striking example was an examination, in August, of racial problems in Memphis; "the steamy city on the Mississippi still seethes in the residue of April's unlearned lessons," *Time* reported, "and the aloof attitude of Mayor Henry Loeb and the other officials hardly helps." Among the latter was located a figure reminiscent of Bull Connor: "chest-thumping . . . Fire and Police Director Frank Holloman, who recently promised an applauding white civic club that if Memphis' Negroes revert to 'lawlessness,' as he put it, 'we'll knock them on their ass.' "[46]

Some of the same thematic elements surfaced in *Newsweek*. It described Hanes as "the strapping ex-mayor of Birmingham in the Bull Connor era and defender of the three Ku Kluxers tried for the murder of Mrs. Viola Liuzzo after the 1965 Selma civil rights march." Ray's racism was demonstrated by the journalistic aside that he had long "felt the tug of [Africa's] white-run bastions."[47]

Much of *Time*'s and *Newsweek*'s coverage represented routine and reasonably accurate journalistic work. Indeed, the details of the manhunt, the capture of Ray, his racial attitudes, and the legal proceedings could not have been avoided. Nor was *Time*'s story about Memphis, while exaggerated and flawed because of omissions, wide of the mark when it came to racial tensions in that city. But the significance of those reports appears not in isolation but in comparison. The magazines explicitly associated King with symbols of southern racism. He was the prophet who had fought Bull Connor and Art Hanes in Birmingham and who had perished in a struggle with their latter-day equivalents, Loeb and Holloman of Memphis. Although not at precisely the same time, the two news weeklies were, during the summer of 1968, disassociating King from the radicalism of the Washington campaign for which, in the main, he was responsible.

It was all but impossible, however, to disassociate King from Solidarity Day. Perhaps for that reason, the respectability that eluded Resurrection City was attached to Solidarity Day, even though the rally's intent and purpose

covered *ibid.*, 22–23; and in "Arrested at Last," *Time*, June 14, 1968, p. 23. On Hanes, see "Two for the Accused," *Time*, June 28, 1968, p. 39. *Time* erred. Hanes, an outspoken segregationist, was still mayor of Birmingham during King's campaign. By contrast, the same article emphasized the legal skills of Russell Parsons, the lawyer for Sirhan B. Sirhan, who murdered Kennedy.

46. "On the Brink in Memphis," *Time*, August 16, 1968, p. 23.

47. See *Newsweek*, "The Defenders," July 1, 1968, p. 30, and "Unanswered Questions," June 24, 1968, p. 32.

differed greatly from those of the placid and idealistic March on Washington five years earlier. The distinction in tone was summarized by a writer for the *Southern Courier*: "In 1963, militant remarks were censored from the speeches," while "the accusations came thick and fast" on Solidarity Day from "representatives of the campaign's Indians, Spanish-American, poor whites, Puerto Ricans, and welfare rights groups."[48] No less striking were the differences in intent. Where the marchers departed Washington after one day in 1963, Solidarity Day was intended to signal King's legions to move into nonviolent battle.

While acknowledging there were differences between the two marches, *Time* and *Newsweek* adopted a tone approaching nostalgia that diluted the radicalism of King. The latter sketched a scene "played out like a memory called up from a simpler, more civil past: the great throng massing beneath the Washington Monument, spilling like a river down to Abraham Lincoln's stately memorial and . . . petitioning the government for the redress of grievances a century or more in the making. Solidarity Day 1968 was no match for the 1963 March on Washington in numbers or eloquence or pristine clarity of purpose. Yet the mere fact that the managers of the luckless Poor People's Campaign brought it off at all was something of a triumph." *Newsweek* resurrected the King of 1963 as a presence during Solidarity Day's culminating event, a march to the Lincoln Memorial. "It was the sort of moment Martin Luther King enjoyed and even lived for; the day otherwise suffered painfully from his absence. His widow, Coretta, . . . was never so affecting as when she quoted King's own words, the peroration of his great 'I have a dream' speech of 1963—and retired, eyes glistening, to her seat." *Time* found a difference in spirit. The hope that had suffused the demonstration in 1963— "that the last vestiges of legal segregation would soon disappear"—had by now yielded "to disillusionment and despair," even, among many, to a "mood . . . of apocalypse."[49] *Time* implied, however, that King was not among those who had surrendered to despair. The rub was that King had become grimmer and more radical in the years since his "I have a dream" speech.

One facet of King's radicalism—his struggle against the war—was ig-

---

48. On the respectability achieved by Solidarity Day, see Offenburger interview, 53–54. *Southern Courier*, June 22–23, 1968, p. 1.

49. "'Let No One Be Denied,'" *Newsweek*, July 1, 1968, p. 20; "Solidarity and Disarray," *Time*, June 28, 1968, p. 17.

nored. Where the *Southern Courier* reported that Mrs. King took up "her late husband's anti-war theme," *Newsweek* noted merely that Mrs. King "uttered her own plea for a woman's crusade to end the war and save the ghettos," and *Time* that she "launched into a twenty-five minute speech dwelling at length on . . . 'the most cruel and evil war in the history of mankind.'"[50] Their silence about King's still-controversial role as an opponent of the war erected a wall between him and the stigma of radicalism.

Another wall separated him from his campaign as the two journals proclaimed to the world the failures of Abernathy to deal with the problems of the Resurrection City specifically and the Poor People's Campaign generally. "King's final enterprise seems close to foundering," *Time* reported, explaining that Abernathy "has bumbled in his efforts to lead the campaign." *Newsweek* was even blunter: "Abernathy & Co." was presiding over a dream-turned-nightmare: "an ill-housed, ill-fed, self-segregated, absentee-run slum afflicted with low morale, deepening restiveness and free-floating violence."[51]

"Abernathy & Co." having botched the job, the implication was that King would have changed things; he had conceived "a model of communal living," which had "fallen into a true-to-life squalor." (That King could have straightened out the mess is doubtful; he was not the sort of executive who could turn to with a fury and bring order out of chaos. Even if he had been, the SCLC lacked the resources and the expertise to run a small city.) Another implication emerged from analyses about the direction the SCLC would take after Solidarity Day. *Newsweek* found that "the campaign's bickersome leadership seemed to have no idea how to end the six-week show short of civil disobedience." The same idea was honed by *Time*: The poor "can now either go home or resort to acts of massive civil disobedience, which Abernathy has long threatened."[52]

If King intended to stop short of civil disobedience, what he put on the record—in a fund-raising letter sent out fewer than seven weeks before his death—indicated otherwise: "We will demand to be heard," he wrote, "and we will stay until America responds. If this means forcible repression of our

50. "'Let No One Be Denied,'" 20; "Solidarity and Disarray," 17; *Southern Courier*, June 22–23, 1968, p. 1.
51. "Solidarity and Disarray," 17. Essentially the same point was made by *Newsweek* in "A Touch of Realism," June 24, 1968, pp. 37–38. See also "'Let No One Be Denied,'" 20–21.
52. "'Let No One Be Denied,'" 20; "Solidarity and Disarray," 17.

movement, we will confront it. . . . If it means jail, we accept it willingly, for the millions of poor already are imprisoned by exploitation and discrimination. We will in this way fashion a confrontation unique in drama but firm in discipline to wrest from government fundamental measures to end the long agony of the hard-core poor."[53] Perhaps this amounted to no more than a pitch calculated to squeeze a few more dollars out of the SCLC's contributors in order to pay for the campaign. Certainly, it might have been wise to regard such bold words skeptically a few years earlier. King had made ringing declarations before and pulled back when he got too near the brink. In the last year or so of his life, however, the once-cautious King was recklessly crowding the edge, excoriating the war, and organizing the radical Poor People's Campaign, and his statements and actions gave no sign that this time he was leaving himself a way out. *He would wrest from the government fundamental measures.*

That grim vision was missing, of course, from the news weeklies. It was absent, even, from *U.S. News*, when King's last campaign began to escalate: "Demonstrations became more militant. Violence erupted. Arrests mounted. Leaders defied the government to oust the poor from their Washington shantytown. The June 19 outpouring of support by fifty thousand people signaled a big change—rather than a quick end—to the weeks-long siege of the federal government." The "new turn" dominated the coverage by *U.S. News*. While *Time* and *Newsweek* had emphasized the events of Solidarity Day, *U.S. News* turned its attention to the demonstrations and the skirmishes between police and protesters. Here seemed to be the "long-threatened" episodes of civil disobedience—"deliberately inviting arrest by blocking the doors of government buildings and lying down in the streets to block rush-hour traffic." And worse might be coming. "Mr. Abernathy declared openly that new tactics were to be employed: 'We will have to engage in what some people call civil disobedience.'"[54] Abernathy said no more than had King. But the most untoward action ascribed by *U.S. News* to King or his family was the refusal of his brother, A. D. King, to pay a restaurant bill. Not even Mrs. King's remarks against the war were reported. Instead, her speech was used to revive memories of her husband's most famous speech and of the 1963 March.

53. King to "SCLC Supporters," February 15, 1968, in Box 6, File 29, Mississippi Valley Collection, Memphis State University.
54. "As the 'Poor Crusade' Takes a New Turn," *U.S. News & World Report*, July 1, 1968, pp. 27, 28.

Abernathy notwithstanding, the campaign was almost over. A few demonstrations were organized after Solidarity Day, but they were tepid affairs. A few score demonstrators were arrested during a protest at the Department of Agriculture on June 20. And Washington police, reacting to reports that a gasoline fire bomb had been hurled at a patrol car early on the morning of June 23, tossed tear gas canisters into Resurrection City while hundreds of men, women, and children were sleeping. Several persons were injured, overcome by gas or trampled as they lay gasping in the pathways. The SCLC had secured an extension of the permit allowing Resurrection City to stay on the federal land until June 23. The day after, almost two thousand policemen surrounded the campsite. A heavily armed riot squad of more than two hundred officers broke down the fence encircling the camp and swept through the area, arresting more than two hundred persons, including some small children, for camping without a license. Government workers later leveled what was left of Resurrection City.[55]

One gambit remained: an attempt to stir up a show of support with a dramatic gesture. Abernathy provoked an arrest and was jailed. Emulating King's example from Albany, Birmingham, and Selma, Abernathy sent out a call, but there was little response. The SCLC began sending home the rest of the demonstrators. At the end, there was a brief flurry of defiance, a hope-against-hope improvisation by the few remaining, who wanted to build a city for poor people. They left as their testament a mimeographed recollection of the scene when Abernathy told them to go home. "People began crying, saying, 'What home?' What did he mean by saying he wasn't going to turn around? What about us who lost everything we owned—our homes in the ghettos of this country, the farm, sharecropping in the Delta? What about us? This was the cry." The hard truth was that it was over. The cries of shock and the dream of a "city of love, freedom, equality, peace, and justice"—"Dr. King's dream," it was called by those defiant few who lingered—would not bring it back.[56] There were two or three attempts to found other Resurrection Cities with the virtues, and none of the vices, of the original. But they

55. See Fager, *Uncertain Resurrection*, 108–10; and *Southern Courier*, June 29–30, 1968, p. 1, and July 6–7, 1968, p. 4.

56. "History of Refugees of Resurrection City, U.S.A., For Human Rights," mimeographed, n.d. [*ca*. July, 1968], in Box 33, File 1, George Wiley Papers, Wisconsin Historical Society, Madison.

vanished, unremembered and unmourned, save, perhaps, by the few for whom the vision remained untarnished by the squalor and crime and quarrels of the original.

What journalists recorded in their first rough draft of history was the undeniable reality of squalor, crime, and bickering. "An ugly, anarchic embarrassment to their cause," *Time* said of Resurrection City, returning to the theme of a crusade that had lost its way, the way of moderation, implicitly the way of King. The SCLC scorned "Bayard Rustin's earlier list of reasonable, attainable goals" and demanded "drastic changes in America's economic system," such as guaranteed income; its leaders refused to push for goals the government could satisfy. "Instead, they snapped at any outstretched administration hand." *Time* noted in passing that other Resurrection Cities might spring up, that one, a handful of tents and tepees in Washington State, had done so. The epilogue was in two parts: Resurrection City's "counterparts may continue to prod the nation's conscience—and occasionally test its patience."[57] *Time*'s patience had long since snapped.

As had *Newsweek*'s, for that matter. Its sympathies were with the demonstrators, so long as they would settle for moderate reform carried out at a moderate pace. No doubt *Newsweek* cherished hopes that the SCLC would return to the way designated by *Newsweek*, the same path it had marked out for King. Washingtonians breathed easier following the closing of Resurrection City; the SCLC was "no less relieved." And *Newsweek* shared the sentiment (if not the precise reasons for it) of Andrew Young of the SCLC: " 'The damned thing . . . just got out of hand. . . . Whoever ran us out did us a great favor.' "[58]

The closing was welcomed by *U.S. News* as the end of "a 'cesspool' which had been taken over by 'thugs and hoodlums' and a place 'from which nothing but further virulence and infection can issue.' " In truth, though, the magazine was more interested in the possibility that the authorities had finally learned the lesson it had taught for years—that only a firm hand would keep society from sliding into anarchy. No longer did King's campaign frighten *U.S. News*. No one was taking seriously the SCLC's threat to stage economic boycotts throughout the nation or the call issued by Abernathy from a jail cell

57. "Balance on Resurrection City," *Time*, July 5, 1968, p. 20.
58. "End of the Dream," *Newsweek*, July 8, 1968, p. 19.

for clergymen to descend upon Washington as they once did for King. To his call, *U.S. News* found, in that terse phrase of dismissal favored by journalists, "no immediate response."[59]

Some questions lingered after the ignominious closing of Resurrection City. If, as *Newsweek* put it, the closing represented the "End of the Dream," or, as *U.S. News* had it, Resurrection City ended as a nightmare, whose dream was it? And whose nightmare?

The nightmare was not King's. None of the three major articles reporting the end of Resurrection City mentioned the man who had conceived it. King appeared in the relatively innocuous role of originator only in an article *U.S. News* reprinted from the *Wall Street Journal*. The article summed up the thrust of what the magazines had stated or implied: King was the leader, Abernathy the blunderer; the dream was King's, the nightmare Abernathy's. The distinction was couched in terms of style and rhetoric, but the article contrasted the two leaders as moderate and radical. "King possessed the ability to cloak his causes in the highest of ethical standards. He could speak of 'freedom' and 'justice' and the 'promised land,' and arouse the idealistic emotions of black and white, rich and poor. Even when he talked tough, he sought a higher level with phrases like 'direct action' and 'confrontation' and 'militant non-violence.'" Similar phrases from Abernathy and his lieutenants seem to be delivered with "more rote than conviction. The real Abernathy mission seems to emerge in threats like 'raising hell,' and 'turning the town upside down,' and 'disrupting the processes of government.'"[60]

Such recognition was late in coming to Abernathy. Except briefly during and after the Montgomery bus boycott, he labored in King's deep and lengthy shadow. That shadow persisted after the assassination. The Poor People's Campaign initially was identified with the martyred prophet, not with his successor; only when things went awry did Abernathy truly become his own man. The goals King established for the campaign were probably unreachable, but King-the-symbol remained untarnished by failure. Perhaps that could be explained as a matter of settling blame on the man who presided over the disaster. But Abernathy proved useful in another way. By showing what Abernathy was, the magazines could demonstrate at the same time what King

59. "Setting a New Course in Meeting Race Violence," *U.S. News & World Report*, July 8, 1968, p. 38.

60. Monroe W. Karmin, "A Crusade Collapses," *U.S. News & World Report*, July 8, 1968, pp. 88–87. This article was continued to the previous page.

was not. The role of pretender implied that Abernathy caused the Poor People's Campaign to lurch off in a direction not chosen by King, when actually the demonstrations were never pressed to the radical point of no return foreseen by King before his death.

What occurred, not only in *U.S. News* but in *Time* and *Newsweek* as well, was a process whereby the symbolic integrity of the prophet was kept whole and the image of King was fixed in time. Not in Chicago, where King had failed and from the rubble of defeat had snatched a radical vision of the poor—black, red, brown, and white—setting forth to visit plague after plague upon the government of the United States. Not in 1967, when he likened the ways his country made war to the ultimate horror of the death camps of the Third Reich. Not in Washington in 1968, when lesser men failed at the radical task he set for them before his death. Not then, but on other days, most of all that summer's day in Washington five years before when so much seemed possible, when that great voice rose, bespeaking an improbable, shimmering dream of justice won and brotherhood realized if only Americans would honor and renew the principles that had made their country great.

The process would not end with the closing of Resurrection City; with an occasional exception it continued through 1968 and beyond. "Year by year," David L. Lewis wrote, "King recedes deeper into the mists of his mountain top . . . [as] in a sense, we have sought to remember him by forgetting him."[61] It was in this sense, of remembering and forgetting, that the news magazines accomplished the symbolic resurrection of Martin Luther King.

61. Lewis, *King: A Biography*, 398.

XII

THE MISTS ON THE MOUNTAINTOP

Perhaps it was inevitable that the concealing mists would swirl
about the figure of the prophet on the mountaintop. Other symbols
far less important to the center than King—Malcolm X, for one—underwent
their own transfigurations during and after the turbulent 1960s. Too much was
at stake for it not to happen in the case of King. He exerted enormous power in
the culture as a symbol, embodying the essential goodness of American
society and reaffirming the consensus about the great principles that ought to
rule it—first by waging nonviolent war on Jim Crow, then by serving as the
symbolic alternative to those who preached revolution or social change that
was too rapid or too drastic, and those who stood against change of almost any
sort at any pace. In the last years of his life, however, King set forth on an
increasingly radical course—leading into Chicago, the anti-war movement,
the Poor People's Campaign—that precipitated a crisis of symbols.

The crisis registered most urgently with *Time*, *Newsweek*, and *U.S. News*
because it was a crisis of the center, and their task was to make sense of the
world for readers drawn from the center. The news magazines, among journalistic institutions, were the definers of the middle class. Their audiences
were middle class, not elite, national rather than local or regional; their
strategies of address undiluted midcult. Freed of the unrelenting tyranny of
the daily deadline, the news magazines engaged in a pseudo-historicity, re-
constituting the world week by week on terms understandable and acceptable

338

to readers who, nuances of ideology aside, resembled each other more than they differed.

Making sense of the world was a daunting task in the 1960s. Everywhere, the center seemed unable to hold; King's defection from the middle way was but one important part of the turmoil, symbolic and otherwise, disrupting American society. Making sense of King the radical required a reconciliation of the crisis of symbols, which the news magazines accomplished even though the essential outline of his radicalism was readily available to them.

U.S. News was a special case among the news weeklies because it had consistently damned King and his cause. On the attack, as in its echo chamber campaign, it struggled against a prevailing definition of him as a voice of reason and moderation. Even *U.S. News* paid tacit tribute, however, to that definition and to King's power as a symbol. It did this by contraposing him on occasion to greater threats in the black movement—a tactic first used in 1959 against the Black Muslims and employed even after King's death when he served the same purpose against the radicals of SNCC. King's assassination changed the magazine's perspective, but not only because he was dead. (The FBI, to take the most obvious example, recognized the power of King as a symbol and continued its attempts to destroy his image even after his death.) It would have been all but impossible for *U.S. News* to resist the definition of King as a reformer after his death. However reactionary its voice, the magazine was bound to the society as constituted by invisible chains of ideology; it sought to preserve the status quo, not alter it. But society had changed and was continuing to change because of what King did as a reformer. The campaigns to win access to public accommodations and to secure the ballot were all but absorbed into the American consensus by the time of King's death; and not merely absorbed but approaching the status of mythic events. More immediately, *U.S. News* could not afford to discard a symbol as powerful as King; it needed that symbol to help foster a vital sense of public order in a society that seemed besieged by radicals of all stripes. Thus, in the face of any number of its own assertions to the contrary, *U.S. News* resurrected King as a prophet of moderation and reason.

No less devoted to public order than to social reform, *Time* and *Newsweek* had found King even more useful over the years as a contrapuntal symbol to an assembly of zealots that came to number Bull Connor and Jim Clark, Adam Clayton Powell and Stokely Carmichael, to mention the more prominent. Nevertheless, King challenged the magazines' capacity to make sense of him and his ways, especially during the campaigns in Birmingham and in Selma. King's determination to create crises cost him their support initially, even though what he set out to do not only was achievable within the consensus but was consonant with it. Because King forced the pace, he took on the coloration of an extremist. Once he got his crises, when the dogs were loosed in Birmingham, when the mounted possemen thundered down on the marchers at the Edmund Pettus Bridge, *Time* and *Newsweek* were forced to reinterpret King. The same process altered symbolically his adversaries Bull Connor and Jim Clark, no longer buffoons but savage racists; it swallowed up and transformed as well Boutwell of Birmingham and the city fathers of Selma, who once represented the way of compromise. Years before King's death, events set in motion by King or others forced reinterpretations scarcely any less striking than his resurrection as a moderate by *Time* and *Newsweek*. Indeed, both magazines, though at different times and with different emphases, urged King to remove himself from struggles, under way or coming, outside the South. In effect, they wished him to become an icon.

In death, King did become an icon. The events of the Memphis garbage strike were critical to the process of making him one. The manner of his death—murdered by a white racist while leading the most downtrodden of blacks in a struggle against the oppressive regime of Henry Loeb—greatly facilitated the symbolic resurrection of King. After King's assassination, *Time* and *Newsweek* created a sense of Selma repeated, of Birmingham relived, by disinterring the villains of the old movement, the most satisfying of which was Bull Connor, and matching them with latter-day villains from the contemporary South. Other adversaries of King's recent past—Daley of Chicago, and Lyndon Johnson, who presided over a war attacked by King in the bitterest of terms—were cast in symbolic roles dissimilar to those of the segregationists; Johnson and Daley, respectively, led the mourning for King and denounced the violence that followed the assassination as besmirching the memory of a prophet of nonviolence.

Similarly, King's highly visible role in the anti-war movement was all but ignored, while his Poor People's Campaign was reduced initially to symbolic insignificance beside a minor strike of municipal employees. King was effectively written out of the picture after the Poor People's Campaign settled onto its disastrous course in the nation's capital. *Time* and *Newsweek* (*U.S. News* as well, with somewhat different motives) separated King from the failure and ensured that his symbolism remained untarnished by the radicalism of Resurrection City. If Resurrection City was but a gleam in King's eye when he was slain, if his lieutenants did what King had not intended and bent his final venture in the direction of civil disobedience, as, respectively, *Newsweek* and *Time* maintained despite the transparent evidence to the contrary, then the symbolic integrity of the prophet could be preserved.

It was fitting, therefore, that King died as he did and where he did, locked in mortal struggle with his foes of old, the white racists of his native South, and not with the larger society, as represented by the national government that was the target of King's most radical and ambitious undertaking. It was fitting that the nation mourn King as its own, the man who had taken honored principles out of the abstract and made them reality in a South sweltering in the heat of oppression. It was fitting that some did not mourn him—Loeb of Memphis, Maddox of Georgia, Wallace of Alabama, all cowed on one occasion or another by the magnificent spectacle of Americans marching for the rights enshrined in the Constitution. It was proper that the radicals and revolutionaries, Carmichael of SNCC above all, be dismissed from the rituals of mourning because they wished to twist the memory of King and make of him something he was not.

And it was important to the American center that all this be done in order to effect the symbolic resurrection of King. Vicariously, its members had witnessed the outrages committed against the black southerner. To King's call, delivered most eloquently at the 1963 March on Washington, the American center had responded, whether in the mundane act of writing contribution checks or letters to congressmen, by marching to Montgomery or watching sons and daughters striding along behind King, or, no less important though less tangible, by confessing their good will for the black man's cause. Their will, translated into law, doomed Jim Crow.

It turned out not to be enough, but that is the nature of the great social movements. One stride along the path gives rise to expectations of still more steps in that direction and down other paths as well. Seeing their lives changed little by the social dramas staged by King in the South, black Americans began to feel keenly the sense of opportunity lost or denied and the sting of injustice more subtle than the thud of a policeman's club. What had been a crusade for simple justice seemed no longer simple, nor so removed from the lives of the middle class. Demonstrations, violence, rioting spilled out of the South and into the rest of the nation, engendering fear, anger, hostility, bewilderment, and any number of other reactions among whites. As blacks continued to push, the driving force behind their movement became increasingly radical or revolutionary rather than reformist. Furthermore, to the black cause were joined a multiplicity of causes, many arising on the nation's campuses where the students seemed bent upon destroying values unquestioned by their elders. In the upheaval of the 1960s, the great middle ground of American society had quite enough with which to contend without the added crisis of a symbol turned on its head.

Thus *Time* and *Newsweek* created a usable past for their readers, resurrecting, in the process, a reassuring symbol taken from simpler times and a simpler quest for justice. Shorn of radicalism, King became the icon he declined to be in life. This done, the centrists could once more honor King as a prophet. By so doing, they could honor America and themselves for what they had done, and for what they thought they had done, to liberate their black countrymen. With his death in Memphis, King became once more a prophet from the South, from another country.

SELECTED BIBLIOGRAPHY

BOOKS AND PAMPHLETS

Adams, Frank. *Unearthing Seeds of Fire: The Idea of Highlander*. Winston-Salem, N.C., 1975.

Adler, Renata. "Mississippi." In *The Civil Rights Reader: Basic Documents of the Civil Rights Movement*, compiled by Leon Friedman. New York, 1967.

Bass, Jack. *Unlikely Heroes*. New York, 1981.

Bayley, Edwin R. *Joe McCarthy and the Press*. New York, 1981.

Belfrage, Sally. *Freedom Summer*. New York, 1965.

Bell, Inge Powell. *CORE and the Strategy of Nonviolence*. New York, 1968.

Bennett, Lerone, Jr. "When the Man and the Hour Are Met." In *Martin Luther King, Jr.: A Profile*, edited by C. Eric Lincoln. New York, 1970.

Bishop, Jim. *The Days of Martin Luther King, Jr*. New York, 1971.

Bradlee, Benjamin C. *Conversations with Kennedy*. New York, 1975.

Branch, Taylor. *Parting the Waters: America in the King Years, 1954–63*. New York, 1988.

Cantor, Norman F. *The Age of Protest: Dissent and Rebellion in the Twentieth Century*. New York, 1969.

Carson, Clayborne. *In Struggle: SNCC and the Black Awakening of the 1960s*. Cambridge, Mass., 1981.

Cleghorn, Reese. "Crowned with Crises." In *Martin Luther King, Jr.: A Profile*, edited by C. Eric Lincoln. New York, 1970.

Colburn, David R. *Racial Change and Community Crisis, St. Augustine, Florida, 1877–1980*. New York, 1985.

Diamond, Edwin. *Good News, Bad News*. Cambridge, Mass., 1978.

Elliott, Osborn. *The World of Oz*. New York, 1980.

Elson, Robert T. *The World of Time Inc.: The Intimate History of a Publishing Enterprise, 1942–1960*. Vol. II. Edited by Duncan Norton-Taylor. New York, 1973.

Erikson, Kai T. *Wayward Puritans: A Study in the Sociology of Deviance*. New York, 1966.

343

Fager, Charles. *Selma, 1965*. New York, 1974.

———. *Uncertain Resurrection: The Poor People's Washington Campaign*. Grand Rapids, Mich., 1969.

Fields, Uriah J. *The Montgomery Story: The Unhappy Effects of the Montgomery Bus Boycott*. New York, 1959.

Foster, Arnold, and Benjamin R. Epstein. *Report on the Ku Klux Klan*. New York, n.d. [*ca*. 1965–66].

Frady, Marshall. *Southerners: A Journalist's Odyssey*. New York, 1980.

———. *Wallace*. New York, 1968.

Frank, Gerold. *An American Death*. Garden City, N.Y., 1972.

Gans, Herbert J. *Deciding What's News*. New York, 1979.

Garrow, David J. *Bearing the Cross: Martin Luther King, Jr., and the Southern Christian Leadership Conference*. New York, 1986.

———. *The FBI and Martin Luther King, Jr.: From "Solo" to Memphis*. New York, 1981.

———. *Protest at Selma: Martin Luther King, Jr., and the Voting Rights Act of 1965*. New Haven, Conn., 1978.

Gitlin, Todd. *The Whole World is Watching: Mass Media in the Making and Unmaking of the New Left*. Berkeley, 1980.

Good, Paul. "No Man Can Fill Dr. King's Shoes—but Abernathy Tries." In *Black Protest in the Sixties*, edited by August Meier and Elliott Rudwick. Chicago, 1970.

Gordon, Bud. *Nightriders: The Inside Story of the Liuzzo Killing*. Birmingham, Ala., 1966.

Gurr, Ted Robert. *Why Men Rebel*. Princeton, 1970.

Halberstam, David. *The Powers That Be*. New York, 1979.

———. "When 'Civil Rights' and 'Peace' Join Forces." In *Martin Luther King, Jr.: A Profile*, edited by C. Eric Lincoln. New York, 1970.

Hall, Stuart. Introduction to *Paper Voices: The Popular Press and Social Change, 1935–1965*, by A. C. H. Smith with Elizabeth Immirzi and Trevor Blackwell. London, 1975.

Heaps, Willard A. *Riots USA, 1765–1970*. Rev. ed. New York, 1970.

Hofstadter, Richard. *The Paranoid Style in American Politics*. New York, 1965.

Jessup, John K., ed. *The Ideas of Henry Luce*. New York, 1969.

Killian, Lewis M. *White Southerners*. New York, 1970.

King, Martin Luther, Jr. *Stride Toward Freedom: The Montgomery Story*. New York, 1958.

King, Martin Luther, Sr., and Clayton Riley. *Daddy King: An Autobiography*. New York, 1980.

Kunstler, William M. *Deep in My Heart*. New York, 1966.

Lawrence, David. *U.S. News & World Report: A Two-Way System of Communication*. New York, 1969.

Lentz, Richard. *Sixty-Five Days in Memphis: A Study of Culture, Symbols, and the Press. Journalism Monographs*, XCVIII (August, 1986).

Lewis, David L. *King: A Biography*. 2nd ed. Urbana, Ill., 1978.

Lincoln, C. Eric. *My Face is Black*. Boston, 1964.

Lomax, Louis E. *The Negro Revolt*. New York, 1962.

———. "When 'Nonviolence' Meets 'Black Power.'" In *Martin Luther King, Jr.: A Profile*, edited by C. Eric Lincoln. New York, 1970.

———. *When the Word is Given*. Cleveland, 1963.

Lord, Walter. *The Past That Would Not Die*. New York, 1965.

McIllwaine, Shields. *Memphis Down in Dixie*. New York, 1949.

Macy, Christy, and Susan Kaplan, comps. *Documents*. New York, 1980.

Mars, Florence. *Witness in Philadelphia*. Baton Rouge, 1977.

Matthews, T. S. *Name and Address*. New York, 1960.

Meier, August. "The Conservative Militant." In *Martin Luther King, Jr.: A Profile*, edited by C. Eric Lincoln. New York, 1970.

Meier, August, and Elliott Rudwick. *CORE: A Study in the Civil Rights Movement, 1942–1968*. Oxford, 1973.

Miller, William D. *Memphis During the Progressive Era, 1900–1917*. Memphis, 1957.

Miller, William Robert. "The Broadening Horizons: Montgomery, America, the World." In *Martin Luther King, Jr.: A Profile*, edited by C. Eric Lincoln. New York, 1970.

Morgan, Charles, Jr. *One Man, One Voice*. New York, 1979.

———. *A Time to Speak*. New York, 1964.

Morris, Aldon D. *The Origins of the Civil Rights Movement: Black Communities Organizing for Change*. New York, 1984.

Muse, Benjamin. *Memphis*. Atlanta, 1964.

Myrdal, Gunnar. *An American Dilemma: The Negro Problem and Modern Democracy*. New York, 1944.

New York Times Biographical Edition. New York, 1973.

Oates, Stephen B. *Let the Trumpet Sound: The Life of Martin Luther King, Jr*. New York, 1982.

Peterson, Theodore. *Magazines in the Twentieth Century*. Rev. ed. Urbana, Ill., 1958.

Prendergast, Curtis, with Geoffrey Colvin. *The World of Time Inc.: The Intimate History of a Changing Enterprise, 1960–1980*, Vol. III. Edited by Robert Lubar. New York, 1986.

Race Relations in the U.S.A., 1954–1968. Keesing's Research Report, No. 4. New York, 1970.

Raines, Howell. *My Soul is Rested: Movement Days in the Deep South Remembered*. New York, 1978.

Roberts, Chalmers M. *The Washington Post: The First 100 Years*. Boston, 1977.

Roshco, Bernard. *Newsmaking*. Chicago, 1975.

Rosten, Leo C. *The Washington Correspondents.* 1937; rpr. New York, 1974.

Rowan, Carl T. "The Consequences of Decision." In *Martin Luther King, Jr.: A Profile,* edited by C. Eric Lincoln. New York, 1970.

Southern Christian Leadership Conference. *Does Martin Luther King, Jr., Have the Right? The Qualifications? The Duty? to Speak Out on Peace.* Atlanta, n.d. [*ca.* April–May, 1967].

Speeches by the Rev. Dr. Martin Luther King, Jr., About the War in Vietnam. New York, n.d.

Swanberg, W. A. *Luce and His Empire.* New York, 1972.

Van Zuilen, A. J. *The Life Cycle of Magazines: A Historical Study of the Decline and Fall of the General Interest Mass Audience Magazine in the United States During the Period 1946–1972.* Uithoorn, Netherlands, [1977].

Viorst, Milton. *Fire in the Streets: America in the 1960s.* New York, 1979.

Waskow, Arthur I. *From Race Riot to Sit-in, 1919 and the 1960s: A Study in the Connections Between Conflict and Violence.* Garden City, N.Y., 1966.

Watters, Pat. *Encounter with the Future.* Atlanta, 1965.

Wiebe, Robert H. *The Segmented Society: An Introduction to the Meaning of America.* Oxford, 1975.

Wills, Garry. *The Second Civil War: Arming for Armageddon.* New York, 1968.

Wise, David. *The American Police State: The Government Against the People.* New York, 1976.

Wofford, Harris. *Of Kennedys and Kings: Making Sense of the Sixties.* New York, 1980.

Wood, James Playsted. *Magazines in the United States.* 3rd ed. New York, 1971.

Woodward, C. Vann. *Origins of the New South, 1877–1913.* Baton Rouge, 1951.

Yglesias, Jose. "Dr. King's March on Washington, Part II." In *Black Protest in the Sixties,* edited by August Meier and Elliott Rudwick. Chicago, 1970. Originally published in *New York Times Magazine,* March 31, 1968.

Zinn, Howard. *Albany: A Study in National Responsibility.* Atlanta, 1962.

———. *SNCC: The New Abolitionists.* Boston, 1964.

PERIODICALS

Bagdikian, Ben H. "The Newsmagazines: I—*U.S. News & World Report.*" *New Republic,* February 2, 1959, pp. 11–16.

Danzig, David. "The Meaning of Negro Strategy." *Commentary,* XXXVII (February, 1964), 41–46.

"Dr. King and the Paris Press." *America,* November 13, 1965, p. 560.

Epstein, Joseph. "Henry Luce and His Time." *Commentary,* XLIV (November, 1967), 35–47.

Fager, Charles E. "Dilemma for Dr. King." *Christian Century,* XVI (March 16, 1966), pp. 331–32.

Friedrich, Otto. "There Are oo Trees in Russia: The Function of Facts in Newsmagazines." *Harper's Magazine,* CCXXIX (October, 1964), 59–65.

Gastil, Raymond D. "Homicide and a Regional Culture of Violence." *American Sociological Review*, XXXVI (June, 1971), 412–27.

Good, Paul. "Chicago Summer: Bossism, Racism, and Dr. King." *Nation*, September 19, 1966, pp. 237–42.

Holloway, Harry. "Negro Political Strategy: Coalition or Independent Power Politics?" *Social Science Quarterly*, XLIX (1968), 534–47.

Kemler, Edgar. "The Lawrence Riddle: The Man or the Times?" *Nation*, March 19, 1955, pp. 234–37.

King, Martin Luther, Jr. "A Testament of Hope." *Playboy*, XVI (January, 1969), 174–75, 194, 232–36.

Kopkind, Andrew. "Serving Time." *New York Review of Books*, September 12, 1968, pp. 23–28.

Lawson, James. "The Meredith March . . . And Tomorrow." *Concern*, July 15, 1966, pp. 1–5.

McGraw, James R. "An Interview with Andrew J. Young." *Christianity and Crisis*, January 22, 1968, pp. 1–6.

"Man of the Year." *Nation*, January 13, 1964, pp. 41–42.

Massie, Robert K. "Don't Tread on Grandmother Peabody." *Saturday Evening Post*, May 16, 1964, pp. 74, 76.

Mayer, Martin. "The Lady as Publisher." *Harper's Magazine*, CCXXXVII (December, 1968), 90–100.

Meier, August, and Elliott Rudwick. "The Boycott Movement Against Jim Crow Streetcars in the South, 1900–1906." *Journal of American History*, LV (1969), 756–75.

"A New Sense of Direction." *Drum Major*, I (August, 1971), 5, 8–9.

Newsweek, various articles, 1956–68. See separate listing below.

"Playboy Interview: Malcolm X." *Playboy*, X (May, 1963), 53–63.

Smith, Donald H. "Martin Luther King, Jr.: In the Beginning at Montgomery." *Southern Speech Journal*, XXXIV (Fall, 1968), 8–17.

Time, various articles, 1956–68. See separate listing below.

Trillin, Calvin. "U.S. Journal: Resurrection City." *New Yorker*, June 15, 1968, pp. 71–80.

Tuchman, Gaye. "Objectivity as Strategic Ritual: An Examination of Newsmen's Notions of Objectivity." *American Journal of Sociology*, LXXVII (1972), 660–79.

U.S. News & World Report, various articles, 1956–68. See separate listing below.

Watters, Pat. "The American Middle Ground in St. Augustine." *New South*, XIX (September, 1964), 3–20.

———. "Beale Street and Points North: Memphis Is Also America." *Nation*, April 22, 1968, pp. 529–31.

Welles, Chris. "*Newsweek* (a Fact) Is the New Hot Book (an Opinion)." *Esquire*, LXXII (November, 1969), 152–54, 242–48.

Yoakum, Robert. "Drew Pearson and Jack Anderson and Martin Luther King and

Robert Kennedy and . . ." *Columbia Journalism Review*, VII (Summer, 1968), 18–19.

Young, Andrew J. "And Birmingham." *Drum Major*, I (Winter, 1971), 21–27.

Newsweek

"Acid Test." June 29, 1964, pp. 26–27.

"Alabama . . . Why Race Relations Could Grow Even Worse." March 5, 1956, pp. 24–26.

"Albany Revisited." January 7, 1963, p. 18.

"An American Tragedy." March 22, 1965, pp. 18–21.

"An American Tragedy, 1967—Detroit." August 7, 1967, pp. 18–20, 25–26.

"As the South Turns the Corner on Integration." September 18, 1961, pp. 71–73.

"Back in Circulation." January 22, 1968, p. 28.

"A Barrier Falls: The U.S. Negro Moves to Vote." August 16, 1965, pp. 15–16.

"Battle of Conscience." November 15, 1965, p. 78.

"Battle of Credentials." September 7, 1964, pp. 26–27.

"Bid for the Jackpot." June 24, 1957, p. 30.

"Big Day—End and a Beginning." September 9, 1963, pp. 19–22.

"The Big Man is Martin Luther King, Jr." July 29, 1963, pp. 30–32.

"Birmingham: 'My God, You're Not Even Safe in Church.'" September 30, 1963, pp. 20–23.

"Birmingham, U.S.A.: 'Look at Them Run.'" May 13, 1963, pp. 27–28.

"Birmingham's Choice." May 27, 1963, pp. 26–27.

"Black Breakthrough." October 16, 1967, pp. 30, 35.

"Black Eye." February 8, 1965, p. 24.

"'Black Power!'" June 27, 1966, p. 36.

"'Black Power': Politics of Frustration." July 11, 1966, pp. 26, 31–32.

"Black Power: Road to Disaster?" August 22, 1966, pp. 32, 34, 36.

"Black Power Summit." July 31, 1967, pp. 19–20.

"Boycott in Birmingham, Ala., Time to Sit Down and Talk." May 14, 1962, pp. 28–29.

"Brown Power." March 25, 1968, p. 37.

"The Bull and the Dogs." May 6, 1968, p. 20.

"The 'Bull' at Bay." April 15, 1963, pp. 29–30.

"By the Book." March 1, 1965, pp. 34, 37.

"'Calculated Risk.'" August 10, 1964, pp. 26–28.

"Changing Order." June 3, 1963, pp. 19–20.

"Chip Off the Chippendale." April 26, 1965, pp. 28–29.

"Churning Conflict." March 18, 1957, pp. 35–36.

"Cleveland and Gary." November 20, 1967, pp. 66–67.

"Close to Home." May 16, 1966, p. 35.

"Colorful Campaign." October 17, 1966, pp. 29–30.

"Connor and King." April 22, 1963, pp. 28, 33.

"Courting Trouble." June 10, 1968, p. 30.

Crawford, Kenneth. "Let the Negro Do It." May 8, 1967, p. 46.

————. "The Non-Debate." April 17, 1967, p. 46.

————. "Right to Vote." March 1, 1965, p. 39.

"Crusade Against Gringos." January 3, 1966, pp. 17–18.

"A Cry of Foul at the Fair." May 4, 1964, pp. 20–21.

"Days of Violence in the South." May 29, 1961, pp. 21–22.

"The Deacons." August 2, 1965, pp. 28–29.

"The Deacons Go North." May 2, 1966, pp. 20–21.

"Death of a Desperado." March 8, 1965, pp. 24–25.

"The Defenders." July 1, 1968, p. 30.

"The Demonstrators: Why? How Many?" November 1, 1965, pp. 25–26, 31–32, 34.

"Disarray in the Ranks." June 17, 1968, pp. 48, 53.

"'Discrimination' in Chicago." October 11, 1965, p. 94.

"Dissenters: Rebels with Many Causes." July 10, 1967, pp. 29–30, 33.

"'Do or Die.'" May 6, 1968, pp. 30–31.

"DP's in the Delta." February 14, 1966, pp. 28, 30.

"'A Dream . . . I Have a Dream.'" September 9, 1963, p. 21.

"An End and a Beginning." June 24, 1963, pp. 29–34.

"End of the Dream." July 8, 1968, p. 19.

"Equality Defined." July 3, 1967, p. 30.

"Explosion in Alabama." May 20, 1963, pp. 25–27.

"Films from Uncle Sam." April 18, 1966, pp. 109–10.

"Fire and Frustration." August 27, 1962, pp. 25–26.

"First Things First." September 11, 1967, p. 24.

"Flashpoint in Watts." May 30, 1966, pp. 30, 33.

"Focus on Washington." June 3, 1963, p. 19.

"Forced March." February 22, 1965, pp. 24, 29.

"Freedom Riders Force a Test . . . State Laws or U.S. Law in Segregated South?"
    June 5, 1961, pp. 18–20, 22.

"'Full-Scale Assault.'" February 29, 1960, pp. 24–25.

"The Gadfly of the Poverty War." September 13, 1965, pp. 30–32.

"Gamble in the Ghetto." January 31, 1966, pp. 24–25.

"Georgia Whodunit." July 23, 1962, pp. 18–19.

"The Great Society—in Uniform." August 22, 1966, pp. 46, 48.

"Growl of the Panther." May 30, 1966, pp. 33, 36.

Harris, Louis. "The 'Backlash' Issue." July 13, 1964, pp. 24, 27.

"Helping Hands." June 28, 1965, p. 24.

"Holy Days and the Atom." April 30, 1962, pp. 21–22.

"The Home-Front War." May 8, 1967, pp. 31–36.

"Homesick in Freedomland." February 13, 1967, pp. 37–38.

"The Hoover-King Meeting." December 14, 1964, pp. 22, 24.

"Hot and Cool." April 22, 1968, pp. 24–26.

"Hotter Fires." July 1, 1963, pp. 19–21.
"How Much of the Way with LBJ?" September 26, 1966, pp. 25–28, 30.
"How Negroes Rank Their Leaders." August 22, 1966, p. 34.
"How the World Press Viewed the Days of Tension." June 5, 1961, p. 22.
Hughes, Emmet John. "A Curse of Confusion." May 1, 1967, p. 17.
"'I Like the Word Black.'" May 6, 1963, pp. 27–28.
"Impact and Anger." March 22, 1965, pp. 21–22.
"Incident in Harlem." September 29, 1958, p. 24.
"The Indignant Ones." July 16, 1962, pp. 22, 25.
"Integration Under Fire." January 7, 1957, pp. 18–19.
"Invasion of the South." April 2, 1956, p. 86.
"'It May Be a Bell Tolling for Me.'" April 22, 1968, pp. 23–24.
"'I've Been to the Mountaintop.'" April 15, 1968, p. 38.
"J. Edgar Hoover and the FBI." December 7, 1964, pp. 21–26.
"Judgment on a Judge." July 26, 1965, pp. 30–31.
"'Keep Walking.'" August 13, 1962, pp. 17–18.
"Kennedy and Baldwin: The Gulf." June 3, 1963, p. 19.
"'King is the Man, Oh Lord.'" April 15, 1968, pp. 34–38.
"King's Last March: 'We Lost Somebody.'" April 22, 1968, pp. 26–31.
"King's Targets." June 22, 1964, pp. 26, 29.
"Kiss and Tell." May 10, 1965, p. 40.
"Larger Battleground." January 10, 1966, pp. 22–23.
"LBJ: Rights are Not Enough." June 14, 1965, pp. 36–37.
"LBJ's Supporters: Varying Plumage." July 10, 1967, pp. 22–24.
"Leaning on HEW." October 18, 1965, p. 98.
"'Let No One Be Denied.'" July 1, 1968, pp. 20–21.
"Line in the Dust." July 18, 1966, pp. 23–24.
Lippmann, Walter. "The Racial Crisis." May 27, 1963, p. 23.
"Long Day." April 6, 1964, pp. 20–22.
"The Longest, Hottest Summer." August 22, 1966, p. 57.
"'Long Live the King.'" April 2, 1956, p. 26.
"Lord of the Doves." April 17, 1967, pp. 44, 46.
"Los Angeles: The Fire This Time." August 23, 1965, pp. 15–17.
"Malcolm's Brand X." March 23, 1964, p. 32.
"The Man from SNCC." May 22, 1967, p. 45.
"Marching Shoes." July 30, 1962, pp. 15–16.
"The March—in Step and Out." July 4, 1966, pp. 14–16.
"The March Meredith Began." June 20, 1966, pp. 27–31.
"Memphis: An Ugly New Portent." April 8, 1968, pp. 33–34.
"The Mess in Memphis." April 22, 1968, p. 33.
"Mr. Justice Marshall." June 26, 1967, pp. 34–36.
"Moderate vs. Militant." June 13, 1966, p. 38.
Moley, Raymond. "Pattern of Revolution." August 8, 1966, p. 84.

"Mopping Up." August 30, 1965, pp. 14–16.

"The Negro Family: Visceral Reaction." December 6, 1965, pp. 38–40.

"The Negro in America." July 29, 1963, pp. 15–17.

"The Negro in America—1965." February 15, 1965, pp. 24–27.

"The Negro View: A Special Anguish." July 10, 1967, pp. 34, 36.

"A New Breed—The Militant Negro in the South." June 5, 1961, p. 21.

"New Crisis: The Negro Family." August 9, 1965, pp. 32, 34–35.

"New Look on the Left: Solidarity Forever?" May 24, 1965, pp. 29–32.

"News and Newsmakers." July 10, 1967, p. 92.

"Newsmakers." May 27, 1968, p. 56.

"Newsmakers." June 24, 1968, p. 59.

"New Wave." February 10, 1964, pp. 24, 27.

"New York, N.Y." July 22, 1963, pp. 22–23.

"Next for the South?" March 28, 1960, pp. 25–26.

"No Bang or Whimper." October 16, 1961, p. 29.

"Nobleman King." October 26, 1964, p. 77.

"No Man's Land." July 6, 1964, pp. 16–17.

"Not Since Dallas . . . ." April 15, 1968, pp. 91–92.

"Now—'The Era of Complexities.'" February 15, 1965, pp. 27–28.

"Off Hoover's Chest." November 30, 1964, pp. 29–30.

"$107 Misunderstanding." April 19, 1965, p. 27.

"One War at a Time." July 19, 1965, pp. 22, 25.

"On the March." September 2, 1963, pp. 17–18, 20–21.

"On to Montgomery." March 29, 1965, pp. 21–22.

"Opening a Second Front." November 8, 1965, pp. 33–34.

"The Other Side." June 10, 1963, pp. 29–30.

"Panther on the Prowl." February 7, 1966, pp. 20–21.

"'Peaceably to Assemble and Petition, . . .'" September 2, 1963, p. 19.

"The Peace Marchers." April 24, 1967, pp. 27–28.

"The Periscope." September 6, 1965, p. 9.

"The Periscope." September 27, 1965, p. 20.

"The Periscope." November 29, 1965, p. 15.

"The Periscope." March 27, 1967, p. 21.

"The Periscope." December 11, 1967, p. 20.

"The Periscope." February 19, 1968, p. 17.

"The Periscope." April 22, 1968, p. 19.

"The Periscope." May 27, 1968, p. 19.

"Prayers and Brickbats." August 6, 1962, p. 19.

"Price of Victory." April 29, 1968, p. 22.

"The Prophetic Ministry?" August 20, 1962, pp. 78–79.

"Reading the Riot Act." April 29, 1968, p. 22.

"Rendezvous with History." February 19, 1968, pp. 23–24.

"Reveille in Washington." July 1, 1963, pp. 17–18.

"The Right to a Job." August 5, 1963, pp. 51–52.

"Road From Selma: Hope—and Death." April 5, 1965, pp. 23–27.

"Rough Trip by Bus." November 26, 1956, p. 49.

"Satan in the Ghetto." November 15, 1965, pp. 130, 132.

"Search for a New Selma." December 20, 1965, pp. 29–30.

"'Secret' Crisis in the Delta." March 7, 1966, pp. 28–29.

"Segregation in the North." September 20, 1965, pp. 56, 58.

"Selma, Civil Rights, and the Church Militant." March 29, 1965, pp. 75–76, 78.

"Selma Revisited." April 25, 1966, pp. 25–26.

"Shades of Bull Connor." February 1, 1965, pp. 21, 22.

"'. . . Shall Now Also be Equal . . .'" July 13, 1964, pp. 17–18.

"Showdown in the Delta." June 6, 1966, p. 67.

"Signs of Erosion." April 10, 1967, p. 32.

"Silent March." February 19, 1968, p. 58.

"SNCC and the Jews." August 28, 1967, p. 22.

"SNCC's 'Dissent.'" January 17, 1966, p. 26.

"The Southern Negro: Two Generations." March 5, 1956, p. 25.

"The Starry Heavens—the Moral Law." March 29, 1965, pp. 19–20.

"Summer Strategy." April 12, 1965, pp. 28, 29.

"Summertime." June 27, 1966, p. 60.

"Surveying Summer '68." March 11, 1968, pp. 44–46.

"'Take Everything You Need, Baby.'" April 15, 1968, pp. 31–34.

"Taking a Gamble." November 7, 1960, p. 36.

"A Talk With the Lord." May 20, 1968, p. 45.

"Tension and Justice." June 12, 1961, pp. 37–38.

"'Testimonial of Love.'" February 15, 1960, p. 90.

"That Summer." May 31, 1965, p. 22.

"Thinking Black." November 20, 1967, pp. 37–41.

"Thunder on the Far Right: Fear and Frustration . . . Rouse Extremists to Action Across the Land." December 4, 1961, pp. 18–20, 22, 27–28, 30.

"Tijerina Brass." June 19, 1967, pp. 37–38.

"Time Runs Out for Big Ben." June 7, 1965, p. 52.

"Top of the Week." March 29, 1965, p. 11.

"'To the Sound of a Different Drum.'" April 27, 1964, pp. 25–26.

"The Touchiest Target." August 15, 1966, p. 29.

"A Touch of Realism." June 24, 1968, pp. 37–38.

"Tough Years Ahead." August 30, 1965, pp. 19–20.

"Trouble, Trouble." September 10, 1962, p. 47.

"Two-Time Loser." January 24, 1966, pp. 26–29.

"Unanswered Questions." June 24, 1968, pp. 32, 37.

"Understanding Violence." June 17, 1968, pp. 43–46.

"Up from Montgomery." December 21, 1964, pp. 40–41.

"U.S. Latins on the March." May 23, 1966, pp. 32–36.

"The U.S.—The Issue and a Showdown." September 15, 1958, pp. 26–28.

"Victory in the North." September 5, 1966, pp. 20–21.

"Vigilantes and Visigoths." February 26, 1968, p. 26.

"The Wall." January 14, 1963, pp. 26–27.

"Washington's Racial Jitters." June 3, 1968, p. 27.

"Waving the Red Flag." April 12, 1965, pp. 30–31.

"The Weaver Case: Negro Views." March 5, 1962, p. 27.

"'We're on Our Way.'" May 13, 1968, pp. 32–33.

"West Side Story." July 25, 1966, pp. 17–18.

"'What Can You Do for Us?'" June 3, 1968, pp. 22–27.

"What Must Be Done." November 20, 1967, pp. 33–37.

"What's Ahead for the Negro." November 28, 1966, pp. 30–31.

"Where Are They Now?" March 29, 1965, p. 14.

"Where is James Earl Ray?" April 29, 1968, pp. 21–22.

"Which Way for the Negro?" May 15, 1967, pp. 27–28, 30, 33–34.

"White Consensus: 'They're Trying to Go Too Fast.'" August 22, 1966, pp. 24–26.

"'White Jesus.'" July 25, 1966, p. 29.

"The White Sit-ins." April 29, 1963, pp. 26, 29.

"Whitney Young, Power Player." May 15, 1967, pp. 28–29.

"Who Won What?" January 1, 1962, pp. 13–14.

"Worried Leaders." July 15, 1963, pp. 19–20.

"'You're Such a Brave Lady . . . !'" April 22, 1968, p. 32.

Time

"Accident in Harlem." September 29, 1958, p. 14.

"Act of Belief." September 7, 1962, p. 45.

"Ahead of Its Time." September 30, 1966, pp. 20–21.

"The Aim: Registration." January 29, 1965, pp. 20–21.

"Another Kind of Fighter." August 18, 1967, p. 22.

"Arrested at Last." June 14, 1968, p. 23.

"The Assassination." April 12, 1968, pp. 18–19.

"The Assassination According to Capote." May 10, 1968, p. 65.

"Attack on the Conscience." February 18, 1957, pp. 17–20.

"At the Breaking Point." July 15, 1966, pp. 15–16.

"Avenging What's-His-Name." April 19, 1968, p. 16.

"'The Awful Roar.'" August 30, 1963, pp. 9–14.

"The Backlash." April 24, 1964, pp. 17–18.

"Back With Humility." November 26, 1956, p. 20.

"Balance on Resurrection City." July 5, 1968, p. 20.

"The Banners of Dissent." October 27, 1967, pp. 23–29.

"Battle of Roosevelt Road." July 22, 1966, pp. 18–19.

"Beginning of a Dream." September 6, 1963, pp. 14–15.

"The Benevolent Dictator." September 3, 1965, p. 71.

"Beyond the Ears of the Greys." August 2, 1963, p. 14.
"Big Jim's Comeuppance." June 3, 1966, p. 19.
"Birmingham Revisited." November 10, 1967, pp. 28–29.
"Black Pocketbook Power." March 1, 1968, p. 17.
"Black Power and Black Pride." December 1, 1967, pp. 20–21.
"Black Power in the Red." July 8, 1966, p. 21.
"Black Separatist." June 21, 1968, p. 24.
"Br'er Fox." June 24, 1966, p. 31.
"Brushfire." March 14, 1960, p. 21.
"The Central Point." March 19, 1965, pp. 23–28.
"César's War." March 22, 1968, p. 23.
"Challenge in Alabama." March 18, 1966, p. 29A.
"Challenging the Pharaoh." May 17, 1968, p. 35.
"Chaos on the Left." September 15, 1967, p. 23.
"Chilling Shift." June 10, 1966, pp. 35–36.
"The Churches' Influence on Secular Society." April 21, 1967, pp. 26–27.
"City of New Hope." May 3, 1968, pp. 22–23.
"City on Trial." March 5, 1956, p. 21.
"Complicated Hospitality." February 22, 1960, p. 20.
"Confused Crusade." January 12, 1962, p. 15.
"Confusing the Cause." July 16, 1965, p. 20.
"The Continuing Confrontation." April 9, 1965, pp. 23–25.
"Cooling the Controversy." December 11, 1964, p. 30.
"A Corner Turned." May 13, 1966, pp. 23–24.
"Court v. King." June 23, 1967, p. 20.
"Covering St. Augustine." July 10, 1964, p. 75.
"Crisis in Civil Rights." June 2, 1961, pp. 14–18.
"Crossing the Red Sea." September 2, 1966, p. 19.
"The Crucible." January 26, 1968, pp. 11–12.
"The Cynical Idealists of '68." June 7, 1968, pp. 78–83.
"The Dangers of Militancy." July 19, 1963, p. 17.
"Death and Transfiguration." March 5, 1965, pp. 23–25.
"Democracy in the Foxhole." May 26, 1967, pp. 15–19.
"Difference of Impact." February 19, 1965, p. 23.
"The Dilemma of Dissent." April 21, 1967, pp. 20–22.
"The Divided Negro Vote." April 29, 1966, p. 30.
"Dogs, Kids, and Clubs." May 10, 1963, p. 19.
"Double-Edged Blade." January 16, 1956, p. 20.
"Electric Charges." March 26, 1965, pp. 19–20.
"End of the Road?" August 25, 1967, p. 18.
"Eulogy for a Woodchopper." March 12, 1965, p. 23B.
"The Faith of Soul and Slavery." April 19, 1968, p. 70.
"The Flop." May 1, 1964, pp. 22–23.

"Freedom—Now." May 17, 1963, pp. 23–25.

"Freeze and Thaw." March 28, 1960, pp. 24–25.

"From Toehold to Foothold." November 18, 1966, pp. 29–30.

"Go Ahead and Say It." March 20, 1964, p. 78.

"'A Great Ride.'" December 31, 1956, p. 10.

"'Hate is Always Tragic': Martin Luther King's Challenge." August 3, 1962, p. 13.

"Heat on Highway 51." June 17, 1966, pp. 26–27.

"Herald of the Dream." October 7, 1966, pp. 36–37.

"Hot and Dry." June 18, 1965, p. 26.

"An Hour of Need." April 12, 1968, p. 17.

"How Not to Have Anything." May 4, 1962, p. 24.

"How to Change Laws You Don't Like." July 17, 1964, p. 63.

"Hurt Pride in Memphis." April 26, 1968, p. 44.

"'In Changing Times.'" August 10, 1962, p. 14.

"Indignation in the North." March 19, 1965, p. 71.

"The Inexorable Process." June 14, 1963, pp. 23–24.

"Inside Snick." April 30, 1965, pp. 73–74.

"Insurrection City." June 14, 1968, pp. 24–25.

"Interpreter in the Front Line." May 12, 1967, pp. 72–74, 77–78.

"Intruders in the Dust." September 23, 1966, p. 26.

"The James Gang Rides Again." October 13, 1967, p. 31.

"The Jungle and the City." July 29, 1966, pp. 11–12.

"Kickbacks." January 7, 1957, p. 15.

"King Moves North." April 30, 1965, pp. 32–33.

"King's Last March." April 19, 1968, pp. 18–19.

"The Law and De Lawd." November 5, 1965, p. 38.

"A Legal History of Negro Progress." June 21, 1963, p. 15.

"Let George Do It." May 13, 1966, p. 24.

"Letter From a Birmingham Jail." January 3, 1964, p. 15.

"A Lincoln Man." February 21, 1964, p. 76.

"The Long March." June 21, 1963, pp. 13–17.

"Man of the Year: Never Again Where He Was." January 3, 1964, pp. 13–16, 25–27.

"The March's Meaning." September 6, 1963, pp. 13–14.

"A Marriage of Enlightenment." September 29, 1967, pp. 28–31.

"'A Meeting of History and Fate.'" March 26, 1965, pp. 20–22.

"Memphis: Pre-Summer Blues." March 15, 1968, pp. 19–20.

"Memphis Blues." April 5, 1968, p. 25.

"Mind Over Mayhem." June 23, 1967, pp. 19–20.

"Mr. Smitherman Goes to Washington." April 16, 1965, p. 26.

"The Moderates' Predicament." April 19, 1968, p. 19.

"The Morning After." November 3, 1967, p. 17.

"Mud in the House." May 7, 1965, p. 27.

"The Nashville Lesson." May 26, 1961, p. 17.

"A Nation Within a Nation." May 17, 1968, pp. 24–32.

"The Negro After Watts." August 27, 1965, pp. 16–17.

"The Negro's New Force." November 12, 1965, pp. 33–34.

"The New Racism." July 1, 1966, pp. 11–13.

"New Sounds in a Courthouse." April 2, 1956, p. 24.

"New Wave of Challengers." December 3, 1965, pp. 66, 68.

"Night of Terror." January 21, 1957, p. 15.

"'No Immunity.'" August 13, 1965, pp. 15–15A.

"Off and On." January 26, 1968, p. 17.

"Off the Chest and Into the Fire." November 27, 1964, p. 31.

"One Word Too Many." January 21, 1966, p. 20.

"On the Avenue." April 23, 1965, p. 73.

"On the Brink in Memphis." August 16, 1968, p. 23.

"On the Difficulty of Being a Contemporary Hero." June 24, 1966, pp. 32–33.

"The Other Ninety-Seven Percent." August 11, 1967, pp. 12–17.

"People." May 27, 1957, p. 40.

"People." June 6, 1960, p. 38.

"People." February 7, 1964, p. 44.

"People." May 15, 1964, p. 50.

"People." December 25, 1964, p. 29.

"People." February 25, 1966, p. 42.

"People." October 13, 1967, p. 42.

"Personalities of 1956: Stars in Their Own Orbits." January 7, 1957, p. 24.

"Pharaoh's Lesson." September 9, 1966, p. 22.

"Poorly Timed Protest." April 19, 1963, pp. 30–31.

"Posthumous Victory." April 26, 1968, p. 19.

"The President's Package." June 28, 1963, pp. 14–15.

"Promise Denied." June 9, 1967, p. 34.

"Protest on Route 80." April 2, 1965, pp. 21–22.

"A Question of Priorities." September 8, 1967, pp. 13–14.

"Race and Realism." July 5, 1963, pp. 77–78.

"Ralph Abernathy: Out of the Shadow." May 31, 1968, p. 15.

"Rampage and Restraint." April 19, 1968, pp. 15–17.

"Rare Tribute." February 5, 1965, p. 24.

"Ray's Odd Odyssey." June 21, 1968, pp. 22–23.

"The Real Black Power." November 17, 1967, pp. 23–27.

"Recipe for Riot." June 30, 1967, pp. 20–21.

"Reckoning in Meridian." October 27, 1967, pp. 32–33.

"Render Unto King." March 25, 1966, pp. 18–19.

"The Resounding Cry." May 24, 1963, p. 22.

"The Revolution." June 7, 1963, pp. 17–19.

"The Right to Dissent and the Duty to Answer." May 12, 1967, p. 23.

"Riot Toll: 1967 and Before." August 11, 1967, p. 11.

"Round Three." May 6, 1966, p. 24.

"The Scene at ZIP Code 20013." May 24, 1968, pp. 28–30.

Shepley, James R. "A Letter from the Publisher." April 12, 1968, p. 15.

"Should Looters Be Shot?" April 26, 1968, p. 18.

"Solidarity and Disarray." June 28, 1968, pp. 17–18.

"Soul Brother Humphrey." May 10, 1968, pp. 28–29.

"Spreading Fire." July 28, 1967, pp. 9–10.

"Stokely's Spark." September 16, 1966, p. 37.

"Studying the Study." March 15, 1968, pp. 16–17.

"Sunday School Bombing." September 27, 1963, p. 17.

"Swift Deliverance." November 7, 1960, p. 30.

"The Talk is Race." August 7, 1964, pp. 17–18.

"Tell It Not in Gath." April 23, 1956, pp. 62–63.

"The Temper of the Times." April 14, 1967, pp. 27–33.

"They Came to Mourn." April 19, 1968, a photographic essay.

"Thinking Big." May 27, 1966, p. 22.

"This Time, Things Changed." July 10, 1964, p. 27.

"A Time of Violence and Tragedy." August 4, 1967, pp. 12–13.

"To Fulfill a Historic Role." July 19, 1963, pp. 18–19.

"Transcendent Symbol." April 12, 1968, pp. 19–21.

"Trigger of Hate." August 20, 1965, pp. 13–19.

"Trouble in Alabama." May 26, 1961, pp. 16–17.

"Trying to Paper It Over." September 4, 1964, pp. 31–32.

"Turmoil in Shantytown." June 7, 1968, p. 28.

"The Turning Point." October 7, 1966, pp. 29–30.

"Two for the Accused." June 28, 1968, p. 39.

"Two Perspectives—One Goal." December 18, 1964, pp. 21–22.

"A Universal Effort." May 2, 1960, p. 16.

"Various Forms of Embezzlement." July 16, 1965, p. 20.

"Victory in Jail." February 12, 1965, pp. 16–17.

"The Vietniks: Self-Defeating Dissent." October 29, 1965, pp. 44, 45.

"Vindicative Victory." October 13, 1967, p. 29.

"Violence and History." April 19, 1968, pp. 44–45.

"Visions of the Promised Land." April 12, 1968, p. 20.

"Waiting for Miracles." August 3, 1962, pp. 12–13.

"What a Year!" August 30, 1968, pp. 20–21.

"What Can I Do?" May 17, 1968, pp. 36–37.

"What the Negro Has—and Has Not—Gained." October 28, 1966, pp. 32–33.

"What Next?" August 11, 1967, pp. 11–12.

"Where the Stars Fall." September 27, 1963, pp. 17–21.

"Who Killed King?" April 26, 1968, pp. 20–21.

"With George and Sam on Capitol Hill." July 26, 1963, pp. 11–12.

"The Worker's Rights and the Public Weal." March 1, 1968, pp. 34–35.

"The Youngest Ever." October 23, 1964, p. 27.
"'Your Future Depends on It.'" August 13, 1965, p. 15.

U.S. News & World Report

"After Alabama . . . Negroes' Next Battlegrounds." April 5, 1965, pp. 37–38.
"After Birmingham Riots—Troubles Linger On." May 27, 1963, pp. 40–42.
"After Birmingham Riots: 'Who Has Gained?'" June 17, 1963, pp. 46–47.
"Alabama's Bus Boycott: What It's All About." August 3, 1956, pp. 82–89.
". . . And a Round of War Protests, Too." April 24, 1967, pp. 10, 12.
"Any Answer to Riots?" April 29, 1968, pp. 34, 36.
"Around the Nation, Racial Violence Erupts." July 4, 1966, p. 8.
"As Alabama Arrests Neared 3,500—." February 15, 1965, p. 10.
"As Cities Prepare for Riots—New Weapons, New Tactics." February 26, 1968, pp. 36–37.
"As Negro Unrest Continues to Spread." July 25, 1966, p. 30.
"As 150,000 Said Farewell to Dr. King." April 22, 1968, pp. 38–39.
"As Racial Conflicts Broke Out Anew—." April 29, 1963, p. 8.
"As Racial Troubles Broke Loose in Alabama . . ." May 13, 1963, p. 8.
"As the 'Poor Crusade' Takes a New Turn." July 1, 1968, pp. 27–29.
"As 200,000 Marched in Washington—." September 9, 1963, pp. 39–40.
"Battle of the Lunch Counters: Latest Drive for Integration." March 7, 1960, pp. 44, 46.
"Birmingham After the Bombing." September 30, 1963, pp. 38–40.
"A 'Black Power' Advocate in a Powerful Post." August 1, 1966, p. 8.
"'Black Power' Threatens a Leading Negro College." July 31, 1967, pp. 38–39.
"'Black Revolution'—Theme in Newark." July 31, 1967, p. 8.
"'Black Supremacy' Cult in U.S.—How Much of a Threat?" November 9, 1959, pp. 112–14.
"Blamed in Crime Rise: Civil Rights Excesses." February 27, 1967, p. 15.
"'Bloody Memphis'—And More to Come?" April 8, 1968, p. 8.
"'Boycotts Will be Used.'" February 24, 1964, pp. 59–61.
"Campus Riots: A Justice Speaks Out." June 3, 1968, p. 8.
"The Changing Mood of America: What a Nationwide Survey Shows." May 31, 1965, pp. 36–43.
"Chicago: A Big City Meets Its Problems." March 28, 1966, pp. 74–78.
"A City Cracks Down on Demonstrations." August 29, 1966, p. 10.
"Civil Rights Tangle: Where It Is Heading." May 25, 1964, pp. 37–38.
"Climax Near in Negro Revolt." March 29, 1965, pp. 27–29.
"Communist Gains Among Youths—J. Edgar Hoover Reports." November 1, 1965, p. 46.
"Communist Influence in March on Washington?" May 13, 1968, p. 45.
"Communists and Civil Rights—How Closely Linked?" July 12, 1965, p. 12.
"Deepening Mystery of Dr. King's Assassination." May 27, 1968, p. 10.

"Dirksen: 'We're Not Sick—We're Just Mismanaged.'" August 19, 1968, p. 34.

"Dispute Between Hoover and King: The FBI's Answer to Criticisms." December 7, 1964, pp. 46, 48.

"Dr. King's Crusade: How He Hopes to End the War." May 8, 1967, p. 14.

"Dr. King's Policy: Invitation to Racial Violence?" October 4, 1965, p. 22.

"Dr. King's Prophetic Words—." April 15, 1968, p. 34.

"A Down-to-Earth Look at a Growing Problem." August 22, 1966, p. 53.

"Editor Says Press Plays Down Northern Discord." March 23, 1956, pp. 48–50.

"'Even If I Die in the Struggle—.'" April 15, 1968, p. 33.

"Everywhere: Tension." March 21, 1960, pp. 72–75.

"Example of the Cloth." August 2, 1965, p. 84.

"Ex-Justice Severs Supreme Court Ties." November 1, 1965, p. 14.

"The FBI and Civil Rights—J. Edgar Hoover Speaks Out." November 30, 1964, pp. 56–58.

"A Former Justice Warns: Return to Law, or Face Anarchy." April 25, 1966, pp. 58–60, 62.

"For the 'Poor March': Detours." June 3, 1968, p. 47.

"'Freedom Riders'—and Mob Violence." May 29, 1961, p. 6.

"From J. Edgar Hoover: A Report on Campus Reds." May 31, 1965, p. 84.

"The Growing March on Washington." May 6, 1968, p. 73.

"Growing Success of Negroes in the U.S.: The Story That's Being Overlooked." July 3, 1967, pp. 54–57.

Harris, Frederick Brown. "'The Blade of a Righteous Sword.'" April 24, 1967, p. 120.

"High Court Ruling that Went Against Dr. King." June 26, 1967, p. 10.

"Home Rule for D.C.? What Johnson Proposes." February 15, 1965, p. 10.

"How Martin Luther King Won the Nobel Peace Prize." February 8, 1965, pp. 76–77.

"How Riots Are Stirred Up." May 6, 1968, pp. 68–71.

"How the Army Got Set to Move into Selma." May 10, 1965, pp. 16–17.

"How the FBI Regards Its Responsibilities." December 7, 1964, p. 48.

"How to Solve Racial Problems—Varying Views of Negro Leaders." September 5, 1966, p. 14.

"How U.S. Reds Campaign for a Vietnam Pullout." May 17, 1965, p. 22.

"Hypocrisy of North Incenses Southerner." February 24, 1956, pp. 47–48.

"If Mob Rule Takes Hold in U.S.—A Warning from Richard Nixon." August 15, 1966, pp. 64–65.

"If Voting is the Problem—A Look Outside the South." April 5, 1965, pp. 39–41.

"An Immoral Law." April 5, 1965, p. 116.

"Inside Story of 'Black Power' and Stokely Carmichael." August 15, 1966, p. 12.

"In South: Racial Trouble—and a Threat of More." March 30, 1964, pp. 8–9.

"Insurrection: Outlook in U.S." April 29, 1968, pp. 38–41.

"Interview with J. Edgar Hoover." December 21, 1964, pp. 36–40.

"Is America Really 'Sick'?" June 10, 1968, pp. 44–49.

"Is Castro Behind Guerrilla War in U.S. Cities?" August 14, 1967, pp. 23–25.

"Is Gift to 'Poor March' Deductible?" May 27, 1968, p. 94.

"Is Insurrection Brewing in U.S.?" December 25, 1967, pp. 32–37.

"Is It All Right to Break the Law?" August 12, 1963, p. 6.

"Is South Headed for Race War?" June 5, 1961, pp. 42–44.

"Is There a 'Sick' Society in the U.S.?" August 28, 1967, pp. 49–51.

"Is Vietnam to Become a Civil Rights Issue?" July 19, 1965, p. 12.

"It Looks Like a 'Hot Summer'—With Selma the Beginning." March 22, 1965, pp. 32–33.

"J. Edgar Hoover Speaks Out on Reds in the Negro Movement." May 4, 1964, p. 33.

"James Earl Ray: Manhunt Ends, but Mysteries Remain." June 24, 1968, pp. 34–36.

Karmin, Monroe W. "A Crusade Collapses." July 8, 1968, pp. 88–87.

"Kennedy Says 'Talk,' Georgians Say 'No.'" August 13, 1962, p. 8.

"Lawlessness in U.S.—Warning from a Top Jurist." July 5, 1965, pp. 60–63.

Lawrence, David. "Are Provocative Demonstrations Really Necessary?" June 20, 1966, p. 112.

———. "Bowing to the New Extremists." March 29, 1965, p. 112.

———. "Church Control of the State." September 23, 1963, pp. 116–15.

———. "The Enemy Within Our Gates." May 4, 1964, p. 108.

———. "Is the Clergyman Changing His Role?" April 19, 1965, p. 116.

———. "Is This the 'Land of the Free'?" July 12, 1965, p. 108.

———. "The Power of Reason." April 15, 1968, p. 108.

———. "The Right to Loot?" September 6, 1965, p. 100.

———. "What's Become of 'Law and Order'?" August 5, 1963, p. 104.

———. "What's Wrong with America?" April 22, 1968, p. 108.

———. "Who is to Blame?" August 1, 1966, p. 84.

———. "The Wrong Way." August 30, 1965, p. 88.

"A 'Liberal' Group Speaks Out Against Draft Violation, Rioting." February 12, 1968, pp. 68–69.

"Long, Hot Summer of Race Trouble Ahead?" May 23, 1966, pp. 34–38.

"A Long Road for the Vanishing Mule." May 27, 1968, p. 8.

"The Looted Merchants Tell Their Story." April 29, 1968, pp. 42–44.

"Man of Conflict Wins a Peace Prize." October 26, 1964, p. 24.

"'The March'—Gains and Losses." September 9, 1963, pp. 33–35.

"'March Leader' Randolph: Struggle Just Begun, He Says." September 9, 1963, p. 24.

"March on Washington—What to Expect." March 18, 1968, p. 44.

"Martin Luther King: Who He Is . . . What He Believes." April 5, 1965, p. 18.

"Martin Luther King's Reaction—A Statement and a Disagreement." November 30, 1964, p. 58.

"Militant Clergy—Critics Fire Back." November 27, 1967, pp. 66–68.

"Militant Public Employees—More Trouble for the Cities." February 26, 1968, pp. 78–79.

"A Million New Negro Voters?" August 16, 1965, p. 8.

"'Mob Law—Let's End It Now.'" August 7, 1967, p. 11.

"Mobs Run Wild in the Nation's Capital." April 15, 1968, pp. 8, 10.

"Montgomery Trouble a Possible Pattern?" March 23, 1956, pp. 44, 46.

"More Campus Unrest—Are Reds to Blame?" May 10, 1965, p. 14.

"More Violence and Race War?" April 15, 1968, pp. 31–34.

"Mounting Concern over Racial Violence." August 22, 1966, p. 6.

"NAACP Head Warns 'Black Power Means Black Death.'" July 18, 1966, p. 34.

"National Police Force? 'No,' Says FBI Chief Hoover." April 12, 1965, p. 20.

"Negroes Move Up in Government." July 3, 1967, pp. 57–58.

"Negro Leader Jailed, Then Freed on Appeal." November 7, 1960, p. 14.

"Negro Leader's Advice to Members of His Race." June 13, 1966, p. 14.

"Negro Leaders Dividing—The Effect." July 18, 1966, pp. 31–34.

"Negro Leaders—More Militant Now?" April 22, 1968, pp. 19–20.

"Negro Leaders Warn: More Race Troubles." May 25, 1964, p. 38.

"Negro Official Speaks Out: A Rebuke to Dr. King?" August 30, 1965, p. 16.

"New Clues in RFK Death—Was There a Plot?" June 24, 1968, p. 36.

"New Negro Threat: Mass Disobedience." August 28, 1967, p. 10.

"New Problem—Puerto Rican Riots." June 27, 1966, p. 8.

"New Tack for Dr. King: Broader Issues, Wider Goals." May 3, 1965, p. 18.

"New Turn in Race Troubles." January 1, 1962, pp. 43–44.

"Next: A National Police Force?" December 7, 1964, pp. 44–46.

"Next Big Integration Drive in the South: 'Freedom Highway' Rides—Led By
    CORE." May 7, 1962, p. 56.

"No Peace for Winner of Peace Prize." February 1, 1965, p. 19.

"Now a March of Tribute, Not Protest." August 16, 1965, p. 12.

"Now a New Shift in '68 Politics." April 22, 1968, pp. 57–58.

"Now, Charges of Orgies on Rights March." April 12, 1965, p. 11.

"Now It's a 'Kneel-in' Drive in the South." August 22, 1960, p. 8.

"Now It's a Negro Drive for Segregation." March 30, 1964, pp. 38–39.

"Now It's Negroes vs. Negroes in America's Racial Violence." March 8, 1965, p. 6.

"Now It's 'Passive Resistance' by Whites—The Albany, Ga., Plan." September 3,
    1962, pp. 43–46.

"Now, Negro Attack on 'Black Power.'" October 24, 1966, p. 14.

"Now the Real Race Begins." September 7, 1964, pp. 27–28.

"101 Suits to Enforce Negro Rights." August 23, 1965, p. 34.

"A Police Chief Talks of 'Police Brutality.'" August 10, 1964, pp. 33–36.

"The Policing Job Washington Now is Trying to Get." August 22, 1966, pp. 38–39.

"'Poor March': Threats, Disputes, and Confusion." June 17, 1968, p. 8.

"'Poor March' on Washington: A City Braced for Trouble." May 20, 1968, p. 11.

"'Poor March' Showdown Nears—Most Demands Still Unmet." June 24, 1968, p. 8.

"The 'Poor People's March': Its Demands, the Prospects." May 13, 1968, pp. 44–45.

"'Poor' vs. Freeman—How Many Hungry?" June 3, 1968, pp. 22, 24.

Powell, Lewis F., Jr. "'Civil Disobedience: Prelude to Revolution?'" October 30, 1967, pp. 66–69.

"The President Talks About 'Poor March,' Taxes, Unity." May 13, 1968, pp. 54–55.

"The Push is on for 'Mixed' Pools and Parks." May 21, 1962, pp. 43–44.

"Race Issue Inflamed Again: Aftermath of Shooting." June 20, 1966, pp. 36–38.

"Race Trouble in a 'Model City.'" February 10, 1964, p. 78.

"Race Violence in the 'Oldest City.'" June 22, 1964, p. 8.

"Racial Problems Ahead." April 22, 1968, pp. 45–46.

"The Real Stakes in Negro-Vote Drive." March 8, 1965, pp. 37–38.

"Reds and Negroes—'An Unhappy Secret.'" April 27, 1964, p. 34.

"Revolt Without Violence: The Negroes' New Strategy." March 21, 1960, pp. 76–78.

"Riot Outlook for '68." July 15, 1968, pp. 30–32.

"Riots, Battles, Power Marches—It's Still a Hot Summer." August 15, 1966, pp. 36–37.

"The Rising Threat of U.S. Communists." August 15, 1966, p. 9.

"The Road to 'Anarchy.'" September 14, 1964, p. 40.

"'Rouse the Masses.'" August 8, 1966, pp. 40–41.

"Search Starts for Cause of Riots in U.S. Cities." November 13, 1967, pp. 53–54.

"Senator Eastland on the 'Freedom Riders.'" June 5, 1961, p. 48.

"Setting a New Course in Meeting Race Violence." July 8, 1968, pp. 38–39.

"Shifting Patterns in Race Problem." August 23, 1965, pp. 32–24, 37.

"Should President 'Risk His Life' for Integration?" June 10, 1963, p. 35.

"Some Gains for 'Poor Marchers,' But Their Troubles Grow." June 10, 1968, pp. 60–61.

"Some New Light on 'Spying' in the Kennedy Era." June 3, 1968, p. 16.

"The Strange March Through Mississippi." June 27, 1966, p. 48.

"Strategy of Integration Leaders." June 5, 1961, pp. 44–45.

"A Summer of Race Violence on the Way?" April 6, 1964, pp. 34–35.

"Tension Growing Over Race Issue." May 20, 1963, pp. 37–39.

"Threat Across the Nation: New Wave of Racial Troubles." September 13, 1965, p. 8.

"A Threat of Anarchy in Nation's Capital." May 20, 1968, pp. 47–49.

"Threats: Negroes' Latest Weapon in Rights Drive." July 1, 1963, pp. 39–40.

"Tomorrow." June 10, 1963, pp. 29–30.

"Tomorrow." September 2, 1963, pp. 15–16.

"Tomorrow." March 29, 1965, p. 21.

"Tomorrow." August 16, 1965, pp. 25–26.

"Tomorrow." September 6, 1965, pp. 23–24.

"Tomorrow." June 24, 1968, p. 21.

"Top Man of the Negro 'Revolution.'" June 10, 1963, p. 21.

"Tough Job for New Leader of Big Protest: Trying to Avoid Violence." June 24, 1968, p. 16.

"U.S. Race Riot Outlook for '67—What Negro Leaders Predict." May 1, 1967, pp. 42–45, 49.

"A Warning Against City Workers' Strikes." February 26, 1968, p. 78.

"Washington Whispers." December 7, 1964, p. 26.
"Washington Whispers." March 8, 1965, p. 22.
"Washington Whispers." March 22, 1965, p. 26.
"Washington Whispers." May 17, 1965, p. 27.
"Washington Whispers." June 7, 1965, p. 32.
"Washington Whispers." September 27, 1965, p. 29.
"Washington Whispers." April 24, 1967, p. 29.
"Washington Whispers." April 22, 1968, p. 22.
"Washington Whispers." May 13, 1968, p. 30.
"Washington Whispers." June 24, 1968, p. 24.
"Were Riots Organized?" April 22, 1968, p. 12.
"What 'Black Power' Leaders are Demanding." August 7, 1967, p. 31.
"What Government Already Has Done for Negroes." August 23, 1965, p. 33.
"What J. Edgar Hoover Says About 'Pressure Groups.'" December 7, 1964, p. 45.
"What Really Happened on Alabama March?" May 10, 1965, p. 17.
"What Southern Editors Say About the Future." June 5, 1961, pp. 45–48.
"What the American Negro Wants." April 29, 1963, pp. 46–52.
"What the Negro Vote Will Do to South." March 29, 1965, pp. 30–32, 34.
"What's Wrong With a 'Poor People's March.'" May 6, 1968, pp. 72–73.
"What Union Won in Garbage Strike." April 29, 1968, p. 82.
"When Dr. King Went to Jail Again." July 23, 1962, p. 10.
"When Federal Registrars Were Last Used in South." March 29, 1965, p. 33.
"When Negroes Tried to Shock a Friendly City—." September 13, 1965, pp. 46–48.
"Where Reds Are Busy on the Campuses." June 7, 1965, pp. 53–54.
Whittaker, Charles E. "Planned Lawlessness Threatens to Get Out of Hand." September 19, 1966, pp. 37–38, 43.
"Will a Racial Protest Tie Up the World's Fair?" April 20, 1964, p. 6.
"Will Negroes Win in the South?" March 14, 1960, pp. 41–45.
"Will Violence Upset '68 Campaign?" January 22, 1968, pp. 46–47.

NEWSPAPERS

Birmingham (Ala.) *News*, October 26, 1962.
Memphis *Commercial Appeal*, March 19, April 7, 1968.
New York *Times*, February 18, March 5, March 15, March 20, March 30, May 25, 1968.
SCLC Newsletter, Atlanta, September, 1962, July-August, October-November, 1964.
Southern Courier, Montgomery and Atlanta, July 30, September 18–19, 1965; June 15–16, June 22–23, June 29–30, July 6–7, 1968.

THESES AND DISSERTATIONS

Hartley, Robert Wayne. "A Long, Hot Summer: The St. Augustine Racial Disorders of 1964." M.A. thesis, Stetson University, 1972.

Hirsch, Arnold R. "Making the Second Ghetto: Race and Housing in Chicago, 1940–1960." Ph.D. dissertation, University of Illinois-Chicago Circle, 1978.

Massoni, Gary. "Perspectives on Operation Breadbasket." M.Div. thesis, Chicago Theological Seminary, 1971.

Ripy, Thomas Beebe, Jr. "Changes in the Formal Structure of Municipal Government and Their Effect on Selected Aspects of the Legislative Process: A Case Study of Memphis, Tennessee." Ph.D. dissertation, University of Kentucky, 1973.

Shelly, Michael Bert. "David Lawrence and Ralph McGill on the Problems of Negro Civil Rights." M.S. thesis, University of Illinois, 1963.

Sorrentino, Frank M. "Bureaucratic Ideology: The Case Study of the Federal Bureau of Investigation." Ph.D. dissertation, New York University, 1978.

Yeakey, Lamont H. "The Montgomery, Alabama, Bus Boycott, 1955–1956." Ph.D. dissertation, Columbia University, 1979.

INTERVIEWS

Mississippi Valley Collection, Memphis State University

Caywood, David, by Anne Trotter and David Yellin, May 20, 1968, tape 141.

Jones, T. O., by Joan Beifuss and David Yellin, January 30, 1968, tape 228.

Manire, James, by Anne Trotter and David Yellin, August 7, 1968, tape 43.

Wurf, Jerry, by Carol Yellin and David Yellin, February 3, 1972, tape 305.

Moorland-Spingarn Research Center, Howard University

Austin, Earnest, by Katherine Shannon, July 9, 1968, tape 264.

Baker, Ella, by John Britton, June 19, 1968, tape 203.

Barry, Marion, by Katherine Shannon, October 3, 1967, tape 54.

Farmer, James, by John Britton, September 28, 1968, tape 317.

Gibson, John, by John Britton, April 26, 1968, tape 176.

Givens, Cornelius, by Katherine Shannon, July 7, 1968, tape 223.

Hill, Norman, by James Mosby, March 12, 1970, tape 532.

Hollowell, Donald L., by John Britton, May 23, 1968, tape 187.

King, C. B., by Stanley Smith, August, 1968, tape 392.

Lucas, Robert, by John Britton, February 20, 1968, tape 155.

Nixon, E. D., by Stanley Smith, February, 1968, tape 139.

Offenburger, Thomas E., by Katherine Shannon, July 2, 1968, tape 227.

Randolph, A. Philip, by Robert Martin, January 14, 1969, tape 384.

Romero, Richard, by James Mosby, June 11, 1968, tape 193.

Shannon, Katherine, by Claudia Rawles, August 12, 1968, tape 297.

Tijerina, Reis, by James Mosby, June 12, 1968, tape 194.

Walker, Wyatt Tee, by John Britton, October 11, 1967, tape 56.

GOVERNMENT DOCUMENTS

Federal Bureau of Investigation. Surveillance File on Malcolm X. 1953–71. Microfilm.

Senate Documents. 94th Cong., 2nd Sess., No. 755.

U.S. Commission on CIA Activities Within the United States. *Report to the President.* 1975.

FILMS

Cohen, Robert Carl. *Committee on Un-American Activities.*

INDEX

Abernathy, Ralph David: Albany Movement and, 60, 66, 70; Birmingham campaign and, 80–81, 83–84; Selma campaign and, 143, 160, 178; at King's funeral, 299; Poor People's Campaign and, 311, 313–17, 320–23, 325–27, 332–37

Alabama: Freedom Rides in, 51, 52–53; Voting Rights Act and, 204–205; black vote in, 207–208; Democratic party in, 207. *See also* Birmingham campaign; Montgomery bus boycott; Selma campaign; names of other cities in Alabama

Albany Movement: importance of, 42–43, 77; problems involved with, 59–60; arrests during, 60–61, 62, 65–66; King's involvement in, 60–63, 66–74; *Newsweek's* treatment of, 60, 63–64, 66, 67–79, 71–73, 79–80; status of blacks in Albany, 60–61; *Time's* treatment of, 60, 61–62, 66–67, 69–70; *U.S. News & World Report's* treatment of, 62–63, 66, 70–71; Pritchett's role in, 68–72, 147

Alinsky, Saul, 267

Alsop, Joseph, 125

American Indians, 263, 272, 308, 321, 324, 331

Anderson, Jack, 328

Anniston, Ala., 51

Astor, Vincent, 11

Atlanta, Ga., 49, 121, 248

Baker, Ella, 46–47

Baker, Wilson, 145, 146, 152, 163, 315, 316n

Baldwin, James, 90, 106, 115

Bennett, Lerone, 235

Bevel, James, 316

Birmingham campaign: as moral drama, 4; violence in, 75–76, 78, 84, 87, 88, 109–10; *Newsweek's* treatment of, 78–83, 85–86, 89, 90–92, 111–12; *Time's* treatment of, 78, 80–81, 82, 84–87, 89, 90, 92–94, 103, 111–12, 293–94; *U.S. News & World Report's* treatment of, 78, 82, 86–88, 94–95, 112; King's involvement in, 79–95; Bull Connor's role in, 83–84, 86–87, 143, 145; arrests during, 84, 87, 88; schoolchildren and, 84–87; settlement of, 88–89

Black families, 188, 188n

Black militancy, 39, 77, 89–91, 97–98, 100, 102–103, 113–18, 184. *See also* Black Power; names of specific organizations and leaders

Black movement. *See* names of specific organizations

Black Muslims, 39, 48, 85, 89–90, 93, 100, 114, 115, 150, 199–200, 209, 307

Black Power, 196, 202–203, 205–206, 208–10, 212–19, 224, 244n, 225–29, 236, 239–40, 246–49, 249n, 252, 253, 261, 265, 284. *See also* names of specific organizations and leaders